CONTENTS

INTRODUCTION 1

AUTUMN 5

WINTER 65

SPRING 121

SUMMER 177

A WELL-STOCKED PANTRY 232

INGREDIENTS 243

CONVERSIONS 245

INDEX 248

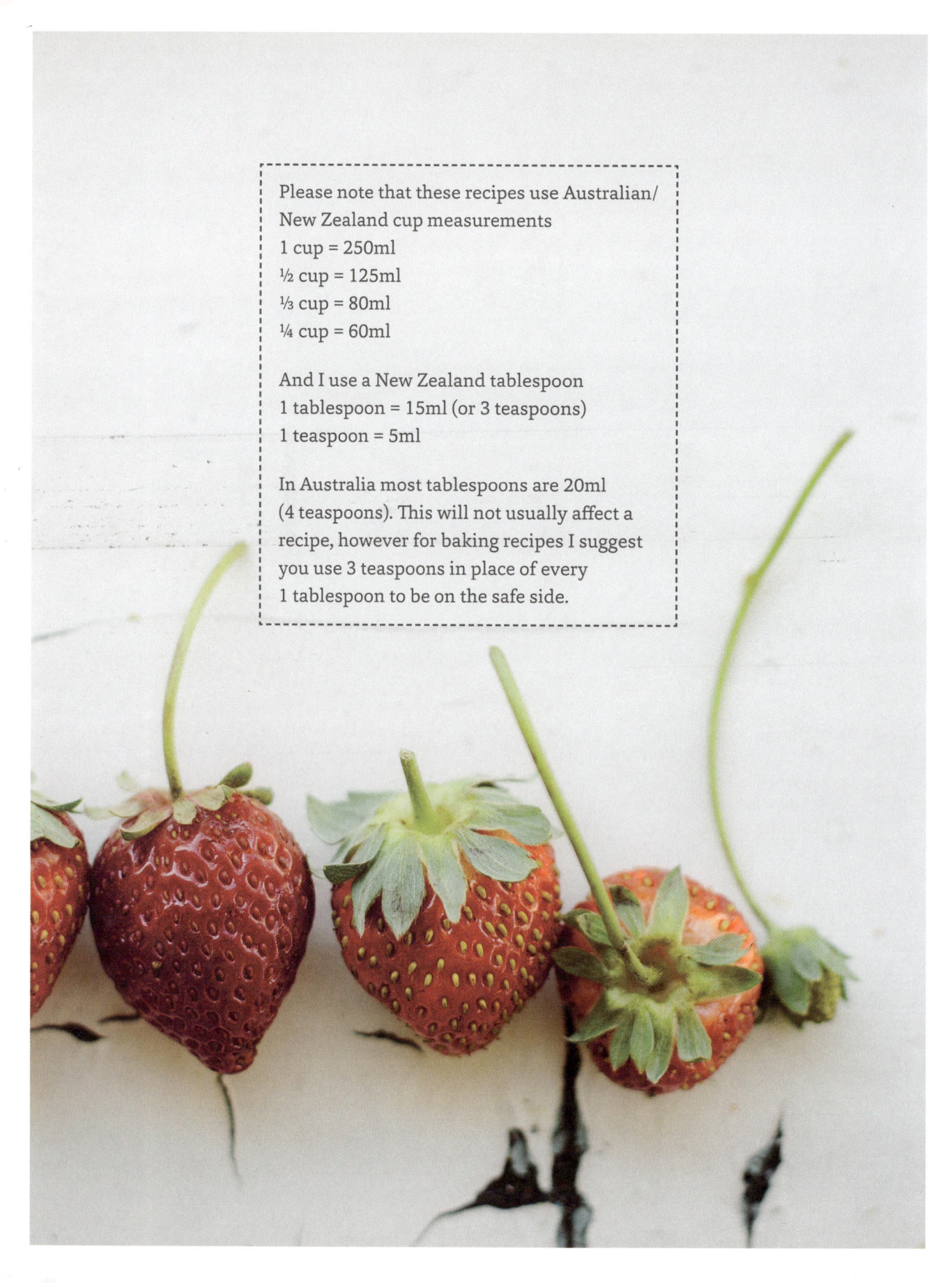

Please note that these recipes use Australian/New Zealand cup measurements
1 cup = 250ml
½ cup = 125ml
⅓ cup = 80ml
¼ cup = 60ml

And I use a New Zealand tablespoon
1 tablespoon = 15ml (or 3 teaspoons)
1 teaspoon = 5ml

In Australia most tablespoons are 20ml (4 teaspoons). This will not usually affect a recipe, however for baking recipes I suggest you use 3 teaspoons in place of every 1 tablespoon to be on the safe side.

INTRODUCTION

I'll admit it, I'm a full-on produce geek.

If anyone was to buy me flowers or chocolates, I'd say thank you and give them a hug. But give me a bunch of rainbow-coloured carrots fresh from the ground or a box of juicy perfectly ripe strawberries and I'll be your friend forever. Growing up vegetarian on an organic vegetable farm and then going on to cook professionally as a chef for many years may have set me up to live the life I now lead, but it's the years of playing in the kitchen with the produce from our little garden and local farmers markets which have left the biggest imprint on my style of cooking – and the food I love to make for and eat with my family today.

Changing our diets when our gluten-intolerant kids were babies only made my drive to cook nourishing locally produced food from scratch even stronger, given the only other option was to use tasteless store-bought gluten-free products, devoid of all nutrients.

Food is life, but it's so much more than sustenance alone, and thankfully people, as a whole, are much more aware of what they put into their bodies nowadays. Taking ownership of what you eat is the single most powerful choice we have as humans and nothing makes me happier than seeing people trying their best to support local growers and artisans, trying their hand at growing their own vegetables and getting back to the simple basic pleasures of cooking real food from scratch. The current trend of growing your own vegetables and eating mindfully is a definite sign that we're all keen to take the power back.

One of the proudest moments I've experienced as a mother was when my dad came to visit a few years back. We were living in Perth at the time, and he took my two kids (then four and six years old) to the supermarket to pick up a few supplies. On their return Dad told me how when asked whether or not they'd like him to buy a few cherries for them to snack on, my eldest asked where they were from. Dad looked at the sign and replied, 'America.' Ada quickly replied, 'We don't eat American fruit,' turned around and walked off without giving it another thought. Now I'm not against American-grown fruits and vegetables at all; on the contrary, if you happen to live in the US then these are exactly what I encourage you to eat! But it is my belief that we should try our best to eat fruits and vegetables produced in our own countries. Of course, as with everything in life, there are times when eating imported food simply can't be avoided. Bananas and pineapples don't grow in New Zealand, but this doesn't stop me enjoying them from time to time. But I prefer to celebrate the sometimes brief season of locally grown produce and then hold out – making it all the more special when their time rolls around again.

In a time of all-year-round growing, by means of hydroponics and glasshouses, it's way too easy for us to forget that each fruit, each vegetable, has its own time and place when it's at its prime. Just as nature intended. Left on the tree or bush until the moment of ripeness and not a second sooner, in-season fruits and vegetables taste much sweeter and juicier than out of season, or those which have travelled for miles. Yes, you can buy a peach in the middle of winter (a far cry from my childhood memories, of peaches eaten in the summer sun with juice dripping down my arms and face!), but if you only knew how far that peach has travelled, how much pesticide residue sits on its skin and the amount of radiation it has been subjected to, you'd probably step away from it rather quickly! Sadly many people nowadays have lost that connection our forebears had with the land and wouldn't be able to even tell you when a tomato is in season.

Chefs harping on about seasonal produce is not something new and I almost feel like I'm repeating the words of so many others, but eating locally, in season and in line with nature is the foundation of everything I do. So it only makes sense that my second book be based around something I hold so dear.

When I wrote my first cookbook, *My Darling Lemon Thyme: Recipes from my real food kitchen*, I initially wanted to have it set out in seasons, purely because this is how I've always cooked. But I didn't want the simple little things, like drinks and breakfasts, to get lost in a book of this kind, so instead I chose to arrange the recipes by meal times. In it I shared all my base recipes and knowledge of wholefood gluten-free vegetarian cooking, along with my story, explaining why I eat like this, and providing an in-depth look at all the different ingredients that grace my pantry shelves (see pantry section on page 232). I love that book and am super-proud of what I shared within its covers. But now that all the basics have been covered, I really want my second book to explore the bounty of the seasons and to give you a glimpse into my kitchen throughout the year.

I've written this book as a simple seasonal guide, and little nudge of encouragement if you will. Of course sticklers for accuracy will note that not all the ingredients fit nicely into their own local season; naturally this will change slightly depending on where you live in the world. Strawberries, for instance, come into season at the end of winter in Western Australia, where I was living while working on this book. But they're not around in other parts of Australia and New Zealand until summer. Many of the recipes found in the autumn section can easily fit into the winter section and vice versa. My aim is to simply give you an outline for living with the seasons and I urge you to get to know what's available where you live.

Life's too short to eat flavourless out-of-season produce. So experiment, make the recipes your own and enjoy good food with the people you love.

Emm xx

A little note on ingredients

- I try to buy organic wherever possible but I don't beat myself up when I can't afford to. Growing your own is by far the best (and usually the cheapest) way to ensure you know exactly what you're eating.
- I always buy local produce over imported.
- I always buy local free-range eggs, from a reputable source. Sadly just because the label says free-range, doesn't necessarily mean the eggs are. Get to know a local producer in your area.
- I buy GMO-free soy products (tofu, miso + tempeh). The same goes for corn products (cornflour, cornstarch and popping corn).

For more detailed notes on ingredients including gluten-free flours, sweeteners, dairy alternatives, rice and grains etc., please see A Well-Stocked Pantry on page 232.

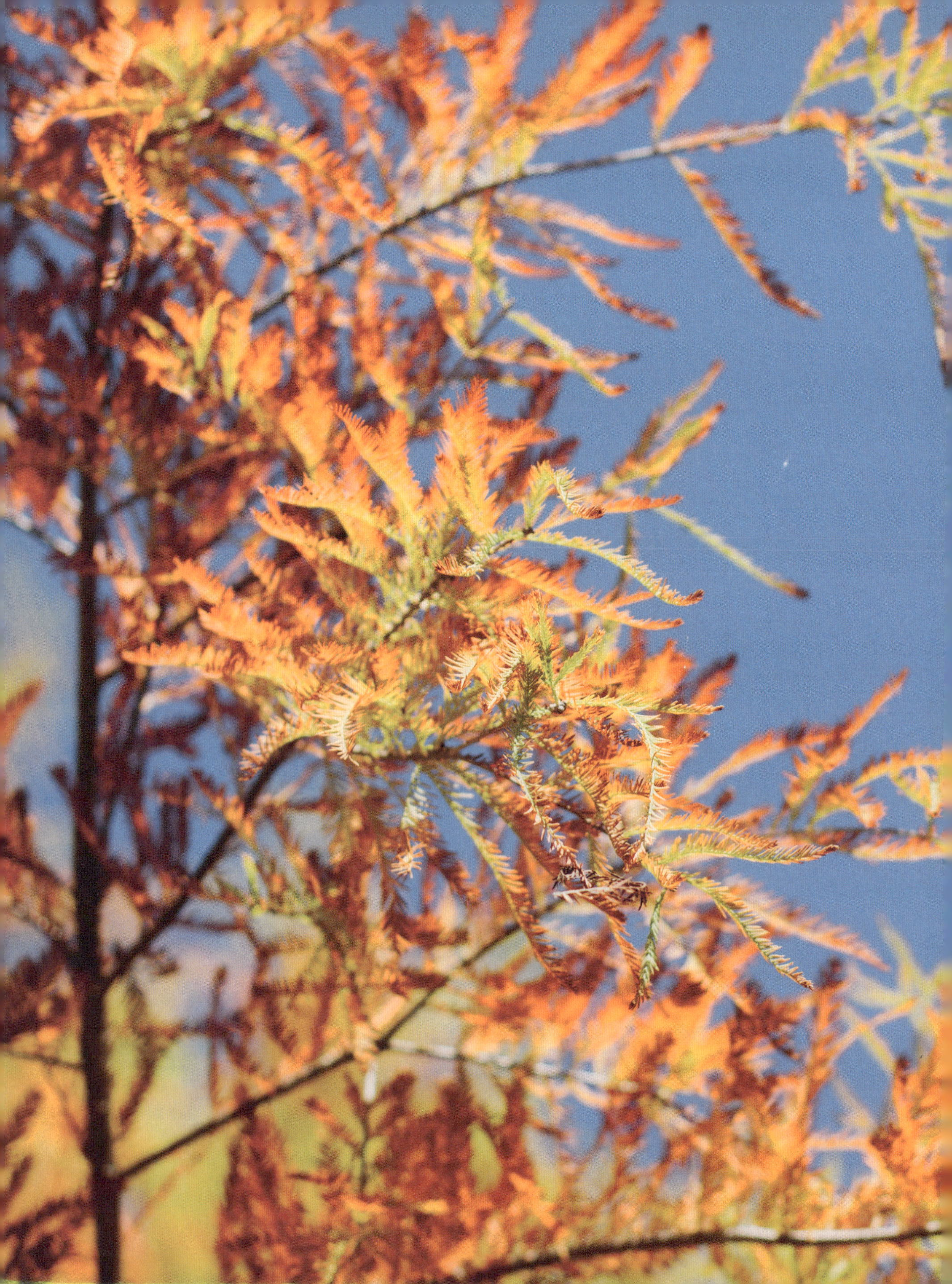

AUTUMN

apple + pear + plum + eggplant + capsicum + fig + tamarillo + feijoa + kumara + pumpkin + persimmon + cabbage + parsnip + mushroom + chestnut + courgette/zucchini + tomato + cauliflower + broccoli + chilli + pomegranate + custard apple/cherimoya + avocado + cumquat + blackberries + quava + passionfruit + papaya + orange + nashi + mandarin + lime + lemon + kiwifruit + quince + rockmelon + jerusalem artichoke + daikon + okra + borlotti beans + onion + fennel + leek + lettuce + silverbeet + spinach + swede + turnip + watercress + radish + brussels sprouts

PUMPKIN + FETA STUFFED JALAPEÑOS

SERVES 4–6 | GLUTEN-FREE

Right at the very beginning of autumn, as the last of the summer vegetables say their farewell and the first of the pumpkins are picked, is the perfect time to make this punchy little snack. Stuffed jalapeños are a big thing in the US, where they're often filled with cheese, coated in crumbs and deep-fried, but here in New Zealand and Australia jalapeños are mostly known in their pickled form (which I'm a huge fan of don't get me wrong, see page 180). The aim with these babies is to prevent this beautiful chilli from being relegated to a mere supporting role. Filled with golden roasted pumpkin, feta, lime and coriander, these stuffed jalapeños celebrate some of my favourite flavours, and are the perfect pre-dinner snack with drinks or served alongside a few other dishes for a substantial meal.

- 500g (approx. ½ small) butternut pumpkin, deseeded, peeled + cut into bite-sized pieces
- 3 tablespoons extra-virgin olive oil
- 1 teaspoon whole cumin seeds
- 12 large jalapeño chillies, halved + deseeded
- 50g feta cheese, crumbled
- 30g (¼ cup) lightly toasted pumpkin seeds + 2 tablespoons extra, roughly chopped
- Handful of coriander leaves, roughly chopped
- 1 teaspoon lemon juice

+ Preheat oven to 200ºC (400ºF). Place pumpkin pieces on a baking tray, drizzle with 2 tablespoons of the oil, scatter over cumin seeds and season well with fine sea salt and freshly ground black pepper. Roast for 30–35 minutes, turning once or twice, until tender and golden.

+ Place halved jalapeños on another baking tray.

+ Transfer roasted pumpkin to a bowl and roughly mash, then fold through crumbled feta, pumpkin seeds, coriander leaves, remaining olive oil and lemon juice. Season well with salt and pepper.

+ Spoon filling into halved jalapeños. Scatter with extra pumpkin seeds and bake for 25–30 minutes until jalapeños are tender. These are lovely served hot, warm or at room temperature.

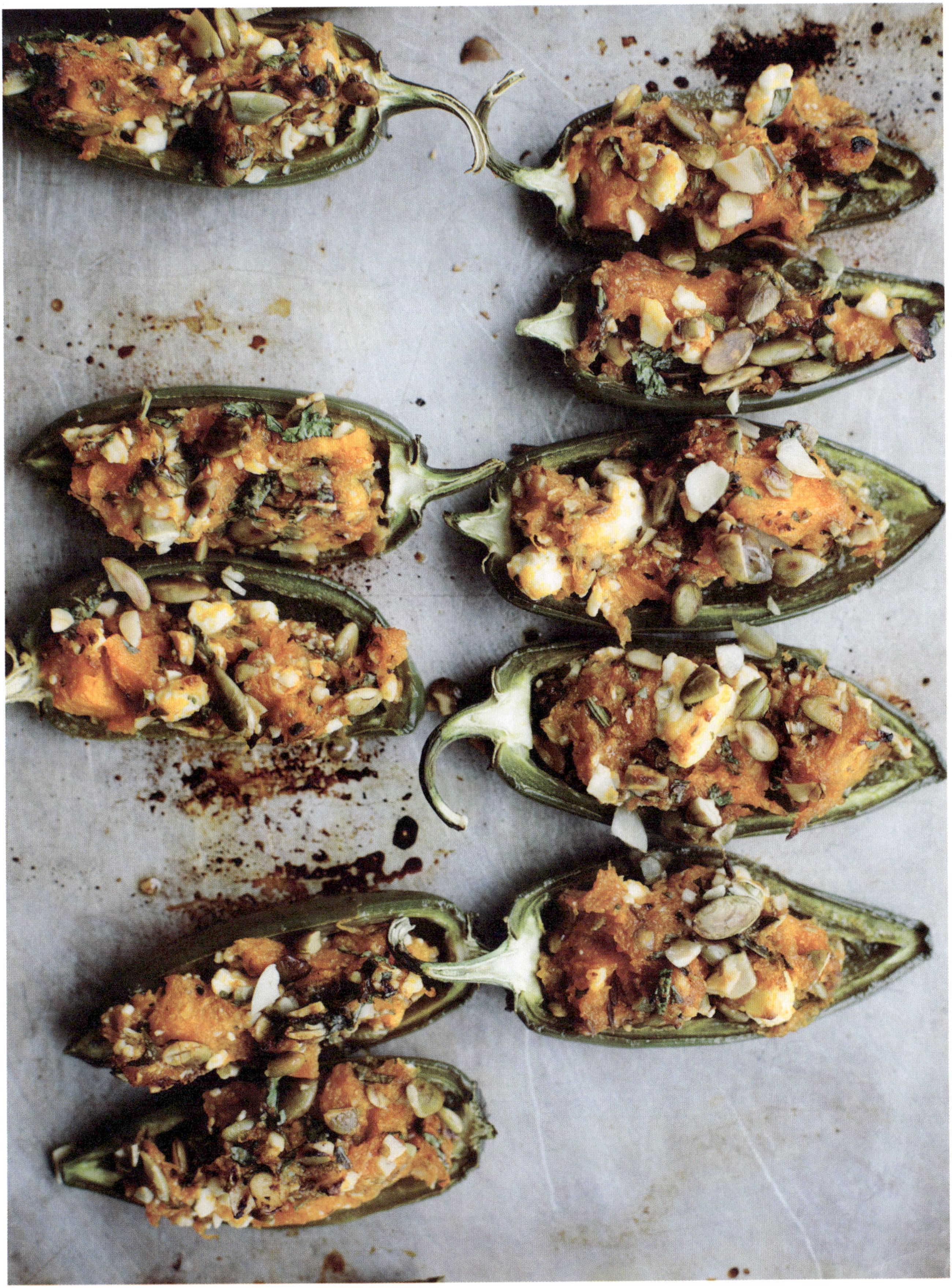

PAPRIKA ROASTED PARSNIPS W/ HAZELNUT ROMESCO

SERVES 4 | GLUTEN-FREE | VEGAN

You will notice that I have a serious thing for roasting vegetables. Roasting gives so much more flavour than any other form of cooking, especially to the humble parsnip – a vegetable which I have loved for as long as I can remember. Treat parsnips as you would carrots, and add to soups, mash and stews. Cook with potato and herbs to make a lovely creamy, warming soup (page 92, Creamy Parsnip Soup) or roast in chunks to add to a hearty cool-weather salad. These paprika roasted parsnips are known in our house as burning trees, aptly named by Ada. I have to agree, the charred ends do look like burnt trees, especially alongside the deep red of the hazelnut romesco. The romesco also makes a lovely spread on bread or served with eggs, rice or quinoa.

1kg (approx. 14 small) parsnips, peeled, ends trimmed + cut into quarters lengthways

2 tablespoons extra-virgin olive oil

1 teaspoon paprika (smoked or sweet)

Good pinch of fine sea salt

Hazelnut romesco

2 red capsicums

1 large ripe tomato, cored + sliced in half horizontally

2 long red chillies

45g (⅓ cup) hazelnuts, toasted + skins removed

3 cloves garlic

1 teaspoon paprika

2 tablespoons red wine vinegar

60ml (¼ cup) extra-virgin olive oil

+ To make romesco, preheat grill to the highest setting. Rub a little olive oil onto the capsicum skins, place on a tray and grill for 10–12 minutes, turning often, until all sides are charred and black. Transfer to a stainless steel or glass bowl, cover with a lid or large plate and set aside to steam.

+ Place tomatoes onto the tray, cut side down, along with chillies. Rub a little olive oil on their skins and grill for 5–8 minutes, turning chillies 1–2 times, until the skins are charred and black. Remove from oven, set tomatoes aside to cool and place chillies in with capsicums. Leave for 15 minutes. Remove skins from tomatoes and roughly chop the flesh. Peel capsicums and chillies, then cut in half and remove seeds.

+ Place hazelnuts in the bowl of a small food processor and pulse until finely ground. Add capsicum, tomato, chillies, garlic and paprika and blend until a rough paste forms. Add red wine vinegar and pulse once more before adding olive oil and blending to a smooth sauce. Season well with fine sea salt. The romesco will store for up to 1 week in the fridge. Bring back to room temperature before serving.

+ Preheat oven to 200ºC (400ºF). Combine parsnips, olive oil, paprika, salt and freshly ground black pepper in a large bowl, mixing well to evenly coat. Spread out onto a large baking tray in a single layer (or use two smaller trays if that's what you have) and roast for 30–35 minutes, turning once or twice during cooking, until tender and golden. If you have larger parsnips you may need to cook them for a little longer. Serve paprika parsnips hot with hazelnut romesco to dip.

NOTE: Large parsnips can have a somewhat stringy, hard centre. To remove this, cut them into quarters lengthways and then slice out the hard centre.

HONEYED EGGPLANT W/ CHICKPEAS + CORIANDER SAUCE

SERVES 4 | GLUTEN-FREE | DAIRY-FREE

This dish is the perfect example of how I love to eat: seasonal vegetables given a little love, served atop a gluten-free grain, then drizzled with a vibrant green herby sauce. It's likely that this will make more coriander sauce than you'll need for the one meal, however, the sauce stores happily in a glass jar in the fridge for 2–3 days and is lovely with roasted vegetables, salad greens, cooked gluten-free grains and so on. Soak your chickpeas the night before if using dried.

- 135g (¾ cup) dried chickpeas, soaked overnight in cold water, or 400g tin cooked chickpeas, rinsed, or 1½ cups cooked chickpeas
- 1 large eggplant, sliced into 1cm rounds
- Extra-virgin olive oil, for shallow-frying
- 2 cloves garlic, roughly chopped
- 1 teaspoon cumin seeds, lightly toasted and roughly ground
- 4 tablespoons lemon juice
- 2 tablespoons honey
- Big handful of coriander leaves + tender stems, roughly chopped
- Cooked millet, quinoa or brown or basmati rice, to serve
- Mint or coriander leaves, to serve

Coriander sauce
- 1 large bunch coriander, stems, roots + all, roughly chopped
- Juice of 1 medium lemon
- 60ml (¼ cup) extra-virgin olive oil
- 2 cloves garlic
- ½–1 long green chilli (deseeded for less heat)
- ½ teaspoon ground cumin
- ½ teaspoon ground coriander

+ Drain and rinse dried chickpeas, put in a saucepan and cover with cold water. Bring to the boil, skimming any foam that rises to the surface. Reduce to a simmer and cook for 25–35 minutes or until tender but not falling apart. Drain well.

+ Sprinkle a little sea salt over each slice of eggplant and set aside for 20–30 minutes.

+ Meanwhile, make coriander sauce. Place all ingredients in a blender and blend on high until smooth. You can add 1–2 tablespoons cold filtered water if you need to, to help things along. Taste and adjust seasoning.

+ Rinse eggplant slices under cold water and pat dry on a clean tea towel. Heat a good glug of olive oil in a large frying pan over medium-high heat and cook eggplant in batches until golden on both sides, adding more oil as needed. Keep in mind that the eggplant will get cooked further later, so don't worry too much if it's not all 100% tender yet. Transfer cooked eggplant to a plate while you continue cooking the rest.

+ Add another glug of oil to the pan and sauté garlic and cumin seeds for 30 seconds. Remove from heat and add lemon juice and honey, then return to heat and stir well. Return eggplant to the pan along with drained chickpeas. Give everything a good stir, then reduce heat, partially cover with a lid and cook for a further 5 minutes, or until the liquid has mostly been absorbed and eggplant is tender. Remove from heat, taste and adjust seasoning if needed, and stir through coriander. Serve hot over cooked millet, quinoa or rice, with a good drizzle of coriander sauce on top and extra to serve. Scatter over fresh herbs, if using.

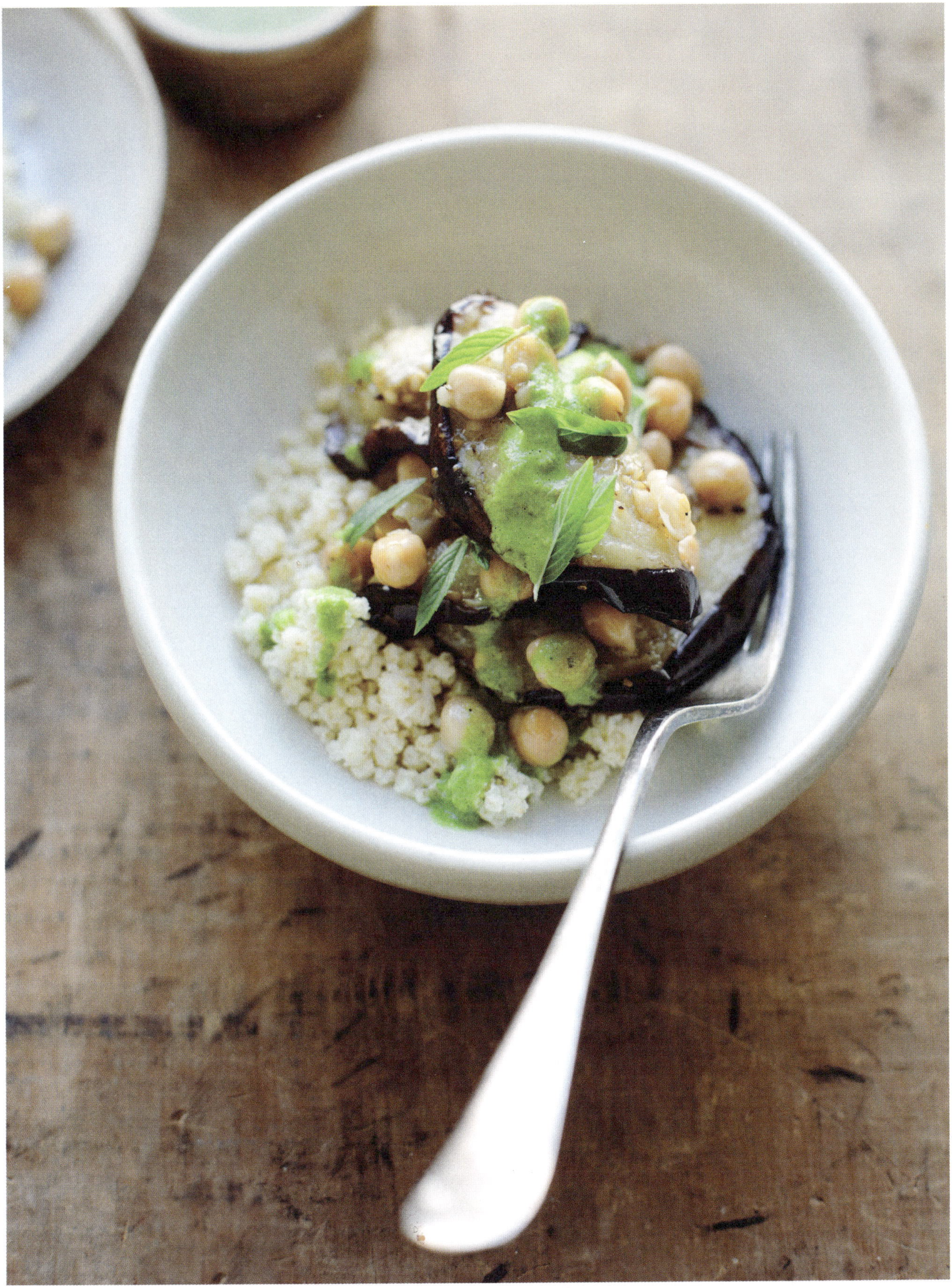

TURMERIC MUSHROOMS w/ CHICKPEA CREPES

SERVES 4 AS A LIGHT MEAL | GLUTEN-FREE | VEGAN OPTION

Soft, gently-spiced chickpea crepes work wonders alongside lemony turmeric-baked mushrooms and a dollop of herby yoghurt. Like all crepes, don't be dismayed if the first is a slight disaster – it usually takes a few goes to get the pan temperature just right. Any leftover batter can be stored in a glass jar in the fridge overnight; just give it a good stir before cooking. Omit herb yoghurt + use olive oil, if vegan.

- 2 tablespoons ghee or olive oil
- 2 cloves garlic, finely chopped
- ½ teaspoon ground turmeric
- 500g button mushrooms, trimmed + wiped clean
- Juice of 1 lemon

Crepes
- 110g (1 cup) chickpea (chana or besan) flour
- 60g (½ cup) white rice flour
- ¼ teaspoon ground turmeric
- ¼ teaspoon fine sea salt
- 410ml (1⅔ cups) soda water
- ½ long green chilli, deseeded + finely chopped
- 1 teaspoon finely grated ginger
- Handful of coriander leaves, finely chopped
- Ghee or olive oil, to cook

Herb yoghurt
- 125ml (½ cup) natural plain yoghurt
- Handful of mint leaves, roughly chopped + extra, to serve
- Handful of coriander leaves, roughly chopped + extra, to serve
- 2–3 tablespoons lemon juice

+ Preheat oven to 190ºC (375ºF). Heat ghee or olive oil in a large ovenproof frying pan. Add garlic and turmeric and mix well before adding mushrooms. Mix to evenly coat mushrooms, season with fine sea salt and freshly ground black pepper and place in oven. Roast, stirring once or twice during cooking, for 25–30 minutes, or until tender. (Alternatively, if you don't own an ovenproof pan, sauté garlic and turmeric in a frying pan for 30 seconds, stir through mushrooms, then transfer to an ovenproof dish before roasting.) Remove from oven and stir lemon juice through. Adjust seasoning if needed.

+ To make crepes, place flours, turmeric and salt in a bowl, whisk in 250ml (1 cup) of soda water, to form a thick smooth batter, before whisking in remaining 160ml (⅔ cup). Add chilli, ginger and coriander.

+ Heat a large frying pan over high heat. Give the chickpea batter a good stir, add a dab of ghee or glug of olive oil to the pan, wipe out any excess with a paper towel then pour in 60ml (¼ cup) of batter, tilting the pan so the mixture coats the base in a thin film. Cook for approx. 1 minute, or until bubbles show on the surface and the underside is golden. Carefully flip using a metal fish slice, then cook for a further 20–30 seconds. Remove from pan and place onto a plate. Wipe out the pan to remove any little bits of batter that may have caught on the bottom, add a touch more ghee or oil and repeat until all the crepes are cooked (aiming for 8–9 crepes).

+ To make herb yoghurt, combine yoghurt, herbs, lemon juice and a good pinch of fine sea salt in a bowl, and mix well. Place 2 crepes on each plate, top with a few spoonfuls of mushrooms, a generous dollop of herb yoghurt and a scatter of fresh herbs.

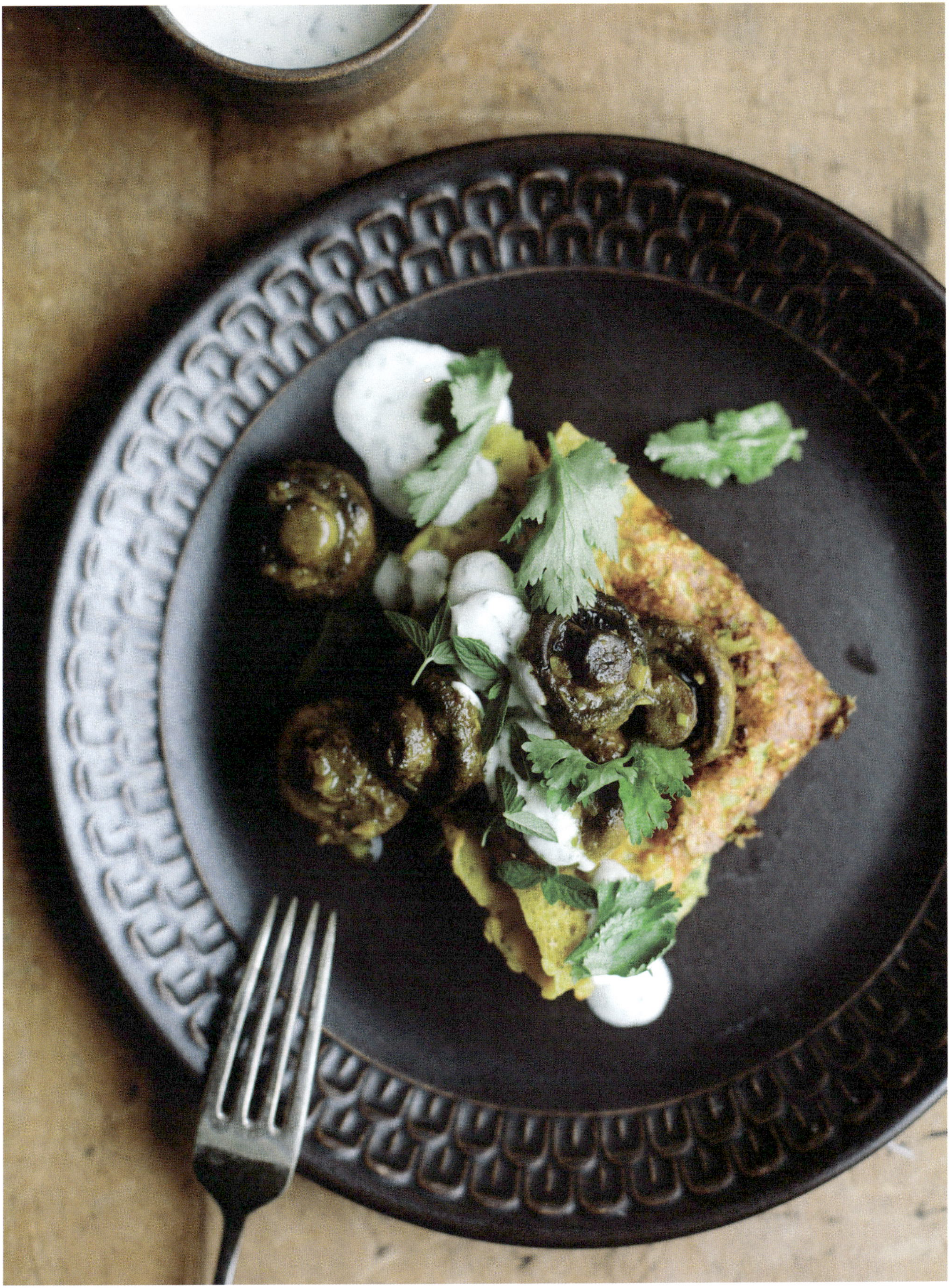

PLUM + ROCKET SALAD W/ ALMOND ZA'ATAR

SERVES 4 AS PART OF A MEAL | GLUTEN-FREE | DAIRY-FREE | VEGAN OPTION

There are a few ingredients which I find myself turning to often to add a little boost of flavour, and za'atar is most definitely one of them. Here, combined with a little nutty crunch of lightly toasted almonds, it adds another dimension alongside sweet end-of-season plums, peppery rocket and a simple lemon juice dressing. You can use any variety of plum, but I find the yellow-fleshed varieties look beautiful against the rocket. Although, on second thoughts, a mixture of both yellow and red would look even better! Use pure maple syrup or raw sugar in place of the honey for a vegan option.

- 1 tablespoon za'atar (page 178), or to taste
- 1 tablespoon slivered almonds, lightly toasted
- 2 big handfuls of rocket
- 4 plums, stones removed + flesh sliced roughly
- ½ teaspoon honey
- 2 tablespoons lemon juice
- 3 tablespoons extra-virgin olive oil

+ Combine za'atar and toasted almonds. Place rocket and plums in a serving bowl. Whisk honey and lemon juice together in a small bowl. Continue to whisk while you slowly drizzle olive oil in a steady stream to form a lovely emulsified dressing. Season to taste with fine sea salt and freshly ground black pepper.

+ Dress rocket and plums with just enough dressing to coat, sprinkle over almond za'atar and serve immediately.

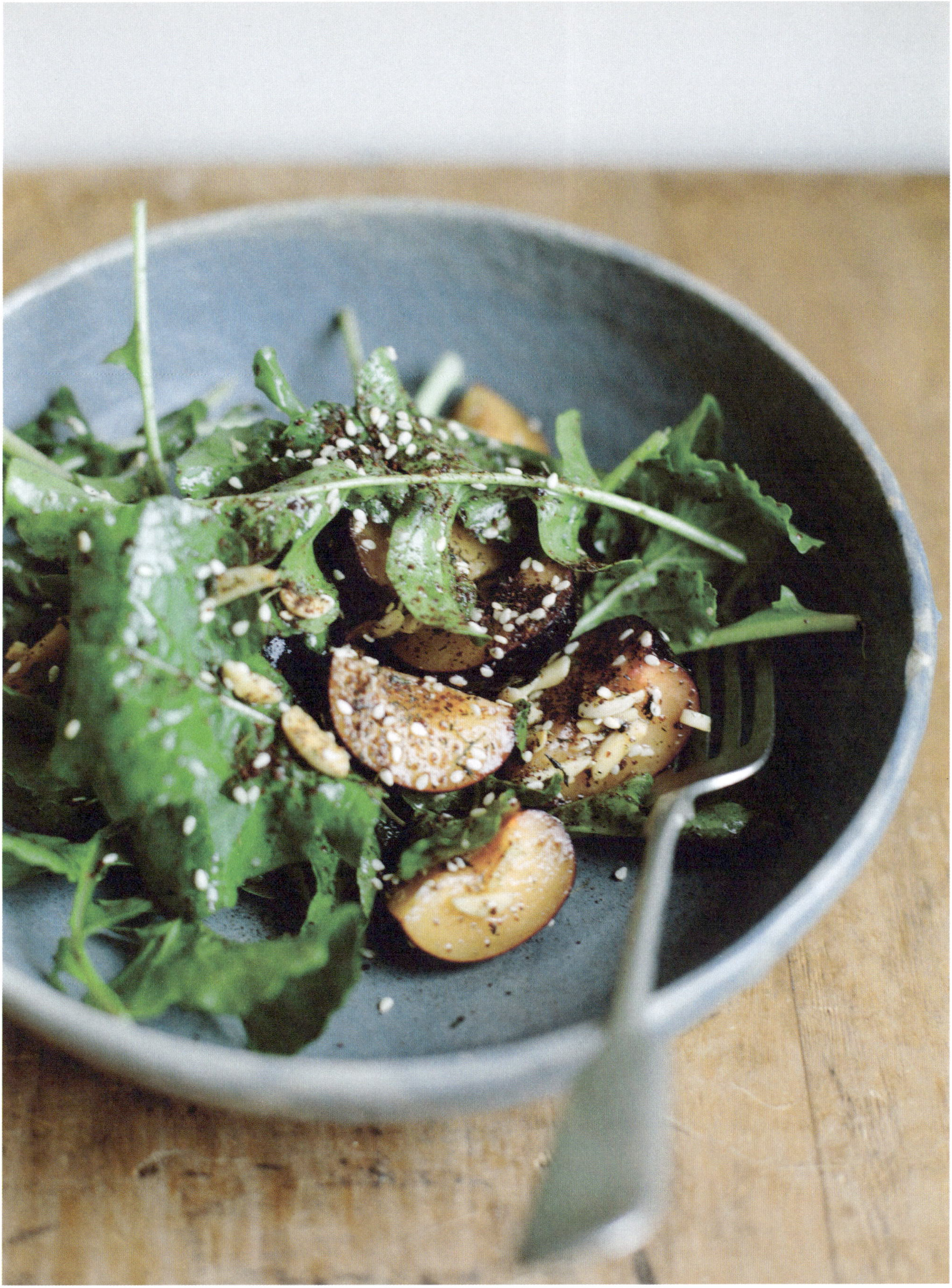

BAKED KUMARA CHIPS W/ OREGANO, PAPRIKA + CHILLI

SERVES 4–6 | GLUTEN-FREE | VEGAN OPTION

When I was a kid we used to go to this local restaurant which served the best kumara (sweet potato) chips around. Dipped into their homemade aioli they became somewhat of a thing in our little town and after a day at the beach they became the snack of choice for many of us teenagers. These baked ones are of course waaaay different from the deep-fried chips of my youth, but are equally as addictive in their spiced coating, with hints of lemon and chilli. For a vegan option, serve with vegan mayonnaise or a cashew-based dip.

- 1kg (4 medium) kumara (sweet potato)
- 60ml (¼ cup) tomato passata (purée)
- 3 cloves garlic, roughly chopped
- 3 tablespoons extra-virgin olive oil
- 1½ tablespoons lemon juice
- 2 teaspoons finely chopped thyme
- 1 teaspoon paprika (smoked or sweet)
- 1 teaspoon dried oregano
- 1 teaspoon whole cumin seeds
- ½ teaspoon dried chilli flakes
- Generous pinch or two of fine sea salt
- Aioli, sour cream, or natural plain yoghurt, to serve

+ Preheat oven to 200ºC (400ºF). Cut kumara into 1cm-wide chips. Combine all remaining ingredients, along with salt and freshly ground black pepper. Add kumara chips and, using your hands, mix well to evenly coat each chip in spice paste. Spread out onto a large oven tray in a single layer (use two if your trays are smaller). Bake for 35–40 minutes, turning once or twice during cooking, until tender and golden. Serve immediately with aioli, sour cream or natural yoghurt.

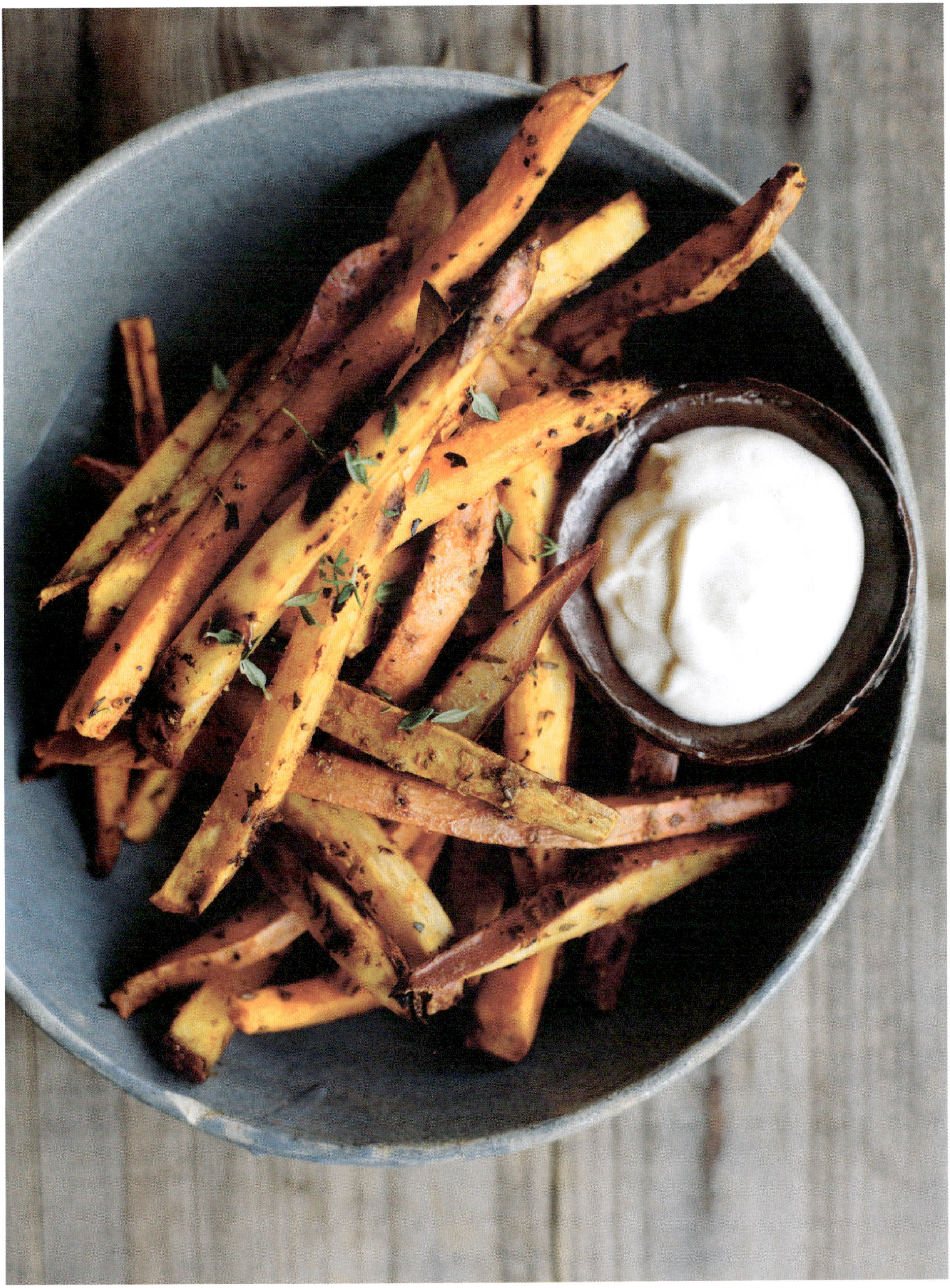

CHICKPEA + TOMATO CURRY

SERVES 4 | GLUTEN-FREE | VEGAN OPTION

As the last of summer's tomatoes ripen, the challenge begins to see how many ways you can use them up! If you grow your own, you'll likely be scrambling to use them quickly, as the dying plants take up precious real estate in your winter garden. And if you shop at farmers markets it's right about now that large boxes of bright red goodness show up, at bargain prices. Make the most of this supply (see NOTE) and you'll be thankful come midwinter, trust me. This is the kind of curry I love to eat. Quick, easy and flavourful it's perfect to serve alongside steamed rice and a simple tomato + cucumber salad, and like most curries, tastes even better the next day. If you've got leftovers that is! Soak your chickpeas the night before if using dried. Use olive oil instead of ghee for a vegan option.

- 270g (1½ cups) dried chickpeas, soaked overnight in cold water, or 2 x 400g tins cooked chickpeas, rinsed, or 3 cups cooked chickpeas
- 4 medium tomatoes, cored, skinned + roughly chopped (see NOTE, page 128)
- 2 cloves garlic, peeled
- 1 teaspoon finely grated ginger
- 2 tablespoons ghee or olive oil
- 2 teaspoons whole cumin seeds
- 2 teaspoons yellow or brown mustard seeds
- 1 onion, finely diced
- 2 teaspoons ground coriander
- 1 teaspoon ground turmeric
- 1 teaspoon garam masala
- 1 teaspoon fine sea salt
- 2 good pinches of unrefined raw sugar
- Pinch of dried chilli flakes
- Juice of ½ lemon
- Steamed rice + coriander leaves, to serve

+ Drain and rinse chickpeas, put in a saucepan and cover with cold water. Bring to the boil, skimming any foam that rises to the surface. Reduce to a simmer and cook for 25–35 minutes or until tender but not falling apart. Drain well.

+ Blend tomatoes, garlic and ginger in a blender or small food processor to a fine purée.

+ Heat ghee or oil in a large frying pan over medium-high heat, add cumin and mustard seeds and cook until mustard seeds start to pop. Add onion, reduce heat slightly and cook, while stirring, for 5–8 minutes, or until onion is tender and golden. Add ground coriander, turmeric, garam masala, salt, sugar and chilli flakes and cook for a further 20 seconds. Add drained chickpeas, tomato mixture and 60ml (¼ cup) water. Simmer over medium heat for 10–12 minutes, stirring often, until the sauce thickens, adding a touch more water if required. Remove from heat, stir through lemon juice and scatter over coriander leaves. Serve with steamed rice.

NOTE: When dealing with an abundance of tomatoes, first, I go crazy cooking all sorts of tomato-based dishes such as these (and the many others you'll see in this autumn section!), then I'll do a good few batches of my simple tomato + basil sauce (see my first cookbook or website for the recipe), which I pack into 500ml containers and freeze for later use in pasta or to top pizzas with. A few batches of tomato relish, chutney and kasundi are a must and oven-roasted tomatoes are the perfect way to use up those cherry tomatoes which often litter our garden throughout the summer and early autumn months.

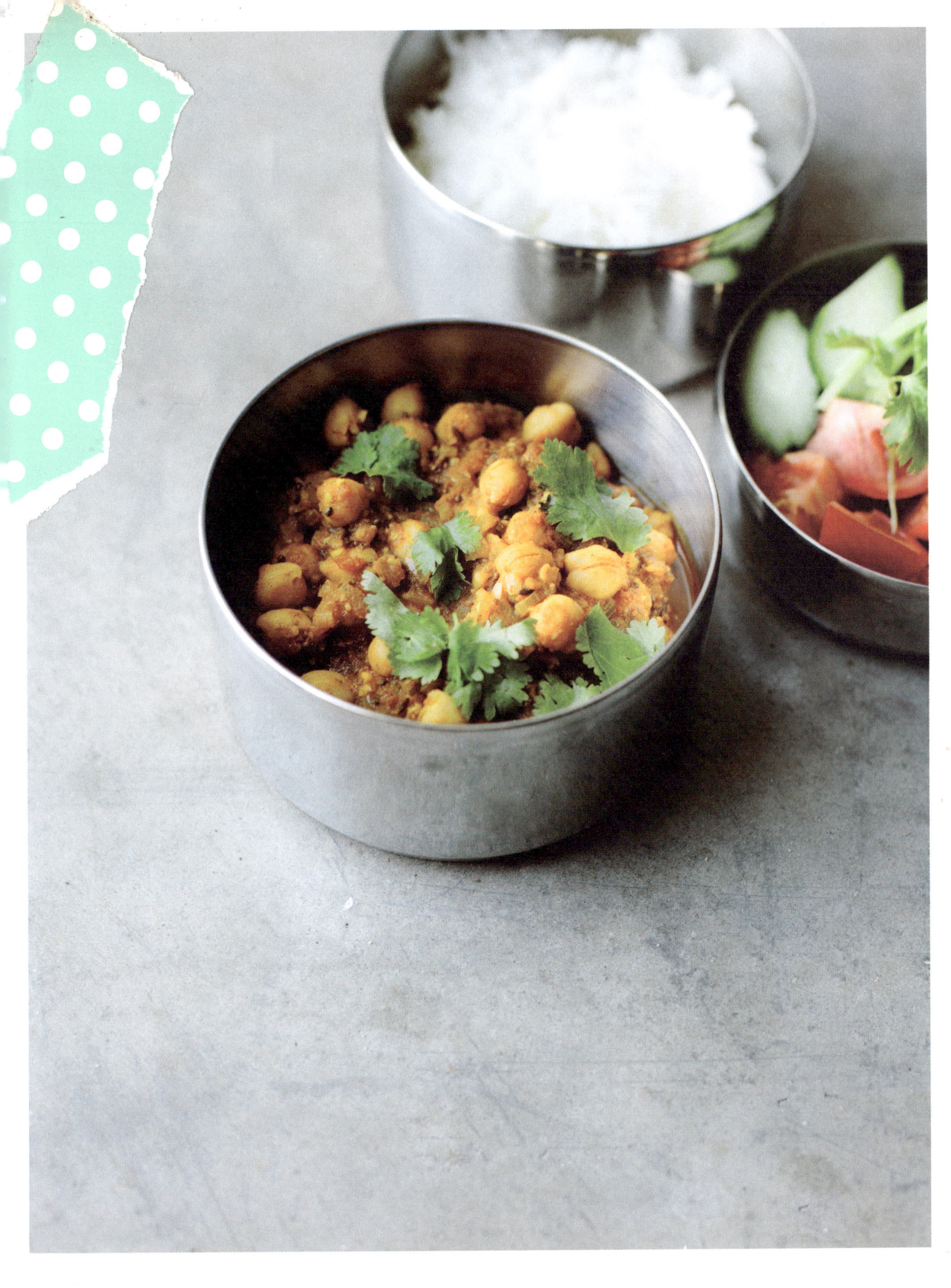

ROASTED KUMARA, PERSIMMON + ROCKET SALAD W/ JALAPEÑO DRESSING

SERVES 4–6 | GLUTEN-FREE | VEGAN

When I think of autumn, the image of bare persimmon trees laden with fire orange ornament-like fruit comes to mind. When most other trees go into hibernation mode as the weather cools, the persimmon stands proud, producing one of my most loved fruits of all time. There are two types of persimmon: Fuju, which are non-astringent fruit best eaten firm, and Hachiya, which are astringent and best left until totally mushy before eating – unless you want your tongue to stick to the roof of your mouth! You're after Fuju for this recipe, where thin slices get tossed with roasted kumara, spices, jalapeño and rocket in one of my favourite autumn salads. The flavours were inspired by a persimmon salsa found in my friend Bryant Terry's cookbook Afro Vegan.

2 medium (approx. 600g) orange (Beauregard) kumara (sweet potato) (see NOTE)

Finely grated zest of 1 lemon

4 tablespoons extra-virgin olive oil

2 persimmons, peeled + cut into bite-sized wedges

2 tablespoons finely chopped chives

1 pickled jalapeño (page 180 or use store-bought), finely chopped

¼ teaspoon ground cinnamon

¼ teaspoon ground allspice

Juice of 1 large lime

Big handful of flat-leaf parsley, roughly chopped

2 big handfuls of rocket

30g (¼ cup) toasted pumpkin seeds

+ Preheat oven to 200ºC (400ºF). Cut kumara into irregular bite-sized pieces and place on a large oven tray along with lemon zest. Drizzle over 2 tablespoons of the olive oil and season well with fine sea salt and freshly ground black pepper. Mix it all up with your hands and roast for 30–35 minutes, turning once or twice during cooking, until golden and tender. Remove and cool to room temperature.

+ Combine sliced persimmon, chives, jalapeño, spices, lime juice and remaining 2 tablespoons of olive oil in a bowl. Season with salt and pepper and set aside until ready to serve (this can be done a good 30 minutes before serving to allow the flavours to develop).

+ To serve, combine roasted kumara, dressed persimmon, parsley, rocket and toasted pumpkin seeds in a large bowl. Mix well to evenly distribute everything and serve.

NOTE: Regular red (Owairaka) or golden (Toka Toka) kumara can be used in place of orange, but I just love the colour and sweetness the Beauregard brings.

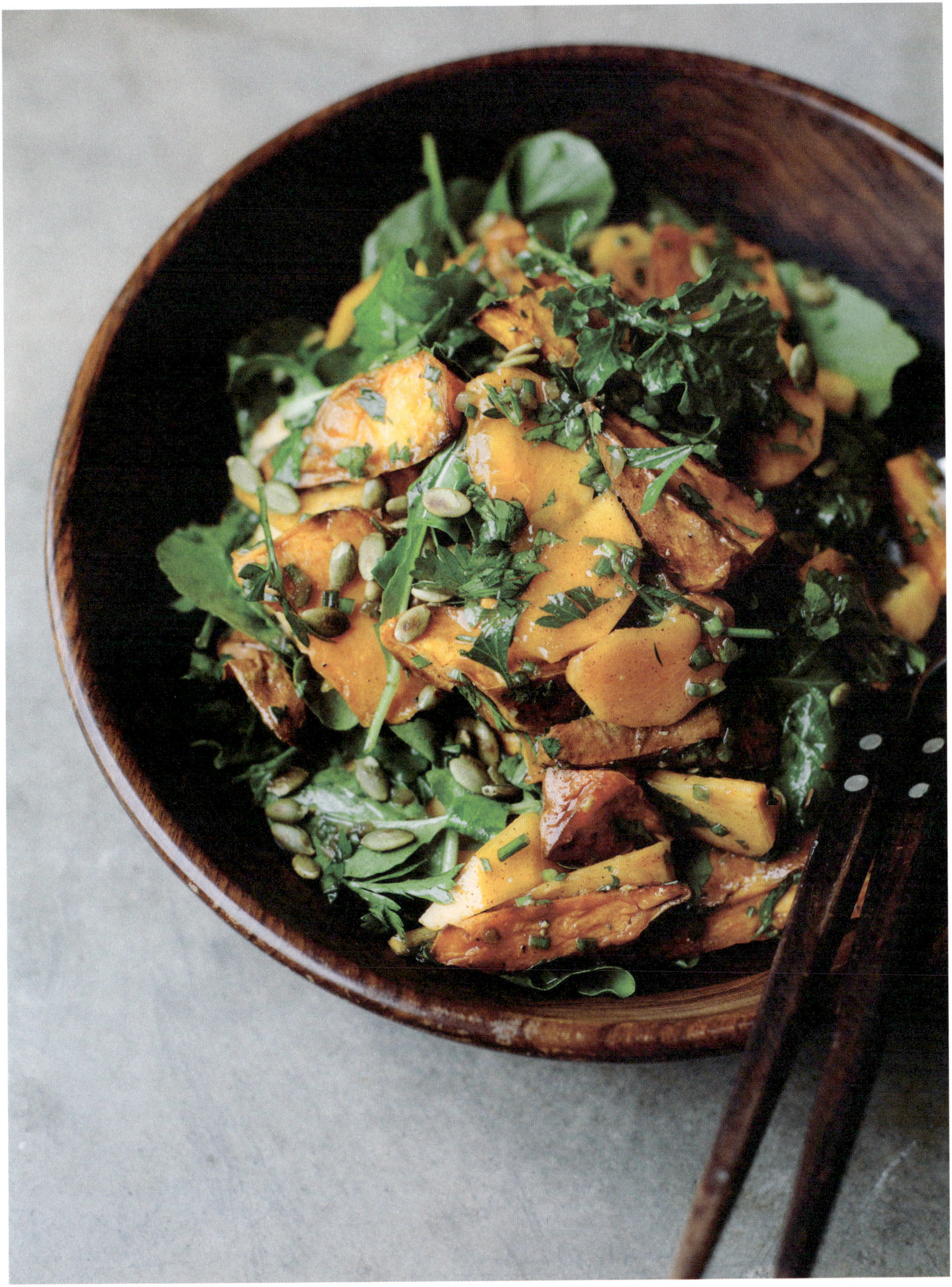

PRESERVED OLIVES

MAKES 1 KILO | GLUTEN-FREE | VEGAN

Having access to an olive tree is a true blessing if you love olives as much as I do. After years of walking past a laden tree, down the road from where we lived in Perth, and watching every autumn as all the olives dropped to the ground uneaten, we finally built up the courage to knock on the door of the house it stood in front of. It turned out the lady who owned the house hated olives and wanted no part of either preserving or eating them. She was only too grateful for us to pick them every year. I always make much more than one kilo of olives at a time, so just use this recipe as a guide. I weigh my olives and write on the lid of the container in marker pen, so I can then calculate the quantities of brine I'll need.

1kg freshly picked ripe olives
800ml boiling water
100g fine sea salt
200ml apple cider vinegar
Extra-virgin olive oil

+ Make a small slit down one side of each olive with a sharp knife, right down to the pip. Place into a large lidded container and cover with cold water (filtered is ideal). Cover and place in a cool, dark spot. Change the water every day for 7–10 days. This removes the natural bitterness of the olives. After 7–10 days (depending on how much water you want to waste!) make the brine.

+ Combine boiling water and salt, stirring until the salt has dissolved, then add vinegar and set aside until completely cold. Pack olives into a large sterilised jar or a bunch of smaller ones and pour in brine solution to 5mm from the top of the rim. Finish with a little layer of olive oil on top, right up to the rim of the jar (this helps to keep the olives submerged in the brine). Screw lids on tightly and keep in a cool, dark place (the pantry is ideal) for at least 1 month before using, but ideally 2–6 months if you can wait. Keep refrigerated once opened. Unopened olives will happily store for 12 months or more.

NOTE: To sterilise jars, place freshly washed and rinsed jars in a preheated oven at 120°C (250°F) for 30 minutes. Remove from oven carefully with a dry tea towel. I find it easiest to set them on an oven tray after being in the oven – when you are filling them with brine any stray drips will be caught in the tray, making clean-up that much easier! To sterilise lids, immerse in boiling water for 5 minutes.

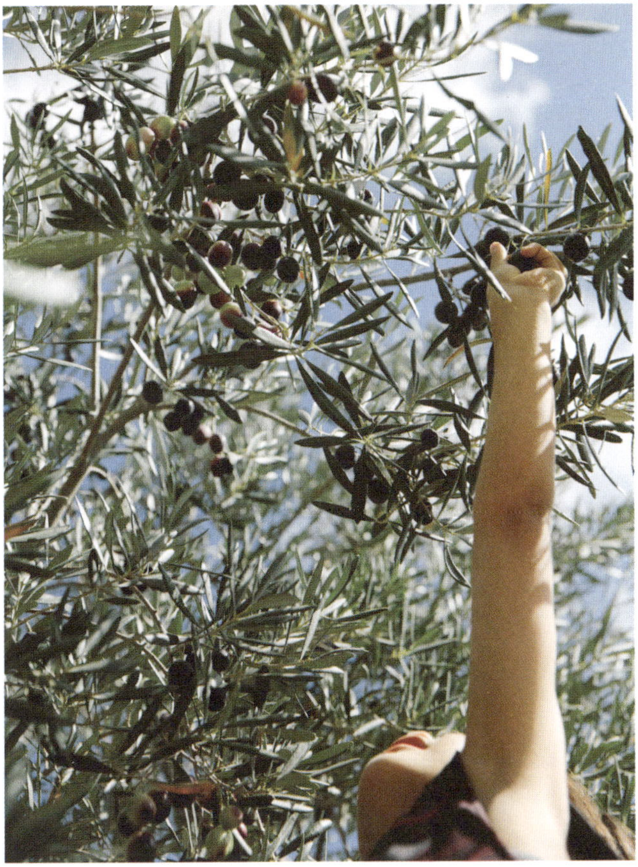
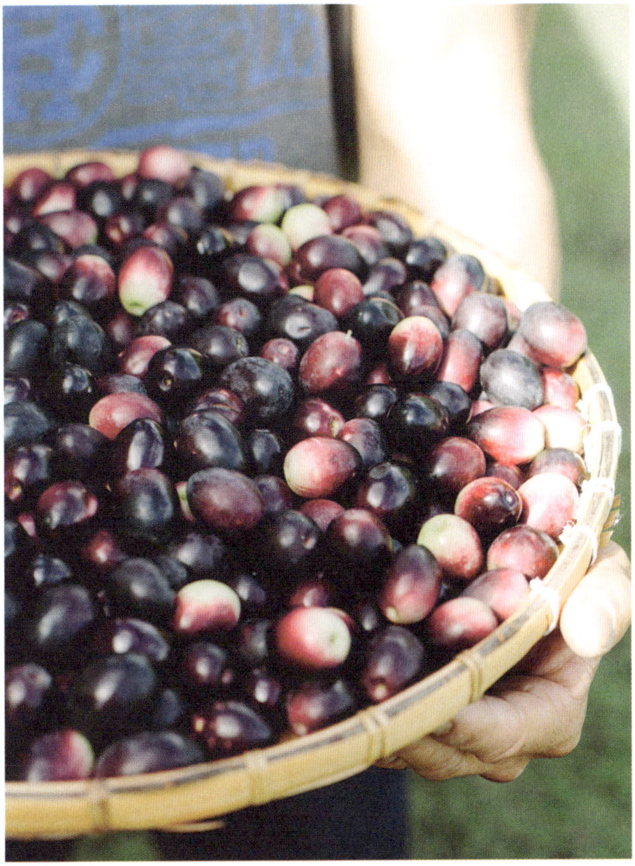
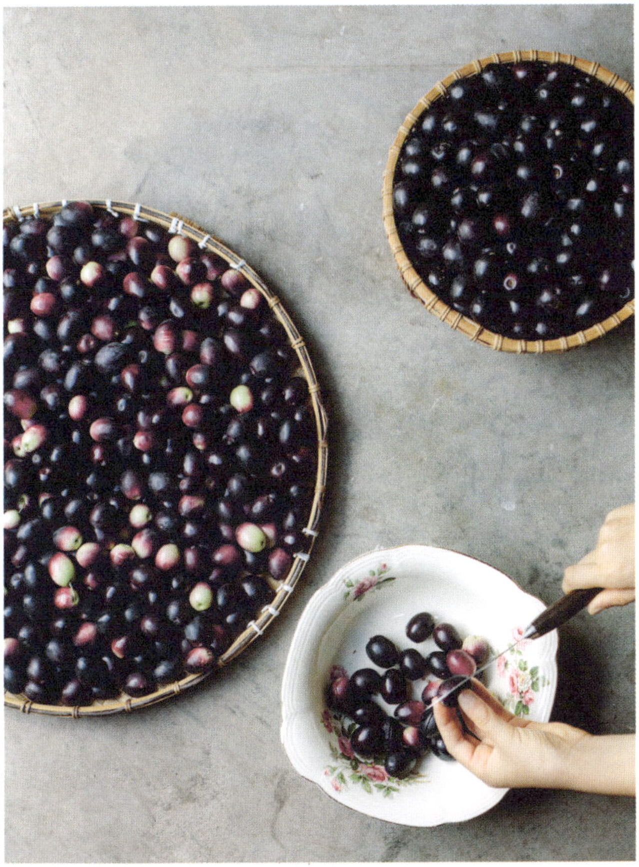
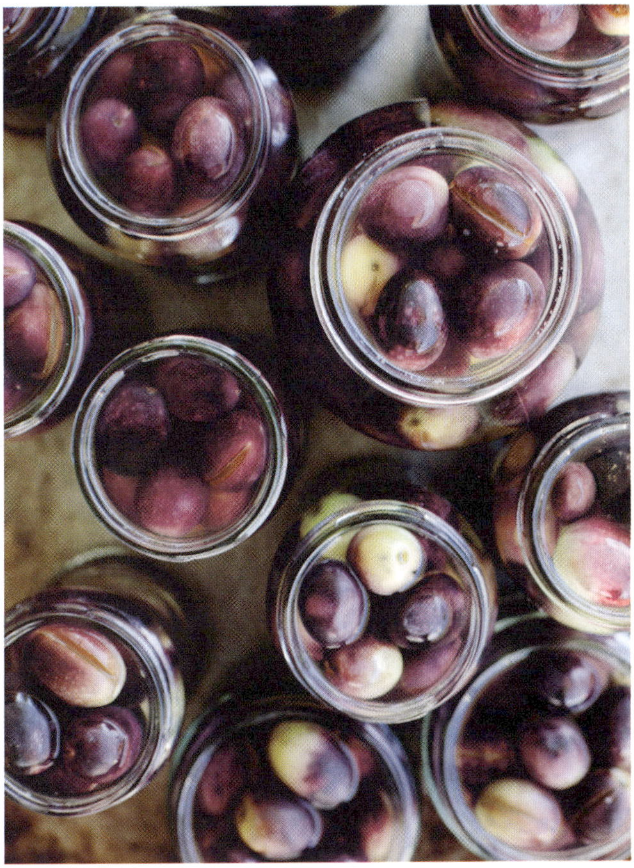

SAFFRON-BUTTERED PUMPKIN W/ HERBED BROWN RICE

SERVES 4 | GLUTEN-FREE | VEGAN OPTION

Don't let this recipe's humble looks deceive you. For beneath its tomatoey goodness lies tender chunks of pumpkin in a sauce rich with saffron, spice and most importantly ... butter! The vinegar-soaked sultanas add a nice piquant note, while the herbed rice not only offers freshness but also mops up all those wonderful juices you won't want to waste. If you're vegan or dairy-free, simply omit the butter and increase the olive oil to 4 tablespoons. To bump up the protein, serve alongside a chickpea or lentil-based dish, or toss cooked chickpeas through the tomato sauce before serving or serve over herbed quinoa instead of rice. Soak the brown rice overnight in the stated water amount before cooking (in the same water) the following day, to improve its digestibility.

300g (1½ cups) brown rice (I use short-grain)
50g (¼ cup) natural sultanas, roughly chopped
2 tablespoons red wine vinegar
30g butter or ghee
2 tablespoons extra-virgin olive oil
3 cloves garlic, roughly chopped
1 tablespoon finely grated ginger
Good pinch of saffron
½ teaspoon ground cumin
½ teaspoon ground coriander
Pinch of ground cinnamon
2 large tomatoes, finely chopped
600g (½ medium) Japanese pumpkin, deseeded + cut into wedges
1 teaspoon fine sea salt
Big handful of flat-leaf parsley, roughly chopped + extra, to serve
Big handful of coriander, roughly chopped

+ To cook brown rice, wash, drain and place in a saucepan with 650ml cold water, cover with a tight-fitting lid and bring to the boil. Reduce heat to lowest setting and simmer, covered, for about 40–45 minutes until the water is absorbed and rice tender. Remove from heat, keeping lid on, and allow to stand for 10 minutes. (Alternatively, cook in a rice cooker following the manufacturer's instructions.)

+ Combine sultanas and vinegar and set aside.

+ Heat butter and olive oil in a large saucepan over medium heat. Add garlic, ginger and saffron and cook, stirring, for 30 seconds until fragrant. Add cumin, coriander and cinnamon, and stir for 10 seconds before adding tomatoes. Cook, stirring, for 5 minutes or until juices have started to release from the tomatoes. Add pumpkin, salt and 250ml (1 cup) water. Cover and bring to the boil before reducing heat to a simmer, then cook for 10 minutes. Remove lid, give it all a good stir and cook for a further 10 minutes or until pumpkin is tender. If you find the sauce is still a little too runny and the pumpkin is cooked, carefully transfer the pumpkin to a bowl, doing your best not to break it all up. Return sauce to heat and simmer for another 5–8 minutes until thick, taste and adjust seasoning if needed, then pour over pumpkin.

+ When ready to serve, mix the chopped parsley and coriander through rice. Serve mounds of rice topped with pumpkin and sauce. Drain sultanas (reserve vinegar for another use, such as to add to a vinaigrette) and scatter over pumpkin along with a little extra chopped parsley.

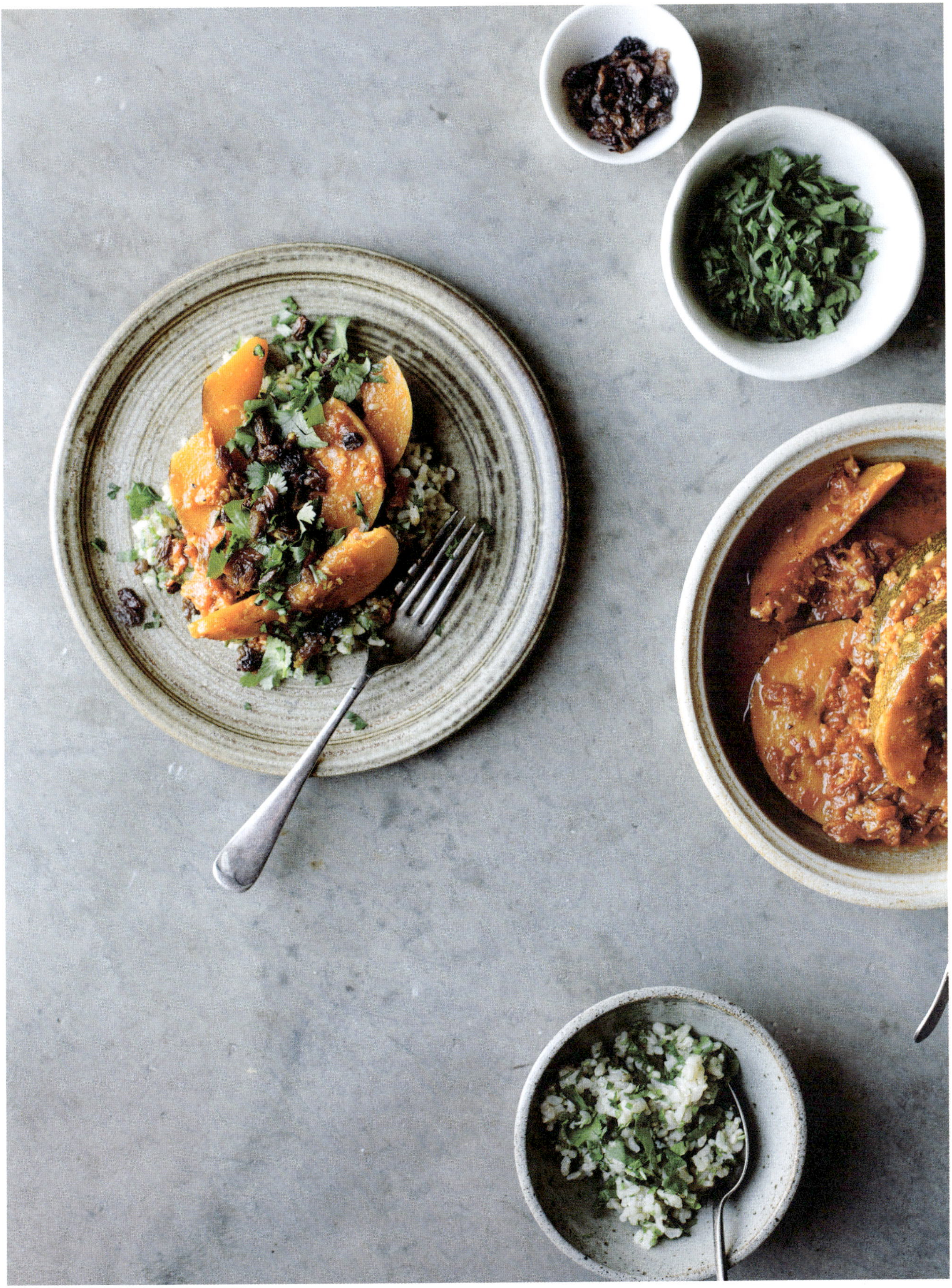

TOMATO, EGGPLANT + BUCKWHEAT BAKE

SERVES 4–6 | GLUTEN-FREE

The idea for this hearty beginning-of-autumn dish came from the Baked Butter Beans with Feta recipe in my first book. The ingredients are totally different, but the premise stays the same: take a wholesome gluten-free protein (in this case, buckwheat), add some in-season vegetables, the last of the summer's tomatoes and top with cheese (in this case mozzarella, but feta would also work wonderfully here if you prefer) and bake until delicious.

- 90g (½ cup) raw hulled buckwheat
- 1 large eggplant, ends trimmed + cut into 1cm dice
- 1 tablespoon fine sea salt
- 60ml (¼ cup) extra-virgin olive oil
- 4 cloves garlic, roughly chopped
- 5 large tomatoes, cored, peeled + finely chopped (see NOTE, page 128)
- Pinch of unrefined raw sugar
- 2 tablespoons tomato paste dissolved in 125ml (½ cup) cold water
- Handful of basil leaves, roughly chopped
- 200g fresh mozzarella cheese, roughly torn

+ Bring 250ml (1 cup) water to the boil with a good pinch of fine sea salt. Add buckwheat, cover with a lid and reduce heat to lowest setting. Cook for 15–20 minutes until water has evaporated and buckwheat is tender. You can remove the lid in the last 5 minutes to evaporate any excess liquid if needed. Remove from heat and fluff up with a fork.

+ While buckwheat is cooking, combine diced eggplant with salt in a large glass or ceramic bowl. Set aside for 30 minutes. Rinse under cold water and drain well. Pat dry with a clean tea towel.

+ Preheat oven to 180ºC (350ºF). Heat olive oil in a large frying pan over medium-high heat (if you have an ovenproof one, such as cast iron, use this). Add eggplant and cook, stirring often, for 8–10 minutes until golden and tender. Add garlic and cook for a further minute before adding chopped tomatoes. Cook for 5–8 minutes until soft, then add sugar, tomato paste mixed with water, and basil. Season with fine sea salt and freshly ground black pepper. Stir through cooked buckwheat. Transfer to a large ovenproof dish if your pan is not ovenproof. Scatter with mozzarella and bake for 25–30 minutes. Serve with a lovely bitter salad, such as rocket leaves dressed with olive oil and lemon juice.

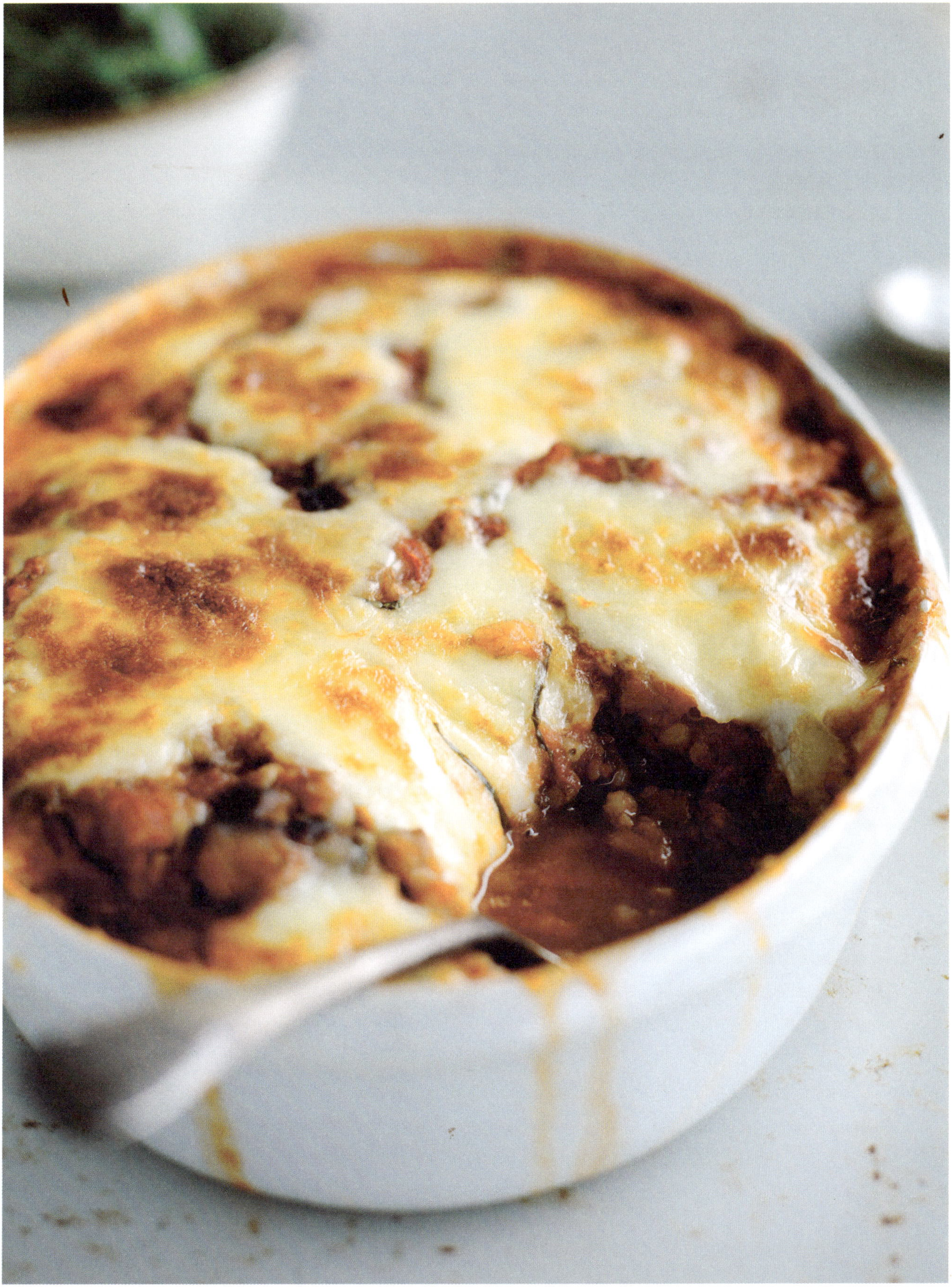

SHIITAKE, PEANUT + TOFU DUMPLINGS

MAKES 40, ENOUGH TO SERVE 4-ISH | GLUTEN-FREE | VEGAN

If you had told me 15 years ago that I'd be making a weekly batch of homemade dumplings, I would have laughed. Yum cha was the domain of my nimble-fingered Filipino friends when I was working in Sydney years ago, and while I did have a go at making the simplest of wontons once, I quickly realised that my big hands were not made for such fiddly work; the look on my friends' faces when they saw my attempts pretty much summed it up. Fast-forward to now, when you have a daughter who'd happily eat dumplings every day of the week, and has to avoid gluten, well, you just suck it up and make them, don't you? I may not be an expert when it comes to shaping, but even I can pinch together the simplest of dumplings and Ada helps me out more often than not too. For the dumpling dough, I get the most consistent results when using Erawan brand white rice and tapioca flour, which you can find at your local Asian grocers for just a dollar or two. Some brands of black (rice) vinegar contain barley, so if you need to eat gluten-free make sure you check the labels carefully. Balsamic vinegar makes an okay substitute if need be.

50g (3–4) fresh shiitake mushrooms (or 15g dried), stems removed + finely diced
125g firm tofu, rinsed, patted dry + cut into 5mm dice
2 spring onions, finely sliced
1 clove garlic, finely chopped
1 teaspoon finely grated ginger
½ long green chilli, deseeded + finely chopped
Handful of coriander leaves + tender stems, roughly chopped
2 tablespoons natural crunchy peanut butter (omit for nut-free)
2 tablespoons gluten-free soy sauce

Wrappers
135g (1 cup) white rice flour
80g (¾ cup) tapioca flour
2 tablespoons peanut or olive oil
160ml (⅔ cup) boiling water

Dipping sauce
2 tablespoons Chinese black (rice) vinegar
1 tablespoon gluten-free soy sauce
¼ teaspoon pure sesame oil
Finely sliced spring onions + dried chilli flakes, to serve

+ If you're using dried shiitake, cover with boiling water and set aside for 20 minutes before draining. Place in a bowl along with diced tofu, spring onion, garlic, ginger, chilli and coriander. Combine peanut butter and soy sauce in a small bowl and mix until smooth before adding to tofu mixture. Season with ground white pepper and mix well.

+ To make wrappers, place rice and tapioca flour in a bowl, and whisk to combine. Add oil and boiling water and, using your hands, mix until the dough starts to come together. Dump onto the bench and knead a few times until a soft smooth dough forms. Cut dough in half, then roll each half out into a long thick rope, approx. 1.5cm thick. Cut off 2cm pieces and, one at a time, roll each piece into a ball, then flatten to a thick circle with the palm of your hand (cover the rest with a clean tea towel to prevent dough from drying out too quickly).

+ Use a rolling pin to roll dough into a 2mm-thick round. Place 1 heaped teaspoon of filling in the centre, use your finger to rub a little water around the edges of the dough, then pull the edges together, squeezing to seal tightly. Transfer to a tray, then continue with remaining dough and filling. If you find the dough pieces are starting to dry out on the outside, give them a quick roll around in your hand to knead slightly, before rolling out and filling.

+ Bring a large saucepan of water to the boil, top with a steamer lined with baking paper. Steam the dumplings in batches for

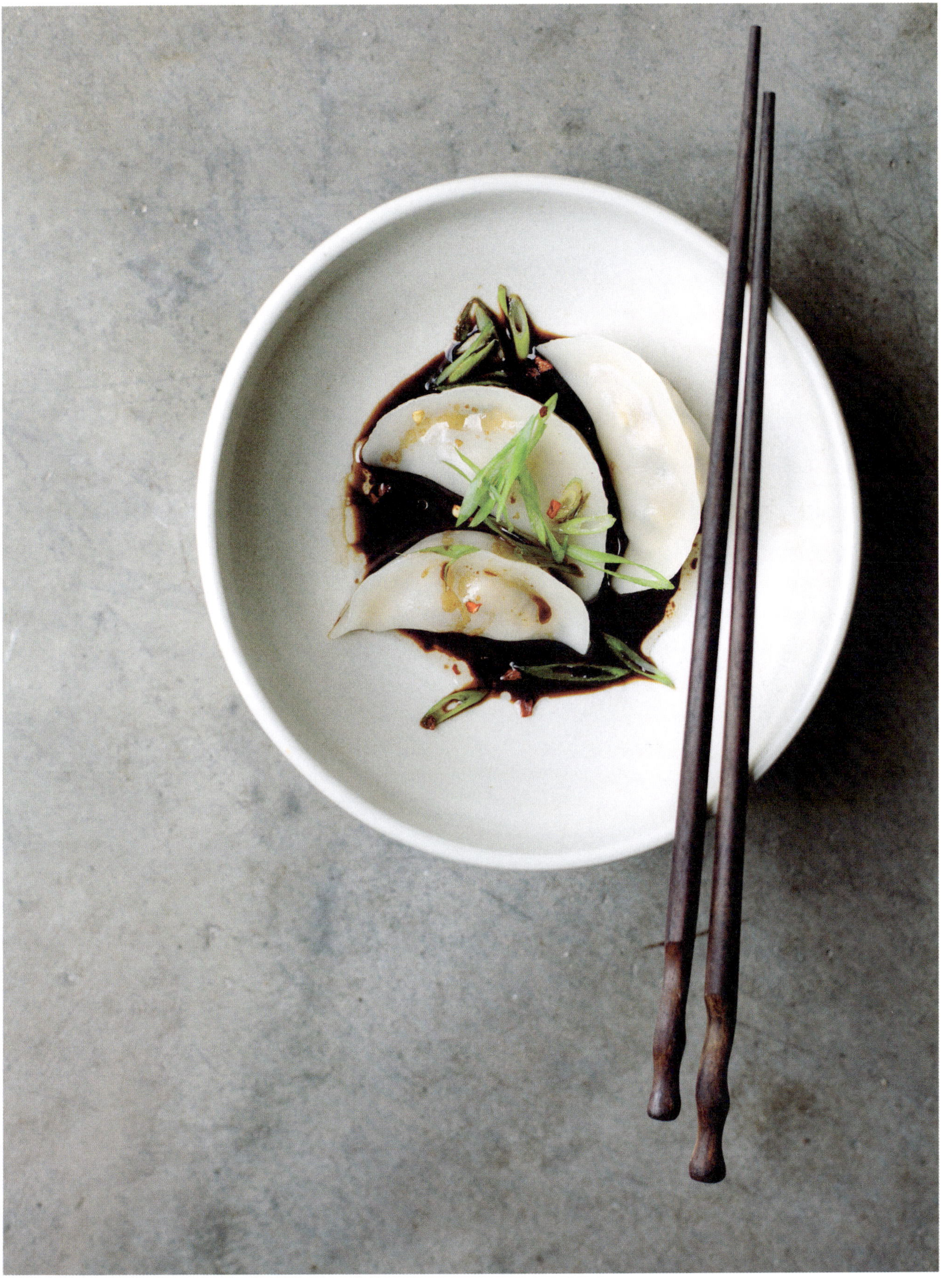

7–10 minutes or until dough is translucent and tender. Make sure you keep the water level topped up at all times.

+ To make dipping sauce, combine black vinegar, soy sauce and sesame oil in a bowl. Serve dumplings with dipping sauce, sliced spring onions and dried chilli flakes.

NOTE: Shaped dumplings can be frozen on a tray in a single layer, then transferred to zip-lock bags once frozen. Cook straight from frozen, adding an extra few minutes to the cooking time. The texture's not quite as good as when fresh, but they're still yum!

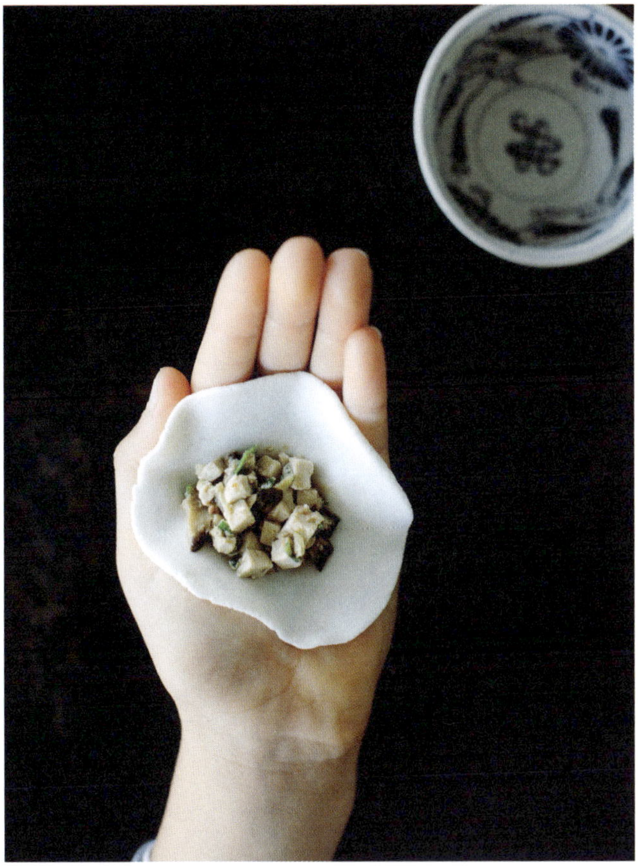
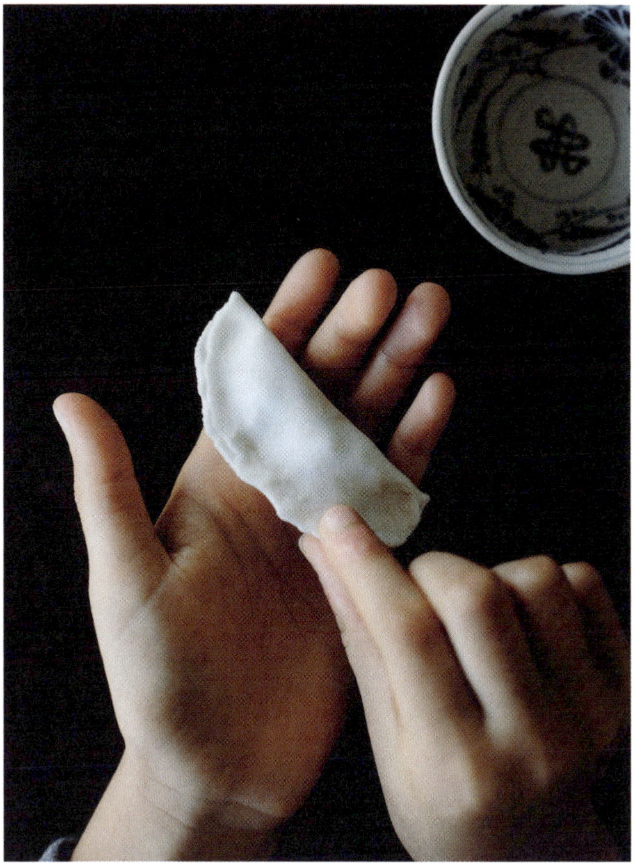
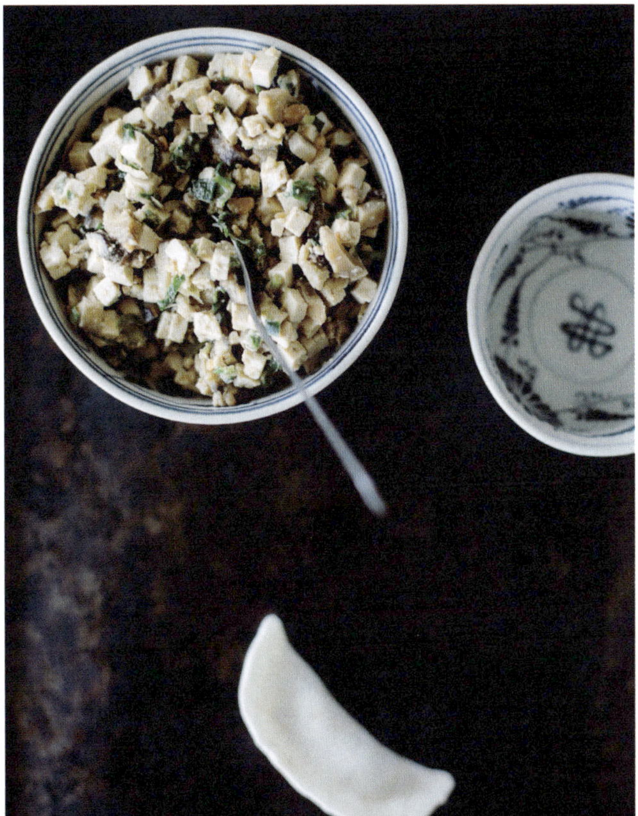
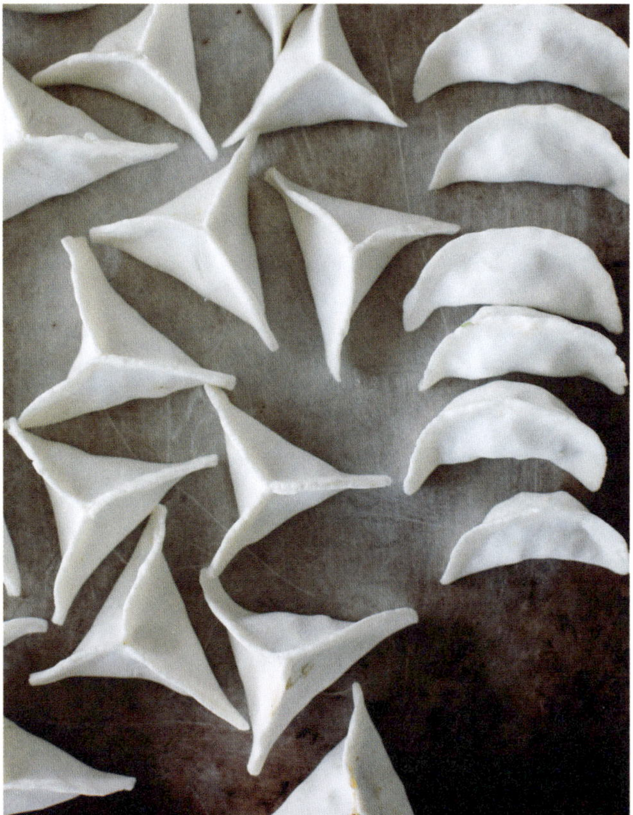

LEMONY MUSHROOM QUINOA W/ CHILLI ALMONDS

SERVES 4 OR MORE AS A SIDE | GLUTEN-FREE | VEGAN

Mushrooms are one of the easiest ways to add a good dose of flavour to any dish – their natural umami characteristic gives such depth and richness to even the simplest of ingredients. Here I've cooked down finely chopped mushroom with a few of its favourite things – olive oil, garlic, thyme and lemon – before tossing through cooked quinoa and sprinkling with crunchy chilli almonds. If you're not a huge chilli fan, scale the amount back to just a pinch. And if you're a fried egg on everything kinda person, this is the perfect place to do just that.

- 185g (1 cup) quinoa, soaked overnight in cold water if possible
- 2 tablespoons extra-virgin olive oil
- 4 cloves garlic, finely chopped
- 2 tablespoons finely chopped thyme
- Finely grated zest + juice of 1 lemon
- 500g Swiss brown or button mushrooms, finely chopped
- Big handful of flat-leaf parsley, finely chopped

Chilli almonds
- 1 teaspoon extra-virgin olive oil
- 65g (½ cup) slivered almonds
- ¼ teaspoon dried chilli flakes
- Good pinch of sea salt

+ Drain quinoa in a fine sieve and rinse well. Bring 250ml (1 cup) water to the boil – increase to 375ml (1½ cups) if using unsoaked – in a small saucepan before adding the quinoa, covering with a lid and reducing heat to a gentle simmer. Cook for 10–12 minutes until the water has been absorbed and quinoa is tender. Remove from heat, leave lid on and set aside to steam for a further 5 minutes before fluffing up with a fork.

+ To make chilli almonds, heat olive oil in a small frying pan over medium-high heat. Add almonds and cook, stirring, for 2–3 minutes or until lovely and golden. Remove from heat and stir in chilli flakes and salt. Set aside to cool briefly before serving. Any leftovers will store airtight for 1 week.

+ Heat a large frying pan over medium heat, add olive oil, garlic, thyme, lemon zest and finely chopped mushrooms. Cook, stirring often, for 8–10 minutes or until most of the liquid from the mushrooms has evaporated and the mixture is relatively dry. Add quinoa and stir well. Check seasoning, squeeze over lemon juice and stir in parsley. Serve topped with a handful of chilli almonds.

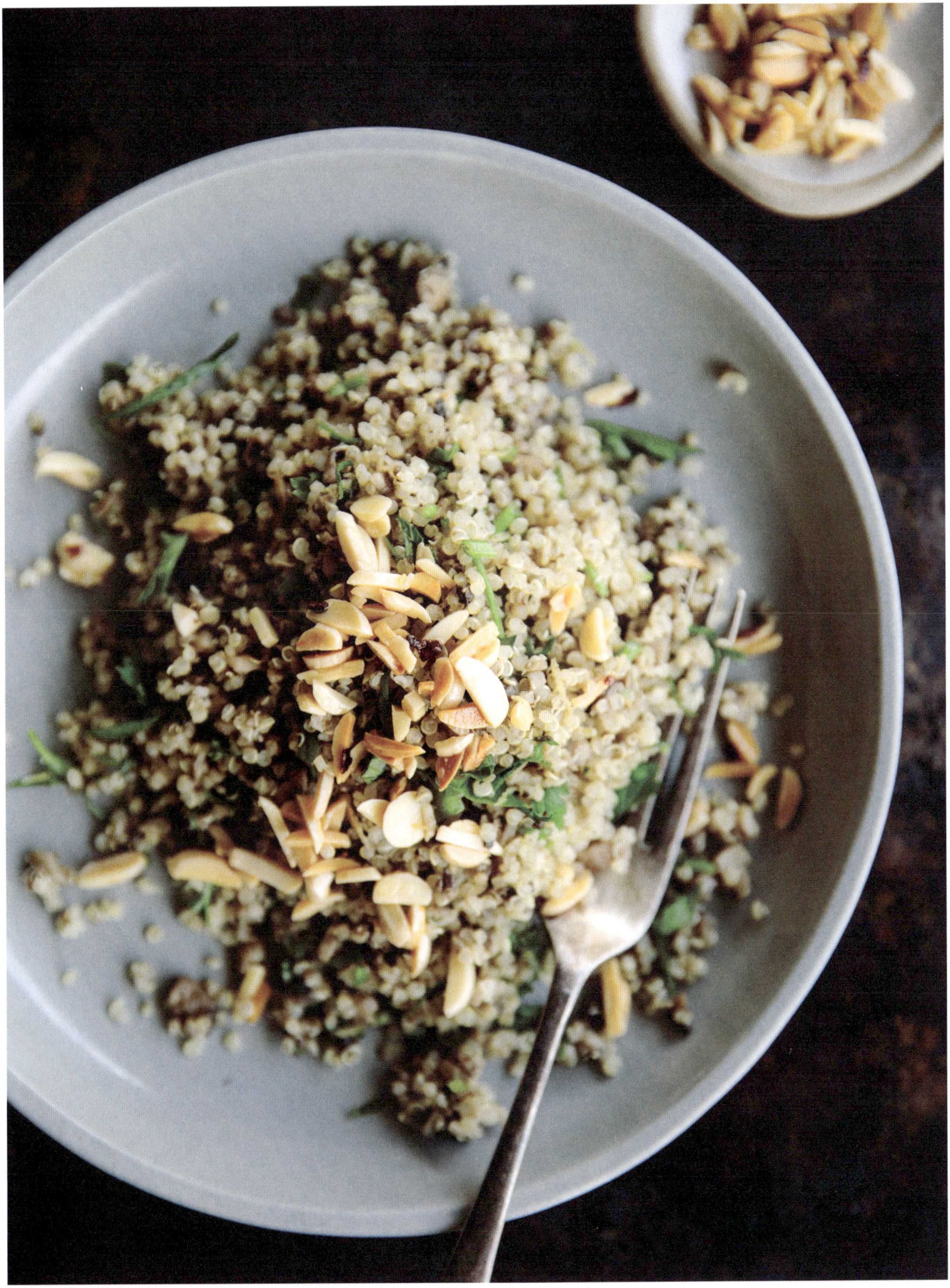

GINGER-ROASTED PUMPKIN + QUINOA SALAD W/ MINT, CHILLI + LIME

SERVES 4 OR MORE AS A SIDE | GLUTEN-FREE | VEGAN

This is my favourite go-to way to eat quinoa. Flavoursome roasted vegetables and a ton of herbs with a bright simple dressing. I buy coriander in large bunches with the stems and roots still attached – the finely chopped roots and tougher stems combined with the pumpkin before roasting adds loads of flavour. Start the night before if soaking quinoa.

- 185g (1 cup) quinoa, soaked overnight in cold water if possible
- 1kg pumpkin, peeled, deseeded + cut into 2–3cm chunks
- 1 tablespoon finely grated ginger
- 2 long green or red chillies, finely chopped (deseeded if you want)
- 2 cloves garlic, finely chopped
- 2 tablespoons olive oil
- 2 teaspoons pure maple syrup
- Handful of finely chopped coriander roots and stems, optional
- Juice of 2 limes (or 1 large lemon)
- Good handful each of mint and coriander leaves
- Toasted pumpkin seeds, to serve

+ Preheat oven to 200°C (400°F). Combine pumpkin with ginger, chilli, garlic, olive oil, maple syrup and coriander roots. Season well with fine sea salt and freshly ground black pepper and turn out onto a large oven tray. Bake for 25–30 minutes, turning once or twice, until the pumpkin is a lovely golden colour and soft right through. Remove from oven and set aside to cool slightly.

+ Meanwhile drain quinoa in a sieve and rinse well. Bring 250ml (1 cup) water to the boil – increase to 375ml (1½ cups) if using unsoaked quinoa – in a small saucepan before adding quinoa, covering with a lid and reducing heat to a gentle simmer. Cook for 10–12 minutes until the water has been absorbed and quinoa is tender. Remove from heat, leave lid on and set aside to steam for a further 5 minutes before fluffing up with a fork.

+ When both pumpkin and quinoa are cooked, combine in a large bowl, making sure you scrape in any lovely bits of ginger and oil from the bottom of the oven tray. Squeeze over lime juice, stir through herbs, season with more salt and pepper if desired and scatter pumpkin seeds over to serve. You can eat this salad warm or cool pumpkin and quinoa first before stirring through herbs and serve at room temperature.

NOTE: I used Queensland Blue pumpkin in this recipe but Crown (NZ) or butternut pumpkin would be great too.

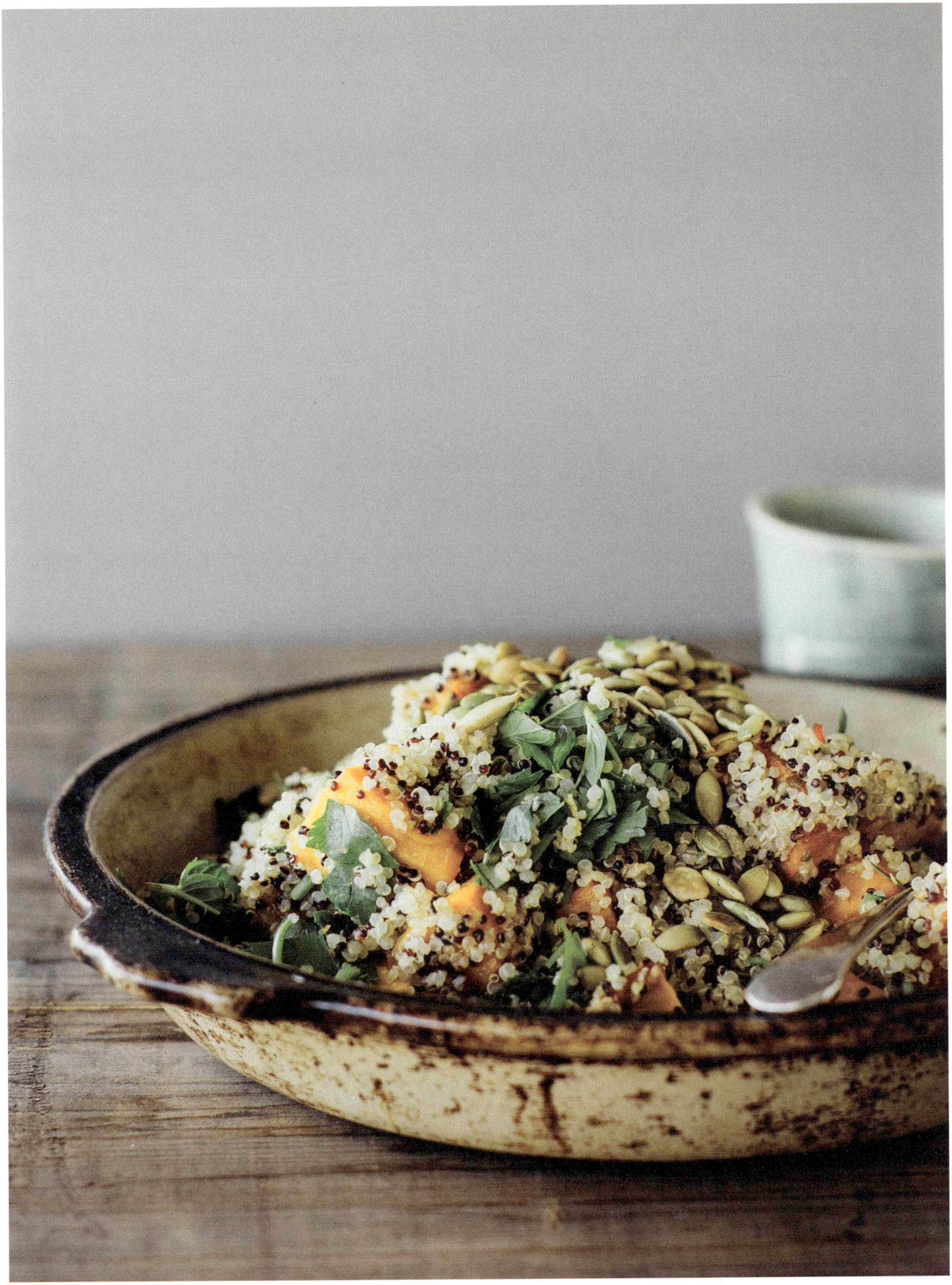

MUSTARDY MUSHROOM + TOASTED QUINOA TAGLIATELLE

SERVES 4 | GLUTEN-FREE | DAIRY-FREE OPTION

It's long been known that mushrooms grown in sunlight are high in vitamin D, but a recent discovery has found that if you place your store-bought mushrooms out in the midday sun for an hour, they'll absorb the sun's rays and naturally charge themselves up on vitamin D! When it comes to mushrooms, I like to keep things simple. A little olive oil, ghee or butter, some garlic, thyme and mustard are all that's required to form a beautiful flavourful sauce to toss through nutty homemade toasted quinoa pasta. A special thank you to my dear friend Shauna Ahern, aka Gluten-Free Girl, who was among the first to develop a gluten- and gum-free fresh pasta, and who invariably inspires me more than she will ever know.

Toasted quinoa tagliatelle
- 60g (½ cup) quinoa flour
- 45g (⅓ cup) fine brown rice flour
- 25g (¼ cup) tapioca flour
- 1 teaspoon psyllium husks
- ½ teaspoon fine sea salt
- 1 large (60g) free-range egg, lightly whisked
- 2 large (30g) free-range egg yolks
- 1 tablespoon extra-virgin olive oil
- 1–2 tablespoons cold water

Mushrooms
- 500g mixed mushrooms
- 1–2 tablespoons extra-virgin olive oil, ghee or butter (or a mixture)
- 3 cloves garlic, finely chopped
- 1 tablespoon finely chopped thyme
- 1 tablespoon wholegrain mustard
- Juice of ½ lemon
- Flat-leaf parsley, to serve

+ Combine quinoa and brown rice flour in a dry pan set over medium heat and cook, stirring often until light golden and fragrant (2–3 minutes). Remove from heat and set aside to cool.

+ To make pasta, place toasted flours, tapioca flour, psyllium husks and salt in a medium bowl and whisk to combine. Make a well in the centre, add egg and extra yolks, olive oil and 1 tablespoon of the water. Using your fingers mix the eggs, slowly incorporating a little flour as you go until the dough forms into one mass. If the dough is a little dry add another tablespoon of water. Turn out onto a lightly rice-floured bench and knead a few times to bring together into a smooth dough. Cover and set aside for 20 minutes.

+ Divide dough in two, keeping one half covered while you roll out the other on a sheet of rice-floured baking paper, flouring as needed, until approx. 2–3mm thick. Cut into 1cm-wide lengths and set aside while you repeat with remaining dough. You can hang the pasta over a couple of wooden spoons or a pasta drying rack (if you have one) at this stage for 1–2 hours, or cook straightaway.

+ Bring a saucepan of salted water to the boil for the pasta. Brush your mushrooms clean, trim ends off stalks and slice any larger ones. Heat olive oil, ghee or butter in a large frying pan over medium-high heat. Add garlic and thyme and sizzle for a few seconds. Add larger mushrooms (button, Swiss brown, shiitake, field) and cook, stirring occasionally, for 3–4 minutes, until slightly tender. Add any softer mushrooms (oyster, enoki) and cook for a further 1–2 minutes or until starting to release their juices and brown. Stir through mustard and lemon juice, and season with fine sea salt and freshly ground black pepper. Cook pasta for 3–4 minutes or until still slightly firm to the bite, drain and drizzle with a little olive oil.

+ Serve mushrooms spooned over piles of pasta and scatter with parsley.

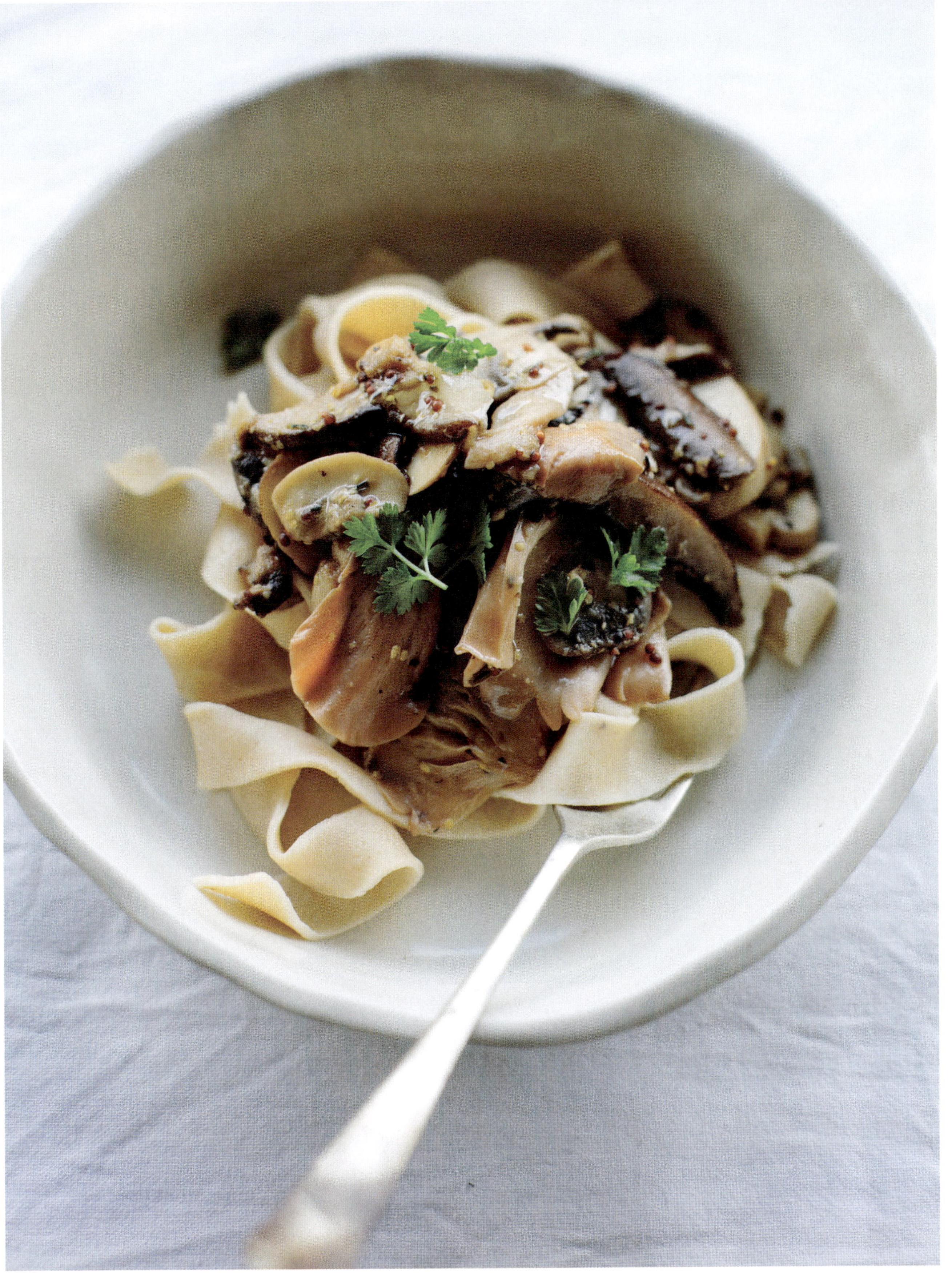

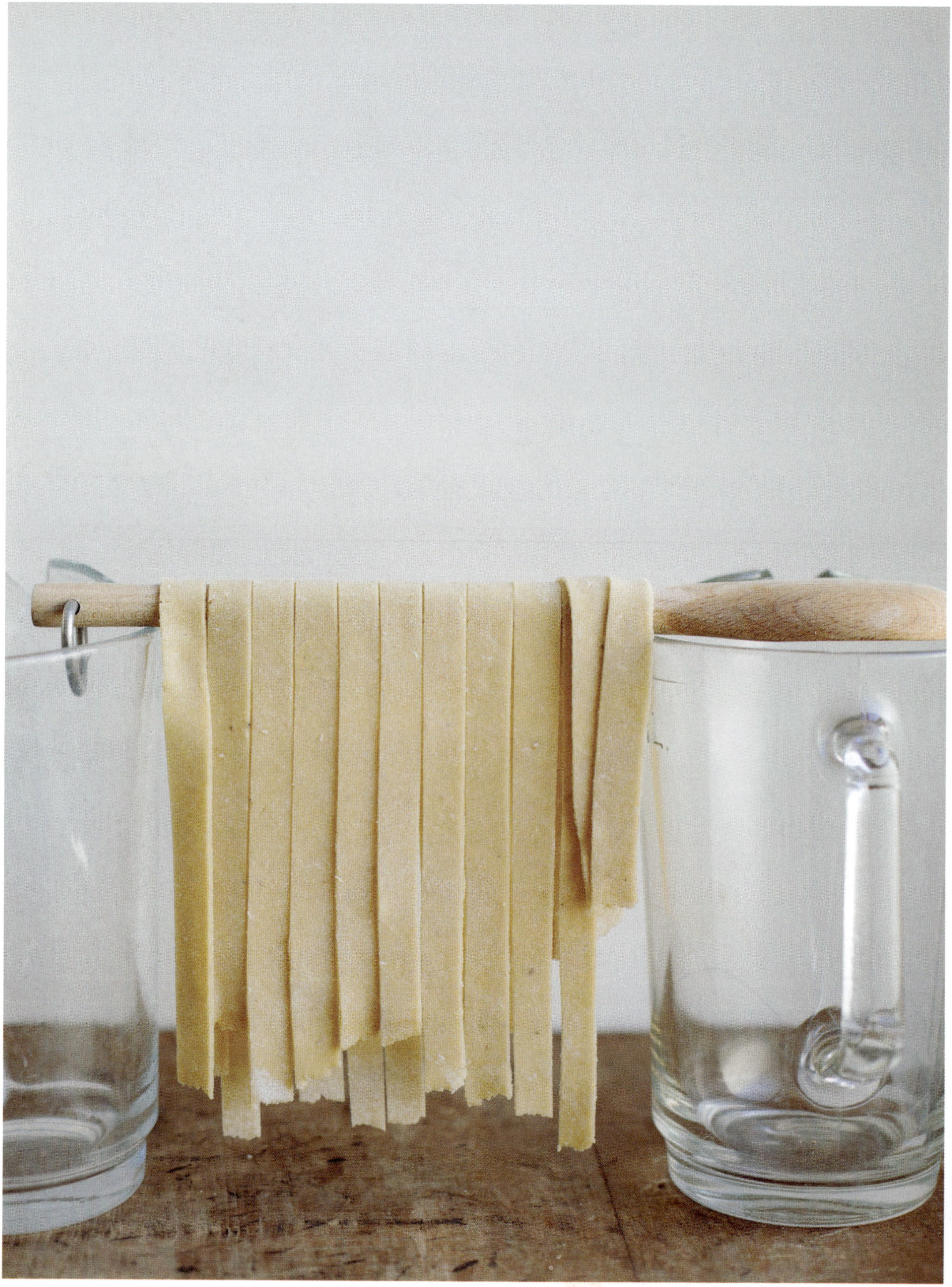

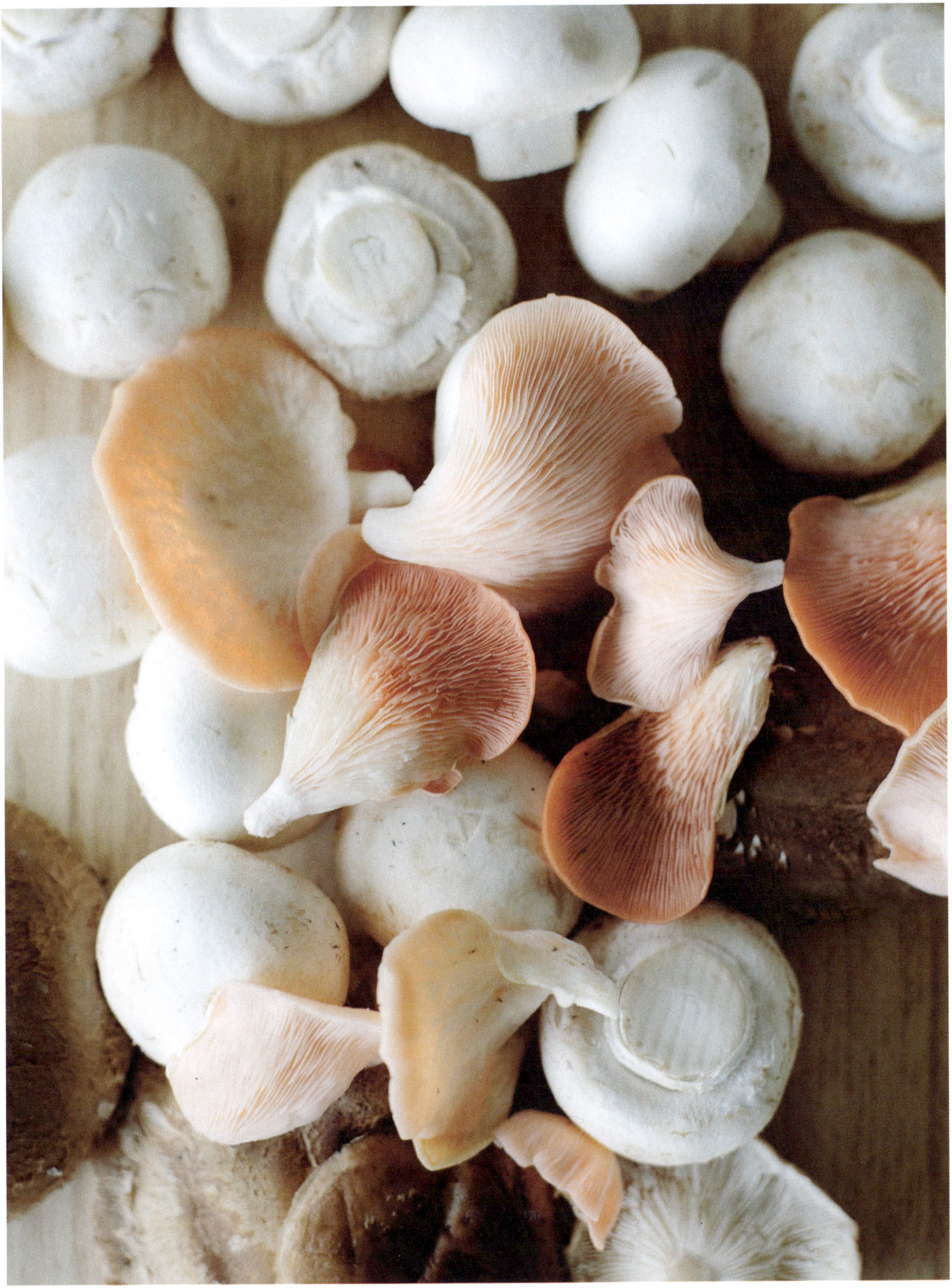

FRIED EGG TORTILLAS w/ PUMPKIN + CORIANDER SALSA

MAKES 4 TORTILLAS | GLUTEN-FREE | DAIRY-FREE

This is the kind of quick and easy meal I love to make for lunch and is something my daughter often requests. A simple fried egg is scattered with a sweet, spicy and sour roasted pumpkin salsa before being wrapped up in a warm white corn tortilla. If you plan ahead and make the salsa, or at least roast the pumpkin beforehand, it will take you mere minutes to prepare. And while I do sometimes make my own corn tortillas (page 204), store-bought ones will also do. I tend to give store-bought tortillas a quick blast in a dry pan, until blistered in places, however, you can also wrap the whole stack in baking paper and heat in a slow oven. The recipe below will make enough filling for 4 single tortillas (to probably serve 2 people), but it can easily be doubled or more to feed a crowd.

Olive oil or ghee, for shallow-frying
4 large free-range eggs
4 white corn tortillas, warmed

Pumpkin + coriander salsa

Approx. 1kg (1 medium) butternut pumpkin
2–3 tablespoons extra-virgin olive oil
2 teaspoons dried oregano
1 teaspoon whole cumin seeds
¼ red onion, finely diced
1–2 pickled jalapeños (page 180), finely chopped
Juice of 1 lime
Handful of coriander leaves + tender stems, roughly chopped

+ Preheat oven to 200ºC (400ºF). To make salsa, cut pumpkin in half, scoop out the seeds, cut into smaller sections and carefully remove the skin. Finely dice the flesh, aiming for approx. 1cm cubes. Transfer to a large oven tray, or a couple of smaller ones, drizzle with olive oil and scatter over oregano and cumin seeds, and season with fine sea salt and freshly ground black pepper. Give everything a good mix up, then spread pumpkin out in a single layer and roast for 25–30 minutes or until lovely and golden, turning once or twice to ensure even cooking. Remove from oven and set aside for 5 minutes to cool slightly. Transfer to a bowl and stir through red onion, jalapeños, lime juice and coriander. Taste and adjust seasoning if you find it needs it.

+ Heat a little oil or ghee in a frying pan and fry eggs to your liking.

+ Place eggs on warmed tortillas and top with a generous spoonful of salsa. Serve immediately.

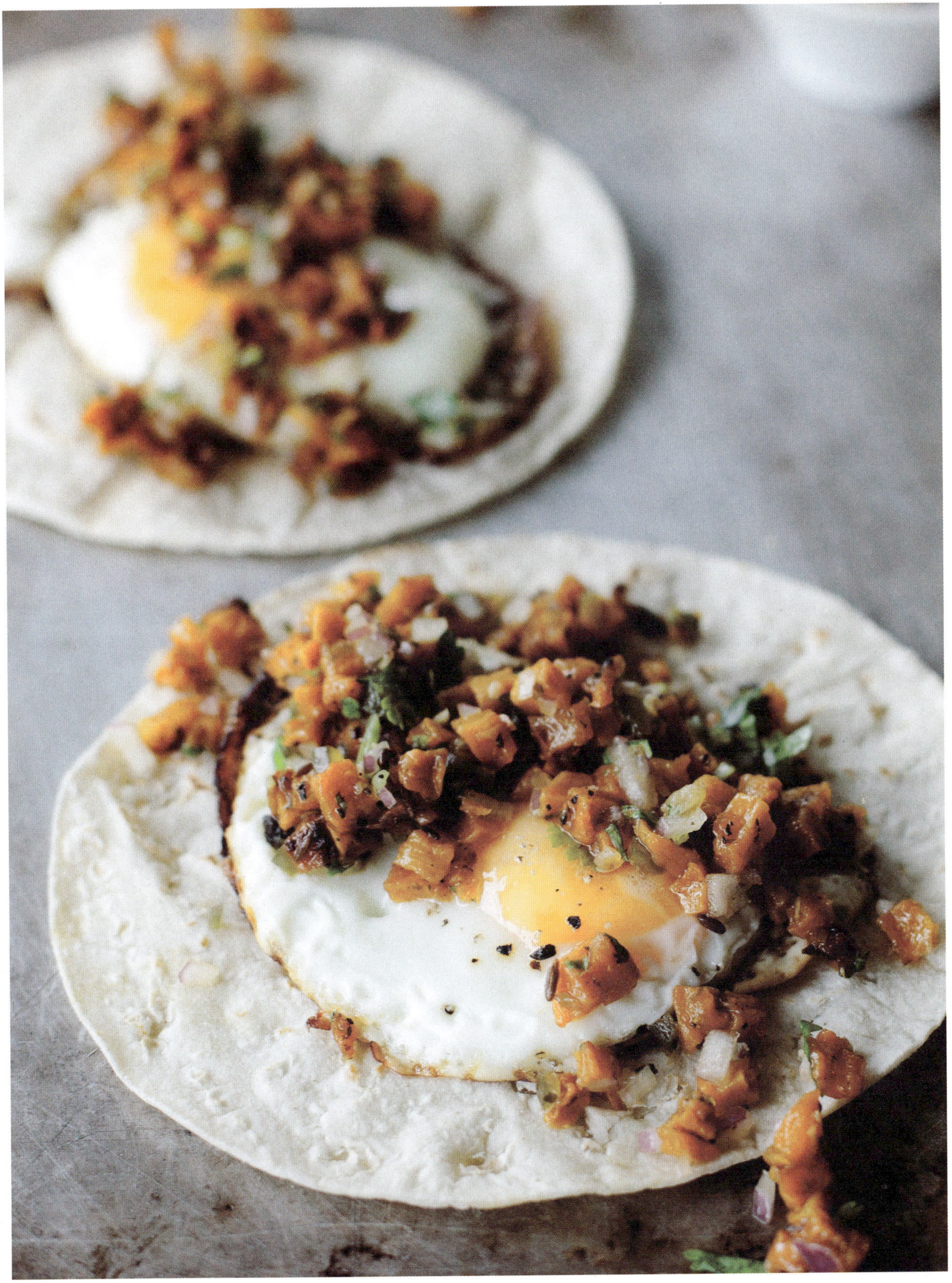

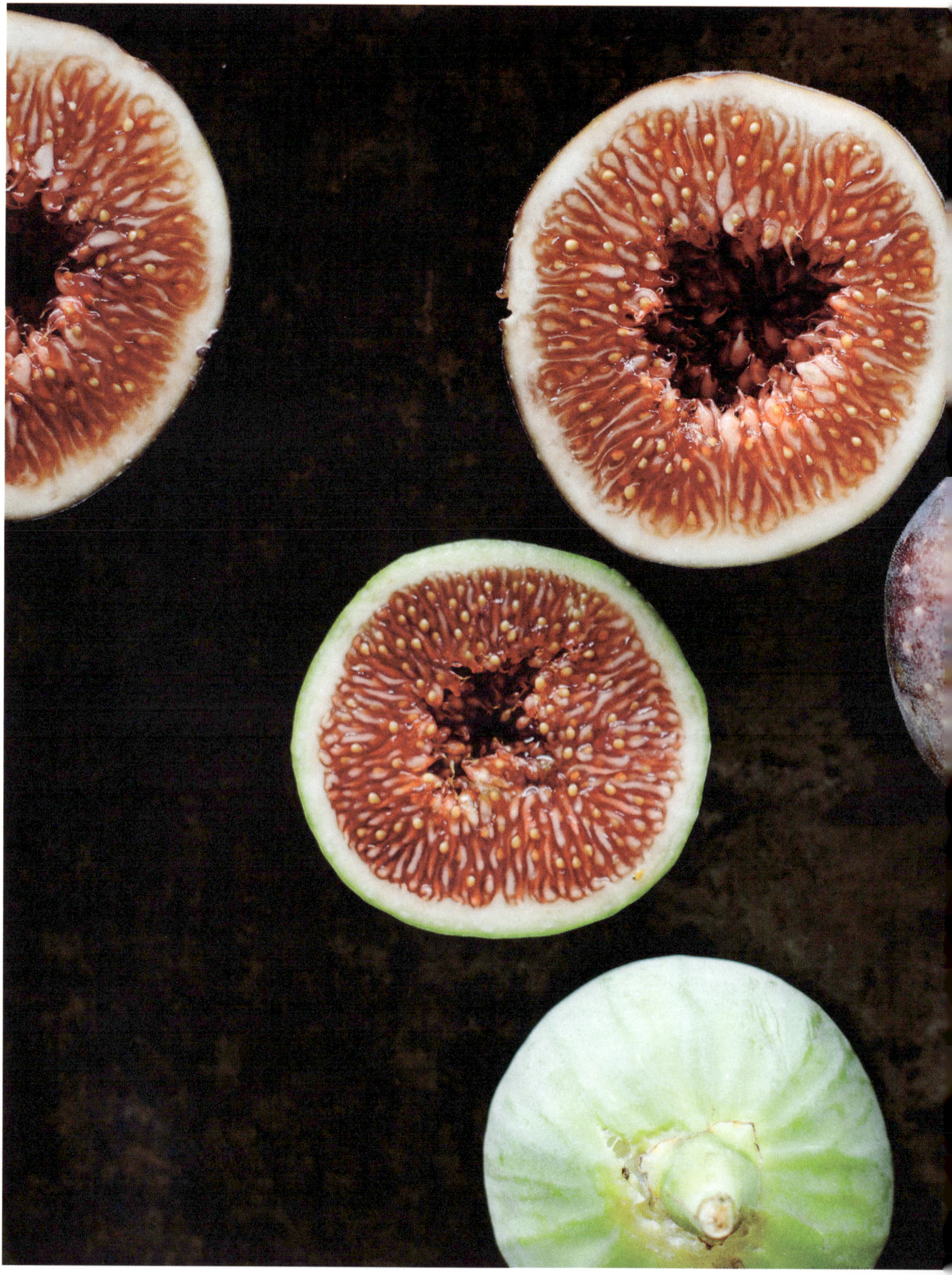

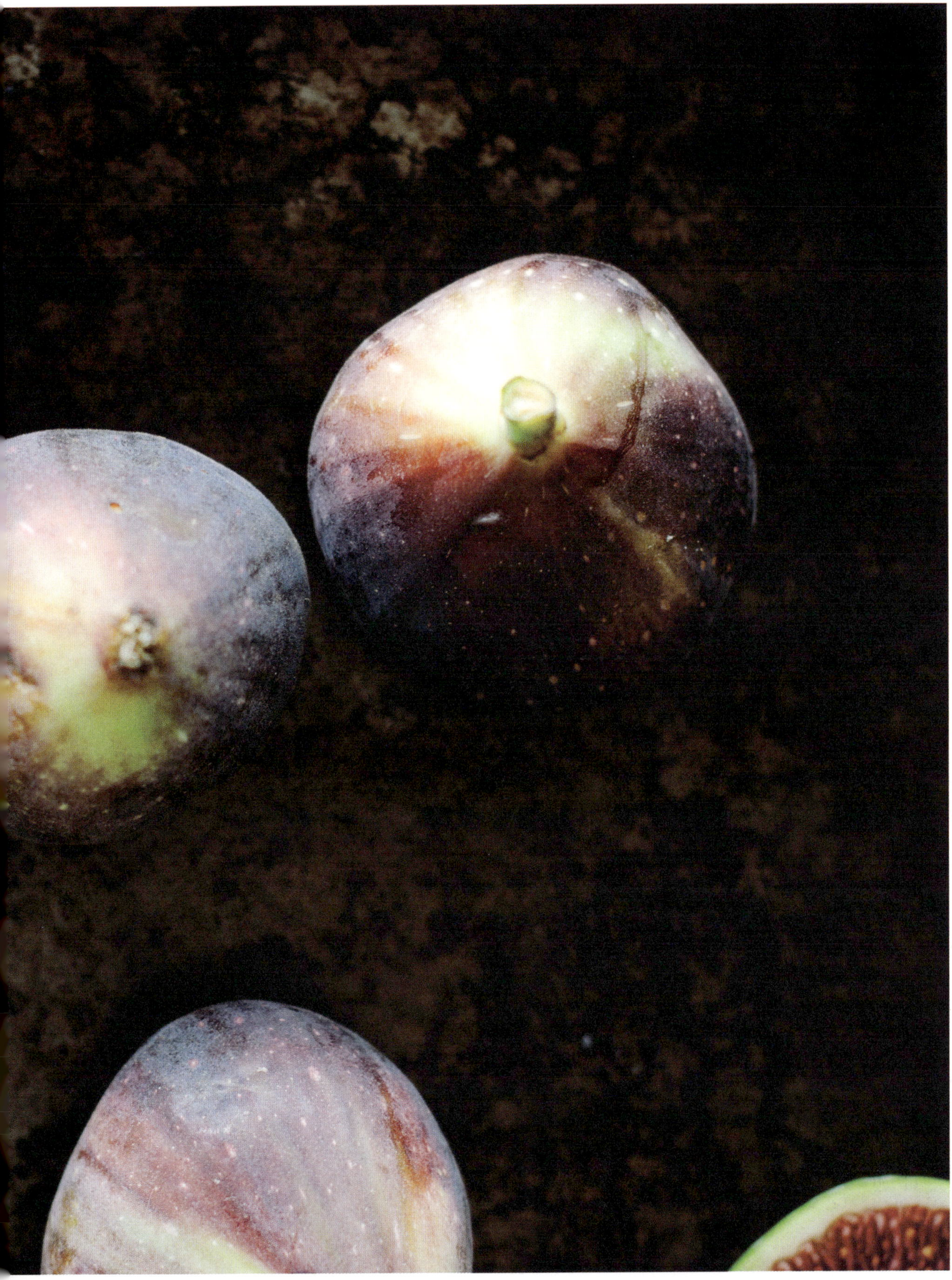

FIG, GINGER + ORANGE LABNEH TART

SERVES 10–12 | GLUTEN-FREE

I've always been one of those people who loves to scrape off the little bits of yoghurt stuck to the sides of the jar – those smears which have naturally drained themselves of excess whey and as a result are lovely, thick and creamy. I guess this is why I adore labneh. The name suggests something exotic and unattainable, that you'd have to spend hours tracking down in a specialty food store, but the reality is something much simpler: it's just strained yoghurt. If you make your own yoghurt it's really cheap too (see page 239). We love eating labneh during summer, for breakfast topped with fresh fruit or compote (page 208), but it also forms the perfect base for this deceivingly decadent tart which is essentially just made from fruit, nuts and yoghurt. We often eat it for breakfast…

2 litres (2kg) natural plain yoghurt
Pinch of fine sea salt
Finely grated zest of 1 unwaxed orange + 1 lemon
60ml (¼ cup) freshly squeezed orange juice (approx. ½ orange)
60ml (¼ cup) freshly squeezed lemon juice (approx. ½ large lemon)
60ml (¼ cup) honey
300g (2 cups or approx. 15) dried figs, hard stalk removed + roughly chopped
200g (1½ cups) sunflower seeds
3 tablespoons virgin coconut oil, melted if solid
1 tablespoon lemon zest
1 tablespoon finely grated fresh ginger
1 teaspoon ground ginger
6–8 fresh figs, sliced into rounds

+ Combine yoghurt with salt. Spoon into a clean square of cheesecloth. Pull up all four corners of the cloth and tie them together. Hang your cloth from a wooden spoon resting over a bowl or large plastic container (to collect the dripping whey). Leave in the fridge overnight. If you can, check the bowl occasionally to make sure it's not overflowing during the first hour or so (see NOTE).

+ Line a 28 x 18cm slice tin with baking paper.

+ Place orange and lemon zest and juice and honey in a small saucepan and bring to the boil over medium-high heat. Continue to boil for 5 minutes or until reduced to a thick syrup. Remove from heat and set aside to cool.

+ Blend dried figs, sunflower seeds, coconut oil, lemon zest, grated and ground ginger and a pinch of fine sea salt in a food processor until finely ground and sticky. Press mixture evenly over base of the prepared tin, using the back of a spoon to smooth it out. Place in the fridge until needed. (Alternatively, you can press mixture into a lined cake tin to cover the base and sides if preferred.)

+ Transfer strained yoghurt to a bowl and swirl through the cooled orange and lemon syrup. Spoon onto the base and top with fresh fig slices. Return to the fridge for 1–2 hours before serving. This tart will store, airtight, in the fridge for 2–3 days.

NOTE: Whey freezes well and can be added to smoothies for an extra vitamin and mineral boost.

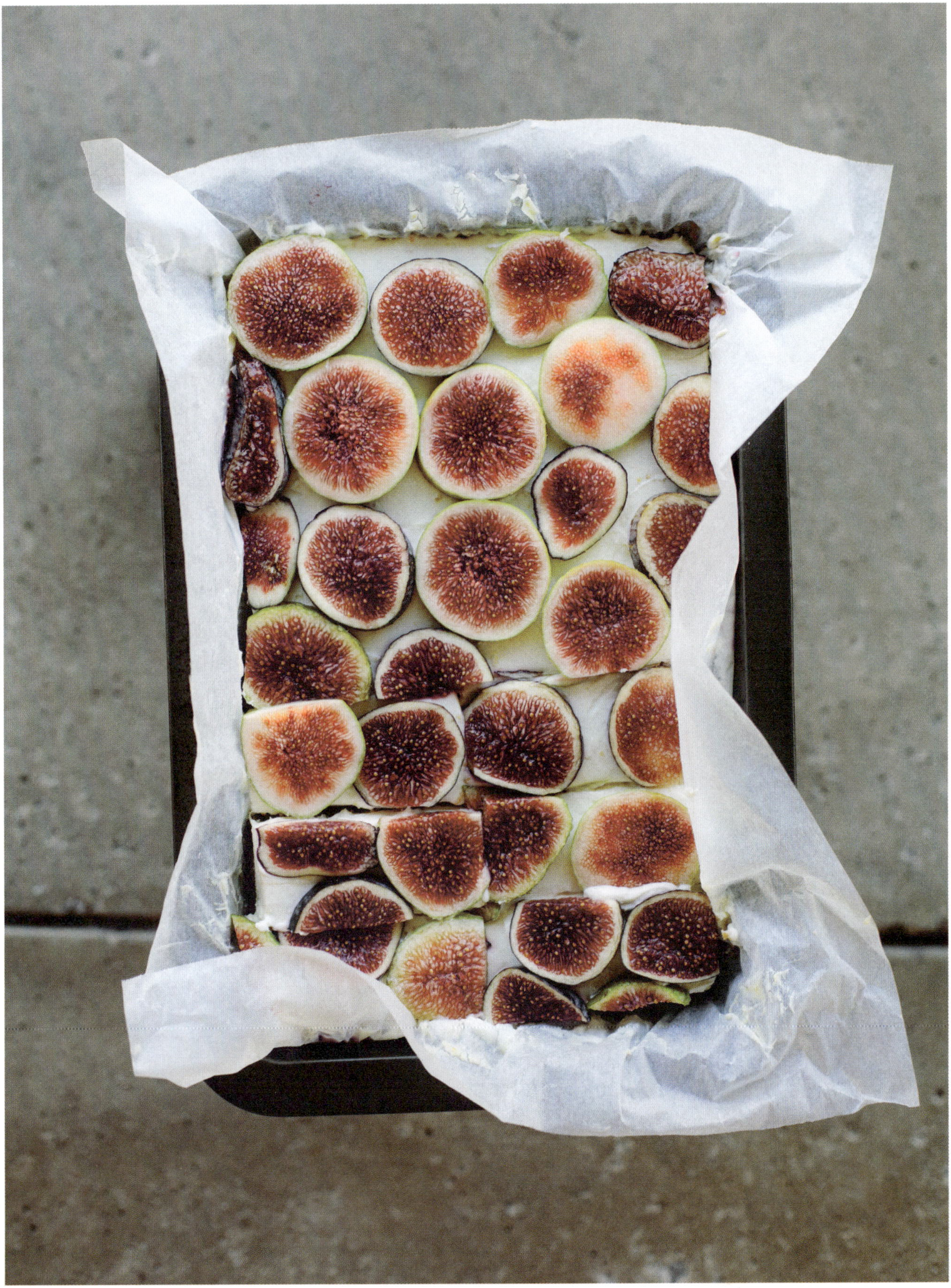

AMARANTH PORRIDGE w/ ORANGE + ROSEMARY PERSIMMON

SERVES 4 | GLUTEN-FREE | VEGAN OPTION

I've long been a fan of alternative grain porridges, as you will have noticed if you own my first book! I grew up eating millet, oat and semolina porridges and then later progressed to eating quinoa and brown rice porridges. Using the somewhat more intensely grassy (and teeny!) amaranth grain is something I got onto a few years back and its fine texture reminds me of the semolina pudding of my youth, which I had to sadly stop eating when we cut out all gluten. Coconut has a lovely way of masking amaranth's grassiness, but you could also add a spoonful of virgin coconut oil for a similar result and then use all almond milk in place of the coconut milk. When I remember, I always try to soak my grains to improve digestibility; the amaranth grain is really small, so you'll have to use a super-fine strainer when draining off the water to avoid tipping all your breakfast down the drain! For a vegan option, choose coconut oil in place of ghee and maple or brown rice syrup in place of honey. You can find amaranth grain at your local health food store.

- 220g (1 cup) amaranth, soaked overnight in cold water if possible + drained
- 500ml (2 cups) almond milk (or ½ almond milk ½ water)
- 250ml (1 cup) coconut milk
- Pinch of fine sea salt
- 1–2 teaspoons honey, pure maple or brown rice syrup

Orange + rosemary persimmon

- 2 Fuju persimmons, peeled + finely diced
- 2 green apples (Granny Smith or Golden Delicious), peeled + finely diced
- 1 tablespoon ghee or virgin coconut oil
- 1 teaspoon roughly chopped rosemary + flowers, to garnish
- 1 tablespoon honey, pure maple or brown rice syrup
- Finely grated zest + juice of ½ orange

+ Place drained amaranth, almond and coconut milk (and 125ml (½ cup) water if using unsoaked amaranth) in a large saucepan with salt. Cover with a lid and bring to the boil. Keep an eye on the porridge as it comes to the boil and remove the lid if it looks like it's about to boil over. Reduce heat to lowest setting and cook for 10–15 minutes, stirring occasionally (it will be a little lumpy before stirring), until amaranth is tender but still has a slight chew, and porridge has thickened. Add a touch more almond milk or water if a tad too thick. Remove from heat and stir in honey or syrup.

+ While porridge is cooking, prepare fruit, taking care to avoid the pips in the persimmons and cores in the apples. Heat a frying pan over medium-high heat, add ghee or coconut oil and rosemary. Cook, while stirring, for about 1 minute or until rosemary is fragrant and slightly crispy around the edges. Add finely diced persimmon and apple and cook, stirring occasionally, for 4–5 minutes or until tender and slightly caramelised around the edges. Add honey or syrup and orange zest. Continue to cook for a further minute until lovely and sticky before adding orange juice and reducing to a slightly sticky glaze.

+ Serve porridge in bowls topped with a generous spoonful, or two, of the persimmon. Scatter with rosemary flowers if you like.

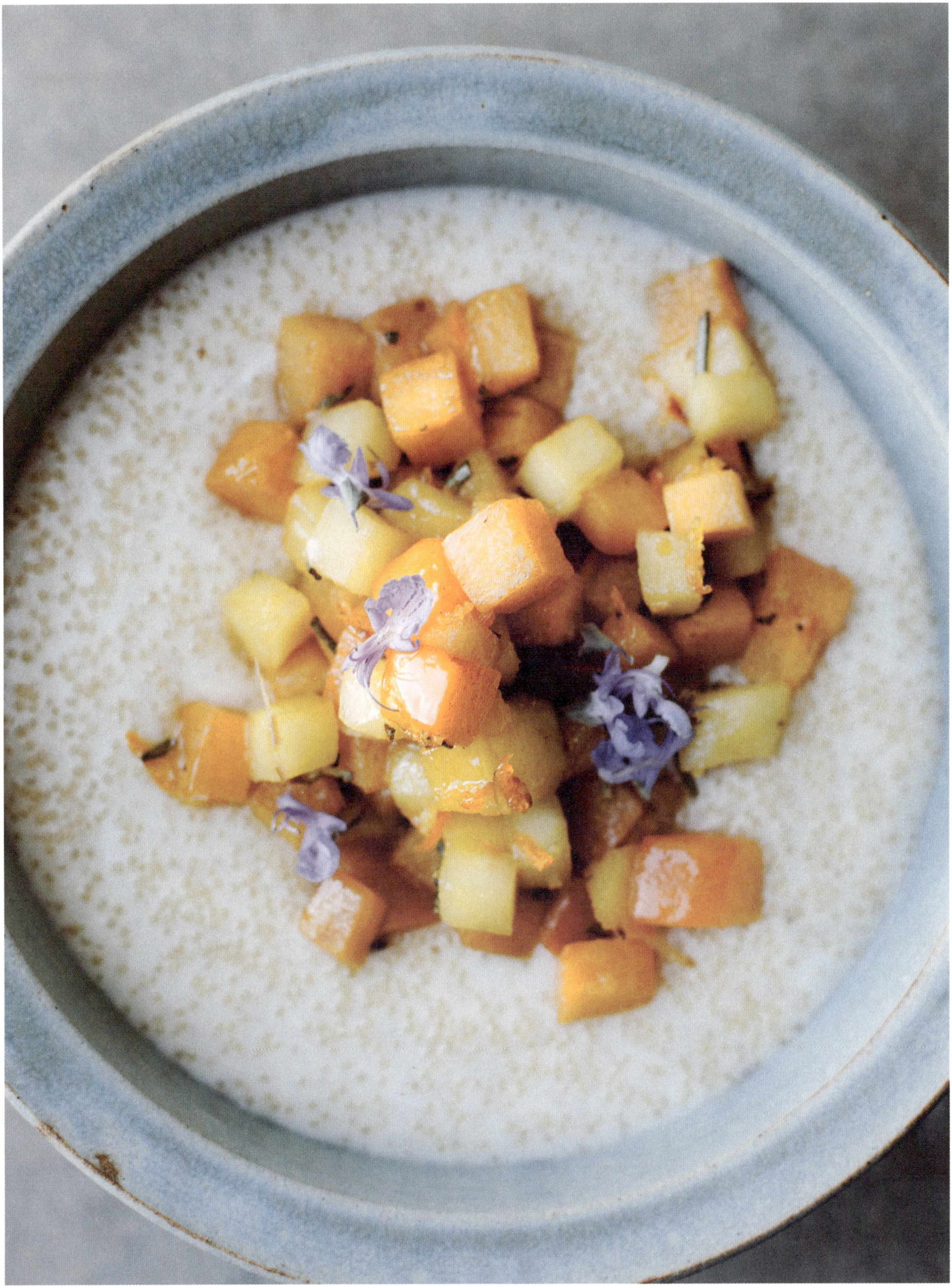

PLUM + TOASTED HAZELNUT CAKE

SERVES 8–10 | GLUTEN-FREE | DAIRY-FREE

As the weather cools, my thoughts often turn to baking and the joy of curling my hands around a steaming mug of tea. Afternoon tea was somewhat of a thing in our house when I was growing up – mugs of Earl Grey tea with a dash of milk and honey were often accompanied by slabs of Mum's banana cake with carob icing, or her peanut brownie cookies that were always slightly singed on the bottom from the wood-fired coal range she cooked in for much of my childhood. This pretty cake, with its toasted hazelnut crumb and generous pieces of jammy end-of-season plums is exactly the kind of thing I love to sit down to and savour with friends and family, over multiple pots of tea.

- 100g (1 cup) ground hazelnuts
- 80g (¾ cup) ground almonds
- 110g (½ cup) unrefined raw sugar
- 50g (½ cup) arrowroot or gluten-free organic cornflour (starch)
- 1 teaspoon gluten-free baking powder
- ¼ teaspoon fine sea salt
- 2 large free-range eggs, at room temperature
- 80ml (⅓ cup) extra-virgin olive oil
- 60ml (¼ cup) almond, rice or coconut milk
- 1 teaspoon vanilla extract
- 4–6 ripe plums, halved + stones removed

+ Preheat oven to 180ºC (350ºF). Grease a 23cm round springform cake tin and line the base and sides with baking paper. Combine ground hazelnuts and almonds in a medium frying pan over medium heat and toast for 5–8 minutes, stirring often, until lightly golden and aromatic. Remove from heat and transfer to a bowl, setting aside for 10 minutes to cool slightly. When cool, add sugar, arrowroot, baking powder and salt and whisk to evenly combine.

+ In another bowl, whisk eggs, olive oil, milk and vanilla. Pour into dry ingredients and mix to form a smooth batter. Pour into prepared tin and arrange plum halves, cut side up, over the batter. Bake for 45–55 minutes or until a skewer inserted into the centre comes out clean. Remove from oven and set aside to cool in tin. This cake stores happily, airtight, for 2–3 days, or in the fridge for even longer.

NOTE: If you can't buy ground hazelnuts, simply toast whole hazelnuts in an oven preheated to 180ºC (350ºF) for 8–10 minutes until golden. Rub off the skins, cool and grind in a small food processor until fine. If you go this route, skip toasting the ground nuts in a pan.

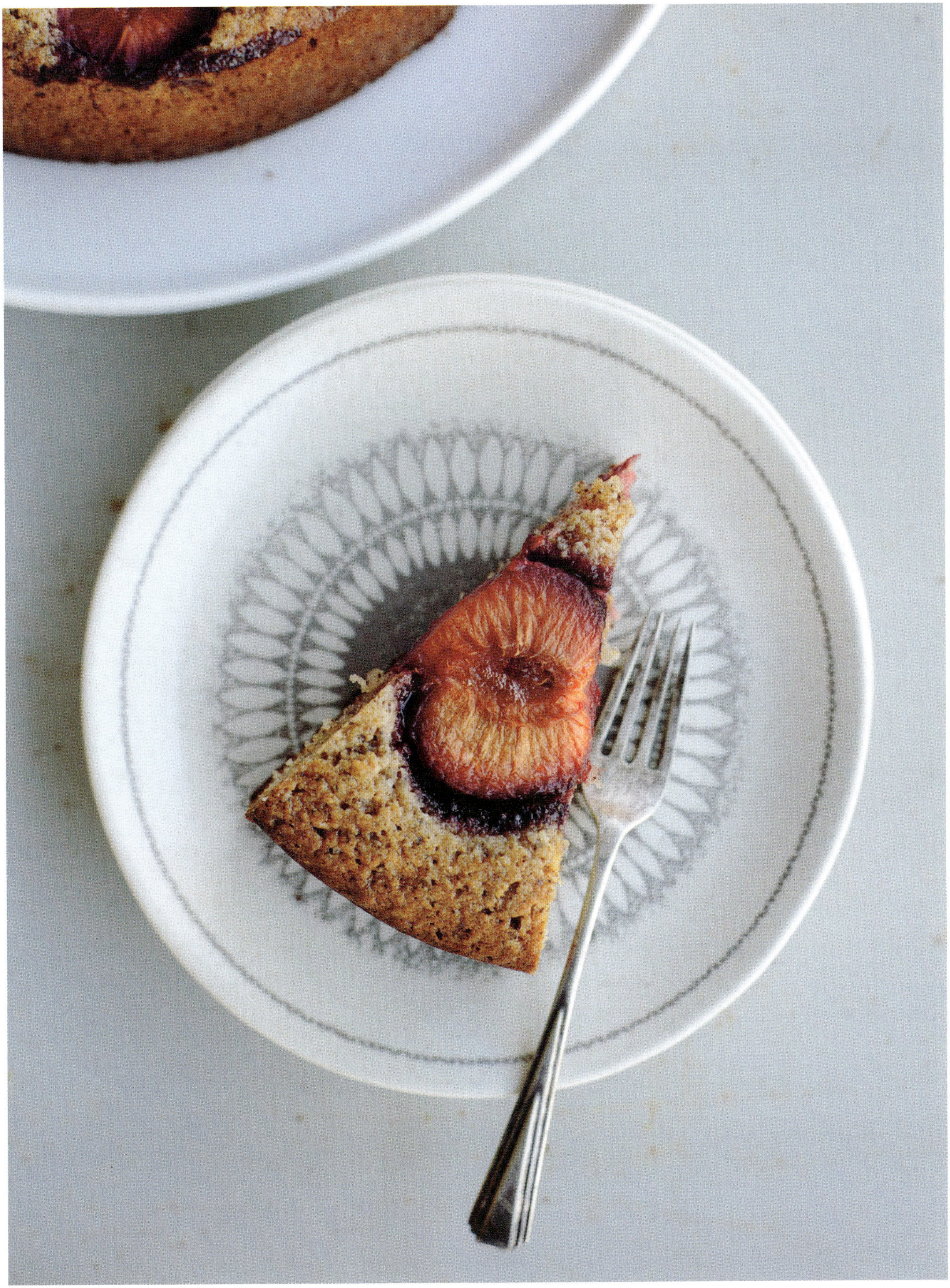

FEIJOA + APPLE SHORTCAKE

SERVES 8–10 | GLUTEN-FREE

Feijoas (also known as pineapple guava) are one of New Zealand's most loved fruits and, far out, have I missed them when I've lived overseas! Growing up we had a whole paddock of feijoa trees, which we'd scramble under every autumn, feasting on just as many fruit as we'd save for later. My dad would sit in front of the TV every night with a bowl twice the size of his head, a knife in one hand to slice them in half, and a spoon to scoop out the flesh in the other. Mum would bottle the surplus with apples in large glass Agee jars, which lined the shelves in our wash-house throughout the year. We'd use them in crumbles or served over homemade yoghurt for breakfast. And the dehydrator was always full to the brim with feijoa slices and homemade feijoa roll-ups. But Mum's feijoa shortcake was the best of all. Converting it to gluten-free was a must as these are the kind of memories I definitely want to pass on to my kids. If you can't get your hands on feijoas, rhubarb alongside the apple makes a good substitute. I love serving shortcake warm from the oven with vanilla ice cream, or it can be cooled and served as a slice.

125g butter, softened

100g (½ cup) firmly packed blended unrefined raw sugar

1 large free-range egg, lightly beaten

50g (½ cup) ground almonds + 1 tablespoon, extra

140g (1 cup) fine brown rice flour

25g (¼ cup) tapioca flour, arrowroot or gluten-free organic cornflour (starch)

1 teaspoon gluten-free baking powder

1 teaspoon ground cinnamon

1 teaspoon ground allspice

6 medium feijoas, peeled + sliced

3 large apples (I use a couple of Pink Ladies for sweetness and a Granny Smith for tartness), peeled + sliced

1 teaspoon finely grated lemon zest

Pure icing sugar to dust, optional

+ To make dough, cream butter and sugar using an electric beater or wooden spoon until light and fluffy. Add egg and beat well. Add ground almonds and sift over flours, baking powder and spices. Mix until a super-soft dough starts to form. Turn out onto a lightly rice-floured bench and bring together with your hands, kneading a couple of times. Shape into a flat rectangle, place in a plastic bag and chill in the fridge for 30 minutes before using. (The dough can be kept in the fridge for 2–3 days or frozen at this stage).

+ Place sliced feijoas, apple and lemon zest in a saucepan and cook over medium heat with the lid on for 8–10 minutes, stirring often, until tender. Remove from heat, transfer to a plate, spreading out the mixture so it cools faster. You can also cook the fruit well in advance, and store in the fridge for up to 2–3 days. The filling needs to be cold before using.

+ Preheat oven to 180°C (350°F). Grease and line a 28 x 18cm slice tin with baking paper, extending up and over the sides by 2cm. Roll two-thirds of the dough out on a lightly rice-floured sheet of baking paper to 5mm thick. Line base and sides of tin with dough, trimming the edges so that it comes approx. 3cm up the sides. Patch up any holes with excess dough. Scatter extra ground almonds over the base, then evenly spread over cold feijoa and apple filling. Roll out remaining dough to 5mm thick, then tear it up into little pieces and scatter it over the top of the filling, to roughly cover.

+ Bake in the centre of the oven for 30–35 minutes, or until golden around the edges and top. Remove from oven and cool in tin. Serve warm dusted with icing sugar and a scoop of ice cream for dessert, or cool completely and serve as a slice for morning or afternoon tea. Best eaten on the day of baking as the dough will soften over time.

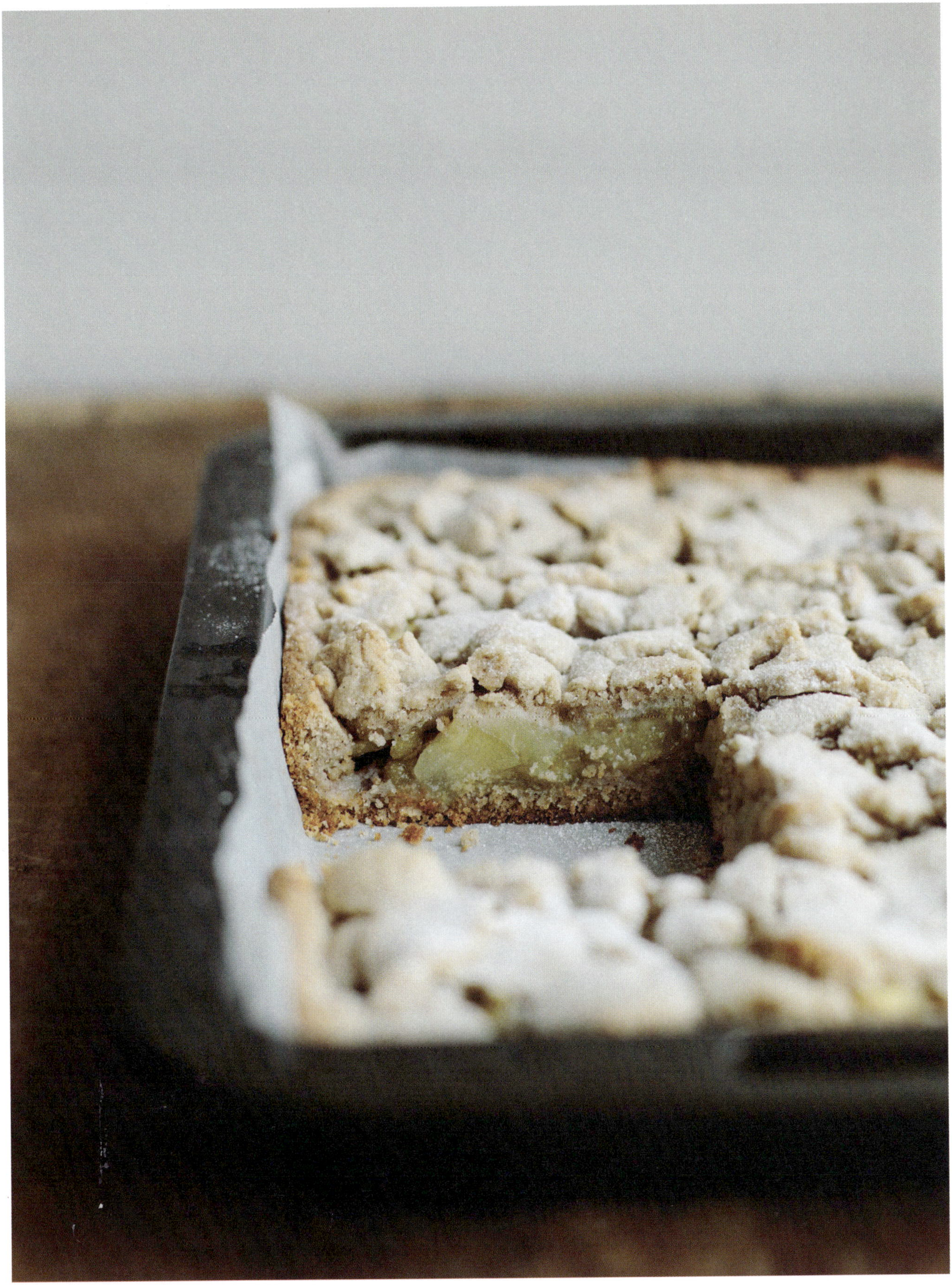

CHESTNUT MAPLE PURÉE

MAKES APPROX. 1½ CUPS | GLUTEN-FREE | VEGAN

Tinned chestnut purée is one of those things you see in European recipes, but is something relatively hard to come across in this part of the world. Instead of feeling sorry for myself I decided instead to make my own. If you're lucky enough to have chestnut trees near where you live, you can forage for your own like we do in New Zealand – just make sure you take sturdy footwear as the spikey outer shells can be quite lethal! If you don't have access to a tree, keep your eyes peeled at the start of autumn, when you'll see them showing up in markets and stores. Look for plump nuts with no cracks or signs of mould on the shells.

I grew up in a household of chestnut roasters, where we'd split the nuts open after they came out of the coal range before slathering them in butter and devouring. My husband, on the other hand, comes from a family of chestnut boilers. After years of trialling which technique makes for the easiest peeling, I merged the two together and came up with what I now think to be the best, tear-free way to shell a chestnut. Don't skimp on the steaming stage, as wrapping them in a clean tea towel after roasting helps to loosen the inner skin. We eat this purée straight from the spoon, but it's also lovely spread over buttered toast or mixed with whipped cream and used to fill cakes or éclairs (page 54).

450g chestnuts
80ml (⅓ cup) pure maple syrup
Pinch of fine sea salt
1 teaspoon vanilla extract

+ Preheat oven to 200°F (400°F). Using a sharp serrated knife, score a shallow cross on the round side of each chestnut. Place in a saucepan, cover with cold water and bring to the boil. Boil for 5 minutes, drain, then transfer to an oven tray and roast for 15 minutes. Remove and immediately transfer to a clean tea towel, wrap up and set aside for 5 minutes to steam and cool enough to handle safely. One at a time, peel each chestnut while keeping remaining nuts wrapped in the towel.

+ Place roasted chestnuts, 375ml (1½ cups) water, maple syrup and salt in a saucepan and cover with a lid. Bring to the boil, then reduce to a simmer and cook for 20 minutes. Transfer everything to a food processor along with vanilla extract and blend on high, adding enough extra water (around ⅓–½ cup) to form a smooth firm purée. Store for up to 1 week in the fridge or freeze for 3–4 months.

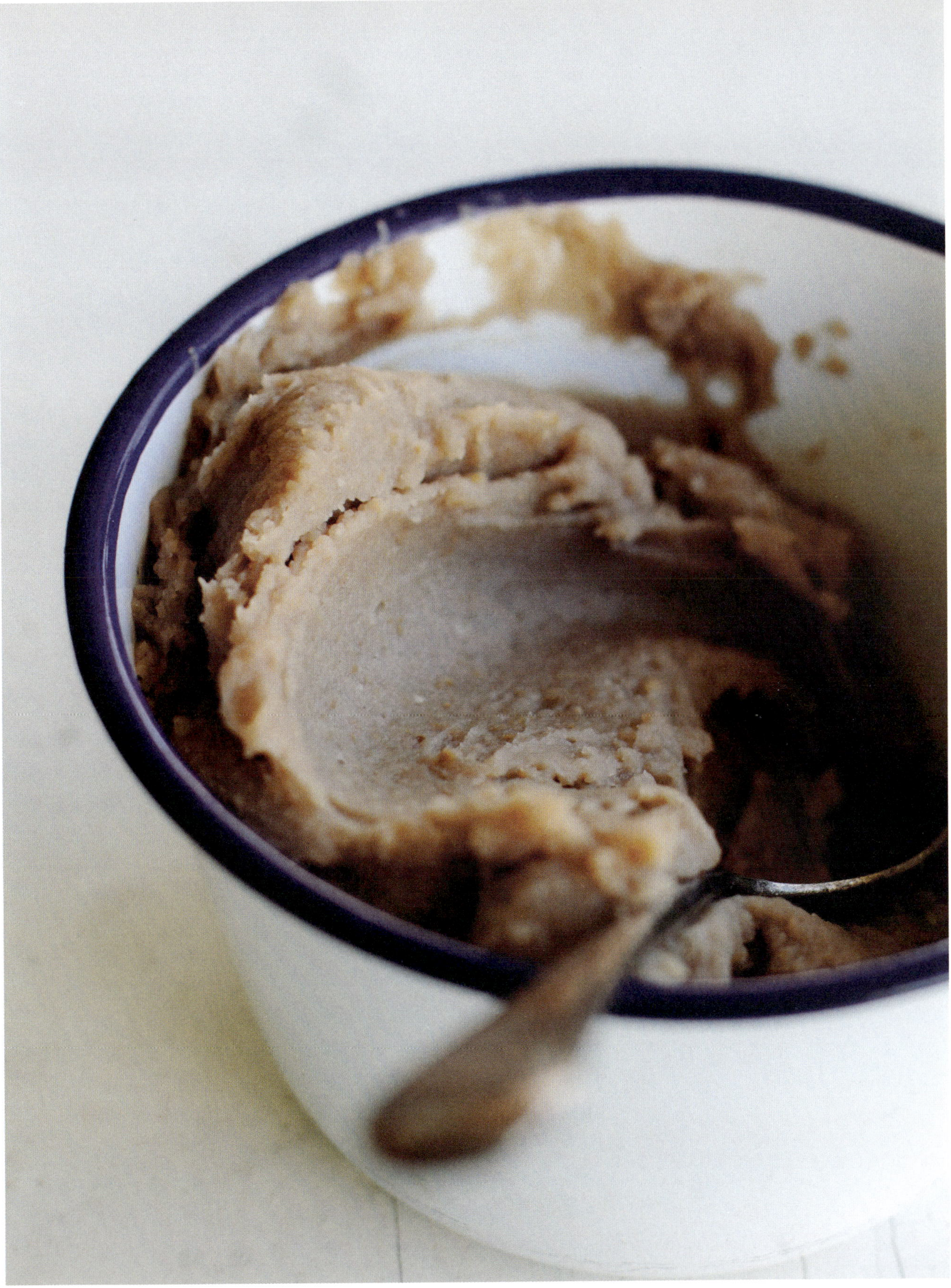

CHOCOLATE ÉCLAIRS w/ CHESTNUT + MAPLE CREAM

MAKES 8–10 SMALL-ISH ÉCLAIRS | GLUTEN-FREE

For those of you who loved the choux puffs I shared in my first book, think of these as their slightly more decadent cousins. Here, the same choux pastry is piped into éclairs, baked until golden, dipped in rich chocolate sauce, before filling with just-sweet homemade chestnut and maple cream. Yum.

50g butter, cut into small cubes
Pinch each of fine sea salt and unrefined raw sugar
35g (¼ cup) fine brown rice flour
20g (⅛ cup) buckwheat flour
15g (⅛ cup) gluten-free organic cornflour (starch)
2 large free-range eggs, lightly beaten
125ml (½ cup) single (pouring) cream
125ml (½ cup) chestnut maple purée (page 52)
1 teaspoon vanilla extract
1–2 tablespoons pure maple syrup, to taste, optional

Chocolate icing
85g dark chocolate, roughly chopped
60ml (¼ cup) single cream
cacao nibs, optional

+ Preheat oven to 200ºC (400ºF). Line 2 baking trays with baking paper.

+ To make éclairs, place butter, salt, sugar and 125ml (½ cup) water in a small heavy-based saucepan over medium heat and bring to the boil. Sift flours into a small bowl and whisk to fully combine. As soon as the water bubbles and comes up to a rolling boil, add combined flours in one go and beat continuously with a wooden spoon as the mixture thickens. Continue beating until the dough is smooth and comes away from the sides of the pan cleanly. It will seem a little greasy and the buckwheat flour will make it look a tad grey – this is okay.

+ Transfer dough to a bowl, flattening it out to help it cool faster and set aside for 5 minutes. Start adding beaten eggs, a little at a time, beating well after each addition with an electric beater or wooden spoon until the mixture falls from the spoon but still holds its shape. You may not need to add the very last little bit of egg – you can use any extra as an egg wash.

+ Transfer mixture to a piping bag fitted with a 1cm plain nozzle and pipe 8cm lengths at least 3cm apart on the lined trays. If you don't have a piping bag, you can put the dough into a zip-lock bag, snip a corner off and pipe that way. Brush tops with any leftover egg if you have it (if you don't, no biggy). Bake for 25–30 minutes or until puffed and golden.

+ Turn off oven and remove éclairs. Pierce a small hole in the side or bottom of each éclair with a knife, letting the steam escape. Put éclairs back into the now cooling oven and leave for a further 15 minutes to dry out. Remove from oven and transfer to a wire rack to cool completely.

+ To make icing, melt chocolate and cream together in a heatproof bowl set over a saucepan of boiling water, stirring with a metal spoon until smooth. Remove from heat and set aside for a few minutes to thicken slightly. Slice each éclair in half lengthways and dip tops into icing before returning to the wire rack to set. Scatter tops with cacao nibs while still wet, if using.

+ To make filling, whisk cream until soft peak forms, add chestnut maple purée, vanilla and maple syrup, if using, and continue to whisk until stiff. Spoon into éclairs and return tops. Serve immediately. Unfilled, un-iced éclairs will store, airtight, for 1–2 days.

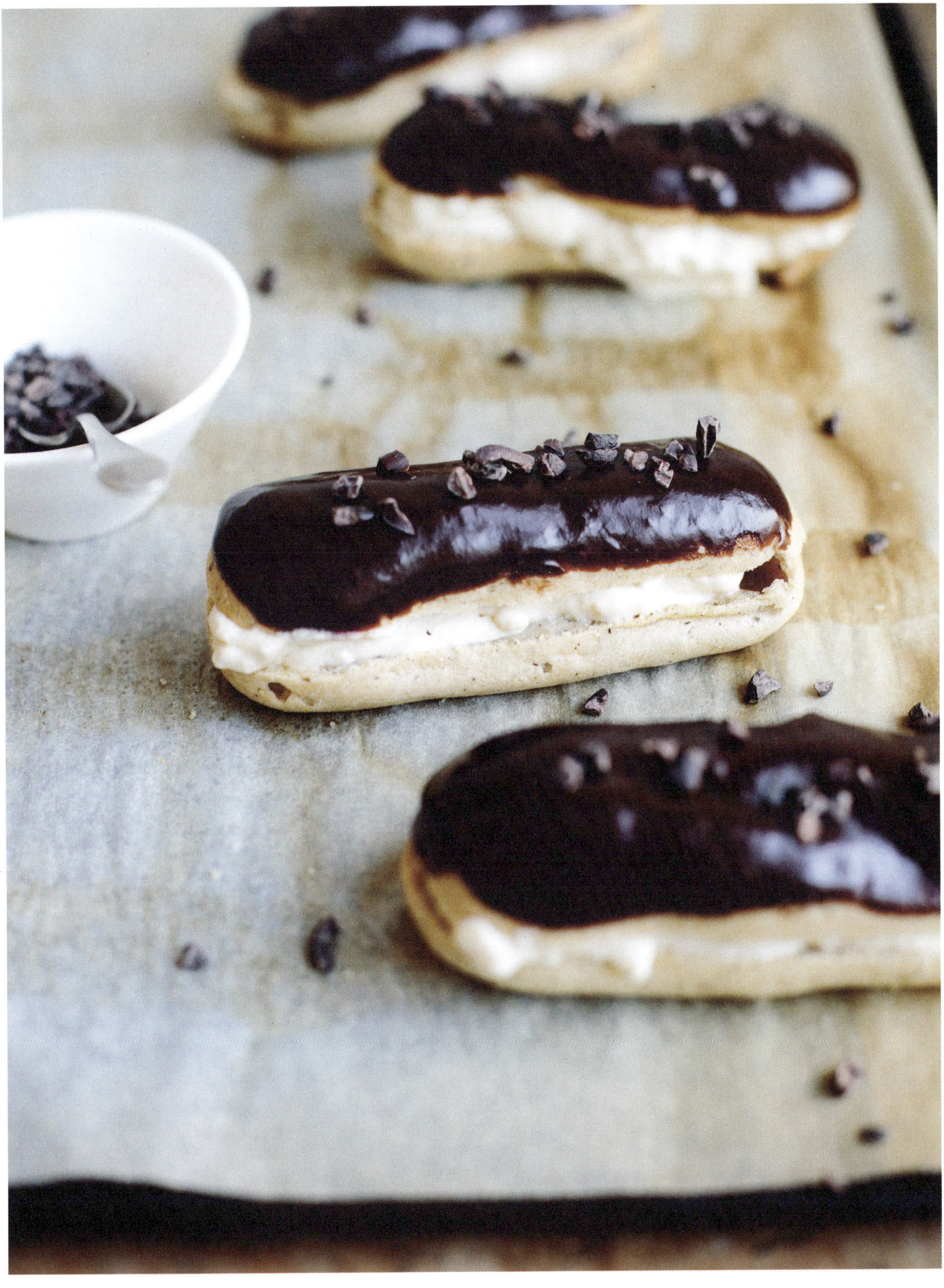

FIG, MILLET + DARK CHOCOLATE BITES

MAKES 25 | GLUTEN-FREE | VEGAN

I've often got treats such as these tucked away in the freezer for times when a little sweetness is needed. They all follow the same theme: nuts, dried fruit, cocoa and coconut oil form the base, to which add-ins get mixed through depending on what I have at hand, or what I'm feeling in the mood for. This combination of mildly-sweet dried figs, almonds, cacao and puffed millet is one of the favourites in our house, especially when dipped in homemade raw chocolate.

150g (1 cup/approx. 7) dried figs, roughly chopped

35g (¼ cup) whole almonds

2 tablespoons almond butter or tahini

1 tablespoon cacao or cocoa powder

1 tablespoon pure maple syrup

1 tablespoon virgin coconut oil (melted if solid)

1 teaspoon vanilla extract

Good pinch of fine sea salt

25g (1½ cups) puffed millet

Chocolate coating

3 tablespoons cacao or cocoa powder

3 tablespoons virgin coconut oil (melted if solid)

2 tablespoons pure maple syrup

+ Place figs, almonds, almond butter or tahini, cacao or cocoa, maple syrup, coconut oil, vanilla and salt in a small food processor and pulse until a thick paste forms. Transfer to a bowl, add millet and, using your hands, mix well. Shape into small cookie shapes, or use an oiled tablespoon measure to shape each bite, tapping onto a board to release them. Place bites onto a tray and freeze for 20–30 minutes.

+ Place coating ingredients in a small saucepan set over low heat, and heat until just melted and combined. Remove from heat, pour into a small deep bowl (I use a Chinese tea cup) and set aside to cool, stirring occasionally, until slightly thickened (approx. 15–20 minutes). Remove bites from freezer and dip half of each into the chocolate, tapping off the excess before returning to the tray. Return to the freezer for 5 minutes until chocolate sets. Store bites in an airtight container in the fridge for 1 week or in the freezer for longer.

NOTE: A little tip for the chocolate-coating stage: allow the dark chocolate mixture to cool down before using – this will ensure you get a good, thick coverage and you won't need to double-dip the bites. Unless, of course, you want to!

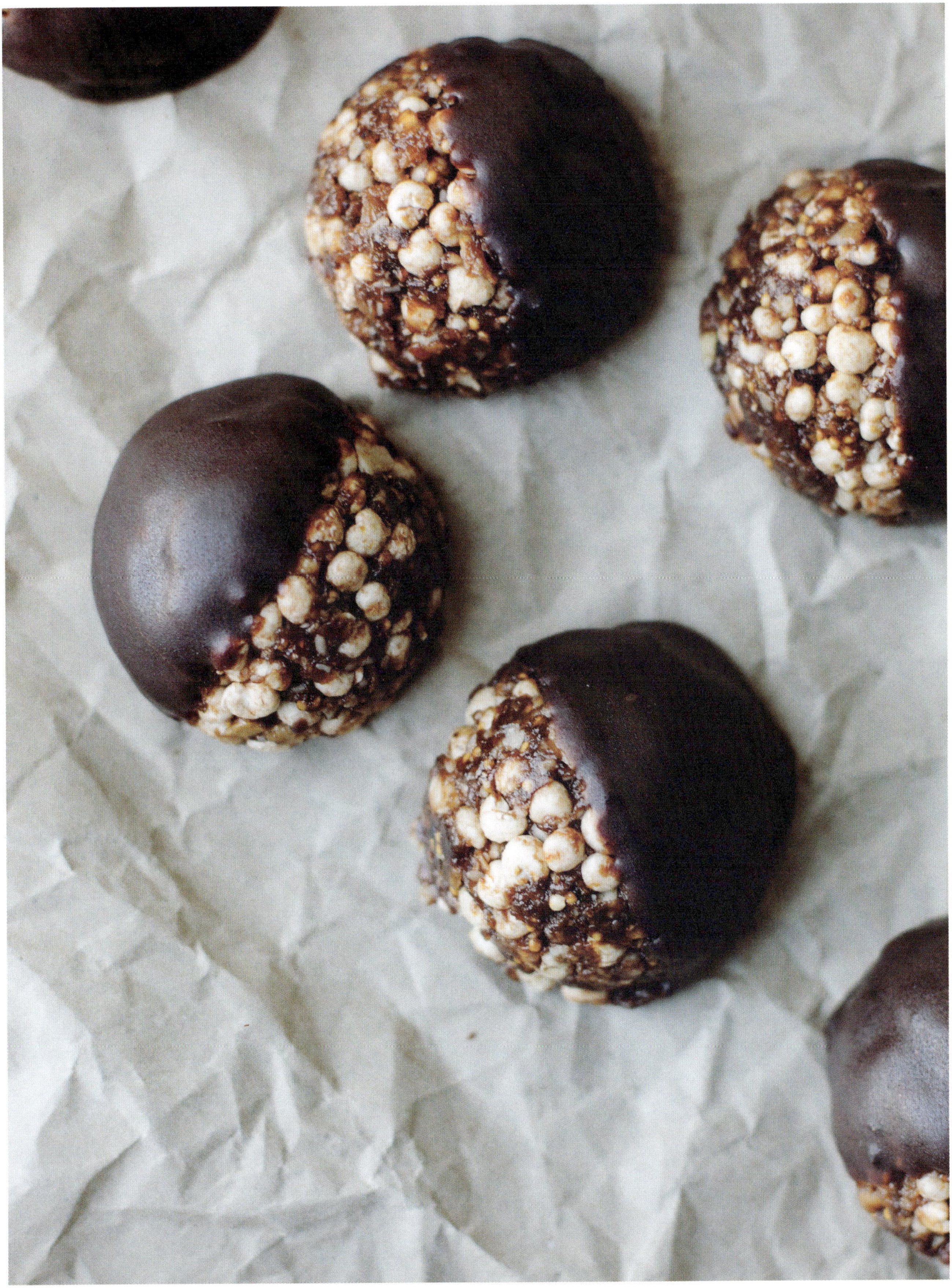

PLUM, CINNAMON + QUINOA BAKE

SERVES 5 | GLUTEN-FREE | VEGAN

This is the kind of thing I like to prepare on cool Sunday mornings in autumn, when there's no rush to be anywhere fast. Plan ahead by soaking the quinoa the night before, then as your oven warms the following morning you can quickly pull the bake together, folding banana and coconut milk through the quinoa, before topping with halves of ripe last-of-the-season plums. When I first started playing around with this idea I used egg to help set it, but found the flavour was not quite right. Replacing the egg with mashed banana not only makes this vegan-friendly but also results in a lovely layer of near-custard-like texture on top, which is Ada's favourite part.

- 185g (1 cup) quinoa, rinsed and soaked overnight in cold water if possible
- 1 large ripe banana, mashed
- 250ml (1 cup) coconut milk
- 2 tablespoons pure maple syrup
- 1 teaspoon vanilla extract
- 1 teaspoon ground cinnamon
- Good pinch of fine sea salt
- 3–4 large plums, quartered

+ Preheat oven to 180ºC (350ºF). Lightly grease 5 x 250ml (1 cup) ovenproof dishes or a 1 litre shallow ovenproof dish with coconut oil.

+ Drain soaked quinoa in a fine sieve, then rinse and set aside to drain well. Combine mashed banana, coconut milk, 125ml (½ cup) water (or 185ml (¾ cup) if using unsoaked quinoa), maple syrup, vanilla and cinnamon in a bowl with salt. Stir through quinoa and transfer to prepared dish or dishes. Scatter over plums and cook for 40–45 minutes for small dishes or 45–50 minutes for 1 large dish, or until golden around the edges and pulling away from the sides of the dish/es slightly. Serve hot or warm.

NOTE: Soaking quinoa overnight in a little cold water with a touch of apple cider vinegar improves digestibility. Drain and rinse well the following day. The easiest way to do this is to put the raw grain into a fine sieve and rinse under running water, then set aside to drain while the water to cook it in comes up to the boil. Rinsing quinoa removes the saponin, a bitter protective coating.

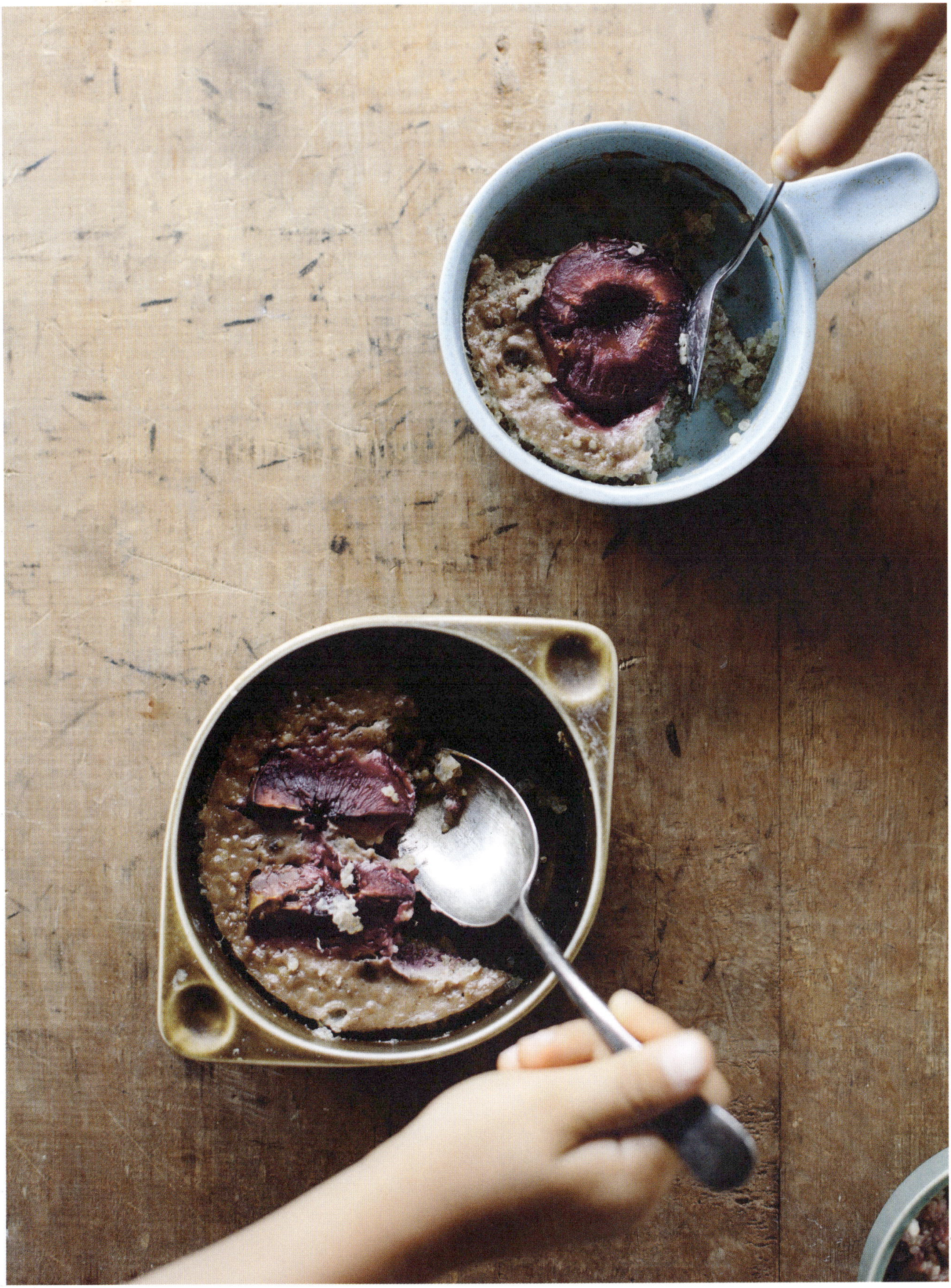

CHOCOLATE ZUCCHINI CAKE

SERVES 10–12 | GLUTEN-FREE | DAIRY-FREE

This is another great recipe to add to your use-up-all-of-the-zucchini arsenal. Grated zucchini gets folded through chocolate-flecked, spice-laden batter to produce one of the most beautiful cakes out. I like to cook mine in a Bundt tin for added drama, but if you follow suit, please make sure you grease the tin well to prevent tears when turning the cake out. A drizzle of dairy-free chocolate icing is a welcome addition and if you're after a chocolate sauce to go with ice cream, this icing moonlights as a good one.

- 105g (¾ cup) fine brown rice flour
- 120g (¾ cup) potato flour
- 25g (¼ cup) cocoa powder
- 1 teaspoon baking soda
- 1 teaspoon ground cinnamon
- 1 teaspoon mixed spice
- 200g (1 cup) unrefined raw sugar
- 25g (¼ cup) ground almonds
- 80g roughly chopped dark chocolate
- ¼ teaspoon fine sea salt
- 3 cups grated zucchini (from approx. 2 medium)
- 3 large free-range eggs, lightly whisked
- 185ml (¾ cup) extra-virgin olive oil or macadamia nut oil
- 1 teaspoon vanilla extract

Chocolate icing

- 85g dark chocolate, roughly chopped + extra, to sprinkle
- 60ml (¼ cup) coconut milk
- 2 tablespoons brown rice or pure maple syrup

+ Preheat oven to 180ºC (350ºF). Grease a 23cm Bundt tin well, making sure you get in all the little nooks and crannies.

+ Sift brown rice flour, potato flour, cocoa, baking soda and spices into a large bowl. Add sugar, ground almonds, chocolate and salt and whisk well to evenly distribute.

+ In another bowl, combine grated zucchini, eggs, oil and vanilla. Pour into dry ingredients and mix until combined. Transfer to cake tin and bake for 50–55 minutes, or until a skewer inserted in the centre comes out clean. Remove from oven and set aside for 10 minutes before turning out onto a wire rack to cool completely.

+ To make icing, bring a small saucepan of water to the boil. Combine chocolate, coconut milk and brown rice syrup in a heatproof bowl and set over the boiling water, making sure the bottom of the bowl doesn't touch the water. Stir until melted and glossy. Remove from heat and drizzle over cake, allowing it to dribble down the creases in the cake. Sprinkle the top with extra chopped chocolate if desired. The iced cake will happily store, airtight, for 2–3 days, or longer in the fridge.

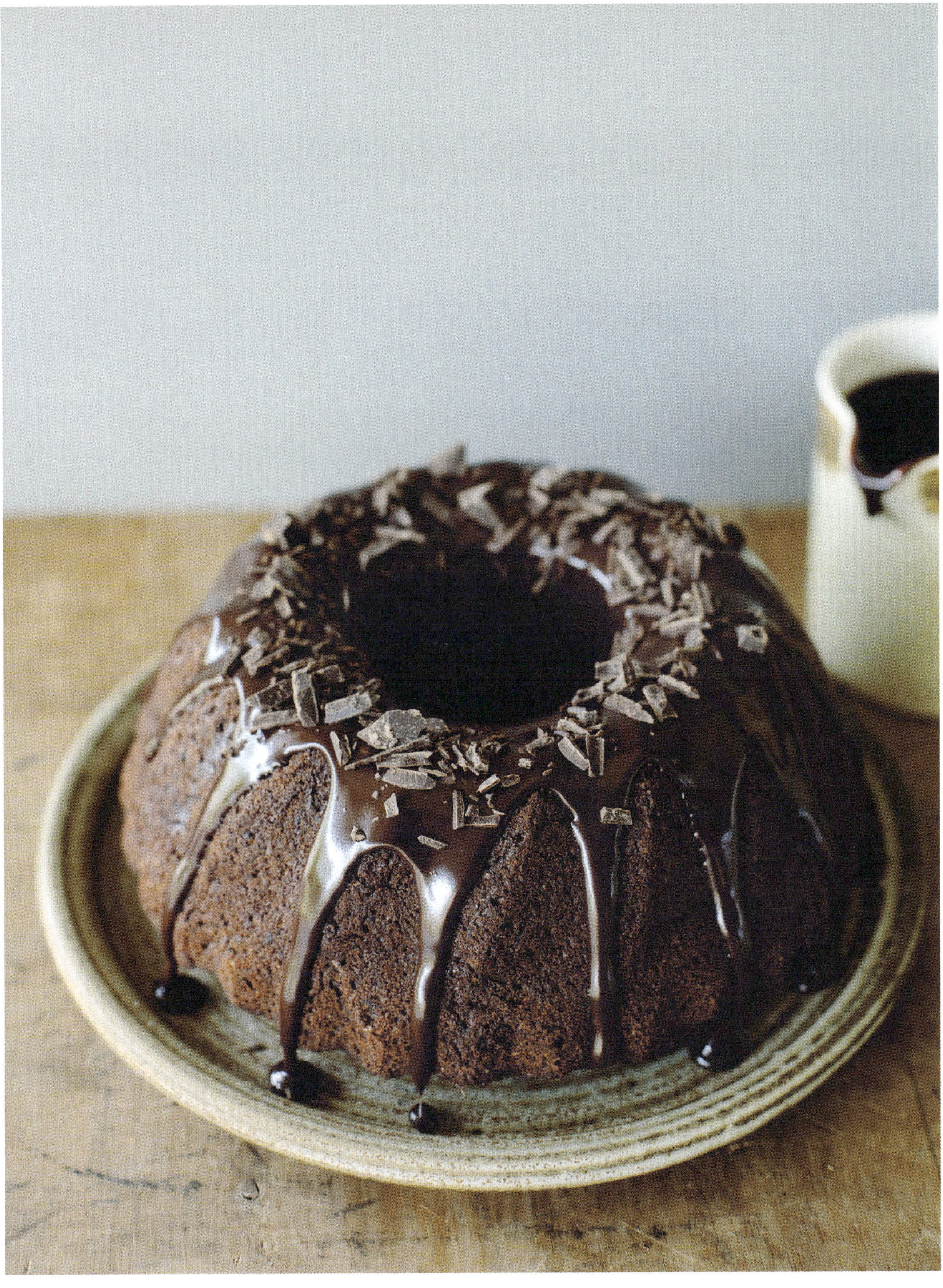

TAMARILLO SPONGE PUDDING W/ VANILLA CUSTARD

SERVES 4–6 | GLUTEN-FREE | DAIRY-FREE

Tamarillos (aka tree tomatoes) are one of my all-time favourite fruits (alongside feijoas, mangoes, berries and stonefruit). Incredibly common in New Zealand, they are sometimes hard to find in other parts of the world, unless you know the right places to shop. We always had trees at the house that I grew up in, both the tart red varieties and the slightly sweeter orange ones. Mostly we'd just slice them in half and scoop out the centre with a spoon, sprinkling with a little raw sugar on occasion. Poached and peeled, with their deep maroon syrup, they are one of the best things to serve alongside a scoop of vanilla ice cream, but it's in this lemony olive oil sponge pudding – inspired by a cake my nana used to make – that I love them most of all. Of course you could always serve this with vanilla ice cream, but I prefer this dairy-free vanilla custard. If you can't get your hands on tamarillos, lightly stewed apples, berries or rhubarb make a lovely substitute.

6–7 tamarillos, peeled + cut in half
2 large free-range eggs
65g (⅓ cup) firmly packed blended unrefined raw sugar (page 235)
Finely grated zest 1 lemon
½ teaspoon vanilla extract
125ml (½ cup) extra-virgin olive oil
70g (½ cup) fine brown rice flour
18g (3 tablespoons) ground almonds
1 teaspoon gluten-free baking powder

Vanilla custard
60g (½ cup) raw cashew nuts, soaked for 4 hours or overnight in cold water + drained
500ml (2 cups) rice milk
1 tablespoon pure maple syrup, brown rice syrup or unrefined raw sugar
½ teaspoon vanilla bean paste, optional
Little pinch of fine sea salt
1 teaspoon arrowroot or gluten-free organic cornflour mixed with 1 tablespoon cold water
½ teaspoon vanilla extract

+ Preheat oven to 180ºC (350ºF). Arrange halved tamarillos, cut side down, in a greased 2-litre ovenproof baking dish. Beat eggs and sugar for 8–10 minutes using an electric beater until thick and fluffy. Add lemon zest and vanilla, then slowly drizzle in olive oil. Stop mixing the second the oil is incorporated. Sift over brown rice flour, ground almonds and baking powder, using a spoon to help get the almonds through the sieve if need be. Gently fold through until just incorporated, doing your best not to knock out all that beautiful air. Gently pour batter over tamarillos and bake for 30–35 minutes or until springy, golden and a skewer inserted into the centre comes out clean. Remove from oven and set aside while you make the custard.

+ Place cashews, rice milk, sweetener of your choice, vanilla bean paste, if using, and salt in a blender and blend until smooth. (If you don't own a high-powered blender, add half of the rice milk, blend until smooth, then add the remaining and blend some more.) Transfer to a saucepan and bring to the boil. Reduce heat and simmer for 3–4 minutes, until mixture thickens slightly. Whisk in arrowroot and water mixture and continue to whisk for a further 30 seconds until thick, before removing from heat. Stir in vanilla extract. Serve scoops of sponge pudding with warm vanilla custard.

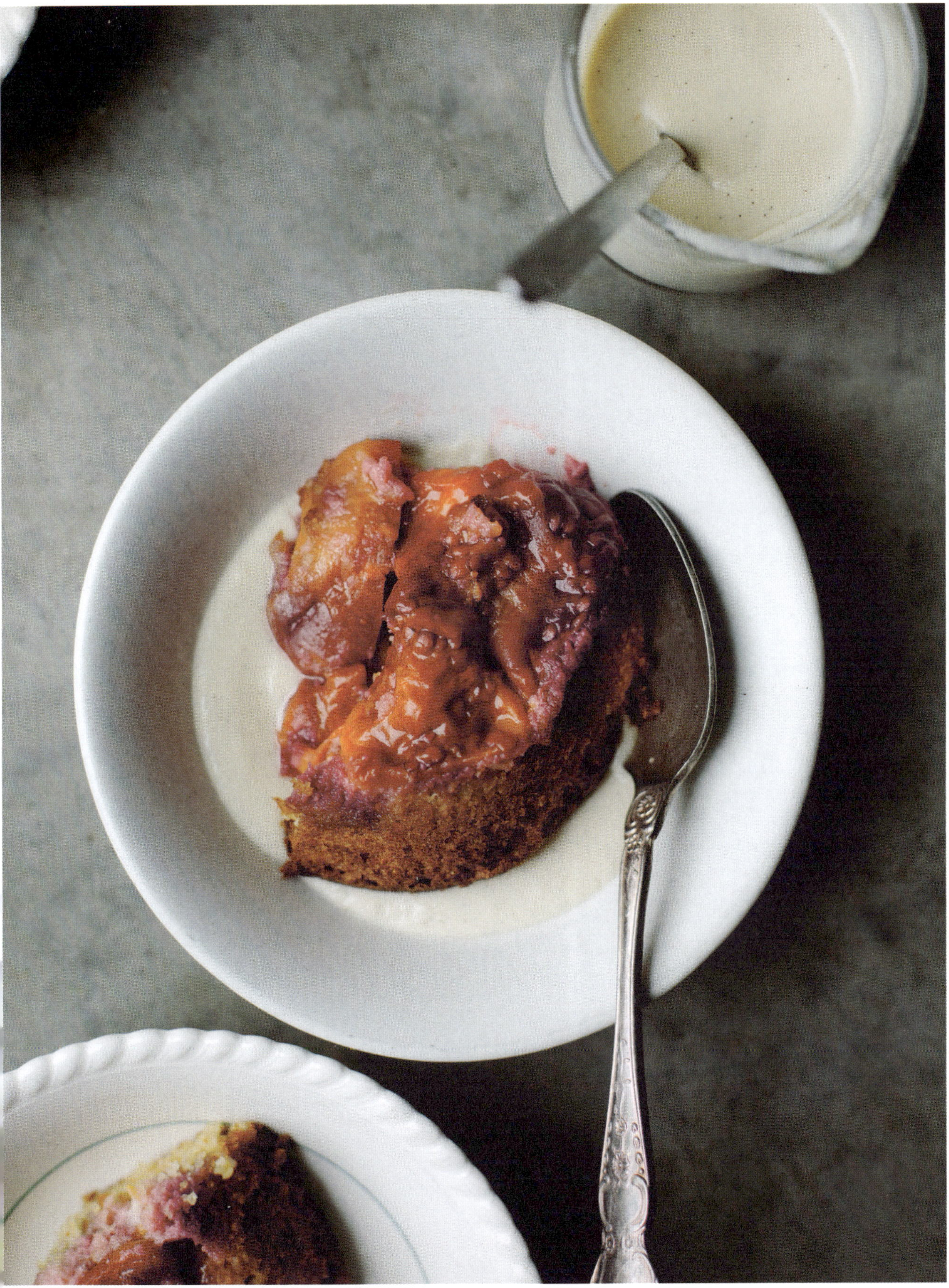

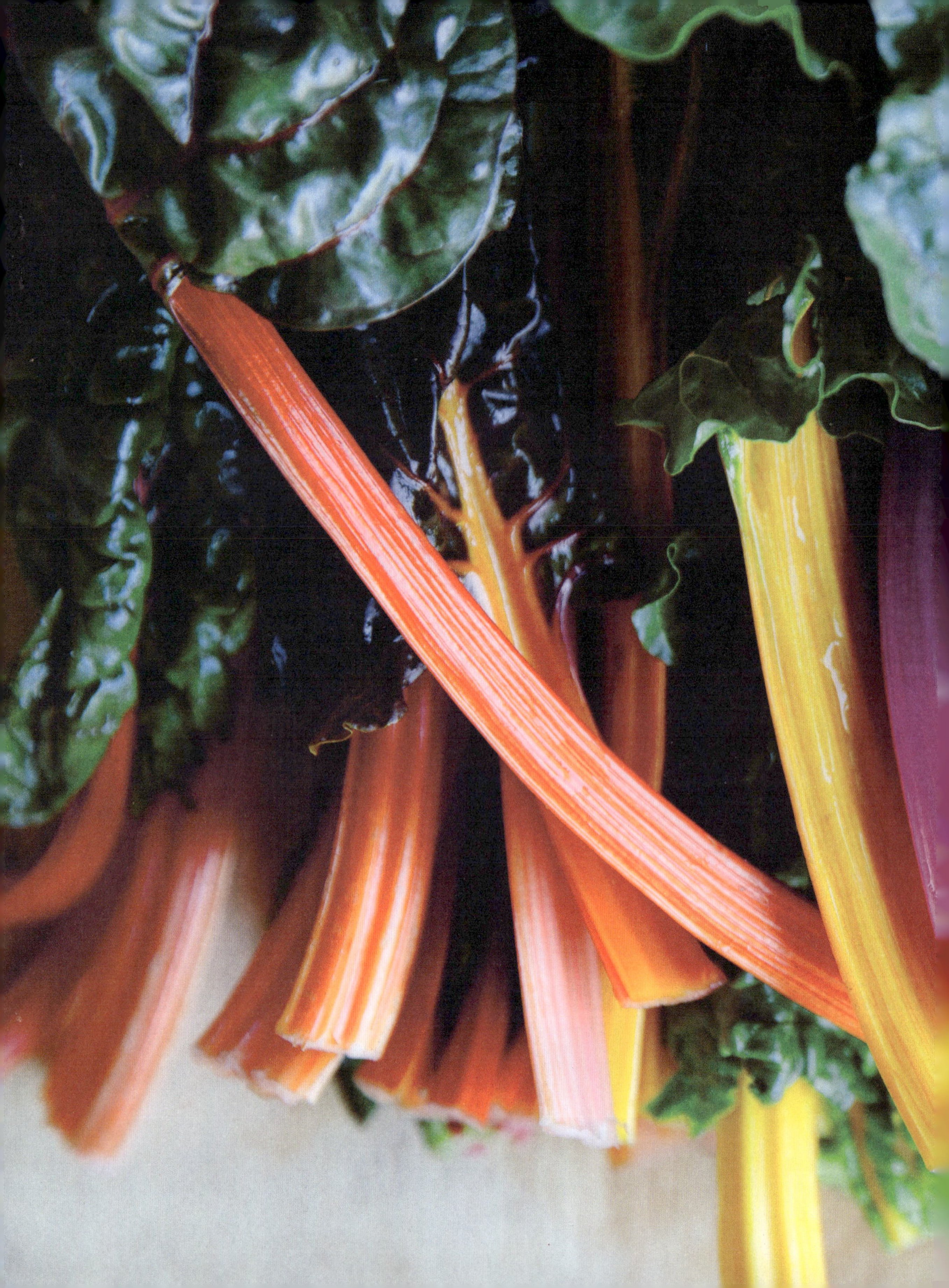

WINTER

cabbage + potato + pumpkin + kumara + orange + apple + cauliflower + lemon + broccoli + pear + avocado + cumquat + custard apple/cherimoya + grapefruit + kiwifruit + lime + mandarin + nashi + persimmon + quince + tangelo + broccolini + brussels sprouts + carrot + celeriac + celery + horseradish + okra + mushrooms + onion + parsnips + silverbeet + swede + kumara + turnip + kohlrabi + chokos

TANDOORI-ROASTED ROOTS W/ FRESH MINT CHUTNEY

SERVES 4–6 | GLUTEN-FREE

My daughter and I eat a lot of roasted vegetables so I often find myself changing things up a bit with the flavours. Adding tandoori spices and yoghurt before roasting root vegetables adds a ton of flavour and the cool thing is you can use whatever root vegetables you have at hand, aiming for around 1.2kg all up. But I suggest you avoid beetroot unless you want everything stained a lovely shade of pink. For added protein, add 1½ cups cooked chickpeas (or a 400g tin, rinsed and drained well) to the vegetables before coating in the spice mixture or serve alongside dhal with rice.

- 200g (¾ cup) natural plain yoghurt + extra, to serve
- 2 teaspoons ground cumin
- 1½ teaspoons ground coriander
- 1½ teaspoons paprika
- 1 teaspoon garam masala
- 1 teaspoon fine sea salt
- ¼ teaspoon chilli powder
- 2 tablespoons extra-virgin olive oil
- 2 tablespoons lemon juice
- 3 cloves garlic, finely chopped
- 2 teaspoons finely grated ginger
- 4 medium potatoes, scrubbed
- 1 small kumara (sweet potato), scrubbed
- 1 parsnip, peeled + ends trimmed
- 3 carrots (orange or purple), ends trimmed

Fresh mint chutney
- 2 cups packed mint leaves
- ¼ cup packed coriander leaves + extra, to serve
- Juice of 1 small lemon
- 2 tablespoons extra-virgin olive oil
- 1 clove garlic
- ½ long green chilli (deseeded if you like)
- ¼ teaspoon fine sea salt
- Pinch of unrefined raw sugar

+ Preheat oven to 200ºC (400ºF). Lightly grease a large oven tray with olive oil. Combine yoghurt, spices, salt, chilli powder, olive oil, lemon juice, garlic and ginger in a large bowl. Chop root vegetables into bite-sized pieces making sure they're all roughly the same size so they cook evenly. Add vegetables to spiced yoghurt and mix well to evenly coat each piece. Spread out onto the tray in a single layer, and drizzle over any excess yoghurt. Roast for 35–45 minutes, turning vegetables 2–3 times during cooking, until golden and tender. The mixture will seem really wet to begin with, but about 15 minutes in the yoghurt will dry onto the roasting veg.

+ While vegetables are roasting, place all mint chutney ingredients in a small food processor or blender and pulse until a rough sauce forms. Taste and adjust seasoning if required. Serve vegetables hot or warm, drizzled with mint chutney, dollops of yoghurt and coriander leaves. Any leftover veg or chutney will store happily in the fridge for 2–3 days in separate containers.

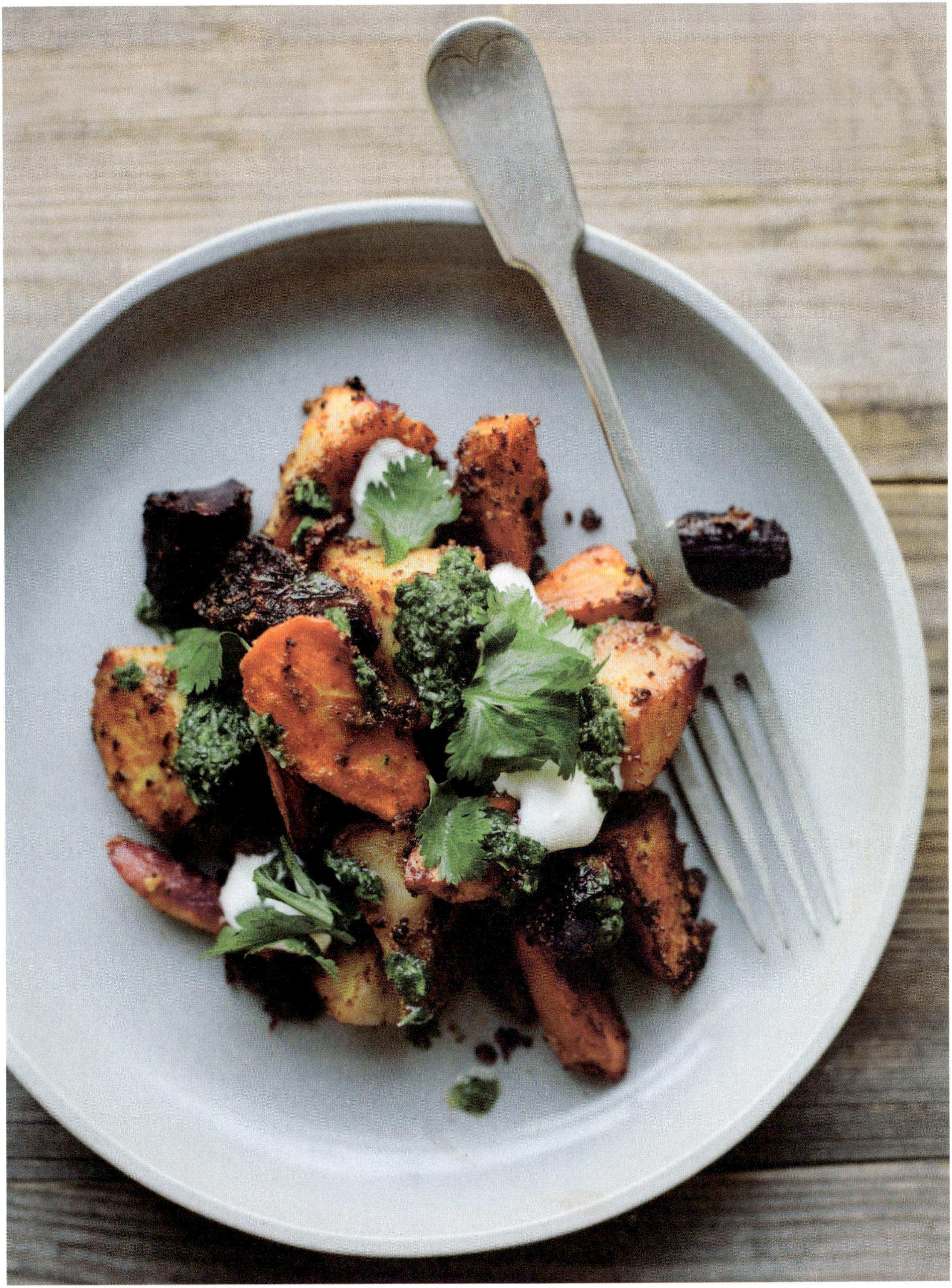

RAINBOW CHARD PILAF

SERVES 4–6 | GLUTEN-FREE | VEGAN OPTION

I love greens of any kind: spinach, kale, beet leaves, you name it and I love it, but it's the humble silverbeet, or chard as it's also known, that is my favourite. In New Zealand, where most houses have a few silverbeet plants growing out back even if nothing else, it's often one of the only greens available during the cooler months (along with kale, of course) when softer leaves such as spinach and lettuce struggle to survive the frosts. Silverbeet has so much flavour that we often just sauté it up with a little butter and garlic and enjoy straight from the pan. It's also lovely in dishes such as this pilaf, especially if you can get your hands on rainbow chard, as its bright stalks add beautiful little pops of colour throughout the spiced rice. I tend to use ghee in any Indian-inspired dish, however, you can also use olive oil to make this dairy free and vegan friendly.

- 285g (1½ cups) basmati rice, washed well
- 1 bunch (approx. 350g) rainbow chard (silverbeet)
- 1 onion, finely diced
- 2 tablespoons ghee or extra-virgin olive oil
- 1 teaspoon cumin seeds
- 1 teaspoon yellow mustard seeds
- 1 long green chilli, finely chopped (deseeded if you like)
- Small handful of curry leaves
- 1 teaspoon ground turmeric
- ½ teaspoon fine sea salt
- 60g (½ cup) toasted unsalted cashew nuts, roughly chopped
- Lemon juice, to taste

+ Bring a large saucepan of salted water to the boil. Add rice and boil for 7 minutes uncovered. Drain in a fine sieve, then return to pan, cover with a tight-fitting lid and set aside for 20 minutes.

+ Roughly slice stalks of the rainbow chard into bite-sized pieces and set aside with onion. Roughly chop leaves and set aside separately.

+ Heat a large frying pan over medium-high heat. Add ghee or olive oil, cumin and mustard seeds. Cook until mustard seeds start to pop, then add onion, chilli, curry leaves and chard stalks and cook, stirring often, for 5 minutes. Add turmeric and salt and cook for a further minute before adding chard leaves. Stir well, cover with a lid and allow to steam for a minute or two until the leaves are wilted and stalks tender. Turn down heat if things are starting to look dry and threatening to burn, or add a touch of water. Remove from heat, stir through cooked rice and cashew nuts. Squeeze over a little lemon juice to taste, and serve.

NOTE: You can find bunches of fresh curry leaves at some supermarkets, Indian grocers or veggie stores. Any excess can be frozen for later use.

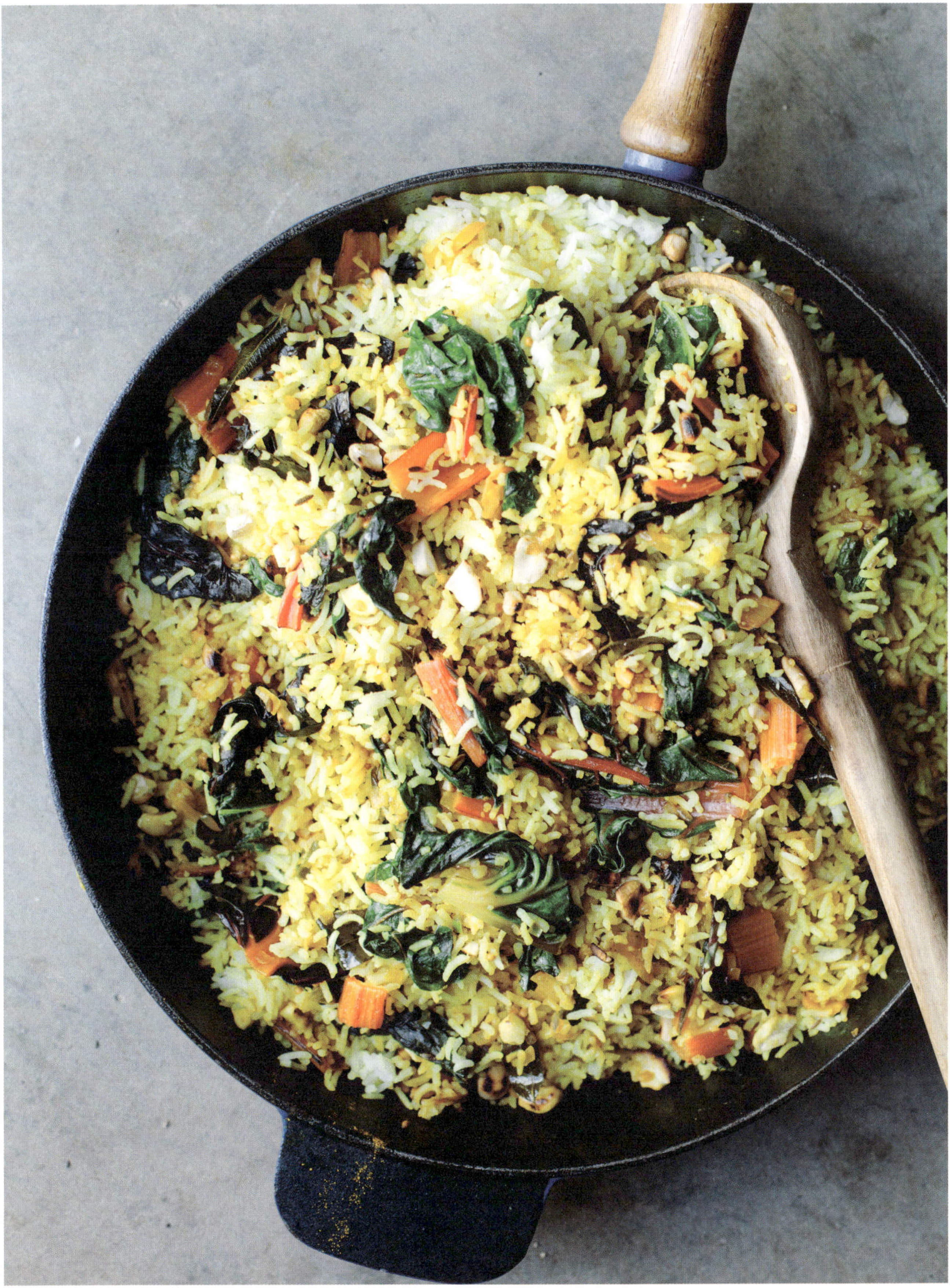

CURRIED KUMARA + COCONUT SOUP

SERVES 4 | GLUTEN-FREE | VEGAN OPTION

I use a beautiful Madras curry powder from my local Indian grocery store in this soup, which doesn't have quite as much turmeric as some curry powders found at the supermarket. So just note that depending on the curry powder used, the colour of your soup will differ slightly from mine – it will still taste yum, don't worry. I prefer to use regular red (Owairaka) kumara, but any kind will do, you'll just get a different coloured soup!

1 tablespoon virgin coconut oil or ghee
½ onion, finely diced
2 cloves garlic, roughly chopped
1 bunch coriander, roots finely chopped, optional
1½–2 teaspoons good-quality curry powder
1 large (approx. 750g) kumara (sweet potato), peeled + cut into bite-sized chunks
185–250ml (¾ cup–1 cup) coconut milk
Turmeric pepitas (page 148), optional, + coriander leaves, to serve

+ Heat oil in a large saucepan over medium heat. Add onion and cook, while stirring, for 5 minutes or until tender and just starting to colour. Add garlic and coriander roots, if using, and cook for a further minute. Add curry powder and stir well. Add kumara and give it a few good mixes before pouring over just enough cold water to cover the kumara. Season with fine sea salt and a few grinds of black pepper, cover with a lid and bring to the boil. Reduce to a simmer and cook for 20 minutes, stirring occasionally.

+ Remove from heat, add 185ml (¾ cup) coconut milk and blend using a stick blender or transfer to an upright blender and pulse until smooth, adding in remaining coconut milk to thin to a nice consistency if needed. Taste and adjust seasoning if needed. Serve hot topped with a sprinkle of turmeric pepitas, if desired, and coriander leaves. Leftovers can be stored in the fridge in a glass jar for 2–3 days; when reheating you will need to add a touch of water or coconut milk to thin the soup down.

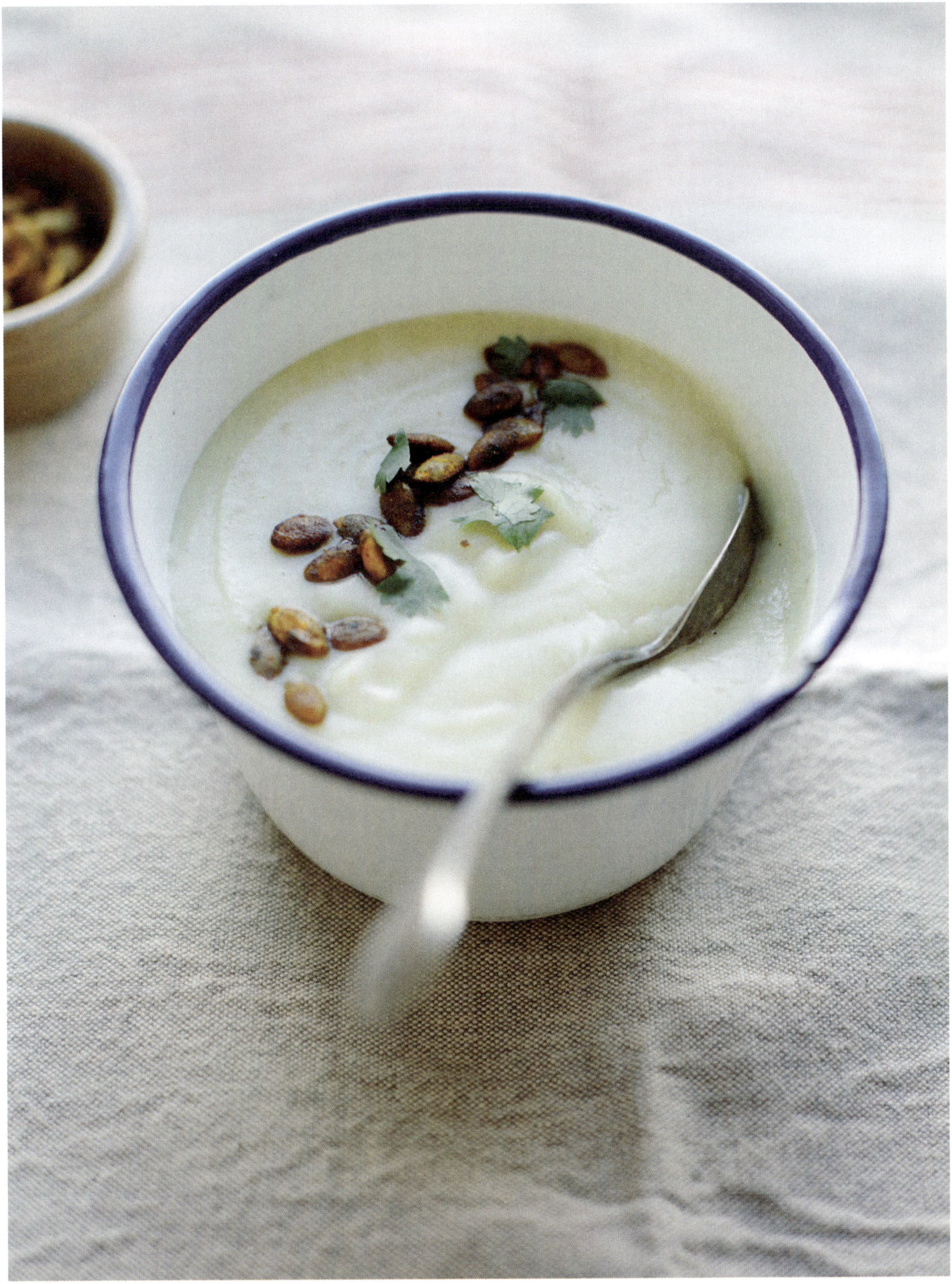

ROASTED BROCCOLINI + TOFU NOODLES W/ PEANUT LIME SAUCE

SERVES 4 | GLUTEN-FREE | VEGAN

We're sticking with the roasting theme throughout winter if that's okay with you? Good, 'cause roasted broccolini (or broccoli if that's what you have) is one of the best things out. Roasting anything means it's essentially evaporating moisture and concentrating flavour, and for the vegetable that is all too often completely decimated by boiling until mushy, let's just say that going the roasting route is kinda revolutionary. Ditto for roasted tofu. The recipe for peanut lime sauce is likely to make twice as much as you'll need; by all means halve it, however, if like me you love the stuff, I'm sure you'll find loads of ways to use up the remaining sauce.

- 300g packet firm tofu, rinsed + patted dry
- 2 bunches (400g) broccolini (or 1 large broccoli cut into small florets)
- 2 cloves garlic, finely chopped
- 2 teaspoons finely grated ginger
- Olive oil, to drizzle
- Cooked rice noodles or jasmine rice, roughly chopped roasted unsalted peanuts, finely sliced spring onion + lime wedges, to serve

Peanut lime sauce
- 2 tablespoons olive oil
- 1 onion, finely diced
- 2 cloves garlic, finely chopped
- 1 tablespoon finely grated ginger
- 1 long red chilli (deseeded if you like)
- 1 teaspoon curry powder
- 185g (¾ cup) natural peanut butter (chunky or smooth)
- 65g (¼ cup) coconut sugar (grated if in solid form) (or muscovado sugar)
- 60ml (¼ cup) freshly squeezed lime juice
- 3 tablespoons gluten-free soy sauce
- 1–2 tablespoons rice vinegar, or to taste

+ Preheat oven to 200ºC (400ºF). Cut tofu into bite-sized squares, slice broccolini in half lengthways if stems are large and then slice in half on a slight diagonal across each one. Place tofu, broccolini, garlic and ginger in a bowl, drizzle with a little olive oil, season with fine sea salt and freshly ground black pepper and mix well with your hands. Spread out on a large oven tray in a single layer and roast for 30–35 minutes or until broccolini is tender and charred in places and tofu is golden. While that's roasting make your sauce.

+ To make sauce, heat olive oil in a heavy-based saucepan over medium heat. Add onion and cook, stirring, for 2–3 minutes until tender but not coloured. Add garlic, ginger, chilli and curry powder and cook for a further minute until fragrant. Remove from heat, add peanut butter, sugar, lime juice, soy sauce and 125ml (½ cup) cold water. Return to heat and bring to a simmer, stirring with a wooden spoon to dissolve the peanut butter. Add rice vinegar – just enough to make it sing – season with salt and pepper and stir in more cold water if needed, thinning it down to sauce consistency. Simmer for 5–8 minutes to develop the flavours, then remove from heat. If not using immediately, cool and store in a glass jar in the fridge for 7–10 days. You may need to add a touch of water before serving as it will thicken up in the fridge.

+ Serve roasted broccolini and tofu over cooked rice noodles or rice, drizzle generously with peanut lime sauce, scatter with chopped peanuts and spring onion, and serve with lime wedges on the side to squeeze over.

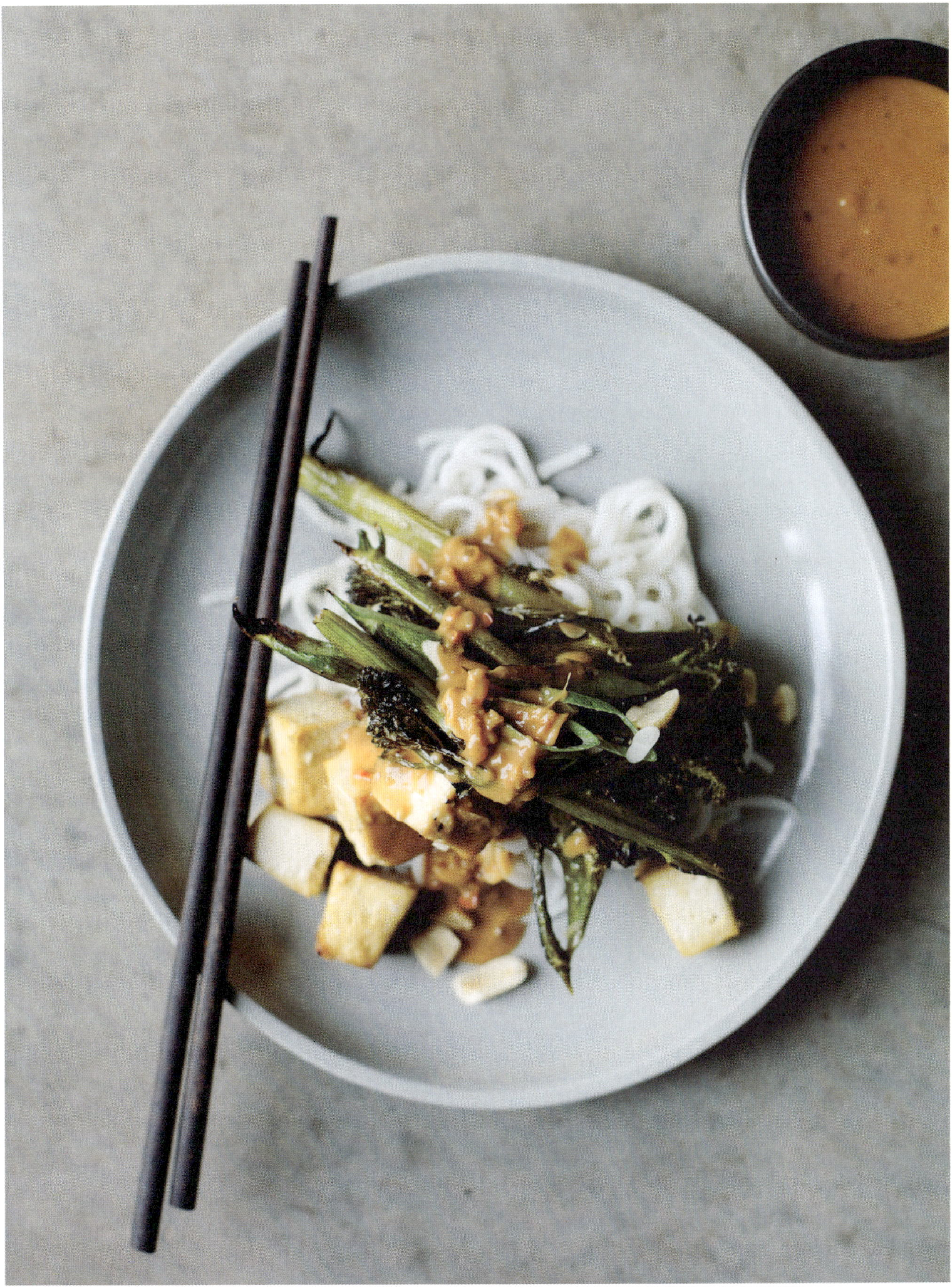

CURRIED LENTIL HAND PIES

MAKES 6 | GLUTEN-FREE

Growing up, my mum's curried lentil potato-topped pie was pretty legendary. So much so, that it inspired these flavour-packed hand pies. If you're wanting to get ahead of yourself, both the filling and pastry can be prepared in advance and stored in the fridge for 2–3 days.

- 2 tablespoons ghee or extra-virgin olive oil
- 1 onion, finely diced
- 2 cloves garlic, finely chopped
- 1 tablespoon finely grated ginger
- 1 long green chilli, finely chopped (deseeded if you like)
- 1 large carrot, finely diced
- 2 teaspoons cumin seeds
- 1 teaspoon ground coriander
- 1 teaspoon garam masala
- ½ teaspoon ground turmeric
- ½ teaspoon fine sea salt
- 2 tablespoons tomato paste
- Small pinch of unrefined raw sugar
- 1½ cups cooked Puy-style or brown lentils, drained well (you'll need to cook ½ cup lentils for this amount; page 78 for cooking instructions lentil patties)
- Juice of ½ lemon
- Big handful of coriander leaves + tender stems, roughly chopped
- 1 x savoury pastry (page 242)
- 1 egg mixed with a dash of milk (any kind), for eggwash

+ Heat ghee or olive oil in a large frying pan over medium-high heat. Add onion and sauté for 5–8 minutes. Add garlic, ginger and chilli and continue to cook for a further 2 minutes. Add carrot, spices and salt and continue to cook for another minute or two, stirring. Combine tomato paste with 125ml (½ cup) cold water and add to the pan along with sugar. Partially cover with a lid, reduce heat and simmer for 5 minutes until carrot is tender and most of the liquid has reduced. Stir through drained lentils, lemon juice and coriander. Taste and adjust seasoning. Set aside to cool. This can be prepared the night before and stored in the fridge. It must be cold when you fill the pastry.

+ Preheat oven to 190ºC (375ºF). Cut pastry disc in half, then, one half at a time, roll out on a large sheet of baking paper dusted lightly with rice flour until approx. 3–4mm thick. Cut out 3 x 14cm circles (I use a small saucer to cut around). Repeat with remaining pastry so you have 6 pastry rounds. Brush the circumference of each circle with eggwash, then place approx. ¼ cup lentil filling on one half of each circle. Fold pastry over, gently pressing the edges to seal before using a fork (dusted in rice flour to prevent it from sticking) to crimp. Transfer to an oven tray and repeat with remaining pastry and filling. Brush tops generously with eggwash and use a sharp knife to cut two small slits in the top (to allow steam to escape).

+ Bake for 20–22 minutes or until golden and crackly on top. If you cook for longer, you will notice the pastry starts to split at around 25 minutes; if this happens don't worry, they still taste delicious! Eat straight from the oven or cool to room temperature. Best eaten on the day of baking.

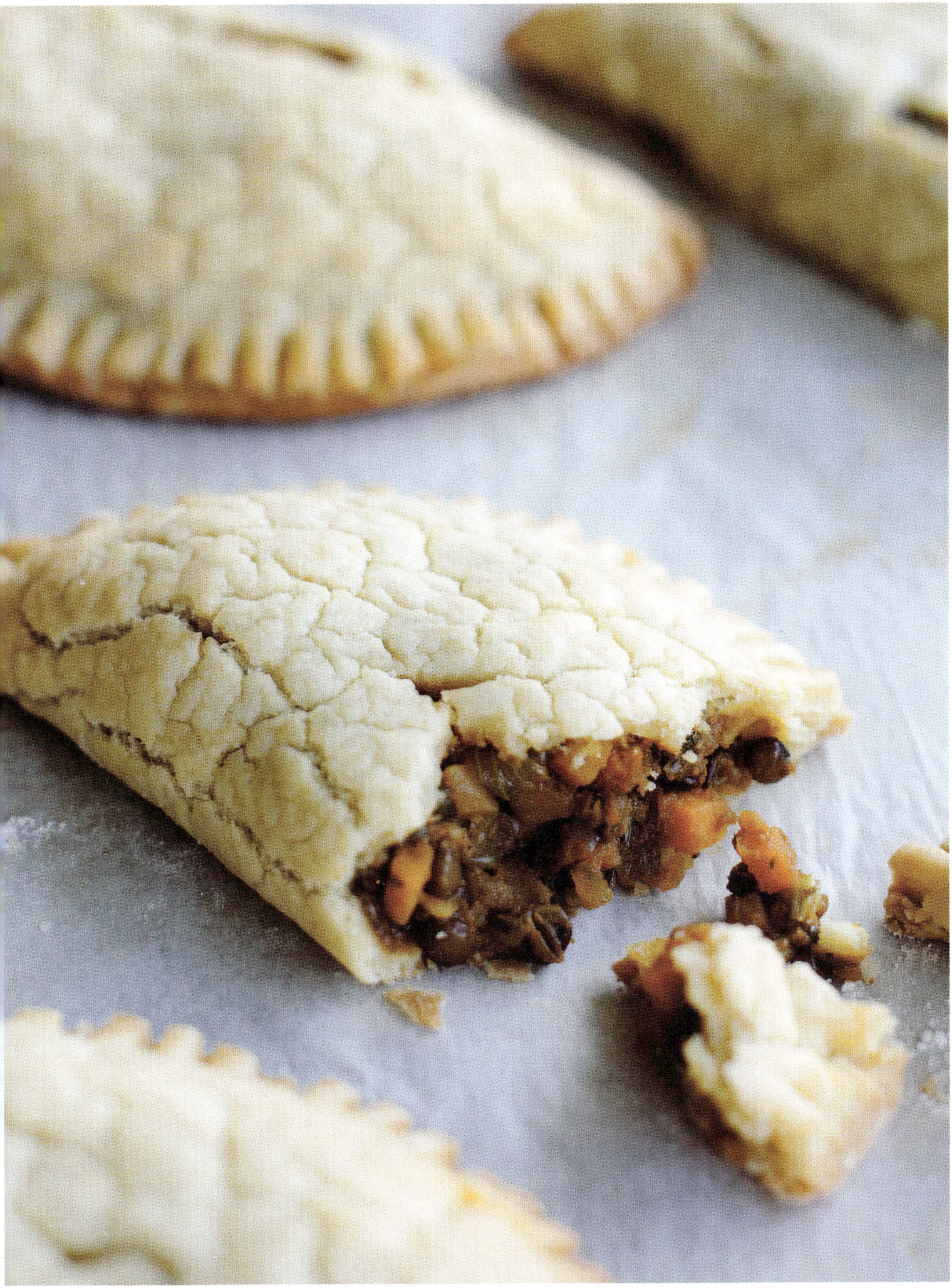

ROASTED CAULIFLOWER, CHICKPEA + QUINOA SALAD W/ JALAPEÑO LIME DRESSING

SERVES 4 OR MORE AS A SIDE | GLUTEN-FREE | VEGAN

Tender golden-roasted cauliflower is combined with quinoa, crispy chickpeas, toasted almonds and a punchy jalapeño-spiked lime dressing in this well-loved salad, which is both comforting and fresh. When I first made this salad out of leftovers I had in the fridge back in 2013, I knew it was a winner. What I didn't know, though, was how many other people would agree! This is now one of the most popular recipes on my website and I've lost count of how many emails, comments and photos I've seen from people making it in their homes. If you're cooking your own chickpeas, allow time for overnight soaking.

135g (¾ cup) dried chickpeas, soaked overnight in cold water, or 400g tin cooked chickpeas, rinsed, or 1½ cups cooked chickpeas

½ large (approx. 800g) cauliflower, cut into small florets

Finely grated zest of 1 lemon

Extra-virgin olive oil, to drizzle

1 teaspoon fennel seeds

90g (½ cup) quinoa (white, red or black or a combination), soaked overnight if possible (see NOTE, page 58)

Handful each of roughly torn mint, flat-leaf parsley + coriander leaves

35g (¼ cup) toasted almonds, roughly chopped

Jalapeño lime dressing

2 pickled jalapeños, finely chopped

Juice of 2 juicy limes

3 tablespoons extra-virgin olive oil

2 tablespoons finely chopped chives

+ Drain and rinse chickpeas. Place in a saucepan, cover with plenty of cold water and bring to the boil, skimming off any foam that rises to the surface. Reduce to a simmer and cook for 25–35 minutes or until tender but not falling apart. Drain well, then lay out on a clean tea towel and pat dry.

+ Preheat oven to 220°C (425°F). Lay cauliflower florets in a single layer on an oven tray, scatter over half the lemon zest, season well with fine sea salt and freshly ground black pepper and drizzle with olive oil. Give it all a good toss and roast for 15–20 minutes, turning every 5 minutes or so, or until cauliflower is golden and tender. On another tray spread out chickpeas, scatter over remaining zest and fennel seeds, season with salt and pepper and drizzle with a little olive oil. Toss well to combine and then roast for 10–15 minutes, turning every 5 minutes or so, or until chickpeas are lovely and crispy golden brown.

+ While cauliflower and chickpeas are roasting, cook the quinoa. Bring 125ml (½ cup) water – or 185ml (¾ cup) if using unsoaked – to the boil in a medium saucepan. Rinse quinoa and drain well. When the water's boiling, add quinoa, cover with a lid, turn down to lowest setting and simmer for 10–12 minutes until all the water has been absorbed and quinoa is tender. Remove from heat, leave lid on and set aside to steam for a further 5 minutes before fluffing up with a fork.

+ Combine dressing ingredients in a small bowl, season with salt and pepper and mix well.

+ Combine cooked cauliflower, chickpeas, quinoa, herbs and almonds in a large bowl, drizzle over dressing, mix well and serve warm or at room temperature.

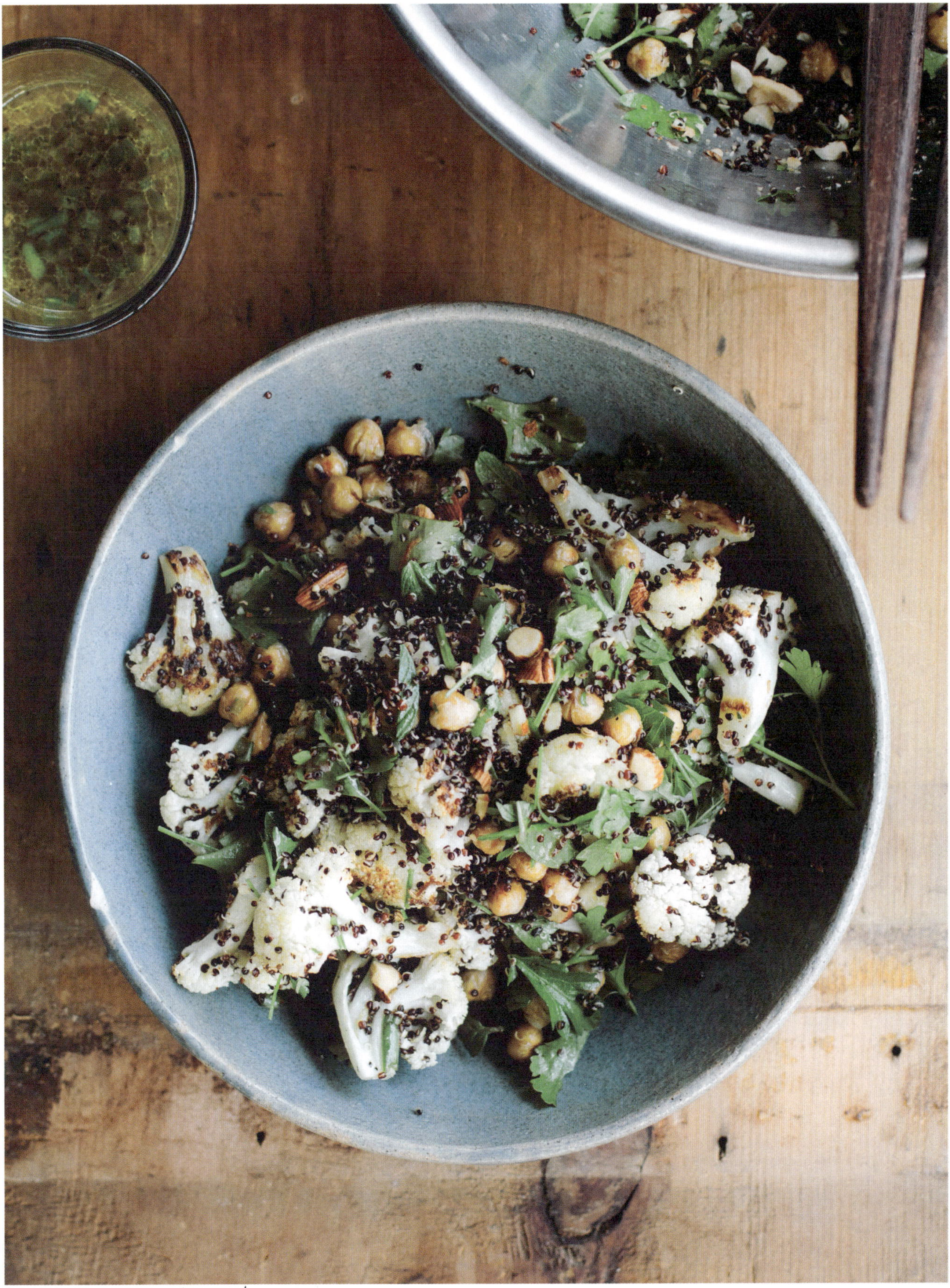

LENTIL PATTIES w/ HORSERADISH MASH + SAUERKRAUT

SERVES 4 | GLUTEN-FREE | VEGAN

This is the kind of meal that makes me think of my mum every time I make it. She's a huge mashed potato fan, a trait that my daughter also possesses, and this is exactly the kind of meal we ate as kids. The lentil pattie mixture can be prepared well in advance, up to two days ahead, and stored in a covered container in the fridge, making these a great easy weeknight meal. If you prefer, serve this alongside a salad such as my Celeriac + beet salad w/ lemon, chilli + mint (page 84) or Cauliflower + apple salad w/ creamy honey mustard dressing (page 94).

200g (1 cup) Puy-style lentils, rinsed
1 fresh or dried bay leaf
1 tablespoon extra-virgin olive oil
1 onion, finely diced
2 cloves garlic, finely chopped
1 tablespoon finely chopped thyme
1 teaspoon dried oregano
2 tablespoons tomato paste
1 tablespoon gluten-free soy sauce
2 slices gluten-free bread, toasted
A small handful flat-leaf parsley, roughly chopped
Sauerkraut (page 80) + rocket, to serve, optional

Horseradish mash

1kg (approx. 5 large) potatoes, peeled + cut into even-sized chunks
Good glug of extra-virgin olive oil
Splash of rice or unsweetened almond milk
1–2 tablespoons grated horseradish, fresh or from a jar, to taste (see NOTE)

+ Place lentils and bay leaf in a saucepan and cover with plenty of cold water. Bring to the boil, then reduce to a simmer and cook for 25–30 minutes or until lentils are tender but not mushy (the timing will depend on the freshness of your lentils and if you soak them overnight to improve digestibility, this time can be cut in half). Drain lentils, transfer to a large bowl and set aside to cool.

+ Heat olive oil in a small frying pan over medium heat and cook onion for 2–3 minutes or until tender and golden. Add garlic, thyme and oregano and cook for a further 30 seconds until fragrant. Add to cooled lentils, along with tomato paste and soy sauce, giving it all a good mix. Roughly tear toasted bread into small pieces, place in a small food processor and blend until fine breadcrumbs form. Add to mixture along with the parsley, season well with fine sea salt and freshly ground black pepper and combine well. Cover and chill in the fridge while you make the mash. The pattie mixture can be prepared in advance up to this stage, covered and chilled for up to 2 days.

+ Cover potatoes with plenty of cold water and add a good pinch of fine sea salt. Bring to the boil and simmer for 10–15 minutes or until fork-tender. Drain. Add extra-virgin olive oil and rice or almond milk and mash until smooth. Add horseradish to taste, then season with salt and ground white pepper. Cover to keep warm.

+ Divide lentil mixture into golf–ball sized portions. Flatten into patties and shallow-fry, in batches, in a frying pan with a little olive oil over medium heat until golden on both sides. Flip gently with a fish slice. Serve patties alongside a good portion of mash, with sauerkraut and rocket.

NOTE: If you are coeliac or super-intolerant to gluten, try to source pure grated horseradish or use fresh horseradish root. Failing that, source gluten-free horseradish cream from the supermarket or simply leave it out.

+ Use Agria (NZ) or Royal Blue (Aus) potatoes for the mash.

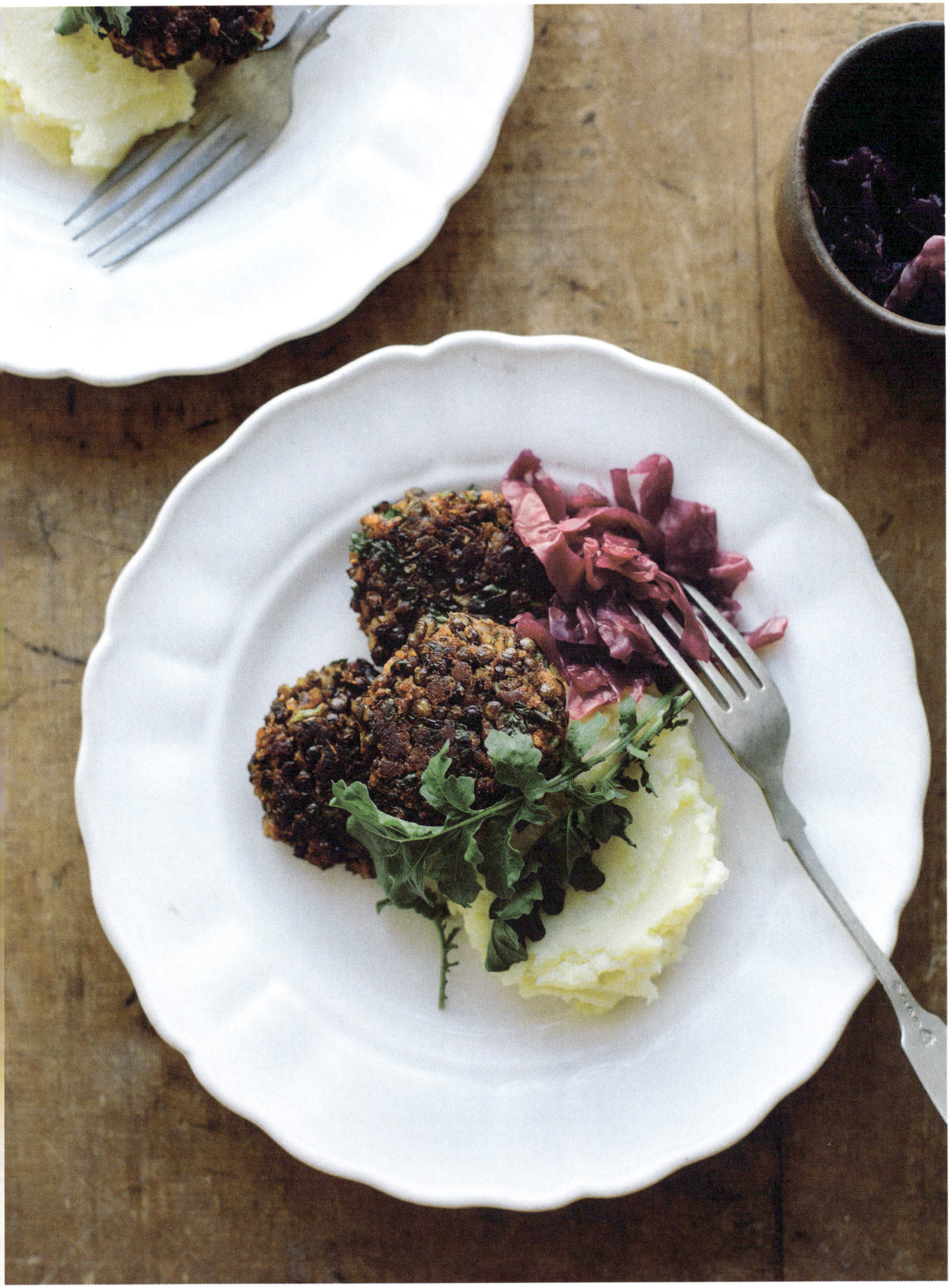

SAUERKRAUT

MAKES 1 JAR | GLUTEN-FREE | VEGAN

Lacto-fermented vegetables are full of gut-friendly bacteria and are super tasty to boot. While it's now possible to find locally made krauts at farmers markets and health food stores, it's also very easy to just make it yourself, which is something I've been doing for the past couple of years, thanks to a few tips I picked up from friend and fermentation guru Holly Davis. I love plain red cabbage kraut, but white cabbage kraut made with finely shredded fennel bulb is pretty magical, as is kraut with ginger and fresh turmeric.

1kg red or white cabbage
20g (4 teaspoons) fine sea salt
Optional add-ins: caraway seeds, fennel seeds, finely grated fresh or ground turmeric, finely grated ginger, finely sliced fennel bulb, cumin seeds

+ Peel off the few tough outer leaves of the cabbage if they look a little tatty (reserving for later use or the compost). Slice cabbage in half, then into quarters, removing hard inner core. Roughly slice into 5–7mm slices and place in a large bowl (ceramic, glass or enamel), along with any optional add-ins. Sprinkle salt over, then massage and scrunch cabbage for 5 minutes or so until it starts to soften and release its juices. Set aside for 5 minutes, then repeat for another couple of minutes until there's a lot of liquid pooling in the bottom of the bowl. Most people will tell you to massage the cabbage for 10 minutes straight, but I find massaging it, then leaving it for those 5 minutes in between allows the salt to draw out the liquid naturally, meaning less massaging time is required!

+ Transfer to a cooled sterilised 1 litre glass jar (see NOTE on page 22), packing it down with your hands as firmly as you can to eliminate any air bubbles and allowing the juices to rise up and cover the cabbage. You should have about 2.5cm of space left at the top of the jar; this is good, as the cabbage needs a little room to expand as the gases form during fermentation. If the cabbage doesn't remain submerged in the liquid you can weight it down. Some people use the outer cabbage leaves, folded up, and then replace these every few days, however I have the perfect-sized glass lid from another jar, which I often place on the top of the cabbage to hold things in place. Other times, when the cabbages are especially juicy, I find I don't need anything. It's a little different every batch.

+ Screw on lid, write the date on the side of the jar with a permanent marker and place in a cool, dark spot for 5–7 days. After a day or two you'll start to see bubbles forming around the cabbage pieces, then by about day 4 or 5 you'll notice the colour change (white cabbage will take on a slight yellow tinge, while red cabbage will turn a bright pink colour). This is a good sign the fermentation process is complete. Have a little taste and if you're happy, transfer the jar to the fridge to slow the fermentation down (if you like it more acidic, screw on lid and leave for another day or two). Your sauerkraut is now ready to eat, however, to allow even more beneficial bacteria to form, leave it in the fridge to slow-ferment for another 3–4 weeks or up to 3 months. Always use clean utensils to remove the desired amount from the jar before using a fork or spoon to repack the contents still in the jar.

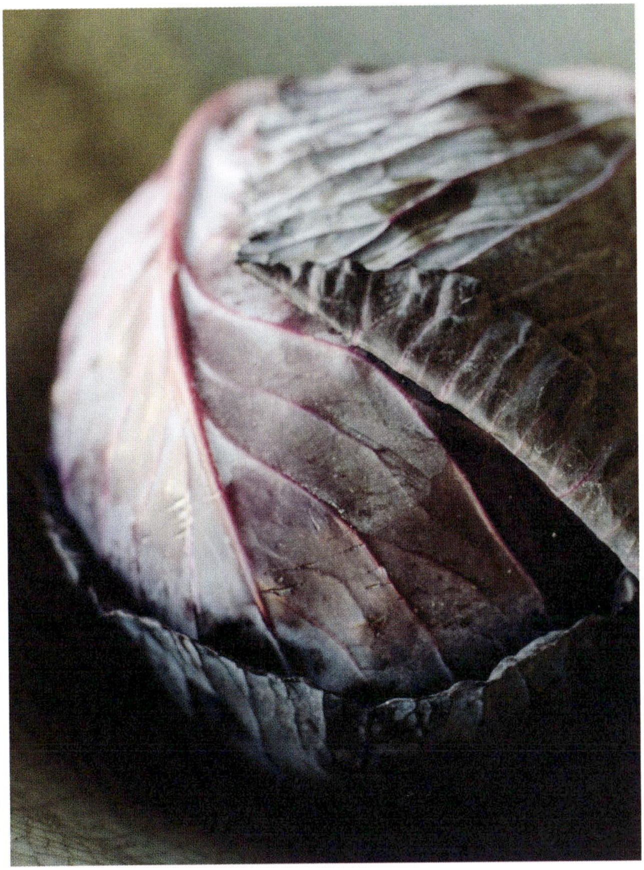
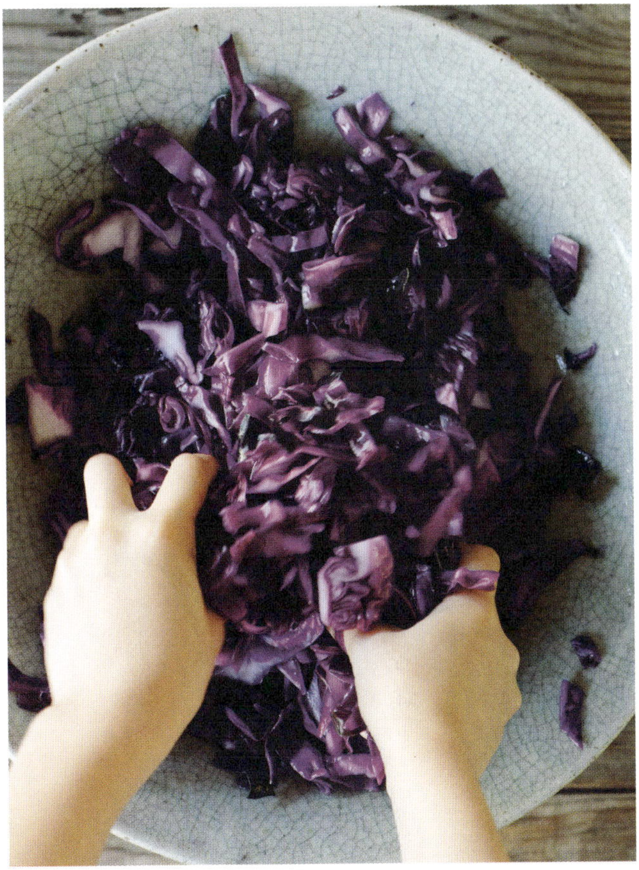
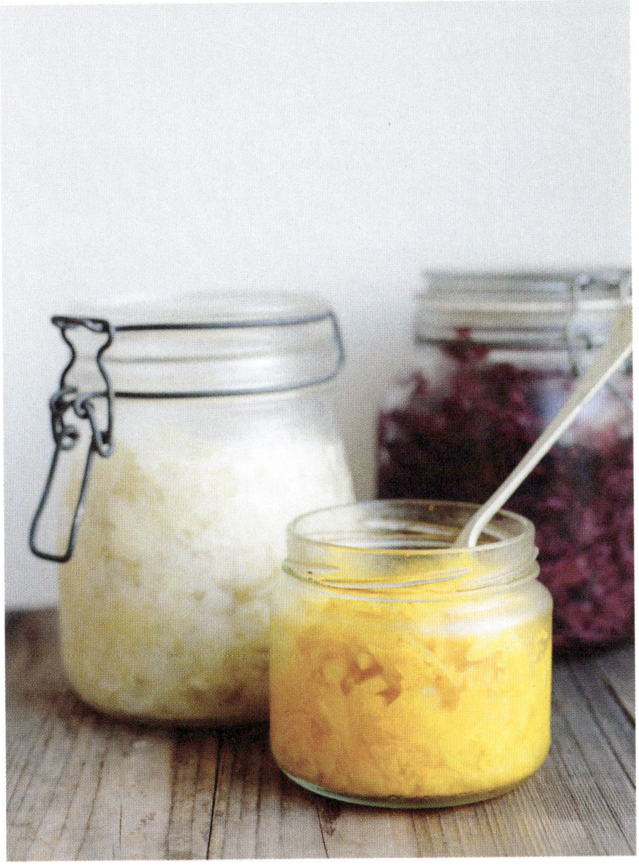
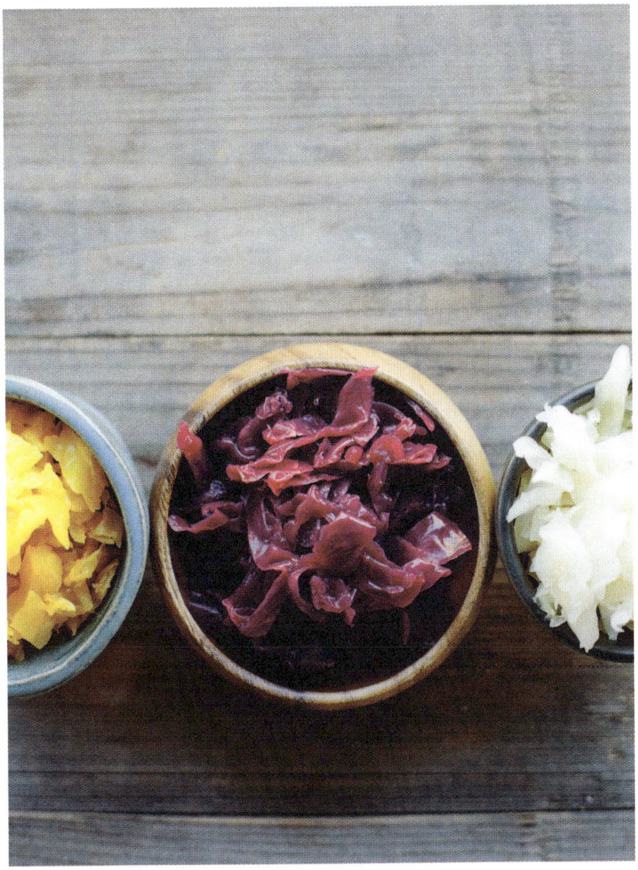

CAULIFLOWER + FENNEL SEED FRITTERS

SERVES 4 | GLUTEN-FREE | DAIRY-FREE/VEGAN OPTION

I'm convinced that chickpea flour, otherwise known as chana or besan flour, is one of the world's most versatile ingredients. Not only does it add a special touch to savoury pastry (page 242), chickpea polenta (page 202) and crepes (page 12), it also makes beautiful fritters without the need for any other flour. And its high protein content means you can get away without even having to add eggs! Mum used to coat large chunks of lightly steamed cauliflower in a fennel-seed flecked batter, before frying until crisp. We didn't have these often, but man it was a good day when we did. The memory of these treats is the inspiration for these simple, spiced fritters. We often eat them plain, straight from the pan when still crisp, but the mint and coriander sauce is well worth making to add a little freshness. Find chickpea flour at your local health food store or Indian grocer (where it's incredibly well priced).

- 1 tablespoon extra-virgin olive oil or ghee + extra, for frying
- 2 cloves garlic, finely chopped
- 2 teaspoons finely grated ginger
- 400g (¼ large) cauliflower, roughly chopped into 1cm pieces (approx. 2 scant cups once chopped)
- 1½ teaspoons fennel seeds, lightly toasted + roughly ground
- 110g (1 cup) chickpea (chana or besan) flour
- ½ teaspoon ground turmeric
- ¼ teaspoon fine sea salt
- ¼ teaspoon baking soda, sifted

Mint + coriander sauce
- Big handful each of mint leaves + coriander leaves + tender stems (approx. 2 cups total)
- 3 tablespoons lemon juice
- 1 long green chilli, deseeded
- 1 small clove garlic, peeled
- Pinch of unrefined raw sugar
- 1 tablespoon coconut milk or natural plain yoghurt

+ Heat oil or ghee in a large frying pan over medium-high heat. Add garlic and ginger and stir for 20–30 seconds until fragrant. Add chopped cauliflower and fennel seeds and continue to cook for 5–8 minutes, stirring continuously, until tender and just starting to colour. Remove from heat and set aside to cool.

+ Place chickpea flour, turmeric, salt and baking soda in a bowl, and whisk to combine before adding 125ml (½ cup) cold water and whisking to form a thick batter. Set aside until cauliflower is cool. Mix cauliflower into batter.

+ Heat a large frying pan over medium-high heat and add a good few glugs of extra-virgin olive oil. Cook large tablespoonfuls of batter in batches, pressing the batter out to form thin fritters (the batter will seem a tad thick, that's okay). Cook until golden on the underside and bubbles appear on the surface. Flip and cook for a further minute or until cooked through. Remove from pan and transfer to a paper towel lined plate. Cook remaining batter.

+ To make sauce, combine all ingredients in a blender along with 2–3 tablespoons water, a good pinch of fine sea salt and blend on high until smooth-ish. Taste and adjust seasoning. Serve hot fritters with mint and coriander sauce on the side.

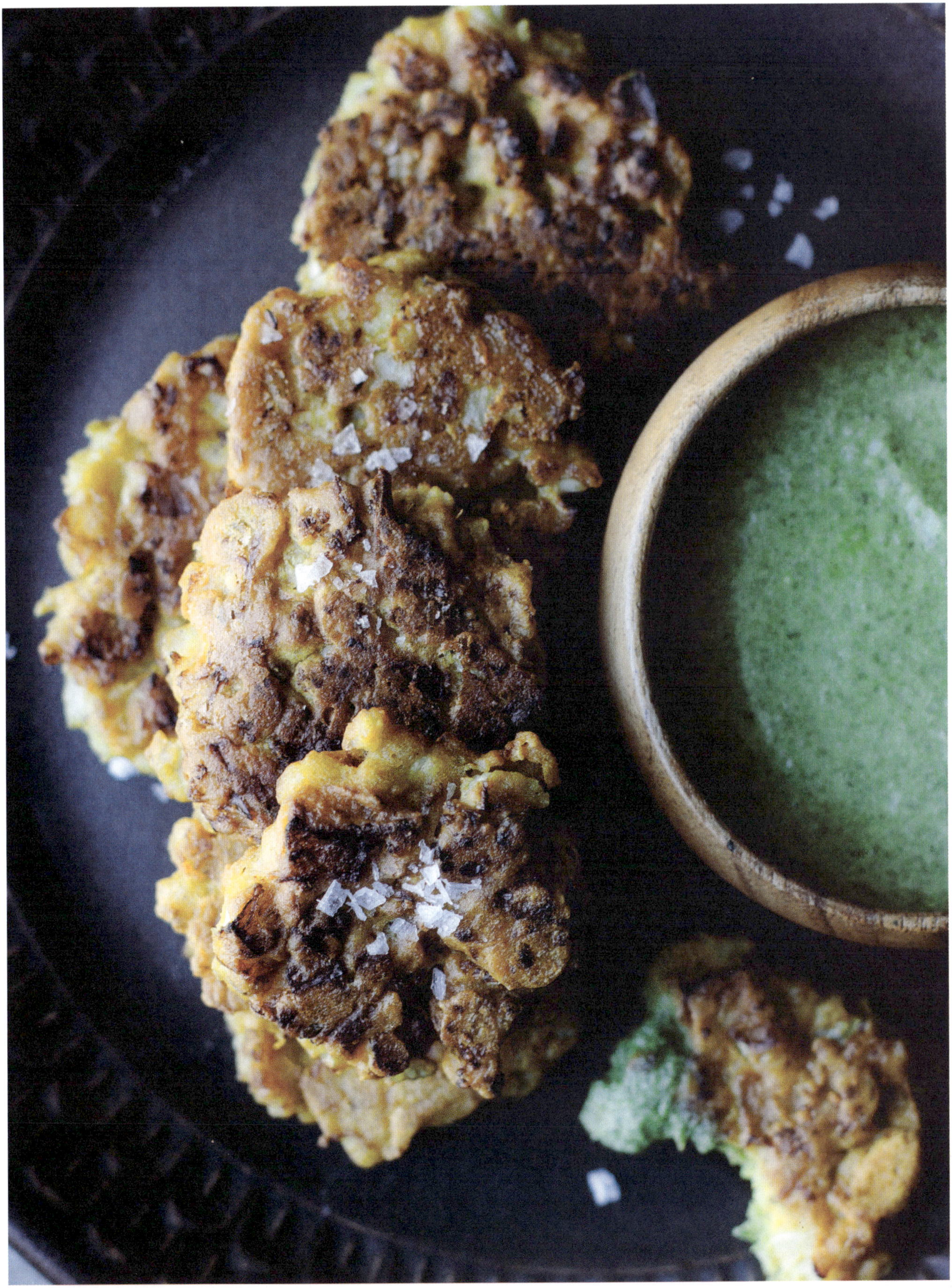

CELERIAC + BEET SALAD W/ LEMON, CHILLI + MINT

SERVES 4–6 AS PART OF A MEAL | GLUTEN-FREE | VEGAN

Inspired by a crunchy salad eaten at Jamie's Italian in Perth, I look forward to making this every year as soon as the first celeriac starts showing up at the markets. I know celeriac isn't always the easiest vegetable to come across, especially in New Zealand (unless you grow your own), but do keep your eyes peeled during the winter months. If you've never eaten celeriac before it can seem a little strange with its knobbly bulb and long celery-like stems, but peeled they reveal a beautiful white flesh that faintly tastes of celery, with a texture close to a carrot. They're lovely boiled and mashed, made into soup, or roasted. I love a good hit of chilli in this salad, but if you're not a huge fan, remove the seeds and membranes to lessen its blow.

1 large carrot, peeled
125g (1 medium) beetroot, ends trimmed + peeled
½ large celeriac, ends trimmed + peeled
Large handful of mint leaves, finely chopped
1 long red chilli, finely chopped (deseeded if you like)
Juice of 1 medium lemon
Few good glugs of extra-virgin olive oil

+ Finely shred carrot, beetroot and celeriac either using a mandolin, grater or your food processor. Combine in a bowl (leave the beetroot out until the end if you don't want it to completely colour everything), add mint and chilli and mix well. Dress with lemon juice and olive oil. Season really well with plenty of fine sea salt and freshly ground black pepper. Serve immediately.

NOTE: If you can't get your hands on celeriac, just use extra carrot or beetroot. Turnip, swede or kohlrabi would also be interesting substitutes, giving a similar colour and texture but completely different flavour.

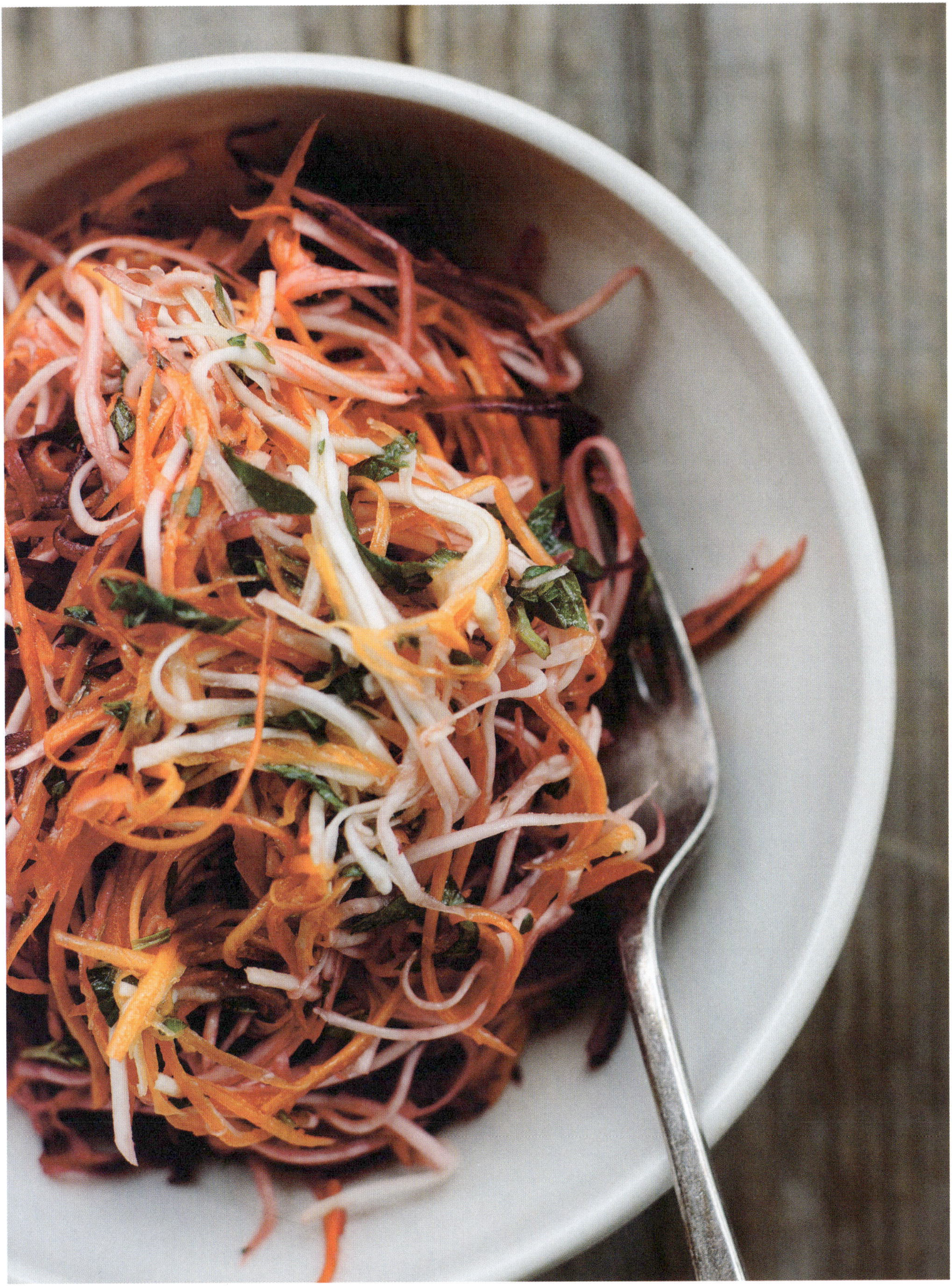

BUCKWHEAT 'RISOTTO' W/ ROASTED PUMPKIN, FETA + CRISPY SAGE

SERVES 4 | GLUTEN-FREE | VEGAN OPTION

Protein-rich buckwheat groats form the basis of this beautiful mid-winter comfort dish. I've used the term risotto loosely, but it gives you an idea of the kinds of flavours and textures involved. Using good-quality ingredients makes all the difference in simple dishes like this. I use homemade vegetable stock, which, unlike meat-based stocks, is really quick and easy to make. To make this dish vegan, use olive oil not ghee and leave out the feta.

1kg pumpkin, deseeded + cut into thick wedges (I use Japanese, but any nice full-flavoured variety will do)

Extra-virgin olive oil or melted ghee

2 tablespoons ghee or extra-virgin olive oil

½ onion, finely diced

2 cloves garlic, finely chopped

270g (1½ cups) raw hulled buckwheat

1 litre (4 cups) vegetable stock, preferably homemade (page 242)

1–2 teaspoons white (shiro) miso paste, to taste

Handful of sage leaves

Crumbled feta cheese, to serve

+ Preheat oven to 200ºC (400ºF). Rub pumpkin wedges generously with olive oil or melted ghee, season with fine sea salt and freshly ground black pepper. Stand upright on a large oven tray and roast for 45–50 minutes or until tender and golden.

+ When pumpkin is about half-cooked, start your risotto. Heat ghee or olive oil in a medium saucepan. Add onion and cook for 1–2 minutes, until translucent but not coloured, then add garlic and cook for a further 30 seconds. Add buckwheat and continue to cook for 2–3 minutes, stirring continuously. Add stock and a good pinch of fine sea salt. Bring to the boil, then pop on a lid, reduce heat to a simmer and cook for 20–25 minutes, stirring a few times during cooking, until buckwheat is tender and a little liquid remains forming a soft 'risotto'. If you prefer a looser risotto you can add a touch more stock or a little water. Remove from heat and stir in miso paste, to taste, along with a little finely ground black pepper.

+ Quickly heat a little ghee or olive oil in a saucepan and fry sage leaves for 15–20 seconds, or until crispy but not too brown. Scoop risotto onto plates, topping with a few pieces of roasted pumpkin each, and scatter over crispy sage with a little crumble of feta.

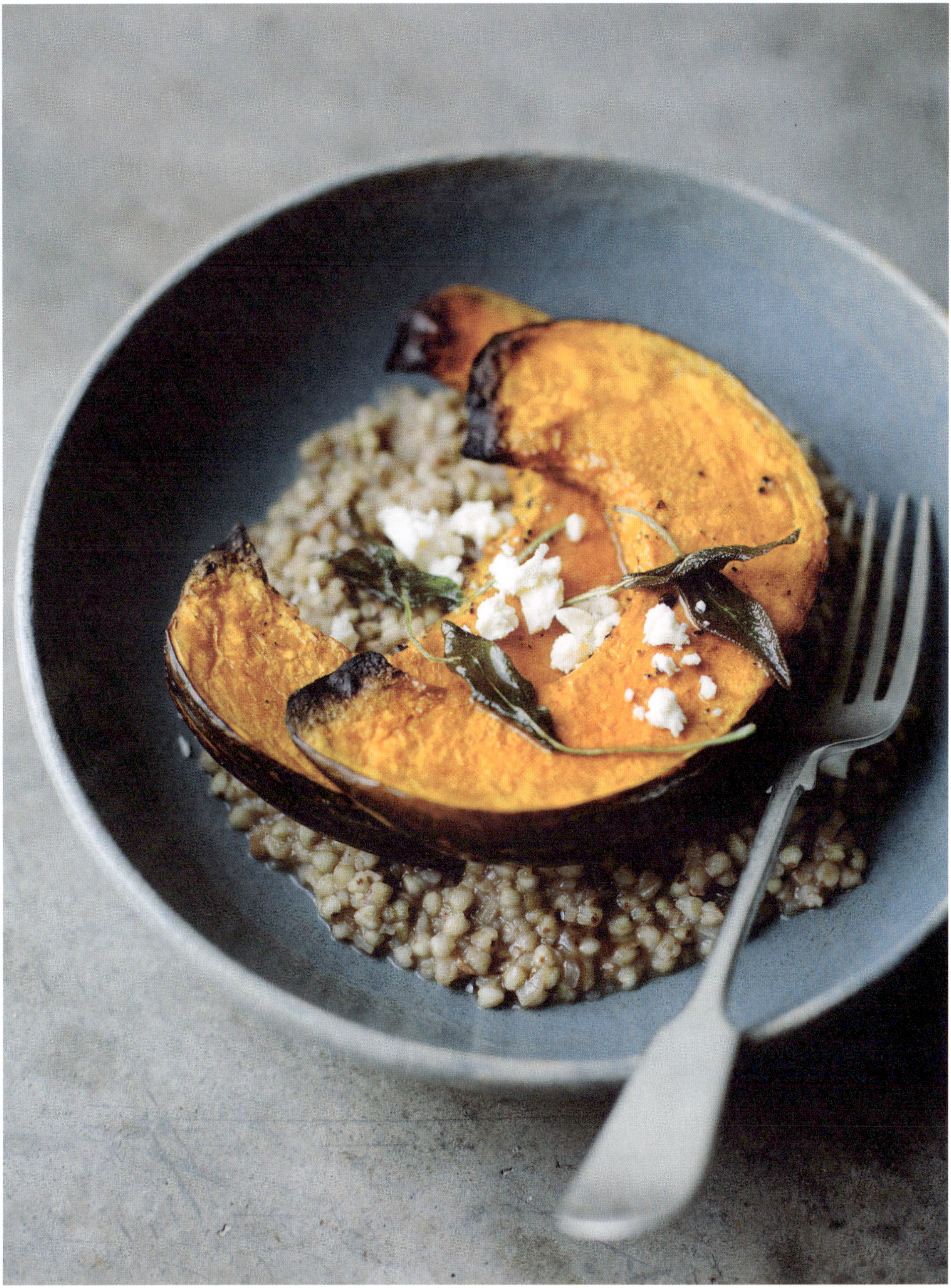

PUMPKIN KORMA

SERVES 4 | GLUTEN-FREE

Rich with warming spices and creamy yoghurt, this pumpkin curry is a real treat. Despite the number of ingredients (most of which are spices!), it's really easy to make and uses everyday items. I recommend grinding your own spices fresh as the flavour cannot be beaten (see NOTE). You can buy cashew pieces at your local Indian grocer for a fraction of the price of whole. In a recipe such as this, where they're just blended, it really makes no difference if they're whole or not.

2–4 dried chillies, soaked in boiling water for 10 minutes
2 onions, peeled
30g (¼ cup) raw cashew nuts
1 tablespoon finely grated ginger
1 clove garlic, peeled
1½ teaspoons fine sea salt
2 teaspoons ground coriander
½ teaspoon ground cumin
½ teaspoon ground turmeric
¼ teaspoon ground cardamom
¼ teaspoon ground cloves
3 tablespoons ghee or extra-virgin olive oil
1kg pumpkin, peeled, deseeded + cut into 3cm chunks
150g (½ cup) natural plain yoghurt mixed with 2 teaspoons chickpea (chana or besan) flour
Cooked basmati rice, quinoa or millet + coriander leaves, to serve

+ Deseed chillies and roughly chop. Finely slice one of the onions and set aside. Roughly chop the other onion and place in a small food processor along with chilli, cashew nuts, ginger, garlic, salt and spices. Pulse until a paste forms.

+ Heat ghee or oil in a large frying pan over medium heat. Add sliced onions and cook for 8–10 minutes, stirring often, until really tender and deeply golden. Add paste and cook for a further 3–4 minutes, continuing to stir often. Add 310ml (1¼ cups) cold water, stirring with a wooden spoon to loosen any bits stuck on the bottom of the pan. Add pumpkin and yoghurt mixture and stir well to coat in paste. Reduce heat to a gentle simmer, cover with a lid and cook for 25–30 minutes, stirring occasionally, until pumpkin is tender, adding a touch more water at any point if needed. Taste and adjust seasoning. Serve with cooked basmati rice, quinoa or millet, and scattered with coriander leaves.

NOTE: If you're grinding your own spices you'll need the seeds from 4 cardamom pods and 4 whole cloves.

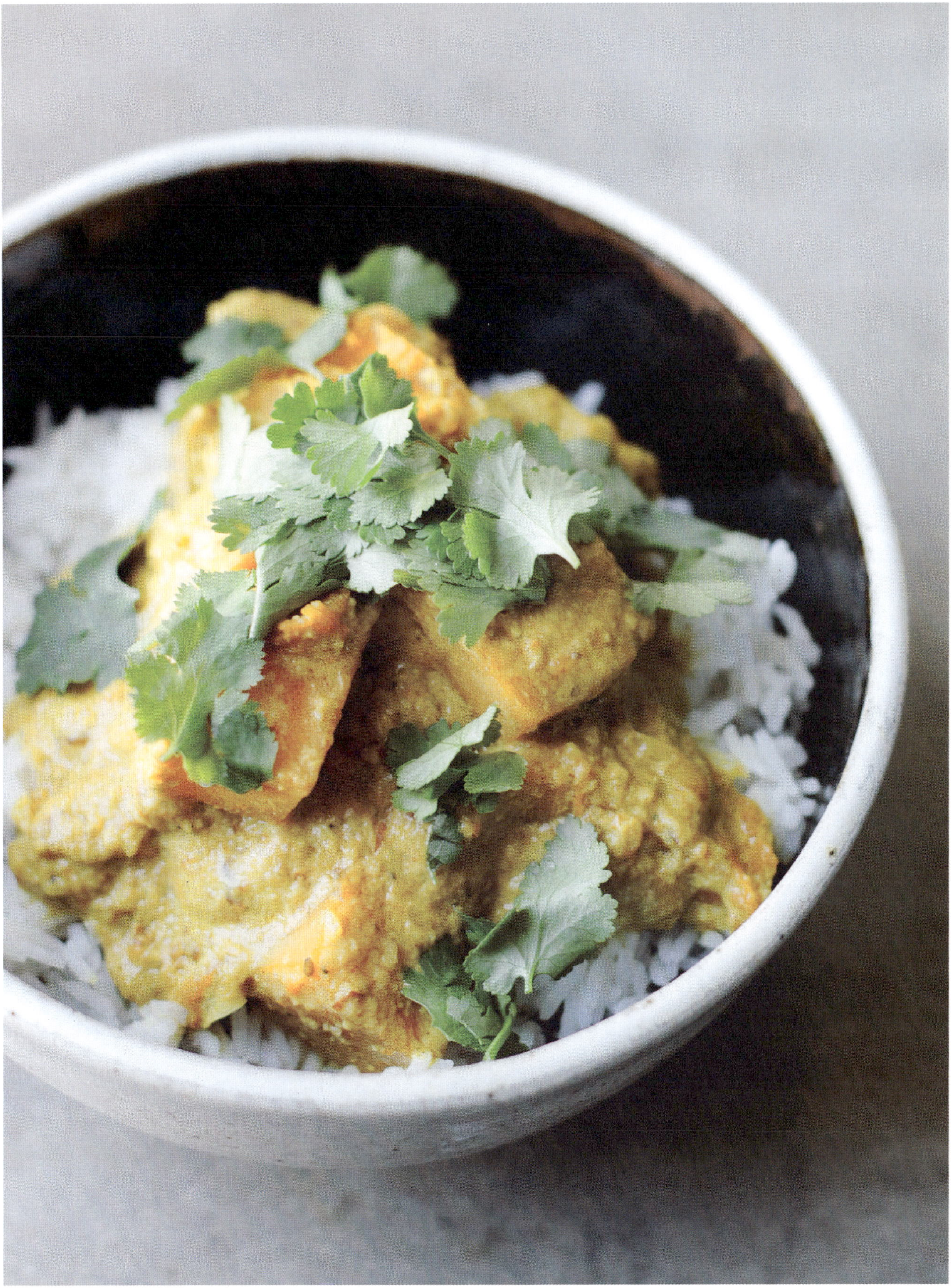

CAULIFLOWER SPAGHETTI W/ LEMON, CHILLI + CRISPY CAPERS

SERVES 4 | GLUTEN-FREE | VEGAN

People often ask me where I get my inspiration from. More often than not it's from the seasons and nature; that beautiful purple cauliflower picked up at the farmers market (page 94, Cauliflower + apple salad), or the rocket out in the garden that needs to be used up quickly before getting too old and peppery. But it turns out I also pick up ideas from eavesdropping! While waiting outside Ada's classroom years ago, I overheard two of the other mums chatting about their favourite ways to prepare cauliflower. My ears instantly pricked up and you can bet ya I went straight home to experiment and I have been making this version of Kristina's recipe ever since. Long and slow cooking creates the most beautiful soft and sweet cauliflower, while the lemon and chilli add a bit of oomph. I like the crunch from the crispy-fried capers, however, a few lightly toasted slivered almonds would work too.

- 60ml (¼ cup) extra-virgin olive oil
- 4 tablespoons baby capers, drained well + patted dry
- 4 cloves garlic, finely chopped
- Finely grated zest + juice of 1 lemon
- Good pinch of dried chilli flakes
- approx. 800g (½ large) cauliflower, cut into roughly 2cm florets
- 340g packet dried gluten-free spaghetti (I use Barilla)
- Handful of flat-leaf parsley, finely chopped

+ Heat olive oil in a large heavy-based frying pan over medium-high heat. Add drained capers and cook, stirring often, for approx. 2 minutes or until crispy. Using a slotted spoon, scoop them out of the oil and transfer to a paper towel lined plate. Return the caper-flavoured oil to the heat, adding garlic, zest and chilli, and cook, while stirring, for 30 seconds. Add cauliflower, mix well, and reduce heat to medium. Cook, stirring often, for 25–30 minutes, by which time the water will have evaporated, concentrating the flavour and cauliflower will be super-tender and golden (and slightly mushy looking – this is okay!) Squeeze over lemon juice and check seasoning.

+ Halfway through cooking cauliflower, set a large saucepan of salted water on to boil. Add spaghetti and cook for 8–10 minutes or until cooked through but still firm to the bite. Drain and drizzle with a touch of extra-virgin olive oil. Serve topped with a big scoop of cauliflower and scatter over crispy capers and chopped parsley.

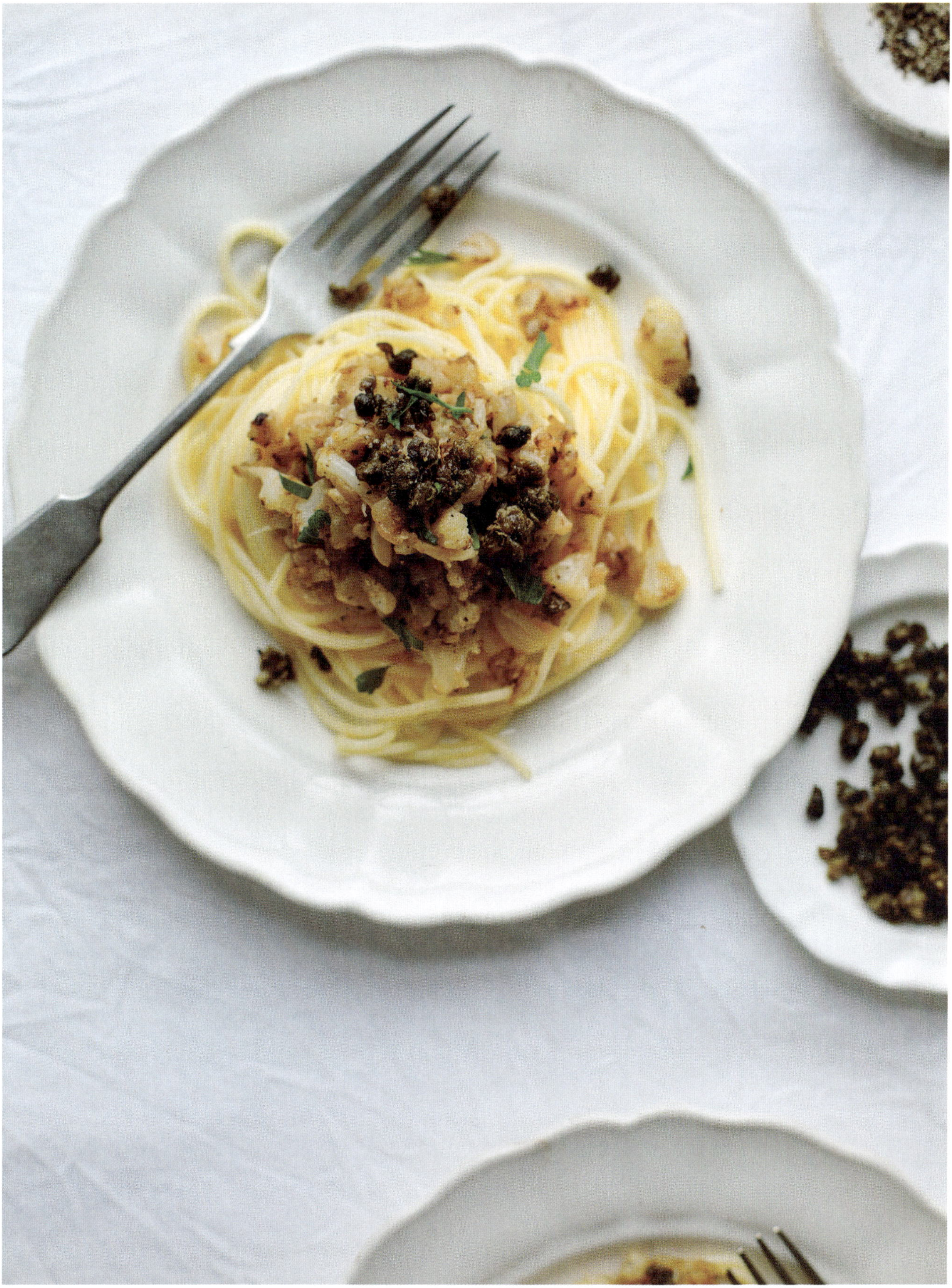

CREAMY PARSNIP SOUP W/ SMOKED PAPRIKA + ALMOND QUINOA

SERVES 4–6 | GLUTEN-FREE | VEGAN

This beautiful creamy cream-less soup is super-easy to make, full of comforting flavours and has a lovely contrast of textures from the silky smoothness of the soup, to the crunch of toasted almonds and little pops of smoky quinoa. The soup is good enough to serve on its own with some buttery toast if you're in a hurry, however, the quinoa adds a lovely boost of protein and flavour punch too.

- 2 tablespoons extra-virgin olive oil
- 1 onion, finely chopped
- 2 cloves garlic, finely chopped
- 1 tablespoon finely chopped thyme
- 1 fresh or dried bay leaf
- 7 medium parsnips, peeled + roughly diced
- 1 small floury potato, peeled + roughly diced
- 1–2 tablespoons white (shiro) miso paste, optional
- 1 tablespoon freshly squeezed lemon juice

Smoked paprika + almond quinoa

- 2 tablespoons extra-virgin olive oil
- 2 cloves garlic, finely chopped
- 1½ teaspoons smoked paprika
- 1½ cups cooked quinoa (you'll need ½ cup uncooked for this amount; see page 32 for cooking instructions lemony mushroom quinoa)
- 35g (¼ cup) toasted almonds, roughly chopped
- Handful of flat-leaf parsley, roughly chopped

+ Heat olive oil in a large saucepan over medium-high heat. Sauté onion, garlic, thyme and bay leaf for 2–3 minutes until translucent. Add diced parsnip and potato and stir well. Pour in just enough water to cover the vegetables, bring to the boil, then reduce to a simmer and cook for 20–25 minutes or until vegetables are soft.

+ Meanwhile, prepare quinoa. Heat olive oil in a large frying pan over medium-high heat. Add garlic and let it sizzle for 10 seconds before adding smoked paprika and cooked quinoa. Stir well and cook for 1–2 minutes to heat through. Remove from heat, stir through almonds and parsley and season with fine sea salt and freshly ground black pepper.

+ Remove soup from heat, remove bay leaf (and compost). Add miso paste and lemon juice and blend with a stick blender until smooth. Serve in bowls topped with a generous spoonful or two of the smoked paprika quinoa. Any leftover soup can be stored in the fridge for 3–4 days, or frozen for longer. When reheating, just give it a good whisk to return it to a smooth soup. Excess quinoa will store in the fridge for 3–4 days.

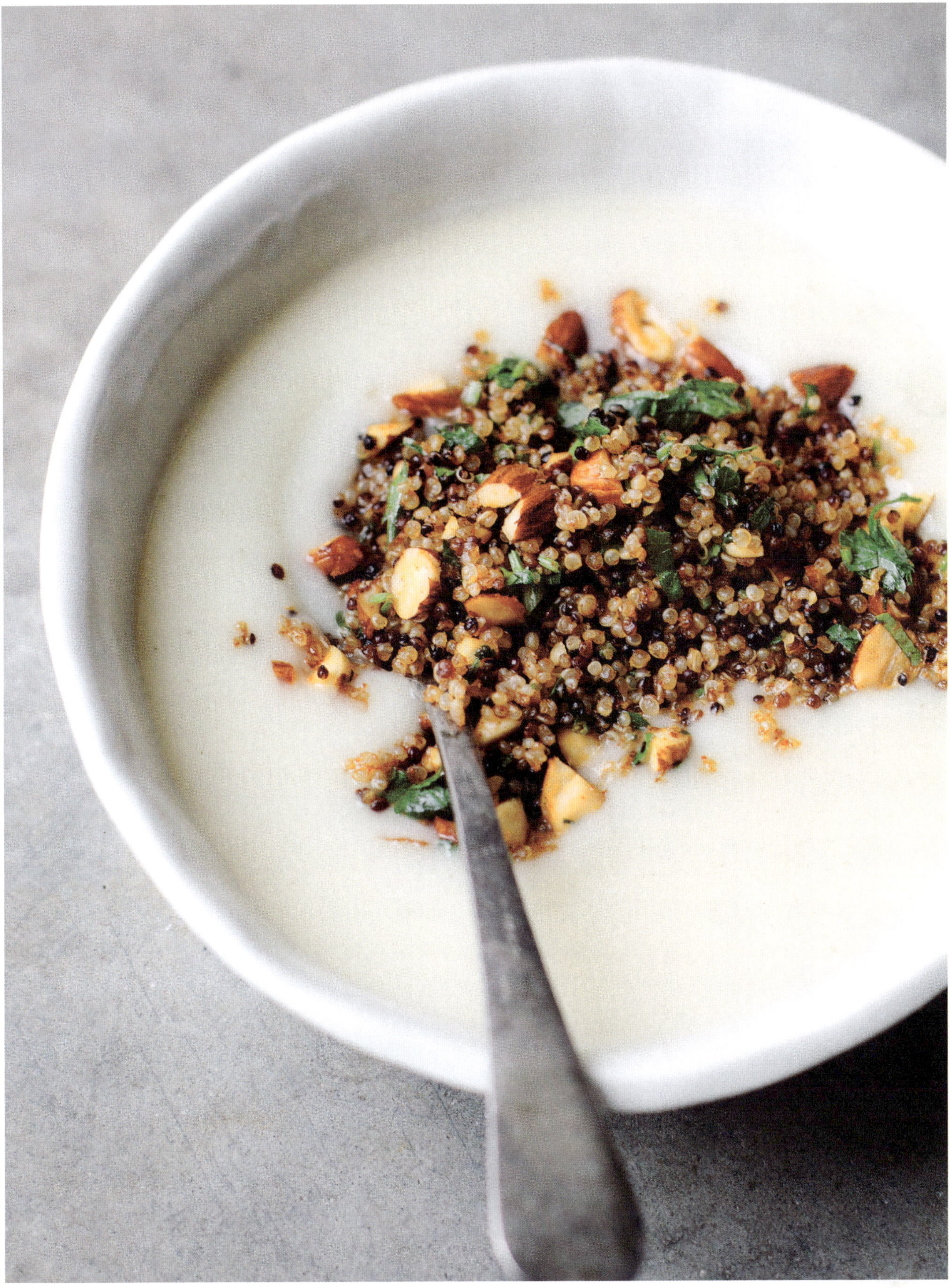

CAULIFLOWER + APPLE SALAD W/ CREAMY HONEY MUSTARD DRESSING

SERVES 4–6 OR MORE AS PART OF A MEAL | GLUTEN-FREE | DAIRY-FREE

You know how I've spoken about being inspired by things I pick up at the farmers markets? Well, this is exactly the kind of recipe I'm talking about. A beautiful purple cauliflower at the farmers markets had me running to the kitchen the moment we got home, with memories of my dad's famous raw cauliflower salad in mind. Purple cauliflower (and purple beans) tend to turn a funny shade of blue when cooked, so I find it's best to eat them in their raw state if you want to keep that beautiful purple hue. I've used Dad's recipe as the starting point, adding in slivers of sweet apple, handfuls of herbs, a little lemon zest and chilli flakes. A little crumbling of feta probably wouldn't go astray here either.

½ large cauliflower, bonus points if you can find purple!
2 Granny Smith apples
Handful of flat-leaf parsley, roughly chopped
Handful of mint leaves, roughly chopped
1 tablespoon lightly toasted sesame seeds
1 teaspoon finely grated lemon zest

Creamy honey mustard dressing
2 teaspoons honey
1 teaspoon Dijon mustard
2 tablespoons apple cider vinegar
1 tablespoon real-egg mayonnaise
90ml (6 tablespoons) extra-virgin olive oil
Good pinch of dried chilli flakes, to taste

+ Cut cauliflower into bite-sized florets, finely slicing the stalks too, and place in a bowl. Cut apples into quarters, core, then finely slice (using a mandolin if you have one). Place in a bowl of water with a squeeze of lemon, to prevent apple from browning.

+ To make dressing, combine honey, mustard, vinegar and mayonnaise in a bowl and whisk until smooth. Continue to whisk while you drizzle in oil. Add chilli flakes to taste and season generously with fine sea salt and freshly ground black pepper.

+ Drain apple slices well and add to cauliflower along with parsley, mint, sesame seeds and lemon zest, mixing well. Add enough dressing to evenly coat, then serve.

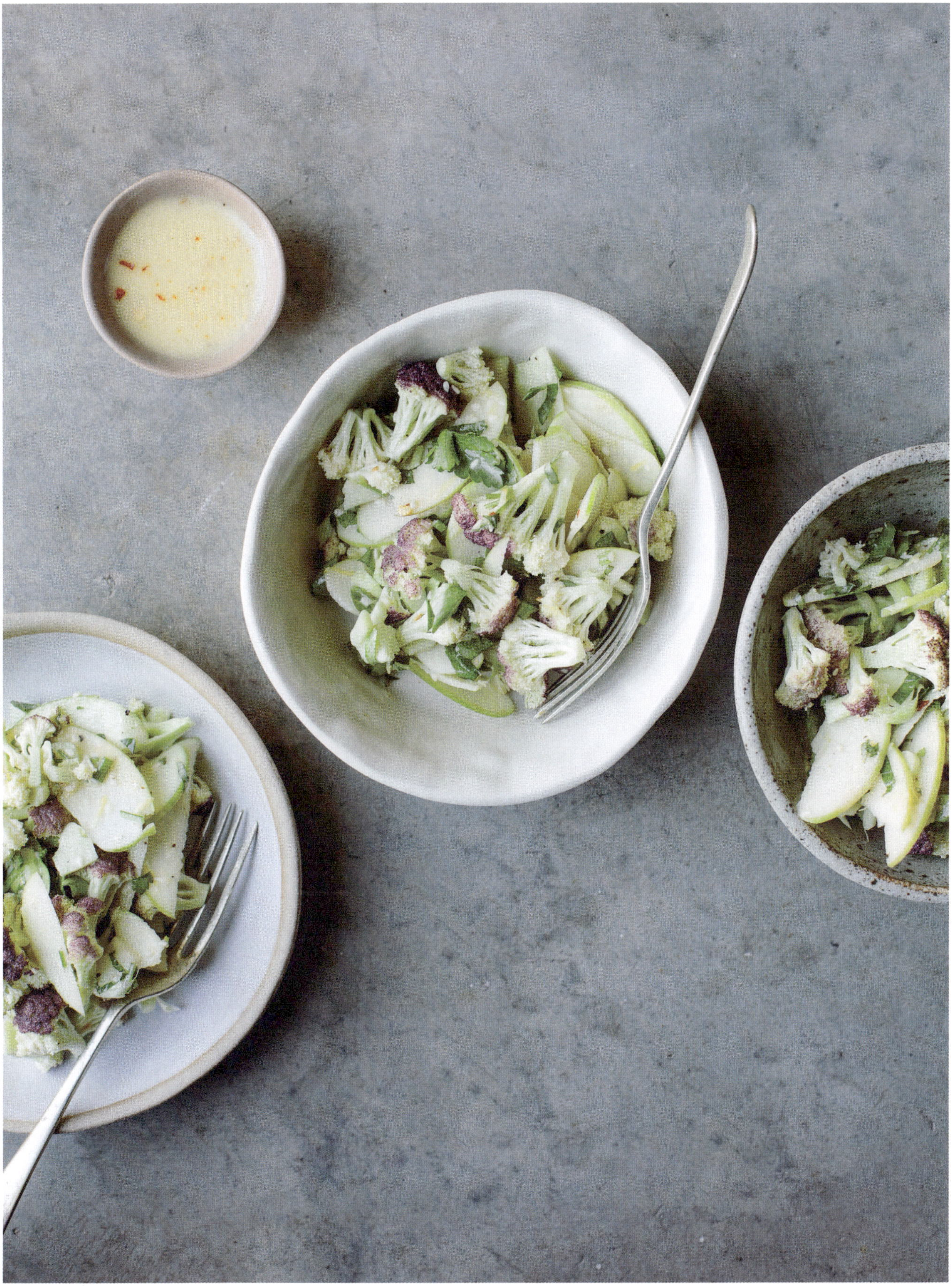

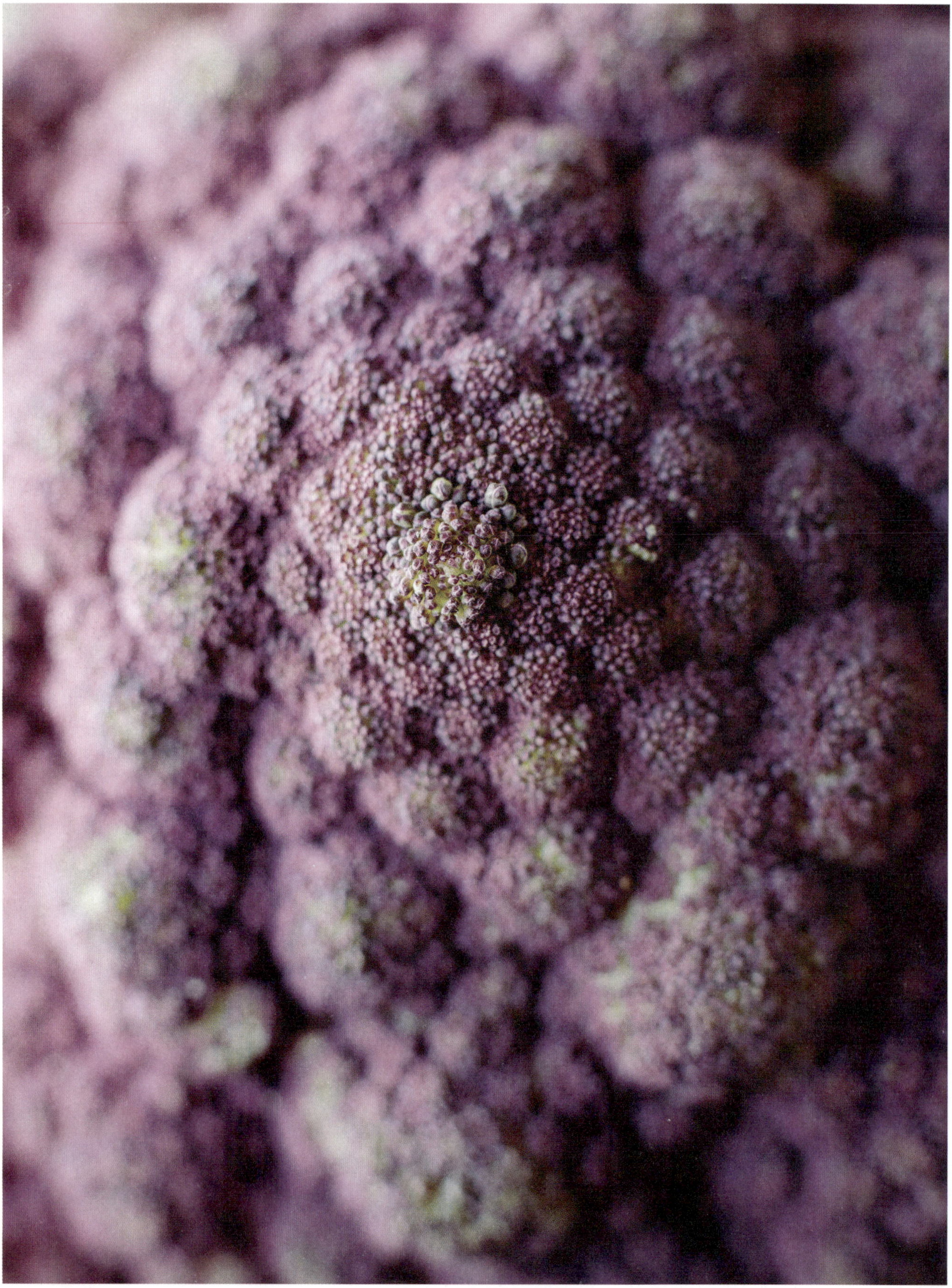

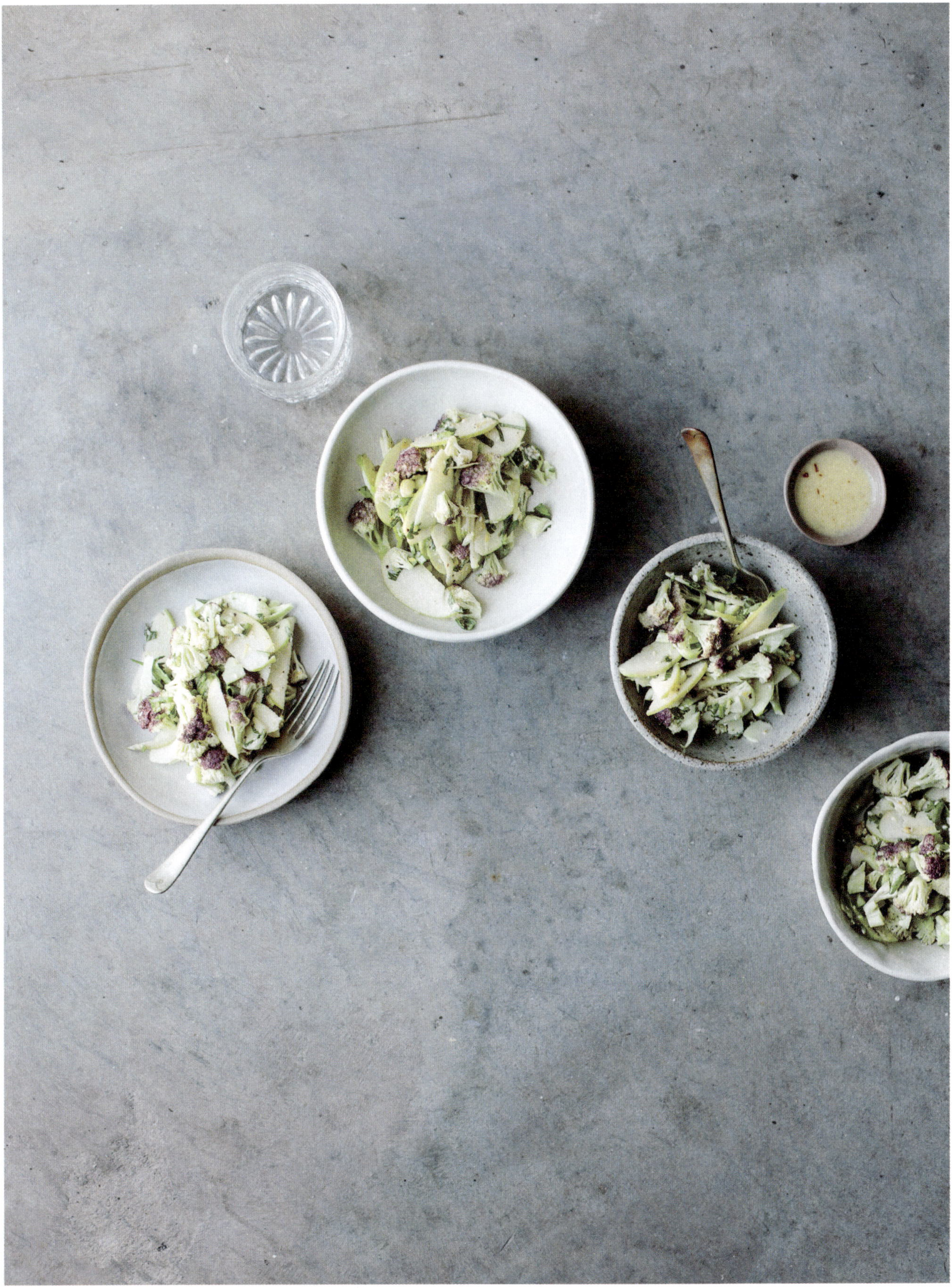

ROSE + CARDAMOM CHAI

SERVES 4 | GLUTEN-FREE | VEGAN

When I was 21 my sister, her partner and I travelled through India, starting in Kashmir at the foothills of the Himalayas. Security was tight as everyone tried to get their head around the horrific events of September 11, only a few days before. The world was on edge, especially India, as many feared they'd be the next target. This sadly meant we didn't get to see much in Kashmir, other than one little chaperoned tour per day. But one of my best memories was of the meals served on the house boat on Dal Lake, Srinagar and, more specifically, of the chai that accompanied every mealtime. Unlike the milky, sweet chai most people are familiar with, Kashmiri chai is made with green tea not black, served without milk and is spiked with saffron (and often crushed almonds or walnuts). I like to add a slight hint of rose to this light, fresh chai and while I think it's the saffron which makes it, if that's out of your price range this drink is still lovely without. (But in saffron's defence, a little goes a long way!)

- 2–3 teaspoons brown rice syrup or unrefined raw sugar
- 1 cinnamon stick
- 6 green cardamom pods, lightly smashed
- 3g (¼ cup) dried rose petals
- Small pinch of saffron
- 2 teaspoons (or 2 tea bags) green tea leaves

+ Place 1.25 litres (5 cups) cold water, sweetener, cinnamon, cardamom, rose petals and saffron in a saucepan and bring to the boil. Reduce heat to a simmer and cook for 5 minutes. Remove from heat, add tea leaves, cover and allow to brew for 1½ minutes. Strain into glasses or cups and serve immediately.

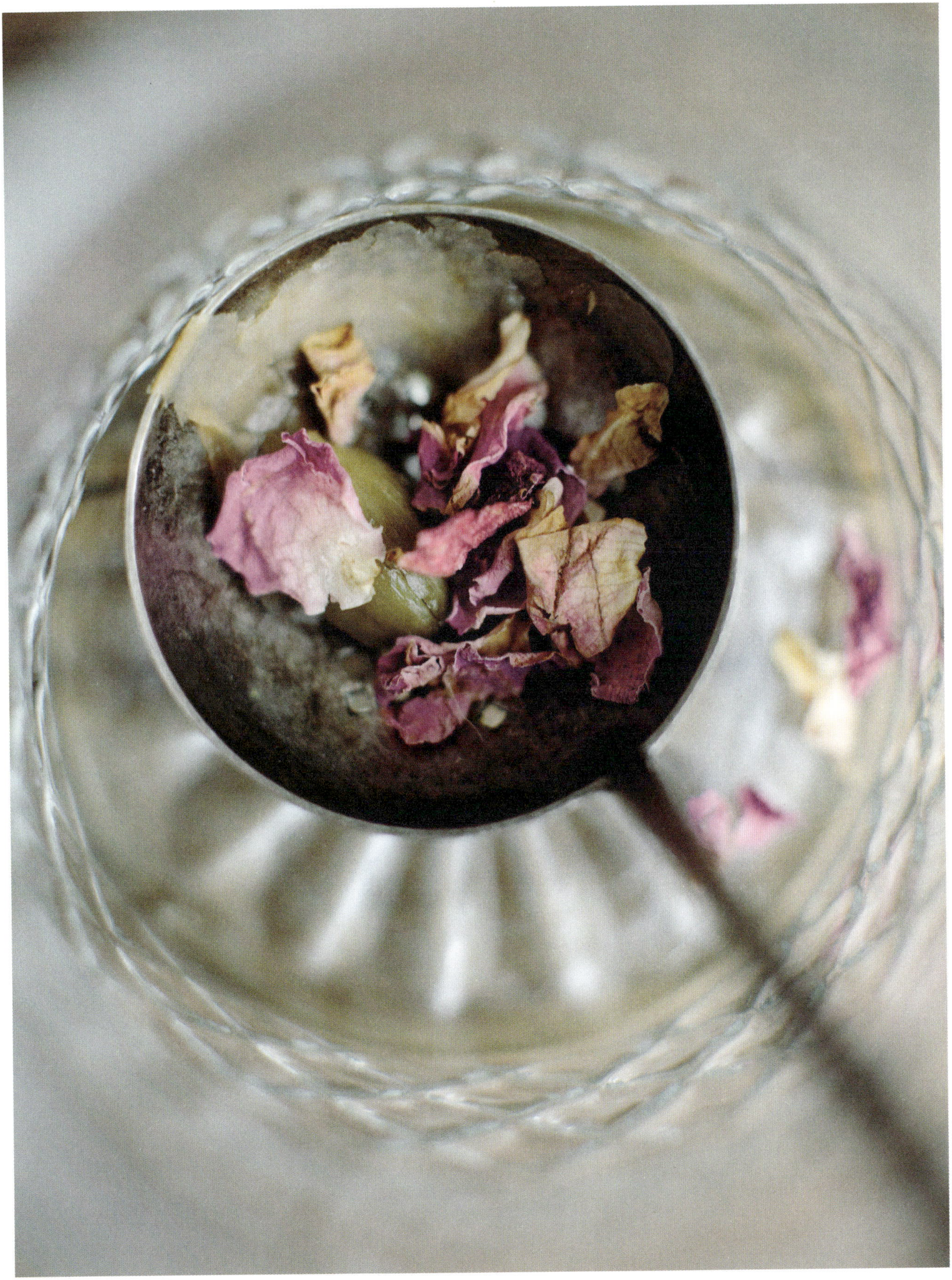

PUMPKIN + CHOCOLATE BROWNIE

MAKES 12–15 | GLUTEN-FREE | DAIRY-FREE

This recipe started out life as a Martha Stewart classic, back before I gave it a gluten- and dairy-free makeover. Dense-chewy brownie mingles with light cinnamon pumpkin cake, the hazelnuts adding a nice little contrast on top. Years ago I got into the habit of steaming or roasting chunks of pumpkin until soft, before puréeing and freezing them in half or quarter cup portions. This way I've always got pumpkin purée at hand to use in recipes like this brownie.

115g dark chocolate, roughly chopped
120ml (8 tablespoons) extra-virgin olive oil
160g (¾ cup) pumpkin purée
1 teaspoon ground cinnamon
¼ teaspoon ground nutmeg
90g (⅔ cup) fine brown rice flour
40g (⅓ cup) quinoa flour
35g (⅓ cup) ground hazelnuts (see NOTE)
1 teaspoon gluten-free baking powder
¼ teaspoon fine sea salt
200g (1 cup) unrefined raw sugar
3 large free-range eggs, lightly whisked
1 teaspoon vanilla extract
40g (⅓ cup) hazelnuts, roughly chopped

+ Preheat oven to 180ºC (350ºF). Grease a 28 x 18cm slice tin and line with baking paper, extending up and over the sides by 2cm. Place chocolate in a heatproof bowl along with 75ml (5 tablespoons) of the olive oil, and set over a saucepan of boiling water, making sure the water doesn't touch the base of the bowl. Stir until chocolate has melted, then remove from heat and set aside to cool slightly. In another bowl combine pumpkin purée, remaining olive oil, cinnamon and nutmeg.

+ Sift flours, ground hazelnuts, baking powder and salt into a bowl, tipping any hazelnut meal that won't go through your sieve back into the bowl. Add sugar, eggs and vanilla and whisk to form a smooth batter. Evenly divide batter between the chocolate and pumpkin bowls and mix each bowl to combine. Dollop big spoonfuls of each batter randomly into the prepared tin, then use a knife to swirl them together. Scatter over chopped hazelnuts and bake for 20–25 minutes or until a skewer inserted in the centre comes out clean. Remove from oven and set aside to cool in tin. This brownie will store, airtight, for 3–4 days, or longer in the fridge.

NOTE: If ground hazelnuts are not available, you can grind your own whole nuts in a small food processor until finely ground or use ground almonds instead.

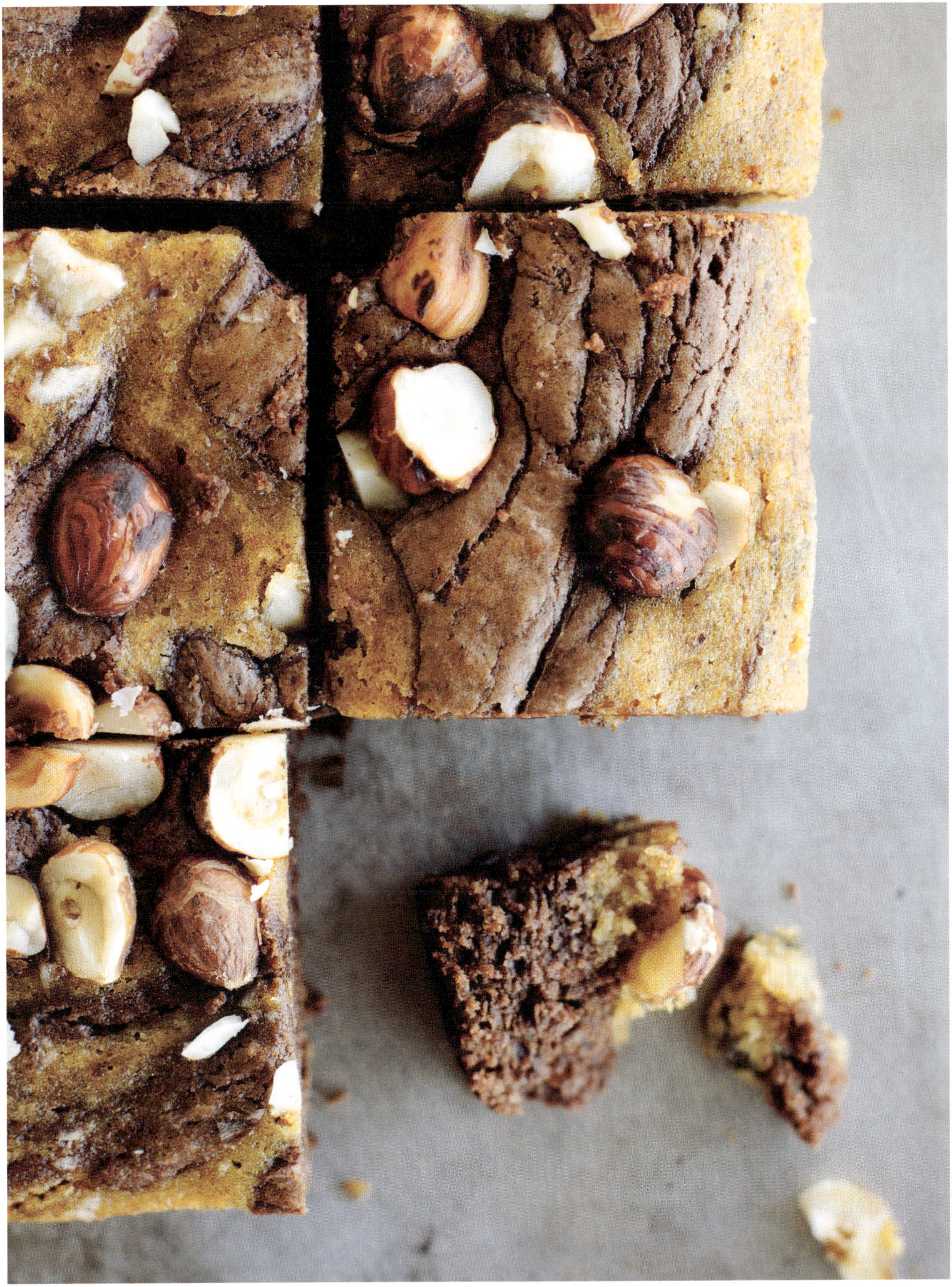

APPLE, LEMON + THYME CRUMBLE

SERVES 4–6 | GLUTEN-FREE | DAIRY-FREE/VEGAN OPTION

I feel that all too often we think of apples merely as the base of a dessert, to which we add berries or other more vibrant fruits. Here I wanted to celebrate the humble apple in all its glory, adding only a little lemon and thyme to accentuate, not cover up, the beautiful natural sweet and sour flavour of in-season apples. For a dairy-free or vegan version, use 60ml (¼ cup) solid virgin coconut oil, plus a pinch of fine sea salt in place of the butter. The results are not quite the same, but still yum. Any leftovers are lovely eaten cold with yoghurt for breakfast, or warmed through if you have the time and/or can be bothered! If like me, you like to plan ahead to make life easier, double up the crumble recipe and freeze half in a zip-lock bag for later use.

- 4 large Granny Smith apples, peeled, cored + sliced
- 4 large Pink Lady apples, peeled, cored + sliced
- Finely grated zest of 1 lemon
- 85g (⅔ cup) sliced almonds
- 70g (½ cup) fine brown rice flour
- 55g (½ cup) ground almonds
- 70g cold butter, chopped into small pieces
- 50g (¼ cup) muscovado or unrefined raw sugar
- 3 teaspoons finely chopped thyme

+ Preheat oven to 180°C (350°F). Place sliced apples and lemon zest in a saucepan, add a little splash of water, cover with a lid and bring to the boil over high heat. Reduce to a simmer and cook for 8–10 minutes, stirring occasionally until apple is tender. Transfer to a 2 litre ovenproof dish (or 4–6 smaller ones if you'd like to make individual crumbles).

+ Place sliced almonds in a dry frying pan over medium-high heat and cook for 3–4 minutes, stirring often until lightly toasted. Remove from heat and set aside. Put rice flour, ground almonds and butter in a bowl. Use your hands to rub in butter until mixture resembles coarse breadcrumbs (it will feel a little more moist than regular crumble at this stage). Stir in sugar, toasted almonds and thyme. Scatter some crumble mixture over apples, then squeeze the rest of the crumble together with your hands to form large clumps before gently scattering on top.

+ Bake for 40–45 minutes for one large dish, or 30–35 minutes for smaller ones, until the top is golden brown and the filling bubbling up and over the crumble in places. Serve warm with vanilla ice cream, vanilla custard (page 62) or natural plain yoghurt (page 239).

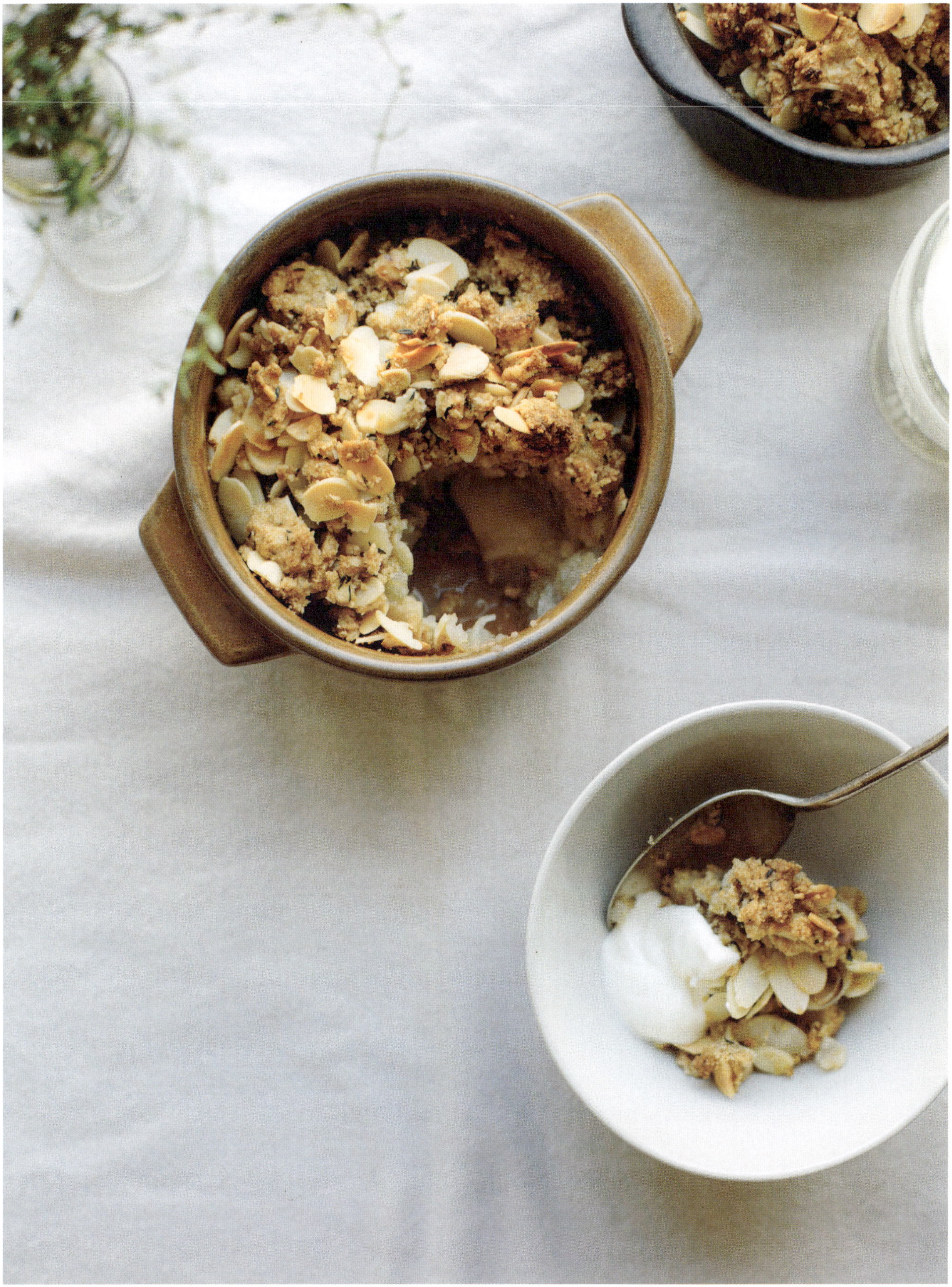

LEMON, LIME + COCONUT TARTLETS

MAKES 4 X 12CM TARTLETS | GLUTEN-FREE | VEGAN OPTION

This tart was inspired by the work of my dear friend, kindred spirit, real food activist and author Jude Blereau, who does the most amazing things with agar-agar. I love experimenting with this ingredient, the vegetarian or vegan alternative to gelatine derived from seaweed (see NOTE). If you're using brown rice syrup in the filling you may need to add another tablespoon, as it's not as sweet as maple or honey. For a vegan option, choose maple or brown rice syrup as the sweetener.

- 250ml (1 cup) coconut milk
- 250ml (1 cup) rice or almond milk
- 60ml (¼ cup) pure maple syrup, honey or brown rice syrup
- 1¼ teaspoons agar-agar powder (see NOTE)
- 2 teaspoons finely grated lemon zest
- 2 teaspoons finely grated lime zest
- 60ml (¼ cup) lemon juice
- 60ml (¼ cup) lime juice
- 2 tablespoons gluten-free organic cornflour

Pastry
- 110g (1 cup) ground almonds
- 45g (½ cup) shredded coconut
- 30g (¼ cup) arrowroot or tapioca flour
- 3 tablespoons virgin coconut oil, melted if solid
- 2 tablespoons pure maple syrup, honey or brown rice syrup

+ Preheat oven to 180ºC (350ºF). Grease 4 x 12cm loose-bottomed tartlet tins. To make pastry, combine ground almonds, shredded coconut, arrowroot, melted coconut oil and syrup or honey in a bowl, mixing well. Divide mixture evenly between the tartlet tins, then, using your fingers, press dough in to line the tins. Place tins onto a baking tray and bake for 8–10 minutes or until golden. Remove from oven and set aside to cool.

+ To make filling, place milks, sweetener of your choice, agar-agar powder, 1 teaspoon each of lemon and lime zest (reserving remaining zest) into a saucepan and bring slowly to the boil, stirring often to prevent the agar from settling on the bottom of the pan. Boil for 1 minute. Combine lemon and lime juice with cornflour and mix well. Add to the pan, whisking as you do. Cook for 1 minute, or until slightly thickened. Remove from heat, strain into a bowl, discarding zest, and set filling aside to cool for 20–30 minutes, stirring often. I leave it until you can no longer see steam rising from the bowl when you mix it, but don't leave the filling so long that it starts to set in the bowl – watch closely.

+ Pour evenly into cases, tapping the tray down on the bench to remove any air bubbles from the mixture. Scatter reserved lemon and lime zest over tops of tarts and allow to cool before chilling in the fridge for 1–2 hours. Best eaten on the day of baking. They're still edible the next day if you have leftovers, however, the pastry will have softened.

NOTE: You can buy agar-agar from your local Asian grocery store, where it's sold in 7–10g packets, but just be sure to buy the uncoloured + unflavoured variety. You can also find it at health food stores. If you're using agar flakes as opposed to the powder you'll need to use more than stated in the recipe. I use the ratio of 1 teaspoon powder equals 6 teaspoons flakes. To activate agar-agar's setting properties it must be boiled for a few minutes in liquid and, unlike gelatine, it will set at room temperature.

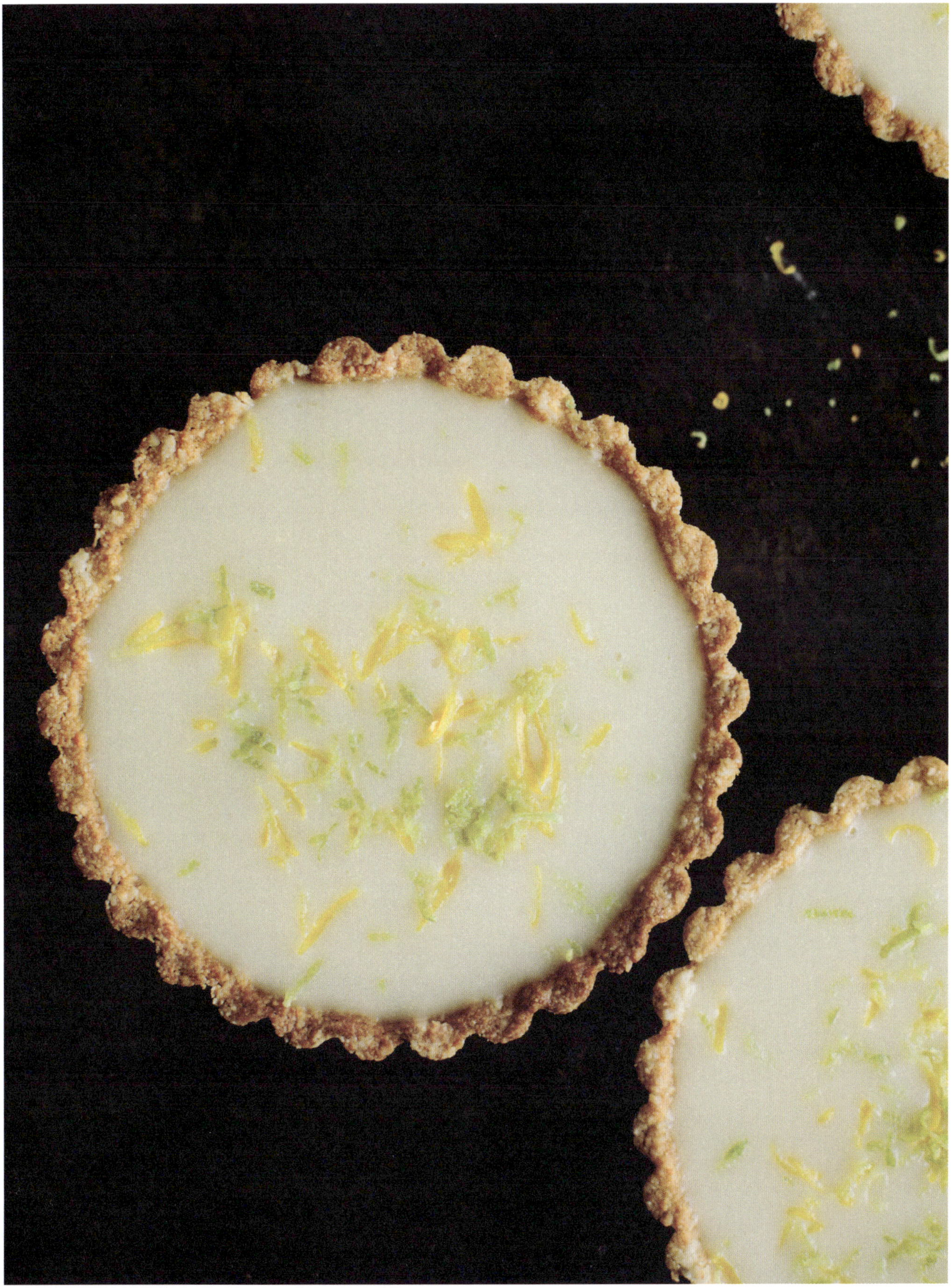

GRAPEFRUIT CURD SLICE W/ ROSEMARY + PINE NUTS

MAKES 12–16 SLICES | GLUTEN-FREE

We're all familiar with lemon curd (or as my nana called it, lemon butter), but it's possible to make curd out of pretty much any fruit. I make mango curd in summer and raspberry curd is another firm favourite, but it's during winter when grapefruit are abundant that I whip up this afternoon tea treat. Tart and ever-so-slightly bitter grapefruit curd is spread over buttery shortbread before being topped off with little flecks of extra dough, rosemary and pine nuts. Make the curd at least one day before baking, to allow it to set.

Grapefruit curd
3 large free-range egg yolks
1 large free-range egg
100g (½ cup) firmly packed blended unrefined raw sugar (page 235)
Finely grated zest of 1 large grapefruit
80ml (⅓ cup) grapefruit juice
3 tablespoons lemon juice
80g butter, cut into small cubes

Shortbread
140g (1 cup) fine brown rice flour
50g (½ cup) tapioca flour or arrowroot
110g (1 cup) ground almonds
100g (½ cup) firmly packed blended unrefined raw sugar
200g butter, softened slightly
2 tablespoons lightly toasted pine nuts, roughly chopped
2 teaspoons finely chopped rosemary

+ To make curd, place egg yolks, whole egg and sugar in a bowl and whisk to combine. Place grapefruit zest and juice, lemon juice and butter in a saucepan, add egg mixture and whisk to combine. Cook over a low heat, stirring continuously with a wooden spoon to melt the butter. Continue to cook over low heat for 6–8 minutes, stirring constantly until mixture thickens enough to coat the back of the spoon. Don't let the mixture boil. Alternatively, if this chef-style shortcut scares you, put all curd ingredients in a heatproof bowl set over a saucepan of boiling water and cook, stirring occasionally, for 20 minutes or until thick. Strain through a sieve, discarding zest, then transfer to a clean jar and cool before sealing and chilling overnight in the fridge (where it will firm up more). Use within a week.

+ To make shortbread, place flours, ground almonds and sugar in a food processor and pulse to combine. Add butter and pulse a few times until a soft dough forms. (Alternatively, whisk dry ingredients by hand in a bowl, and rub in butter with your hands.) Transfer to a lightly rice-floured bench, knead a few times then transfer a third of the dough to a bowl. Shape remaining dough into a flat disc, place in a zip-lock bag and set aside. Add half the pine nuts and rosemary to the dough in the bowl (reserving the rest for later) and mix well to combine. Shape into a flat disc, wrap, then chill both portions of dough in the fridge for 1 hour, or overnight.

+ Preheat oven to 180°C (350°F). Grease a 28 x 18cm slice tin and line with baking paper, extending up and over sides by 2cm. Tear plain dough into pieces and scatter over base of tin, then press in firmly. Bake for 15 minutes or until golden around edges and just cooked through. Remove from oven, turn off oven and set base aside for an hour or so until completely cold.

+ Preheat oven again to 180°C (350°F). Spread grapefruit curd evenly over shortbread base, tear off little pieces of chilled rosemary and pine nut dough and scatter over curd, mostly covering it all, leaving just a few little bits of curd peeping through. Scatter remaining pine nuts and rosemary on top. Bake for 30–35 minutes or until top is golden and cooked through. Remove from oven and set aside to cool completely before cutting. Best eaten on the day of baking, however, the shortbread will store, airtight, for 2 days.

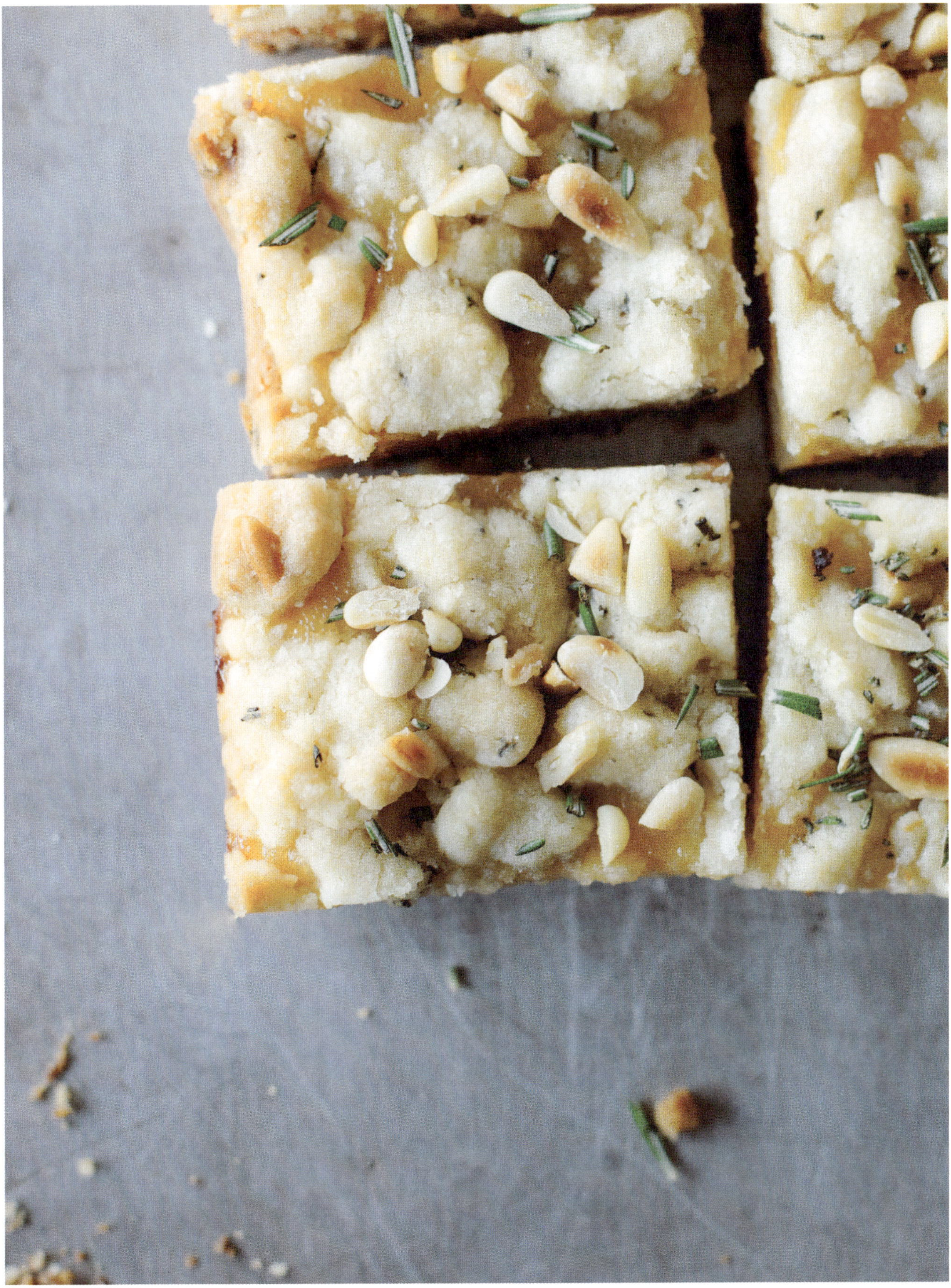

GINGERBREAD LOAF W/ COCONUT ICING

MAKES 1 LOAF | GLUTEN-FREE | DAIRY-FREE

This date-sweetened, spice-heavy, ginger-laced loaf is one I've been making ever since our kids were little, and for a long time it was the only 'cake' we ate while I got my head around gluten- and dairy-free baking. I often serve it un-iced, but for special treats a super-simple coconut butter-based icing gives it a slightly more luxe vibe. If you use maple syrup or honey to sweeten the icing just note that the colour will be ever-so-slightly darker. I love the intense flavour crystallised ginger gives, but if you are wanting a completely cane-sugar-free loaf, simply use freshly grated ginger and omit the molasses.

- 90g (¾ cup) dried pitted dates, roughly chopped
- 110g (1 cup) ground almonds
- 90g (⅔ cup) fine brown rice flour
- 3 teaspoons gluten-free baking powder
- 2 teaspoons ground ginger
- 1 teaspoon ground cinnamon
- ½ teaspoon ground allspice
- ¼ teaspoon fine sea salt
- 1 tablespoon finely chopped crystallised ginger (or 2 tablespoons finely grated fresh ginger)
- 125ml (½ cup) almond, rice or coconut milk
- 80ml (⅓ cup) extra-virgin olive or macadamia nut oil
- 2 large free-range eggs
- 1 tablespoon molasses
- 1 teaspoon vanilla extract

Coconut icing
- 180g (2 packed cups) shredded coconut
- 2 tablespoons brown rice syrup or pure maple syrup or honey
- ½ teaspoon vanilla extract
- 1 tablespoon lemon juice

+ Preheat oven to 180ºC (350ºF). Grease a loaf tin and line with a strip of baking paper that extends over the sides by about 2cm. I use my deep 20 x 10.5 x 7.5cm bread tin, but any loaf tin will do. Place dates and 80ml (⅓ cup) water in a saucepan, cover with a lid and simmer for 2–3 minutes over medium heat or until dates are soft and water has been absorbed. Add a touch more water and cook for a further minute if they aren't quite soft yet. Remove from heat and mash with a fork to form a paste. Set aside to cool slightly.

+ Place ground almonds in a bowl, then sift over rice flour, baking powder, spices and salt. Add crystallised or fresh ginger and whisk to combine. In another bowl, whisk milk, olive oil, eggs, molasses, vanilla and date paste together. Pour into dry ingredients and whisk until a smooth-ish batter forms. Transfer to the loaf tin, smooth off the top and bake for 50–55 minutes or until a skewer inserted in the centre comes out clean. Remove from oven and set aside to cool in tin for 10 minutes before transferring to a wire rack to cool completely.

+ To make icing, place shredded coconut in a food processor (I use the small processor attachment of my stick blender) and blend on high for 5–10 minutes (depending on the power of your processor). At first the coconut will look like fine powder, then it will go clumpy (stop and scrape down the sides a couple of times to assist blending) and finally it will turn smooth-ish and runny once the oils are released. Blend in brown rice syrup, vanilla, lemon juice and 2 tablespoons warm water. Add another tablespoon of water if needed to achieve a lovely icing consistency. Immediately pour over cooled loaf, allowing it to drip over the sides a little. It will set almost immediately unless you're making this in the middle of summer. Best eaten on the day of baking, however, this loaf will store, airtight, for 2–3 days.

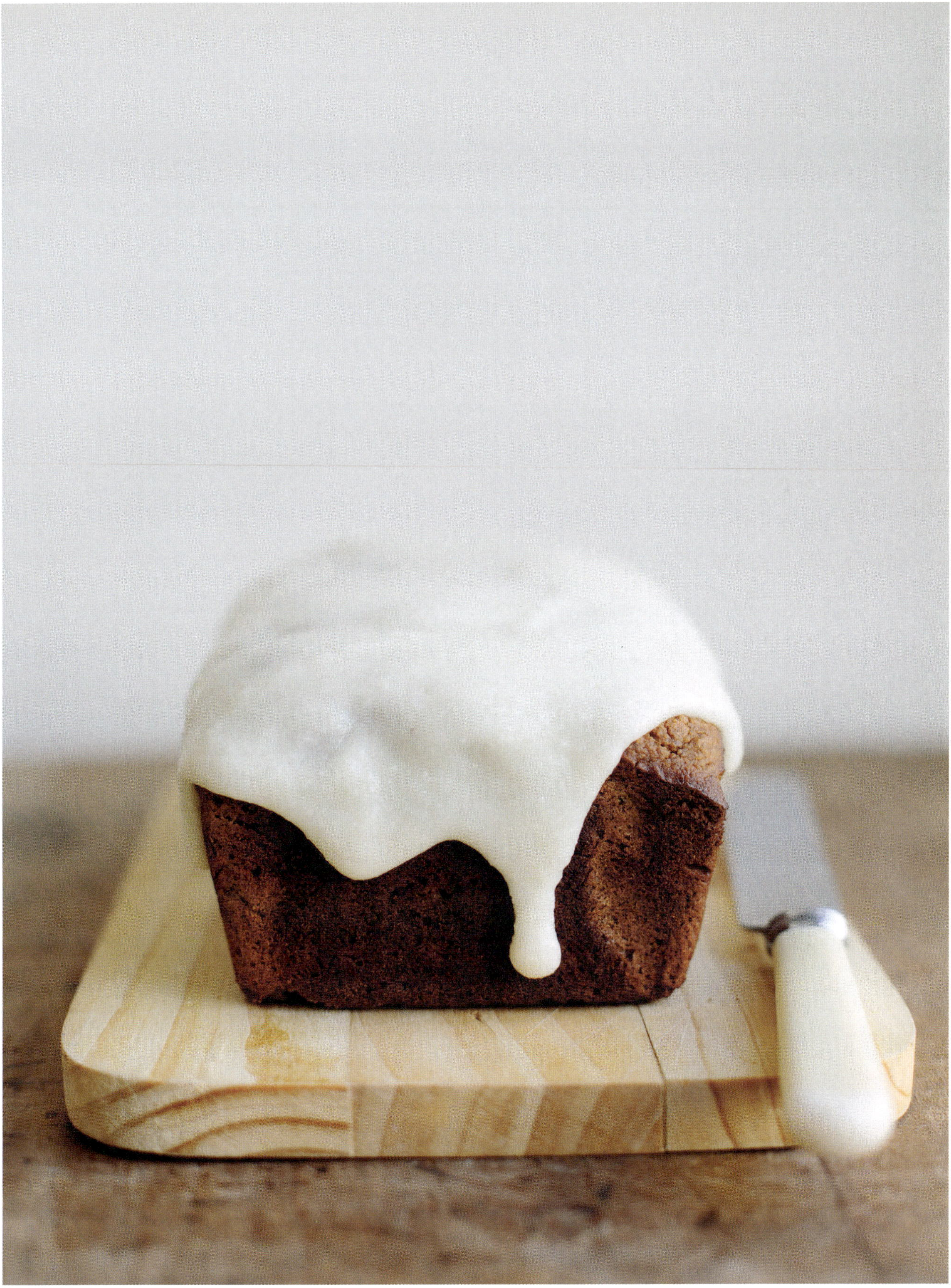

FLOURLESS CHOCOLATE TORTE

SERVES 12–16 | GLUTEN-FREE | DAIRY-FREE

Way back in 2011 I shared a recipe for black bean brownies on my website. At the time similar recipes had already done the rounds online so I decided not to include the brownie in my first book, thinking it was already passé. Little did I know, a few years later with the current health food craze in full swing, that the brownie recipe would become the most popular, commented on and requested on my site! I felt I'd be doing my readers a disservice if I didn't include it in some form in this book. So here I've used the brownie recipe to create an incredibly decadent torte, with two layers of flourless black bean cake sandwiched together with a layer of chocolate coconut cream. You can serve it like this and feel totally happy with yourself, however, if you want to take things over the edge of chocolatey goodness, smother the top with chocolate coconut ganache too. You'll need to start this recipe the night before if you don't already have a tin of coconut milk chilled and to soak the beans if using dried. If you don't own two cake tins of the same size, it's totally okay to just cook one torte, cool, remove from the tin and then use it again to cook the other one. That's what I do!

135g (¾ cup) dried black beans, soaked overnight in cold water, or 400g tin cooked beans, rinsed, or 1½ cups cooked beans

75ml (5 tablespoons) virgin coconut oil, melted if solid, or olive oil

3 large free-range eggs

130g (⅔ cup) muscovado sugar

55g (½ cup) ground almonds

30g (½ cup) cocoa powder

1 teaspoon vanilla extract

½ teaspoon gluten-free baking powder

Chocolate coconut cream

400ml tin coconut milk, refrigerated overnight (see NOTE, page 172)

100g dark chocolate, chopped

1 tablespoon muscovado sugar, pure maple or brown rice syrup, optional

Good pinch of fine sea salt

Chocolate coconut ganache

85g dark chocolate, roughly chopped

60ml (¼ cup) coconut milk

2 tablespoons brown rice syrup or pure maple syrup

+ Place tin of coconut milk in the fridge overnight. Soak black beans if using dried. The following day, drain and rinse beans, put into a saucepan and cover with cold water. Bring to the boil, then reduce to a simmer and cook for 35–45 minutes or until beans are tender but not falling apart (check them from around the 35 minute mark, the cooking time will vary depending on their freshness and how long they've been soaked). Drain well and set aside to cool before using.

+ Preheat oven to 180ºC (350ºF). Grease 2 x 23cm round springform cake tins and line the base and sides with baking paper. Blend cooked, cooled beans and oil in a food processor until a fine paste forms, you may have to stop and scrape the sides down to assist blending (or add one of the eggs if things really aren't moving). Add eggs, sugar, ground almonds, cocoa, vanilla and baking powder and pulse until a smooth batter forms. Evenly divide mixture between the two tins, it won't look like much but that's as it should be. Bake for 10–12 minutes or until firm to the touch and a skewer inserted in the centre of each cake comes out clean. Remove from oven and set aside to cool for 5 minutes, before transferring cakes to a wire rack to cool completely. Don't be surprised at the small size of the cake, once stacked up with cream in the centre it's the perfect torte height. Promise.

+ To make cream, melt chocolate in a heatproof bowl set over a saucepan of boiling water, making sure the base of the bowl doesn't touch the water. Set aside. Carefully transfer one cake back into the cake tin. Open the chilled tin of coconut milk, and carefully scrape off the thick layer of coconut cream on top (you should have approx. 1 cup),

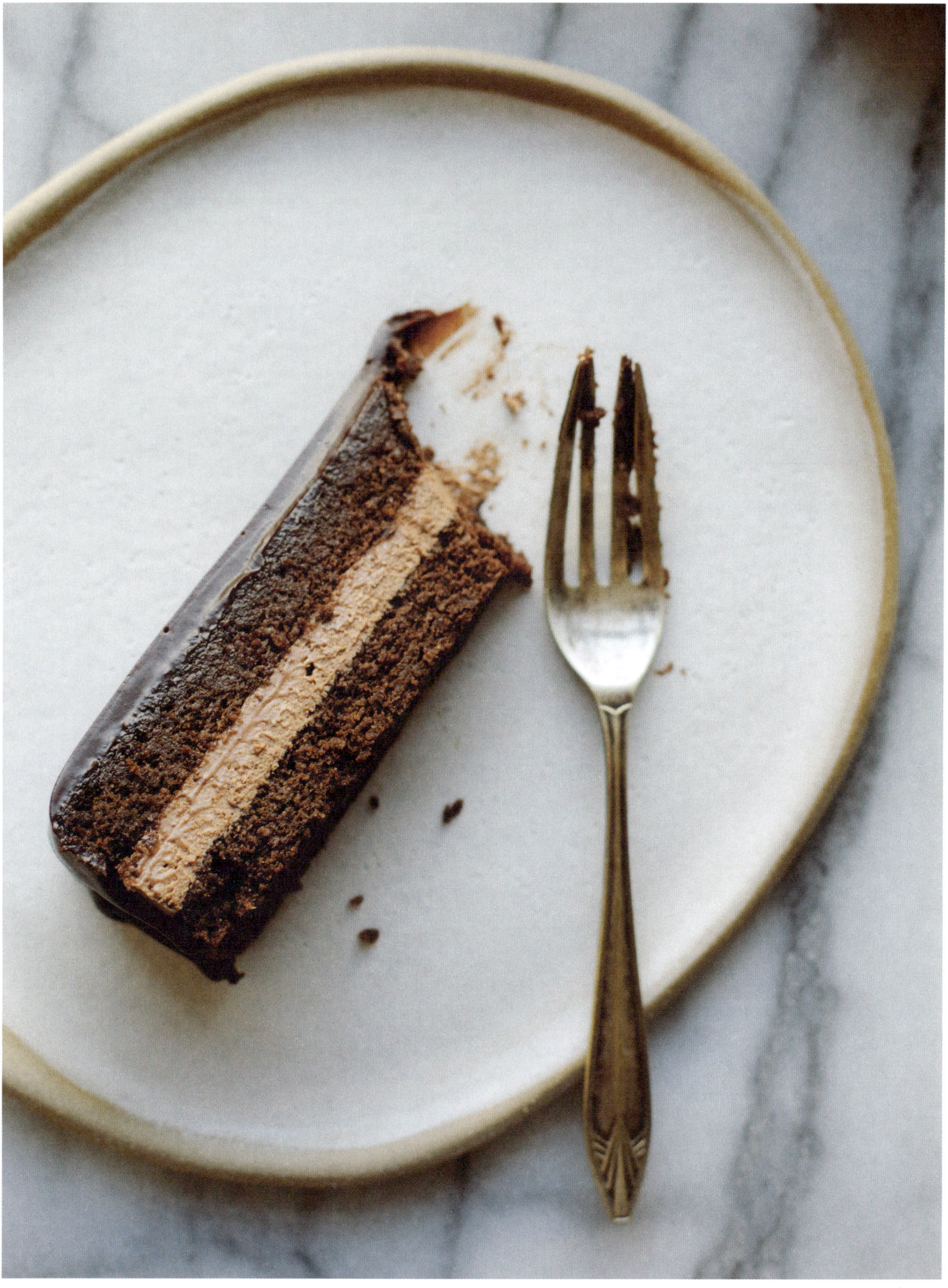

placing it in a bowl and reserving liquid from the bottom of tin. Whisk cream until smooth, adding in a touch of the reserved liquid if it's super-thick, until it reaches approximately whipped cream consistency (reserve the rest of the liquid for another use; I add it to smoothies or porridge). Whisk in melted dark chocolate, muscovado sugar or maple syrup and salt. Spoon onto the cake, smoothing it out evenly before topping with remaining cake. Cover and chill for 4 hours in the fridge, or overnight.

+ Carefully remove cake from tin and transfer to a serving plate. To make ganache, place all ingredients in a heatproof bowl set over a saucepan of boiling water and stir until chocolate has melted and ganache is smooth. Remove from heat and set aside, stirring occasionally for 5–10 minutes until mixture has thickened slightly (but not set). Pour ganache over cake to coat the top, then leave until set. You can speed this up by placing the whole cake in the fridge for 5–10 minutes. Cut into thin slices with a hot knife to serve. The torte will keep for 7–10 days in an airtight container in the fridge, depending of course on who lives in your house and how much they love chocolate!

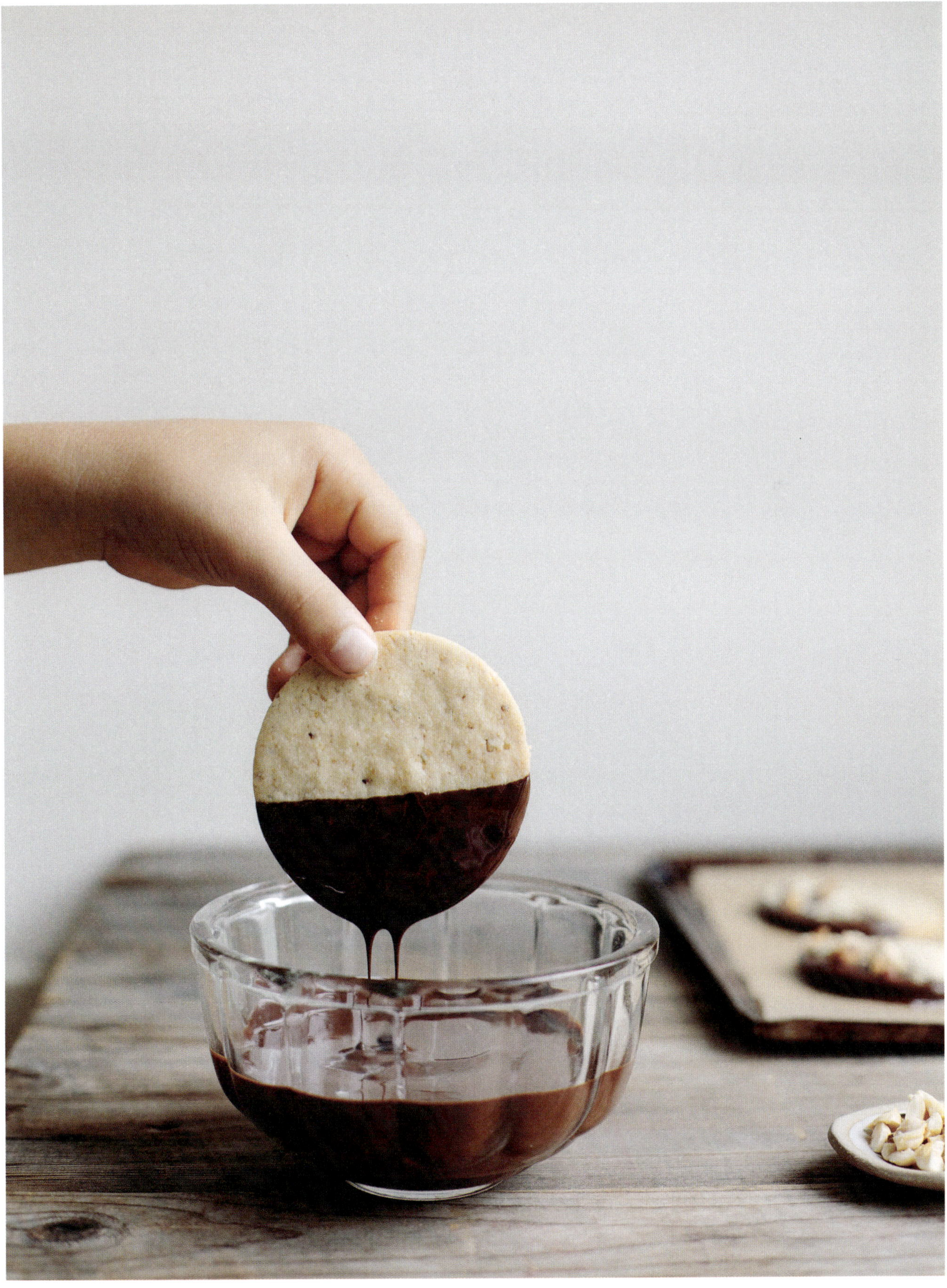

CHOCOLATE-DIPPED HAZELNUT BISCUITS

MAKES 24 | GLUTEN-FREE

I had initially intended for this recipe to appear in the autumn section as that is the time of the year when nuts are harvested, however, it's also the time of the year for fleeting fruits such as tamarillo, feijoa, figs and chestnuts, some of which are only around for a few weeks. So I decided to bump recipes such as these hazelnut-laced, chocolate-dipped biscuits back a few months, as nuts keep a lot longer. That said, you can make these slightly addictive biscuits all year round if your heart so desires. I like sprinkling roughly chopped toasted hazelnuts over the chocolate before it sets to add a little crunch, but if you're making for kids (big or small) who aren't huge nut fans, you can always leave them off.

- 60g (½ cup) toasted hazelnuts, skinned + 2 tablespoons extra, roughly chopped
- 60g (½ cup) quinoa flour
- 70g (½ cup) fine brown rice flour
- 50g (¼ cup) arrowroot or gluten-free organic cornflour (corn starch)
- 100g (½ cup) firmly packed blended unrefined raw sugar (page 235)
- 115g butter, at room temperature
- ½ teaspoon vanilla extract
- 185g dark chocolate, roughly chopped
- 2 teaspoons extra-virgin olive or macadamia nut oil

+ Place hazelnuts in a small food processor and pulse until finely ground. Tip into a large bowl. Sift over flours and arrowroot. Add sugar and whisk to combine. Rub in butter with your hands, add vanilla, then turn mixture out onto a clean bench and knead a few times to form a somewhat dry dough. Shape dough into a disc, wrap in baking paper or place in a zip-lock bag and chill in the fridge for 20 minutes.

+ Preheat oven to 170ºC (335ºF). Line 2 baking trays with baking paper. Roll dough out to 5mm thick on a sheet of baking paper lightly dusted with rice flour (you can roll half the dough at a time to make it a little easier to handle). It will seem a tad drier than most biscuit doughs, this is okay. Cut out biscuits using a 6cm round cookie cutter and transfer to trays. Reroll scraps of dough and cut out as many biscuits as you can, aiming for around 24. Use a fork to prick a few holes in the top of each biscuit to prevent them from puffing up when cooking. Bake for 10–12 minutes or until lightly golden around the edges, swapping the trays around in the oven halfway through cooking to ensure even baking.

+ Cool on trays for 10 minutes before transferring to a wire rack to cool completely.

+ Melt chocolate and olive oil together in a heatproof bowl set over a saucepan of boiling water, stirring with a metal spoon until smooth. Transfer to a small deep bowl and dip half of each biscuit into the chocolate. Transfer to a tray, sprinkle with roughly chopped hazelnuts and leave to set (or place in the fridge for 5 minutes in hot weather). These biscuits will store, airtight, for 2–3 days or frozen for up to 3 months. (They can be eaten straight from the freezer!)

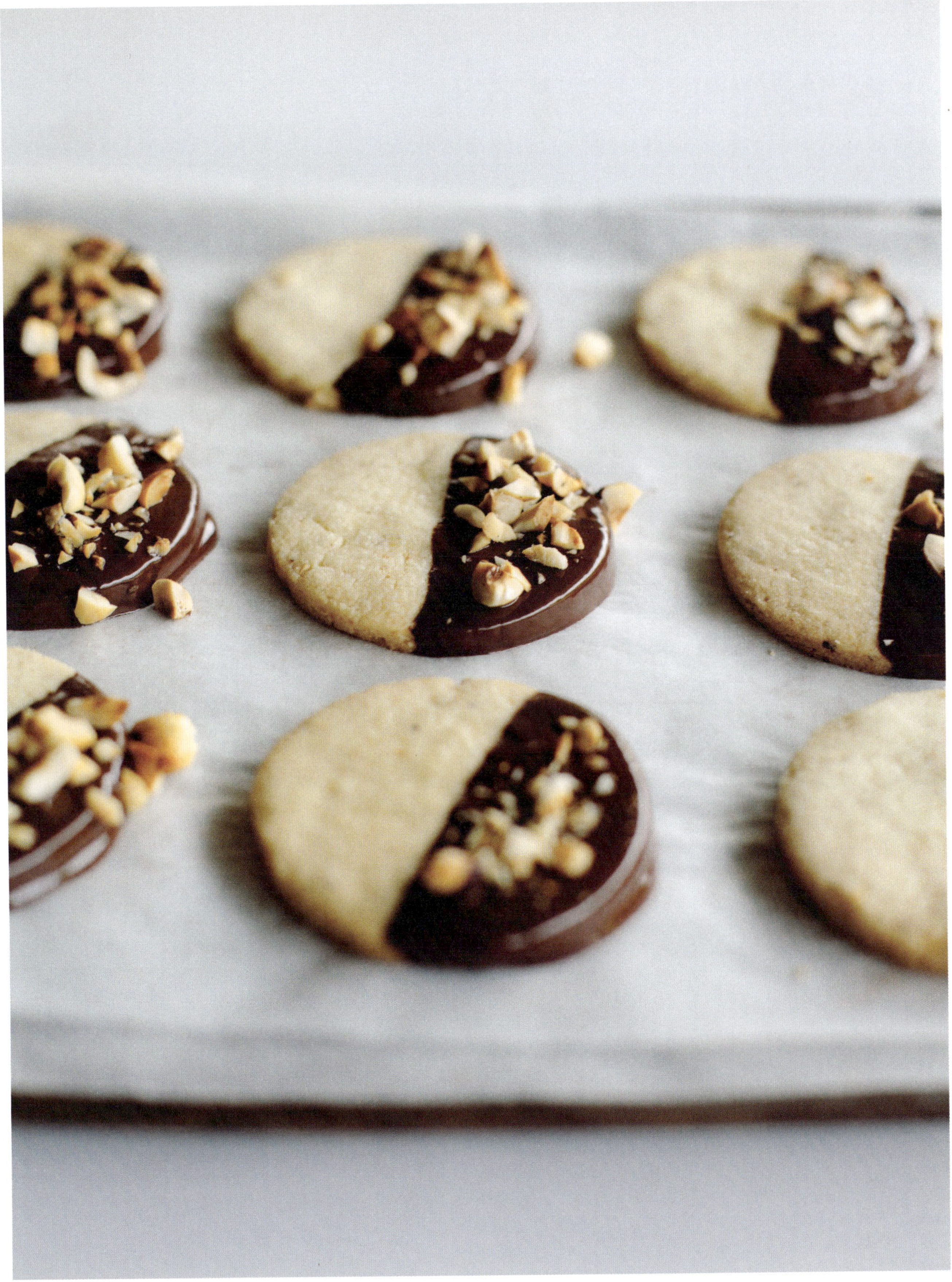

CHOCOLATE, CHILLI + ALMOND COOKIES

MAKES 24 | GLUTEN-FREE | DAIRY-FREE

Spiked with a good dose of chilli, cinnamon and roasted almonds, these brownie-esque cookies are full to the brim with all of my favourite things. They're also really straightforward to make, containing only one naturally gluten-free flour – nutrient-dense buckwheat. When buying buckwheat flour, more often than not in Australia or New Zealand you will find the lighter coloured hulled raw buckwheat flour, and this is what you want. The dark brown, strong-flavoured toasted unhulled buckwheat flour that's common in the US (and now showing up down here these days) is too strong in flavour and it's not one that I ever use in my recipes.

- 200g dark chocolate, chopped
- 30ml (2 tablespoons) virgin coconut oil
- ¼ teaspoon fine sea salt
- 2 large free-range eggs
- 130g (⅔ cup) blended unrefined raw sugar (page 235)
- 1 teaspoon vanilla extract
- 35g (¼ cup) buckwheat flour
- 1 teaspoon ground cinnamon
- ¼–½ teaspoon chilli powder
- ¼ teaspoon gluten-free baking powder
- 75g (½ cup) roasted almonds, finely chopped

+ Place chocolate, coconut oil and salt in a heatproof bowl set over a saucepan of boiling water, making sure that the bottom of the bowl doesn't touch the water. Stir until melted, then set aside to cool slightly. Meanwhile, whisk eggs, sugar and vanilla for 4–5 minutes or until slightly thick and pale, using either an electric beater or by hand. Sift over flour, cinnamon, chilli and baking powder, add chocolate mixture and fold through until just combined. Stir through almonds, cover and chill dough in the fridge for 4 hours or ideally overnight.

+ Preheat oven to 180°C (350°F). Grease or line 3 baking trays with baking paper. Roll tablespoonfuls of mixture into balls and place them (8 per tray) on the trays about 2–3cm apart, allowing plenty of room for spreading. Don't flatten, as they will do this themselves during baking. Bake for 10–12 minutes until puffed and cracked on top, swapping trays halfway through to ensure even cooking if you have a temperamental oven. Remove from oven and set aside to cool on trays. Best eaten on the day of baking, however, these biscuits will store, airtight, for 3–4 days, or longer in the fridge (where they turn lovely and fudgy).

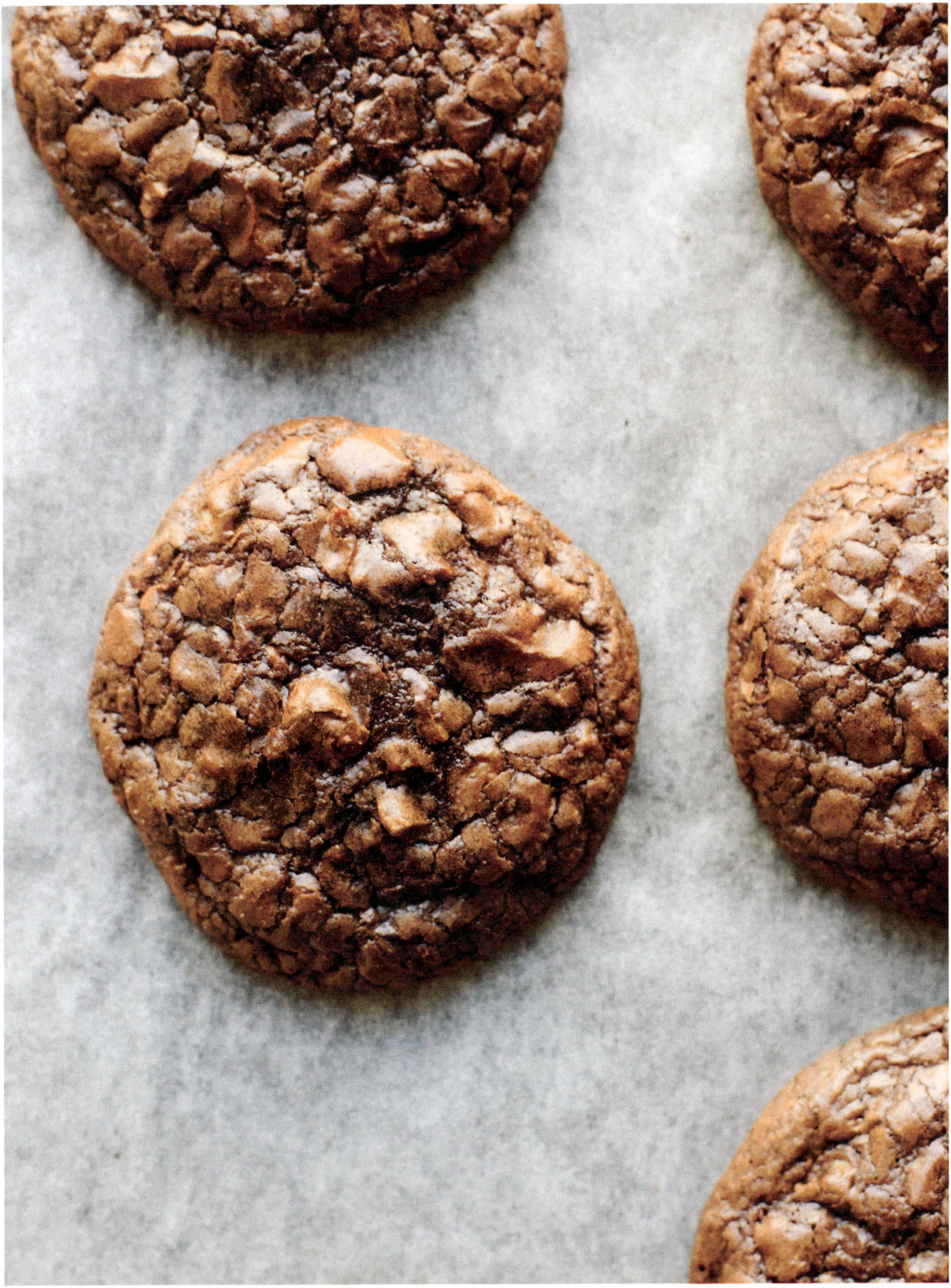

DARK CHOCOLATE, PEAR + PISTACHIO CAKE

SERVES 10–12 | GLUTEN-FREE | DAIRY-FREE

Studded with chunks of pear, dark chocolate and vibrant local pistachios, this easy mix-and-bake cake is one of the simplest I have in my repertoire. There's no creaming butter and sugar or beating eggs, instead high-protein buckwheat and ground almonds form the base along with the special flavourings, before eggs and olive or macadamia nut oil are simply whisked in. This barely sweet un-iced cake is the perfect snacking cake to take to picnics or to simply have at hand when friends pop over. I love eating it fresh from the oven while the little pockets of chocolate are still melted, but it's also lovely eaten cold.

70g (½ cup) buckwheat flour
25g (3 tablespoons) potato flour
1½ teaspoons gluten-free baking powder
55g (½ cup) ground almonds
130g (⅔ cup) unrefined raw sugar
Good pinch of fine sea salt
150g dark chocolate, roughly chopped
80g (½ cup) pistachio nuts, roughly chopped
1 pear, peeled, cored + diced
Finely grated zest of 1 orange
3 large free-range eggs, at room temperature
125ml (½ cup) extra-virgin olive or macadamia nut oil
1 teaspoon vanilla extract

+ Preheat oven to 180ºC (350ºF). Grease a 23cm round springform cake tin and line the base and sides with baking paper. Sift buckwheat flour, potato flour and baking powder into a medium bowl. Add ground almonds, sugar and salt, and whisk to evenly combine. Add chocolate, pistachios, diced pear and orange zest and mix well. (Reserve a little handful of pistachios and/or chocolate to scatter on the top of the cake if you like.) In another smaller bowl, whisk eggs, olive or macadamia nut oil and vanilla. Add to dry ingredients and mix until evenly combined. Transfer to prepared tin and smooth off the top, scattering over reserved pistachios and chocolate.

+ Bake for 45 minutes or until a skewer inserted in the centre comes out clean. Remove from oven and set aside to cool for 5 minutes before transferring to a wire rack to cool further. Serve warm or at room temperature. Best eaten on the day of baking, however, the cake will store, airtight, for 2–3 days.

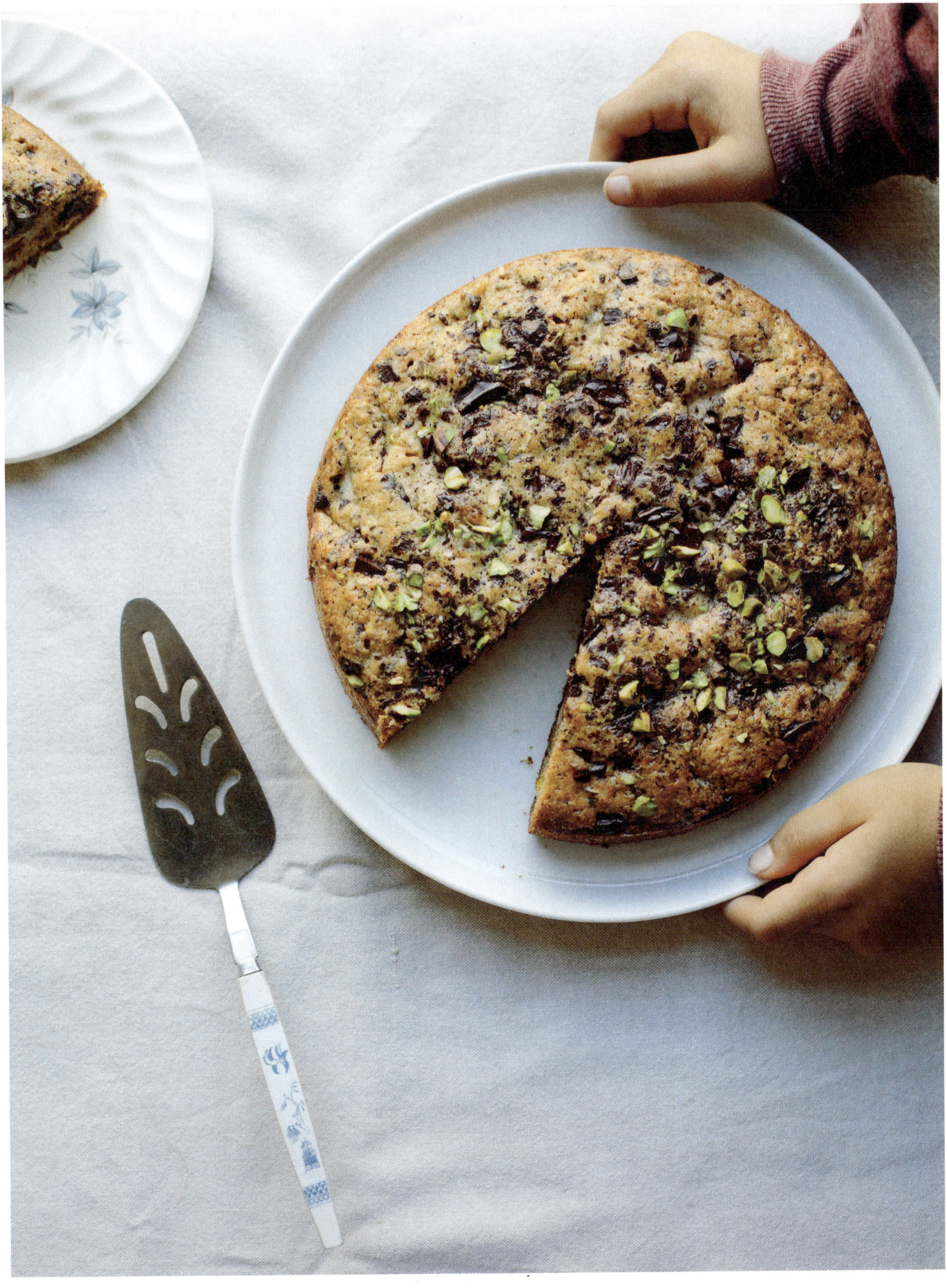

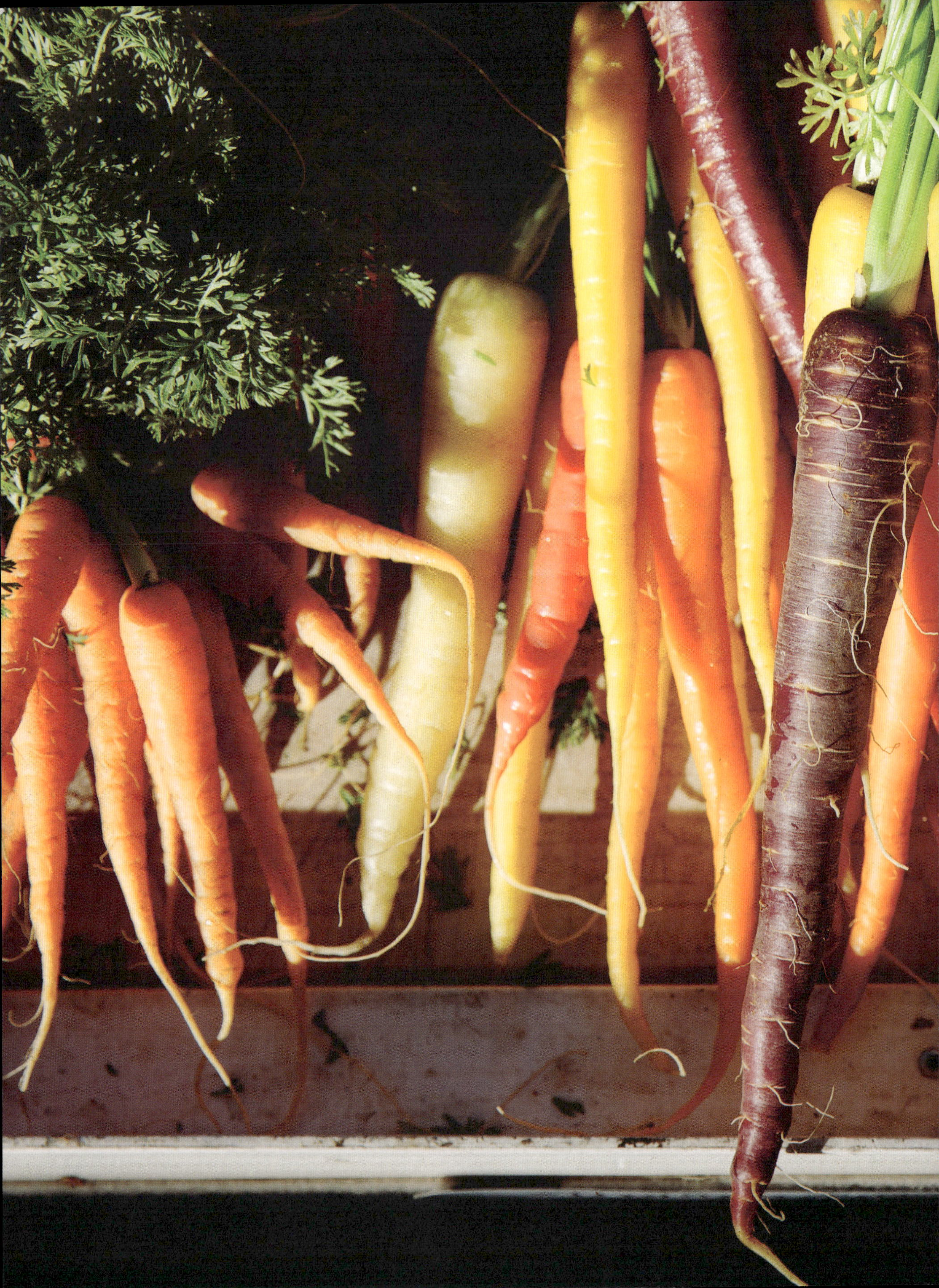

SPRING

rhubarb + avocado + banana + blueberries + grapefruit + cumquats + honeydew + kiwifruit + lemon + globe artichoke + broad beans + green beans + beetroot + broccoli + brussels sprouts + lime + loquat + lychee + mandarin + mulberries + orange + papaya + carrot + cauliflower + cabbage + fennel + leek + spring onion + lettuce + choko + celery + peas + radish + apple + strawberries + tangelo + silverbeet + spinach + watercress + parsnip + daikon

BEETROOT GNOCCHI W/ CAPER GREMOLATA

SERVES 4 | GLUTEN-FREE | DAIRY-FREE

It had been well over ten years since I'd eaten gnocchi when I started working on this recipe. While I remembered being a huge fan of their pillowy potato goodness, years of avoiding gluten had faded the memory of their unique texture, which I wanted to perfect if I were to share the recipe. Thankfully I have a dear friend, Emiko, who is an expert on all things Italian, so I asked her to test these gnocchi for me. At the time she'd just moved back to Italy with her little family after a few years in Australia. She made the recipe with her Italian mother-in-law and much to my delight they not only got Emiko's but an Italian nonna's seal of approval too. She even asked for the recipe!

500g (2 medium) old floury potatoes, scrubbed
150g (½ cup) rock salt
80g (½ cup) potato flour
45g (⅓ cup) white rice flour
20g (2 tablespoons) buckwheat flour
250g (2 medium) beetroot, scrubbed
1 large free-range egg yolk
½ teaspoon fine sea salt
Extra-virgin olive oil
Micro greens, to serve, optional

Gremolata
4 tablespoons capers, drained well
2 tablespoons finely grated lemon zest
2 cloves garlic

+ Preheat oven to 200ºC (400ºF). Pierce each potato 3–4 times with a sharp knife. Spread rock salt out on a small oven tray, place potatoes on top and roast for 1 hour, or until soft.

+ Meanwhile, sift flours into a bowl and whisk to thoroughly combine. Set aside. Trim beetroot stems to 2–3cm long. Place in a small saucepan, cover with plenty of water, and bring to the boil. Turn heat down and simmer for 45–60 minutes or until tender. Drain and set aside to cool for 5 minutes. Peel and roughly chop, then place in a small food processor and purée, stopping to scrape down the sides a few times to ensure even blending.

+ To make gremolata, finely chop capers, lemon zest and garlic together. Set aside.

+ Remove potatoes from oven and set aside to cool for 5 minutes, just enough to handle. Peel and either push through a potato ricer or mash well. Stir beetroot purée through mashed potato along with egg yolk and salt. Add flours and mix to form a soft dough. The dough will still seem a little tacky, but shouldn't stick to your hands. Turn out onto a clean lightly rice-floured bench and knead a few times until dough comes together in a ball. Cover with a tea towel and leave for 10 minutes.

+ Bring a large saucepan of salted water to the boil. Cut dough into 4 pieces, rolling each into long ropes approx. 2cm wide. Use a rice-flour-dusted knife to cut off 3cm lengths. Cook gnocchi in pan for 1–2 minutes or until they float to the surface. Depending on the size of your pan, you may need to do this in a few batches. Remove gnocchi using a slotted spoon and transfer to a large bowl with a good glug of olive oil, tossing well to coat. Add gremolata and mix well. Serve immediately scattered with micro greens, if using.

NOTE: Floury potatoes such as Desiree, Russet, Royal Blue, Laura (Aus) or Agria, late season Ilam Hardy, Red Rascal (NZ) are best for gnocchi.

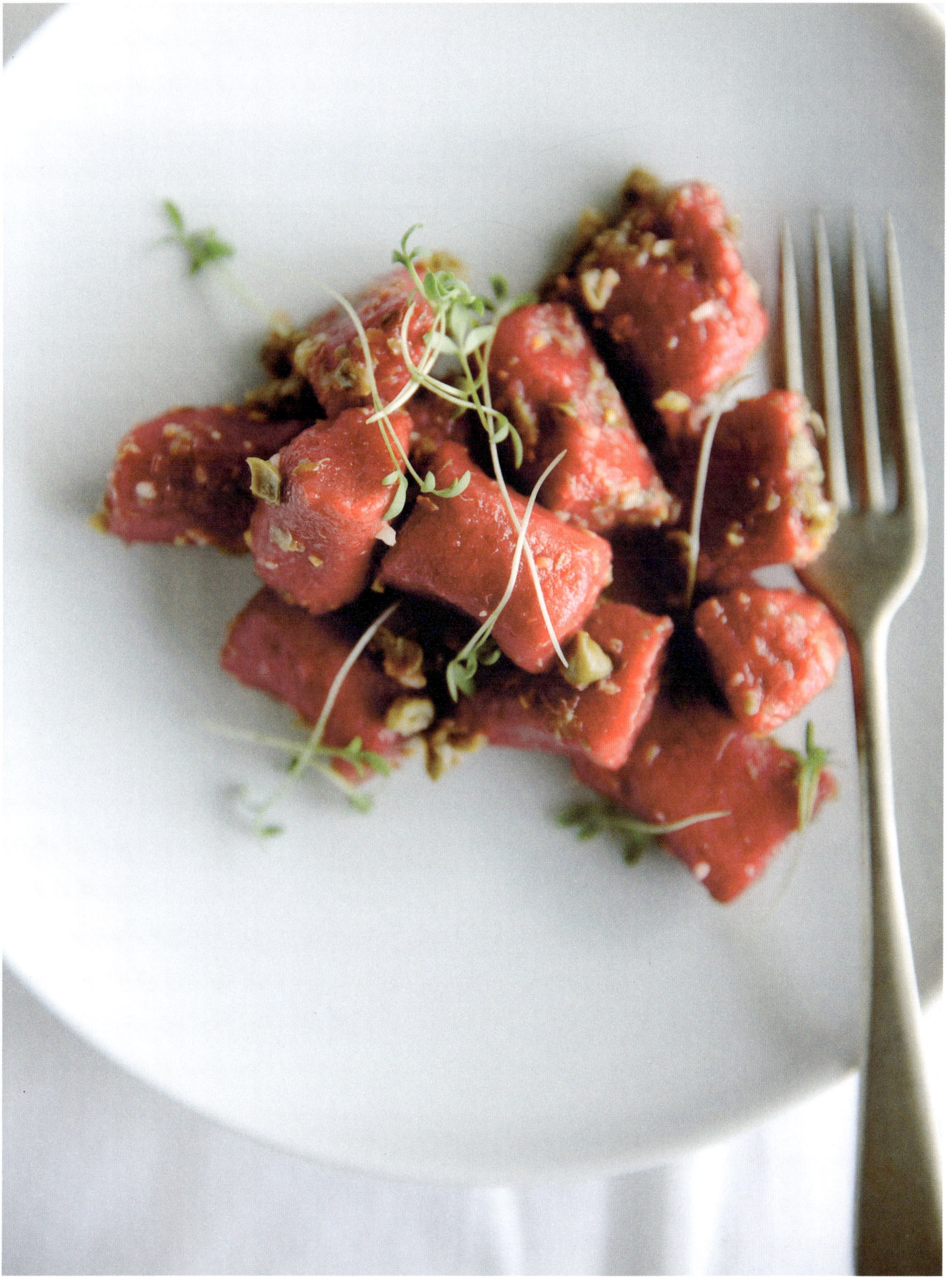

CHICKPEA + CARROT BURGERS w/ GUACAMOLE

MAKES 6 | GLUTEN-FREE | VEGAN

These chickpea and carrot patties are just the kind of quick and easy thing I love to make. You basically dump everything into a food processor and pulse until roughly ground, mix in a little chickpea flour to hold things together, shape and chill while you get onto the other components. I've included my recipe for homemade burger buns below, which do take a little bit longer to make, but I can assure you they're very straightforward and produce a lovely sturdy but light and pliable bun, which is not only gluten-free, but vegan too. You can freeze the buns, but I've found they can be a little bit crumblier once defrosted, so I tend to just make them fresh. Leftover buns do make great croutons though (page 136). The patties themselves are also lovely served with the guacamole and a generous side salad or some grilled asparagus and beans. They will also keep, covered, in the fridge for 2–3 days, making it super-easy to plan ahead. If you're using dried chickpeas, soak them the night before.

Burger buns
- 2 teaspoons (7g packet) dried yeast
- 2 teaspoons unrefined raw sugar
- 2 tablespoons extra-virgin olive oil
- 2 teaspoons apple cider vinegar
- 140g (1 cup) fine brown rice flour
- 110g (⅔ cup) potato flour
- 70g (½ cup) buckwheat flour
- 1½ tablespoons psyllium husks
- 1 teaspoon fine sea salt
- Olive oil
- Toasted sesame seeds, to sprinkle

Chickpea + carrot patties
- 270g (1½ cups) dried chickpeas, soaked overnight in cold water (or 2 x 400g tins cooked chickpeas, rinsed, or 3 cups cooked chickpeas)
- 1 large carrot, grated
- 2 cloves garlic, finely chopped
- Handful of chives, finely chopped (or 1 spring onion)
- 1 teaspoon ground cumin
- 1 teaspoon ground coriander
- 1 teaspoon dried oregano
- Stems + roots of 1 bunch coriander, finely chopped (just under 1 cup), reserve leaves for slaw
- 1 tablespoon lemon juice
- 1 tablespoon olive oil
- 2–3 tablespoons chickpea (chana or besan) flour
- Olive oil, to shallow-fry

To assemble
- 2 cups finely shredded red cabbage
- Squeeze of lemon or lime juice
- Flesh of 2 large perfectly ripe avocados
- 1 clove garlic, finely chopped
- 1 green jalapeño or long green chilli, finely chopped (deseeded if you like)
- 3–4 tablespoons lime or lemon juice
- Tomato relish, to serve

+ To make burger buns, combine yeast, sugar and 310ml (1¼ cups) warm water in a bowl, cover with a tea towel and leave to ferment for 5 minutes until foamy. Add olive oil, vinegar, flours, psyllium husks and salt and whisk to form a thick smooth batter. Cover with a plate and set aside in a warm spot for 20–30 minutes.

+ Drain and rinse chickpeas, put into a saucepan and cover with cold water. Bring to the boil, skimming any foam that rises to the surface. Reduce to a simmer and cook for 25–35 minutes or until tender but not falling apart. Drain well.

+ Preheat oven to 200ºC (400ºF). Line a baking tray with baking paper. Divide dough into six portions, shaping each into a ball with well olive-oiled hands. Place on the tray, allowing enough space on all sides for spreading. Flatten each ball into a dome, approx. 1.5cm thick, brush tops generously with olive oil and sprinkle with toasted sesame seeds. Cover loosely with cling film or an upturned large container and set aside to prove for 15–20 minutes (double the time in winter) until well risen.

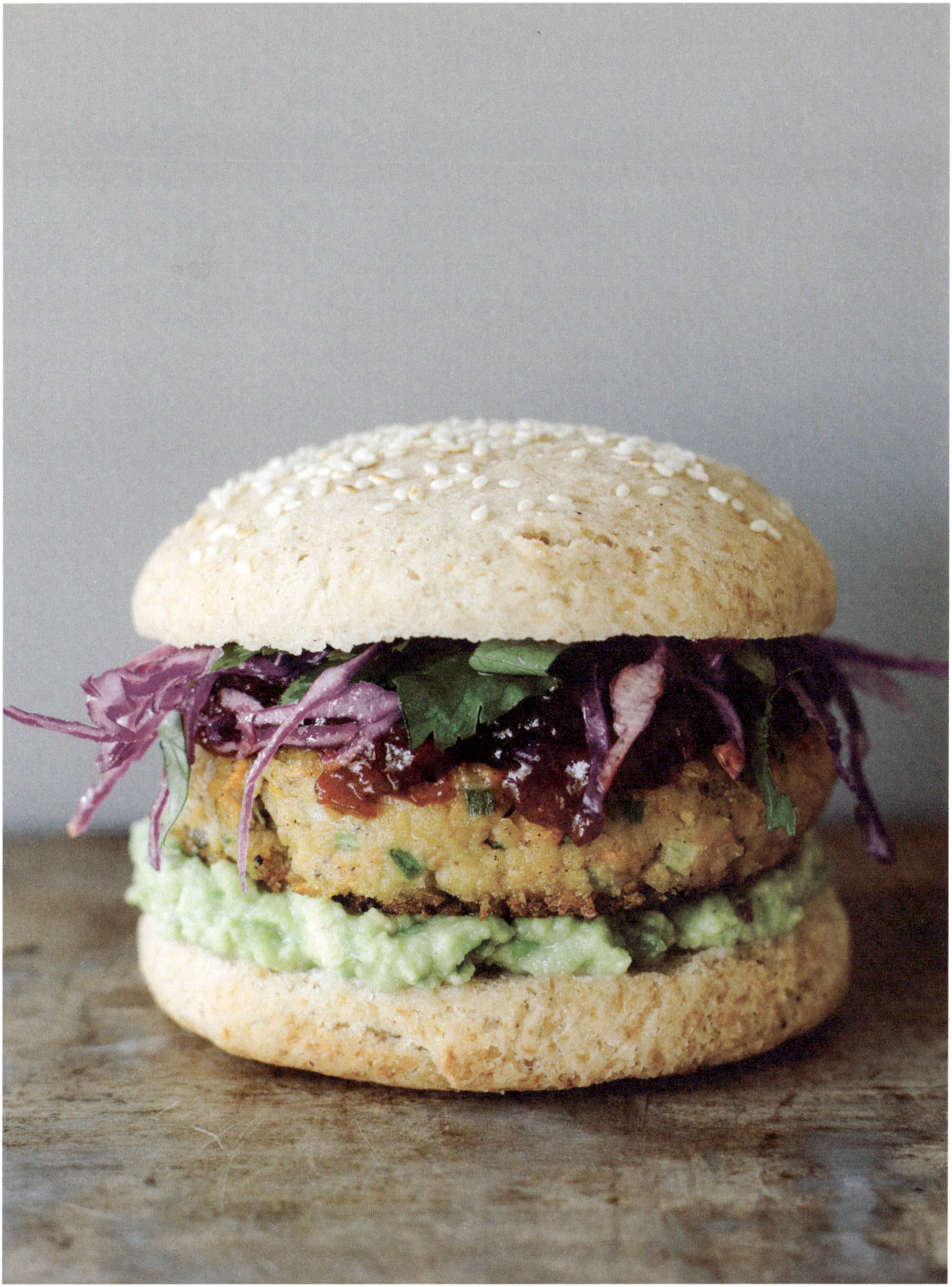

Bake for 20–25 minutes or until risen and golden around the edges and underside. Remove from oven, then transfer to a wire rack to cool.

+ Meanwhile, prepare patties. Place cooked chickpeas, grated carrot, garlic, chives, spices, finely chopped coriander stems and roots, lemon juice and olive oil in the bowl of a food processor. Pulse until finely ground. You want some of the chickpeas to be fully blended, as they act as the binder, but don't pulse them so much that there's no texture left to the mixture. Transfer to a bowl, season with fine sea salt and freshly ground black pepper and add 2 tablespoons of the chickpea flour. Mix with your hands, adding 1 more tablespoon chickpea flour if the mixture still feels too wet. Shape into 6 even-sized patties, place on an oven tray and pop in the fridge for 20–30 minutes, while you get the remaining components ready.

+ To make slaw, combine red cabbage and coriander leaves in a bowl, add a glug of olive oil, a squeeze of lemon or lime juice and season with salt and pepper.

+ Mash avocado roughly in a bowl, add garlic, chilli and lime or lemon juice. Season with salt and pepper.

+ Heat a little olive oil in a large frying pan over medium-high heat. Cook patties for 2–3 minutes on either side or until crispy and golden. Lightly toast buns, to warm through. Spread bun bases with guacamole, top with a chickpea pattie, a dollop of tomato relish, a little slaw and the top of the bun. Serve immediately.

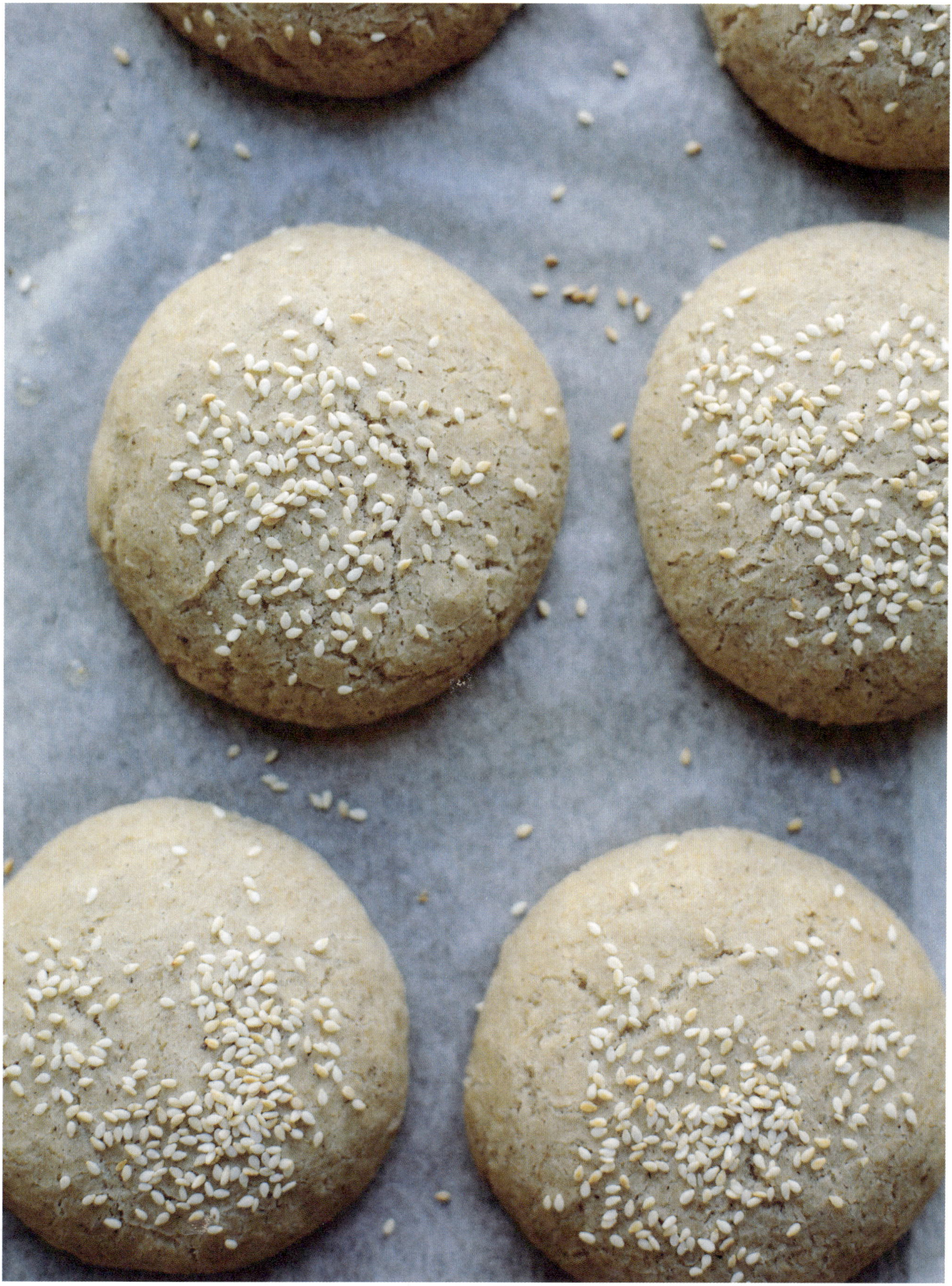

LEEK, FENNEL + WHITE BEAN STEW

SERVES 4 | GLUTEN-FREE | VEGAN

If like me you're a fan of all things fennel, you'll want to try this super-simple dish. Braised in an olive oil and tomato base, spiked with hints of leek, garlic, lemon and coriander this is the kind of dish that makes you realise how uncomplicated food ought to be. Serve alongside a protein-rich grain such as quinoa or simply with bread to mop up all those flavoursome juices. A side of peppery lemon and olive oil dressed rocket wouldn't go astray too. Butter beans are also sometimes known as Lima beans.

- 60ml (¼ cup) extra-virgin olive oil
- 1 large leek, finely sliced
- 4 cloves garlic, roughly chopped
- 2 medium fennel bulbs, trimmed + sliced into thin wedges, tender fronds reserved
- 2 teaspoons coriander seeds, lightly toasted + finely ground
- Finely grated zest of 1 lemon
- 1½ cups cooked butter beans, or 400g tin butter beans, well rinsed + drained
- 2 tomatoes, peeled + finely diced
- Good pinch of fine sea salt
- Juice of ½ lemon

+ Heat oil in a large heavy-based frying pan over medium-high heat. Add leek and garlic, and cook, stirring often, for 5 minutes. Add fennel bulbs, coriander and lemon zest, and cook for a further 5 minutes, stirring often. Add cooked butter beans, diced tomatoes, 125ml (½ cup) water, salt and freshly ground black pepper. Give the stew a good stir, cover with a lid, reduce heat and simmer for 10 minutes, or until liquid has reduced and fennel is tender. Add a touch more water if needed. Remove from heat. Add lemon juice, adjust seasoning, stir through finely chopped reserved fennel fronds and serve.

NOTE: If cooking beans from scratch, soak ¾ cup dried beans overnight in plenty of cold water at room temperature. In hot weather put in the fridge. The next day, drain off water and refill with plenty of fresh cold water. Bring to the boil, skimming off any foam that rises to the surface, and simmer gently for approx. 1 hour, or until tender but not falling apart. Top up with extra water if needed. Add a few pinches of sea salt and cook for a further 5 minutes before draining well.

+ To core, peel and chop tomatoes, remove the core from the flat end of the tomato with a sharp knife. Cut a cross on the opposite (round) end. Put tomatoes into a bowl, pour enough boiling water in to cover them and leave for 1 minute, or until you start to see the skin lifting off. Drain and cover with cold water. Leave until cool enough to handle. Slip the skins off and roughly chop tomatoes into 1cm pieces.

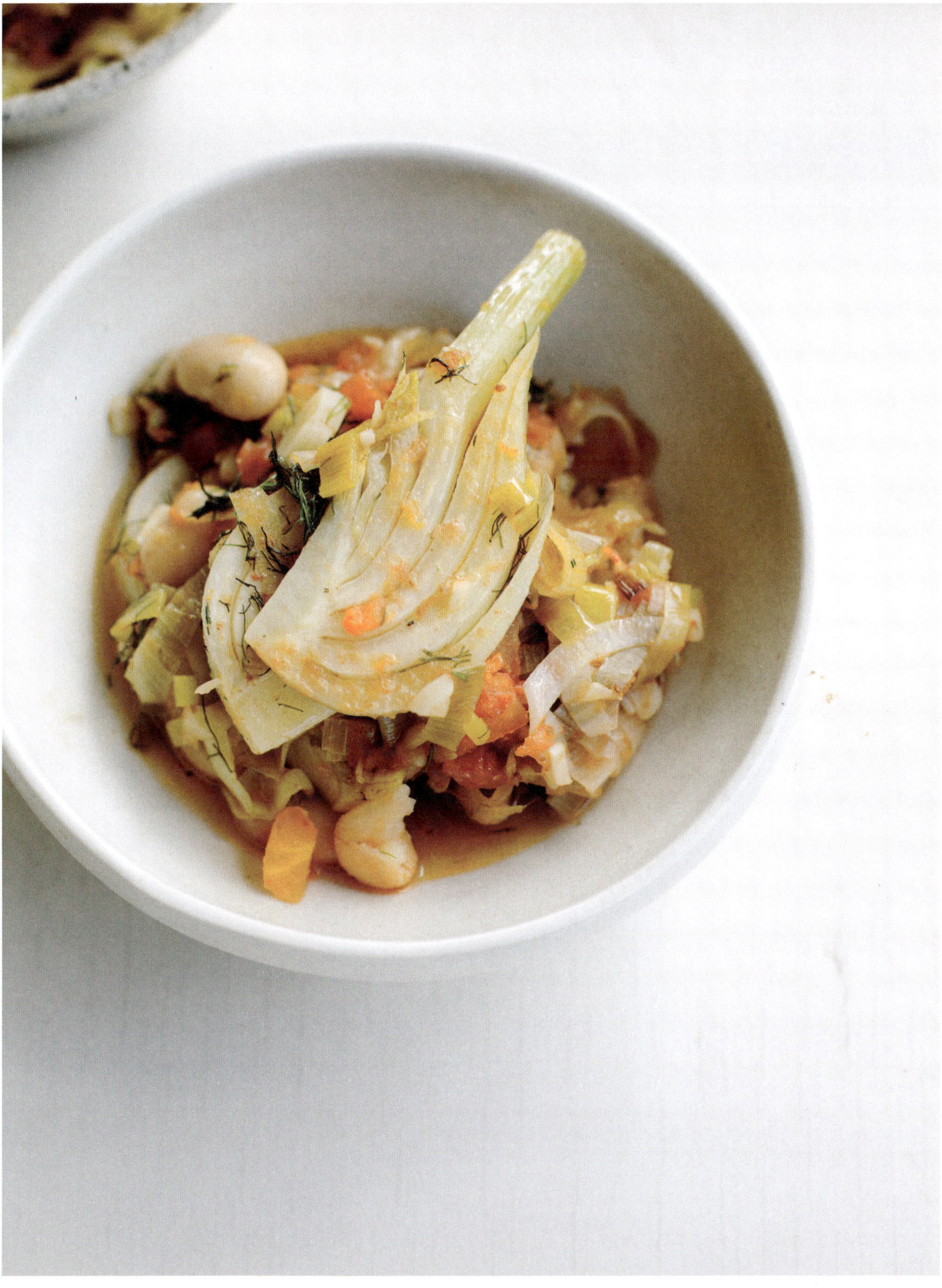

SILVERBEET + FETA GÖZLEME

MAKES 4 | GLUTEN-FREE | DAIRY-FREE + VEGAN OPTION

These Turkish specialties are essentially stuffed pizzas cooked in a heavy-based frying pan or on the hot plate of a barbecue until golden and crispy. You can fill them with any number of things: grilled eggplant, capsicum, feta and a scatter of toasted pine nuts, or keep them as simple as you like with spinach and a cheese of your choice. I've made mine into single-portion sizes which easily fit into a frying pan. If the dough tears a little, don't stress, just pinch it back together and carry on – a lot of their beauty lies in their rustic presentation! You can keep gözleme warm in a slow oven while cooking the rest if you like, or eat straight from the pan. Omit feta for dairy-free + vegan option.

Dough
140g (1 cup) fine brown rice flour
85g (¾ cup) chickpea (chana or besan) flour
40g (¼ cup) potato flour
½ teaspoon fine sea salt
1 tablespoon psyllium husks
½ teaspoon raw sugar
1 teaspoon dried yeast
1 tablespoon extra-virgin olive oil
Olive oil, to pan-fry
Lemon wedges, to serve

Filling
1 tablespoon extra-virgin olive oil
4 large silverbeet leaves with stems, roughly chopped, stems + leaves kept separate
1 red onion, thinly sliced
2 cloves garlic, roughly chopped
½ teaspoon dried mint
80–100g crumbled feta cheese, to sprinkle

+ To make dough, sift flours into a large bowl, add salt and psyllium husks, and whisk to combine. Combine 225ml warm water, sugar and yeast in a small bowl, cover with a tea towel and set aside for 5 minutes until foamy. Add extra-virgin olive oil and whisk in dry ingredients to form a smooth, wet dough. It will seem ridiculously wet, but go with it. Cover with a clean tea towel and set aside to prove for 30 minutes (you can place the dough in a covered container at this stage and chill for up to 4 hours. Chilled dough is much easier to handle).

+ Meanwhile, prepare filling. Heat olive oil in a saucepan over medium heat, add silverbeet stalks, onion and garlic. Cook, stirring often, for 2–3 minutes until tender. Add silverbeet leaves and dried mint and cook, stirring often, until just wilted. Season with sea salt and freshly ground pepper, then transfer to a plate to cool.

+ Turn dough out onto a lightly rice-floured bench. Knead gently, incorporating just enough flour to stop the dough from sticking to your hands (1–2 tablespoons maximum). Divide into 4 equal portions, working with one while you cover the rest with a tea towel. Roll out dough between 2 sheets of lightly rice-floured baking paper to form a long oval, approx. 4mm thick. The dough will be sticky so I find it easiest to pull the paper off a few times on each side and re-flour as I go. When dough is at the desired thickness remove the top layer of paper and brush off excess flour with a dry pastry brush. Place a quarter of silverbeet mixture over the lower half of the dough, scatter over a little crumbled feta cheese, then, using the baking paper, flip over the top half of the dough to enclose filling. Press edges together to seal. Repeat with remaining dough and filling.

+ Preheat a heavy-based frying pan or barbecue plate over medium heat, add 1–2 teaspoons olive oil and cook gözleme for 3–4 minutes on each side or until crisp and golden (you'll have to cook in batches if using a pan). Remove to a serving plate and serve with lemon wedges.

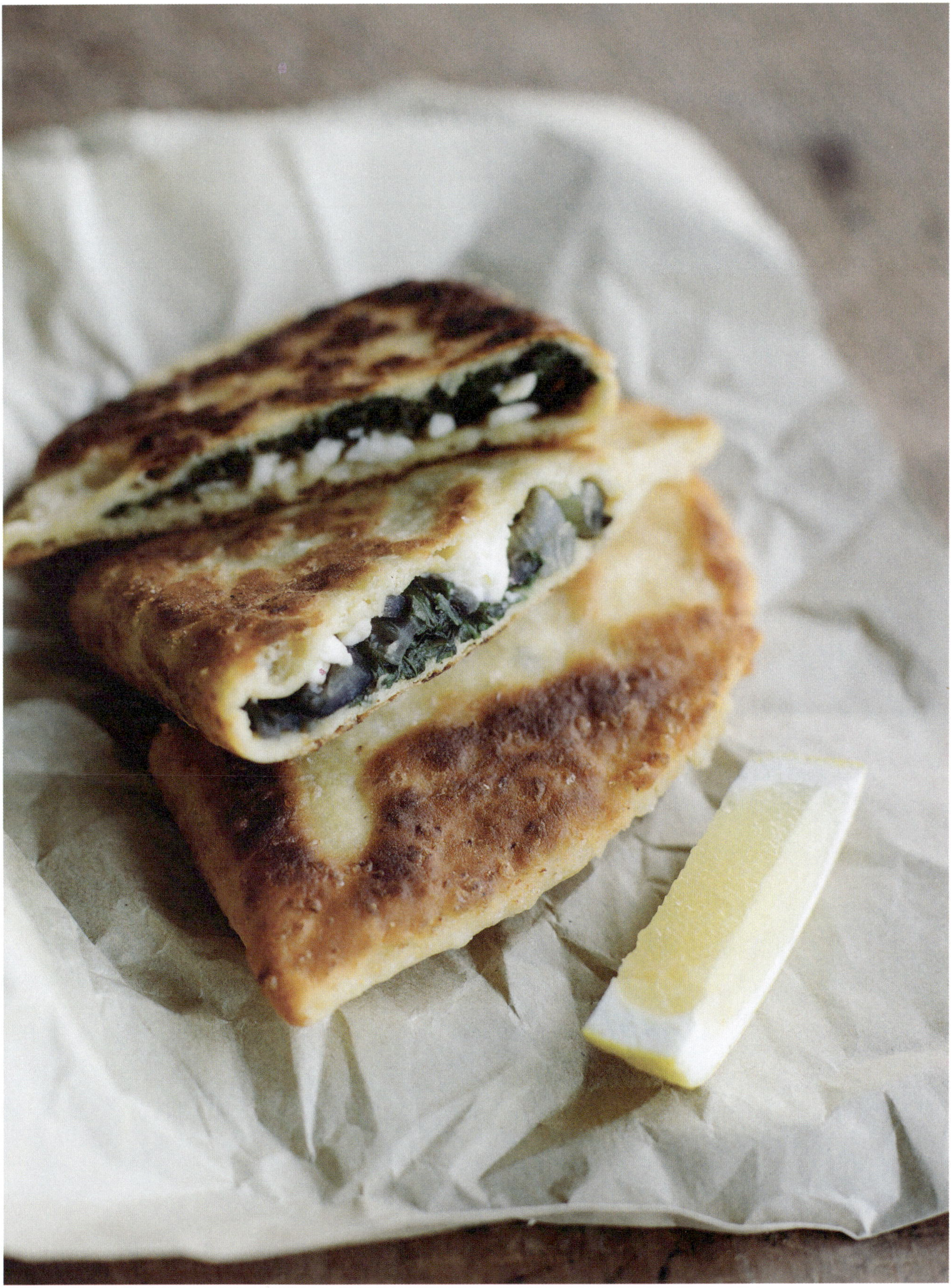

MINTY PEA + FETA PURÉE w/ BUTTERED ASPARAGUS ON TOAST

SERVES 4 (ENOUGH FOR AROUND 8 PIECES OF TOAST) | GLUTEN-FREE

For those toast fans out there, this one's for you! The vibrant green pea purée is something I also love to have at hand to add to salad bowls or roasted vegetables, so feel free to double up the recipe. It will keep in the fridge for 2–3 days. The salty 'n' sour hit of preserved lemon adds something special (they're available at specialty food stores or find the recipe for making your own on my website), however, finely grated lemon zest works a treat here too. Frozen peas are perfectly acceptable as I know fresh ones usually get eaten before you have a chance to cook them! Adding a soft poached egg on top would make for a perfect breakfast if, like me, you love eggs like a crazy person.

- 360g (3 cups) podded fresh or frozen peas
- 1 tablespoon ghee, butter or extra-virgin olive oil
- 4 cloves garlic, finely chopped
- 2 bunches asparagus, woody ends snapped off
- 100g soft Danish-style feta cheese
- Big handful of mint leaves, roughly chopped
- 2 teaspoons lemon juice
- 1 tablespoon butter or ghee
- Gluten-free toast, extra crumbled feta cheese + pea shoots, to serve
- Finely chopped preserved lemon or finely grated lemon zest, to serve

+ Bring a large saucepan of salted water to the boil. If using frozen peas, run them under warm water to thaw before using and drain well. Heat ghee, butter or oil in a frying pan over medium-high heat, add half the garlic and let it sizzle for a few seconds before adding peas. Cook, while stirring, for 2–3 minutes or until peas are tender. Remove from heat and set aside to cool for 5–10 minutes. When the water has come up to the boil, cook asparagus for 1–2 minutes until just tender before draining and plunging into iced or cold water to stop it cooking further.

+ Place cooled peas, feta, mint and lemon juice in a small food processor and pulse until puréed.

+ Slice asparagus spears in half on a slight diagonal. Heat butter or ghee in a large frying pan, add remaining garlic and sizzle for a few seconds before adding asparagus to the pan. Cook, while stirring, for 2–3 minutes or until asparagus is warmed through. Serve minty pea purée spread on toast, top with asparagus, extra crumbled feta, pea shoots and preserved lemon or lemon zest.

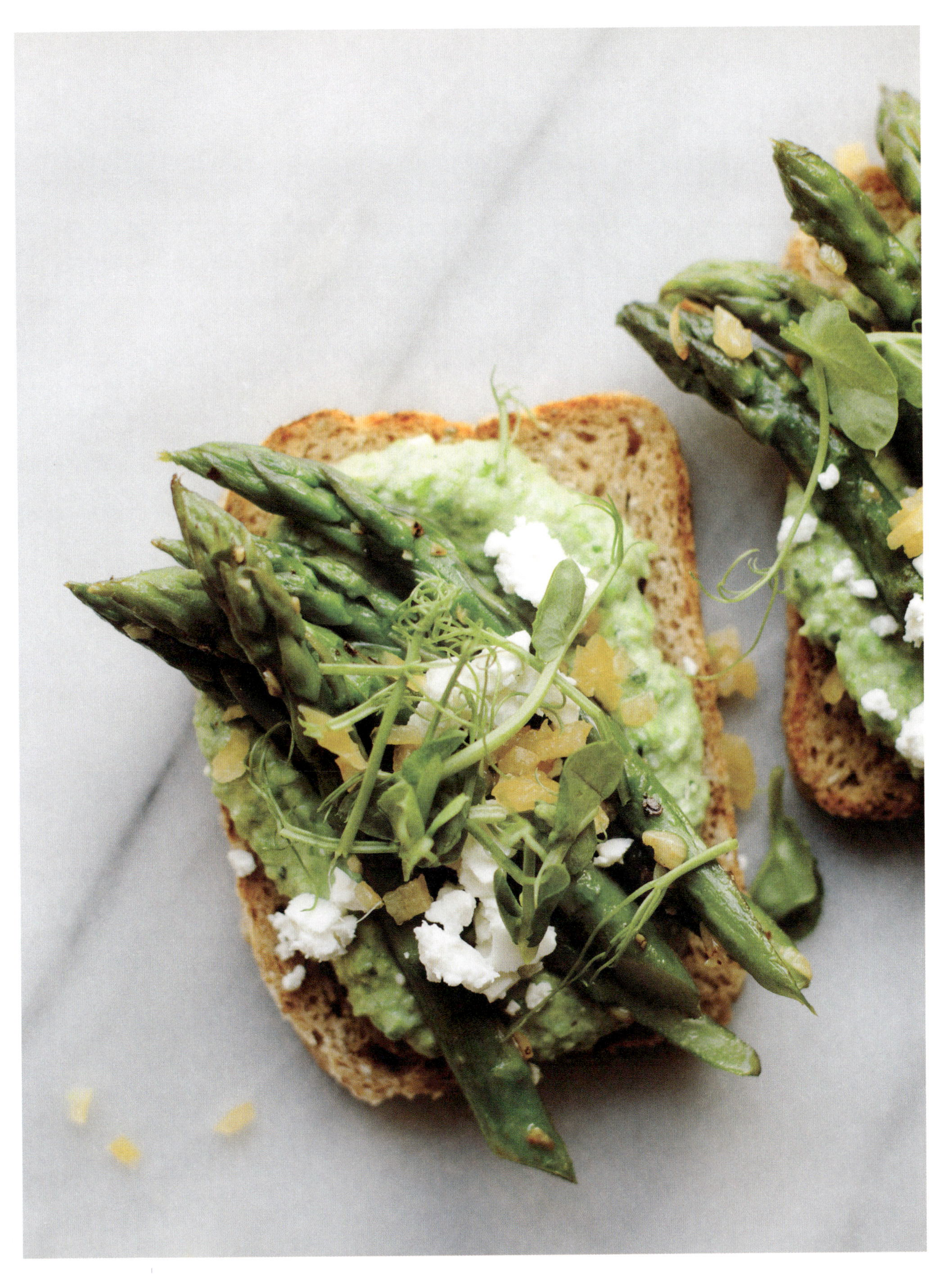

SPICY COCONUT NOODLE SOUP

MAKES 2 GENEROUS SERVINGS OR 3–4 SMALLER ONES | GLUTEN-FREE | VEGAN

A trip to your local Asian grocery store will likely be in order to make this soup, where you'll find candlenuts, fermented tofu, lemongrass and kaffir lime leaves. While you're there, pick up a packet of your favourite rice noodles. I love using thick rice vermicelli, but feel free to use whatever rice noodles you like, and simply follow the cooking instructions on the packet. If you have leftover kaffir lime leaves, these can be frozen and used straight from the freezer next time. If you can't find candlenuts, raw macadamia nuts are a good substitute. They don't taste the same, but do give the same texture to the soup. Please note: raw candlenuts are slightly toxic, so don't be tempted to have a little nibble! You can add some grilled tofu to the soup for extra protein, if desired.

400g packet rice noodles
2 tablespoons virgin coconut oil
1 lemongrass stalk, white part only, bruised
4 kaffir lime leaves
1 large carrot, peeled and cut into thin matchsticks
400ml tin coconut milk (see NOTE on page 240)
1 bunch Asian greens
Juice of 2 limes + extra lime wedges, to serve
Finely sliced chillies and Thai basil, to serve, optional

Spice paste
5 candlenuts or macadamia nuts
1 shallot or medium red onion, finely sliced
3 cloves garlic
1 long red chilli, finely sliced (deseeded if you like)
1 tablespoon finely grated ginger or galangal
1 teaspoon ground coriander
½ teaspoon turmeric powder
½ teaspoon fine sea salt
3 tablespoons drained fermented tofu

+ To make the paste, place candlenuts or macadamias in the bowl of the small food processor and pulse until finely ground. Add shallot or onion, garlic, chilli, ginger, ground coriander, turmeric and salt and pulse until finely ground. Add fermented tofu and blend to form a paste. (Alternatively, you can make the paste using a mortar and pestle and a little elbow grease if you don't own a food processor.)

+ Bring a large saucepan of water to the boil, add rice noodles and cook according to the packet instructions. Thin noodles will only take a few minutes, whereas thick rice vermicelli will take 3–5 minutes. Drain and rinse under cold running water. Divide between four deep bowls and set aside.

+ Heat oil in a large saucepan over medium heat. Add spice paste and cook for 3 minutes or until fragrant. Add lemongrass, kaffir lime leaves and carrot, and cook for a further minute or two, stirring constantly. Add coconut milk and 400ml cold water. Bring to the boil, stirring constantly to prevent the coconut milk from splitting. Add Asian greens, stirring until just wilted (1–2 minutes). Remove from heat, add lime juice and check seasoning, adding more salt or lime juice, to taste. Pick out lemongrass stalk and kaffir lime leaves and compost. Ladle hot soup over your noodles, evenly dividing the greens and carrot between the bowls. Scatter with sliced chilli and basil and serve with extra lime wedges to squeeze over if desired.

+ To store leftovers: cool, then transfer the soup and veg to one container and keep the noodles in another. Cover and refrigerate for up to 2–3 days. Reheat soup gently in a pan, then pour over noodles to reheat.

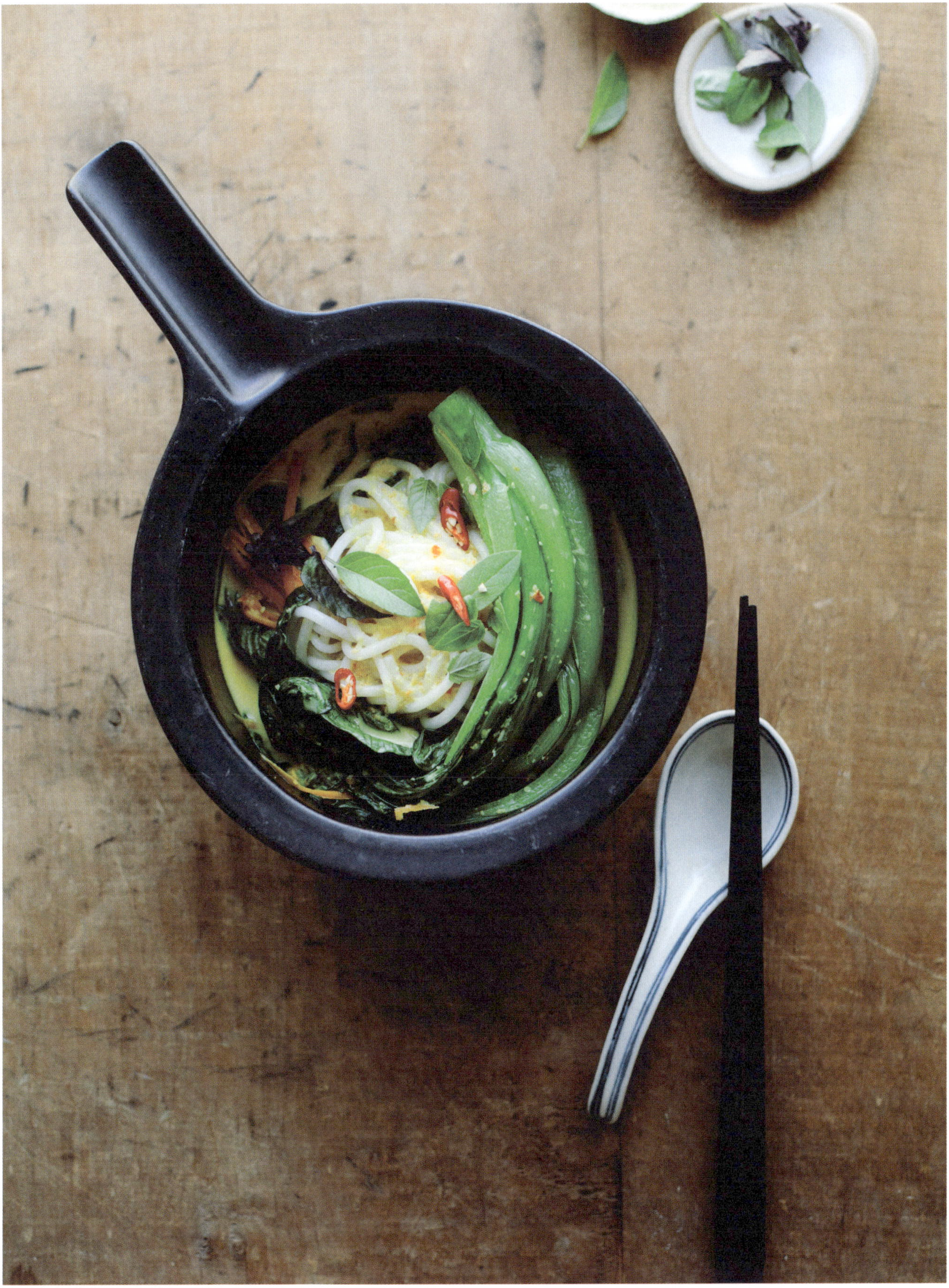

BEETROOT + FENNEL SOUP W/ WHIPPED FETA CROUTONS

SERVES 4–6 | GLUTEN-FREE | DAIRY-FREE / VEGAN OPTION

Every café I've ever worked in made some form of whipped feta dip, which I've paired here with croutons. I always added cumin seeds to the dip but after working with a chef, Rachel, who added fennel seeds, I now use them more often than not. The fennel seed-flecked feta ties in perfectly with the fennel bulb used in this deeply satisfying bright purple beetroot soup. You can use store-bought bread or burger buns (gluten-free if required) if you're after the same look as my croutons, or use the burger bun recipe (page 124) to make your own. (Freeze any leftover for later or double up on croutons for extra snacks.) Omit whipped feta if dairy-free or vegan.

1 tablespoon olive oil
1 red onion, finely diced
2 cloves garlic, finely chopped
2 small fennel bulbs, ends trimmed + thinly sliced, fronds reserved
4 medium beetroot, peeled + roughly diced
1 medium floury potato, peeled + roughly diced
1 fresh or dried bay leaf
Good pinch of fine sea salt
Juice of ½ lemon

Croutons
2 gluten-free burger buns (store-bought or homemade, page 124), sliced vertically into 5mm slices
60ml (¼ cup) extra-virgin olive oil
1 clove garlic, crushed

Whipped feta
100g soft Danish-style feta cheese
2–3 tablespoons natural plain yoghurt
½ teaspoon fennel seeds, lightly toasted + roughly ground

+ To make soup, heat olive oil in a large saucepan over medium-high heat. Sauté onion, garlic and fennel for 4–5 minutes until tender. Add beetroot, potato, bay leaf and just enough water to cover (approx. 1.25L or 5 cups). Add salt, bring to the boil, then reduce heat. Simmer for 35 minutes with the lid ajar. Top up the water level if it gets too low at any point.

+ Meanwhile, preheat oven to 180ºC (350ºF). To make croutons, place bread slices on 2 baking trays in a single layer, combine olive oil and garlic and brush each piece of bread liberally on both sides. Sprinkle with a little fine sea salt and freshly ground black pepper and bake for 15 minutes, swapping the trays over halfway through cooking, until golden and crispy. Remove from oven and set aside to cool.

+ To make whipped feta, place all ingredients in a small food processor and pulse until smooth, starting with 2 tablespoons of the yoghurt and adding more if needed to get a good smooth consistency without it becoming too runny. This amount will vary depending on how firm your feta is.

+ Remove soup from heat, compost bay leaf, add lemon juice and blend until smooth, taste and adjust seasoning. Thin with a touch more water if it's a tad too thick. Serve soup hot with croutons spread with whipped feta and scatter over reserved fennel fronds. Any leftover croutons will store, airtight, for up to 1 week. Store leftover whipped feta in a jar in the fridge for 1 week.

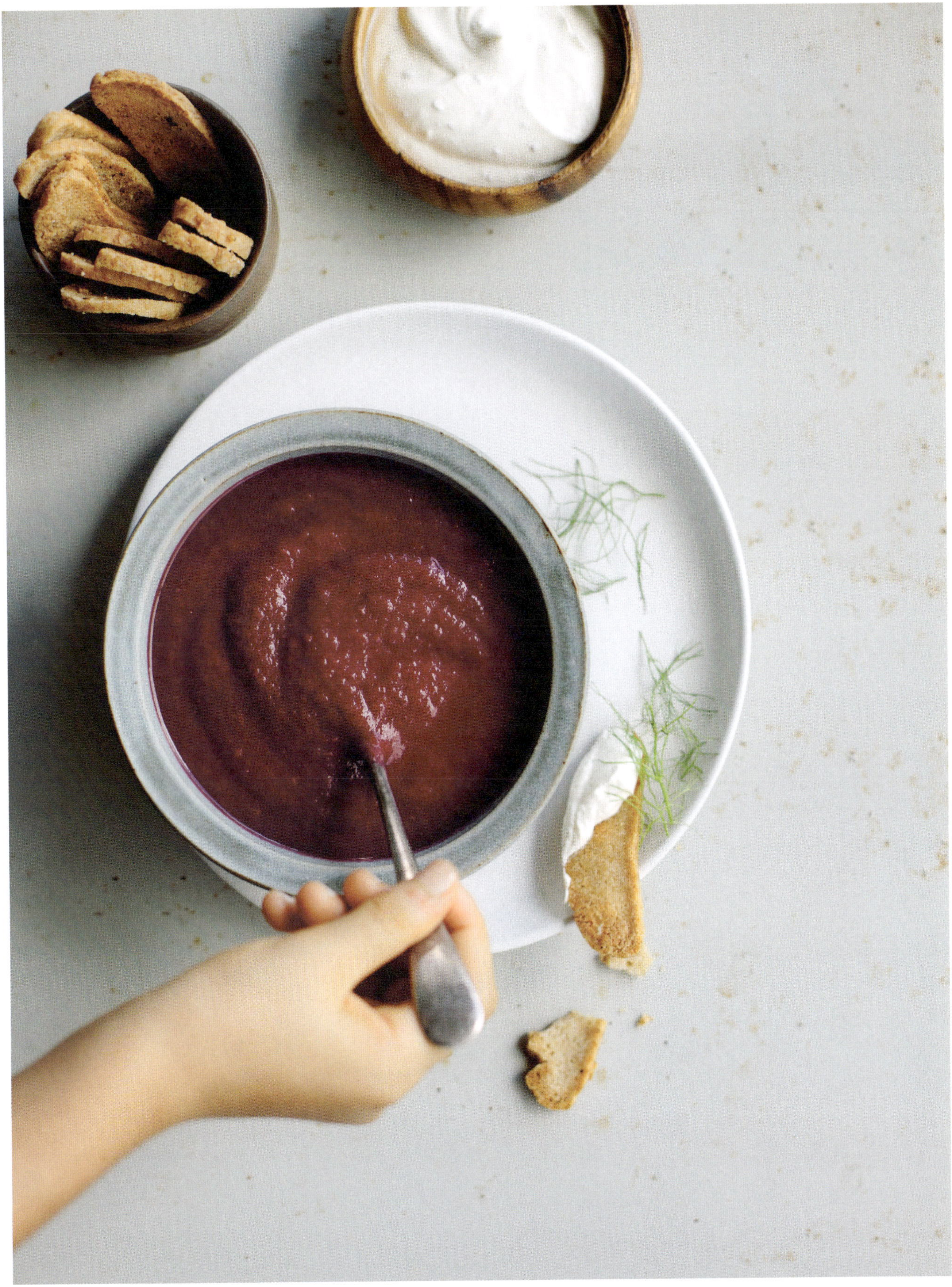

GARLICKY PEAS + BROAD BEANS W/ EGG, FETA + DILL

SERVES 2–4, DEPENDING ON HOW MANY EGGS YOU WANT | GLUTEN-FREE | DAIRY-FREE OPTION

I love any vegetable cooked in a pan along with egg and this recipe is kinda a staple meal in our house, not only for breakfast, but for quick dinners too. In winter I do a potato version with crisp chunks of par-boiled potatoes, smoked paprika and eggs, but in spring, when the broad beans and peas are abundant, I make this bright herby version. I find it's nice served on buttered toast, or with a side of roasted potatoes. You can omit the feta cheese for a dairy-free option.

250g (2 cups) shelled broad beans (see NOTE)
200g (2 cups) podded fresh or frozen peas
2 tablespoons extra-virgin olive oil
4 cloves garlic, finely chopped
4 large free-range eggs
Handful of crumbled feta cheese
Dried oregano, to sprinkle
Roughly chopped dill, to serve

+ Bring a saucepan of lightly salted water to the boil. Cook broad beans for 30–45 seconds until just starting to float to the surface. Drain and transfer to a bowl of iced water to stop the cooking process. When cold, drain well and remove the thick outer skins. If using frozen peas, add these to the water with the beans and drain at the same time.

+ Heat olive oil in large heavy-based frying pan over medium heat. Add garlic and cook, while stirring, for 45–60 seconds until tender, fragrant and golden. Add prepared broad beans and peas to the pan, give it all a good stir and cook for 1–2 minutes until peas are vibrant green and just tender. (If using blanched frozen peas, just cook them for a minute to heat through.) Make four little indents in the mixture and crack one egg into each hole. Scatter over feta, a good sprinkling of dried oregano and season well with fine sea salt and freshly ground black pepper. Cover with a lid and reduce heat to low. Cook for 2–4 minutes, depending on how well cooked you like your eggs. Scatter with chopped dill and serve immediately (either 1 egg each to serve 4, or 2 eggs each to serve 2).

NOTE: If you're not bothered, you can leave the thick outer skin on your broad beans, which I do with fresh young beans from the garden. The aesthetics aren't quite as nice, but you get more bulk in the dish and avoid a fiddly, often time-consuming job.

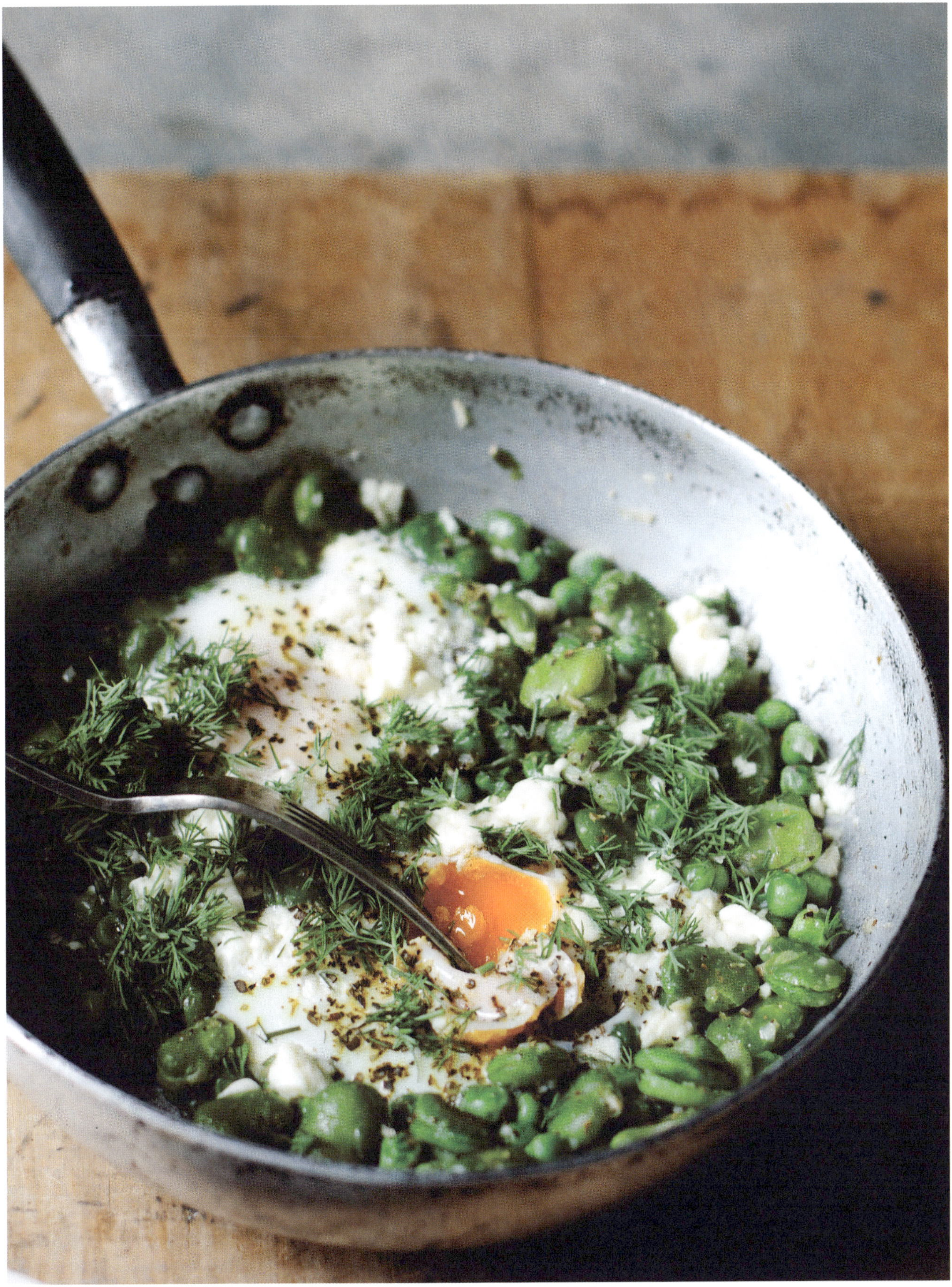

TEMPEH CURRY W/ CHILLI KANG KONG

SERVES 4 | GLUTEN-FREE | VEGAN

It's a well-known fact that I adore curries. I'll happily dig into any curry so long as there's heat, spice and a good hit of sour. Making your own curry paste may at first seem daunting, but I can guarantee once you've made your own you'll never go back to store-bought. I always make sure my freezer is stocked up with grated ginger, whole chillies, coriander roots and stems (leftover from when only the leaves are required) and kaffir lime leaves. We grow our own lemongrass in huge pots, but if you don't, you can either finely slice or grind up market or store-bought stems in a food processor and freeze in small bags. All these ingredients can be used straight from frozen, so making curry from scratch is really not a big deal (see NOTE). And if you can't get hold of tempeh, firm tofu is a great substitute. Any Asian greens such as bok choy, choy sum or even regular English spinach could be used in place of kang kong (aka water spinach) if you can't track it down.

300g tempeh, cut into 1cm dice
Virgin coconut oil, to cook
250ml (1 cup) coconut milk
2 kaffir lime leaves
1 tablespoon finely chopped palm sugar
2 teaspoons gluten-free soy sauce
Juice of 1–2 limes
3 cloves garlic, roughly chopped
1 long red chilli, thinly sliced
500g (approx. 2 large handfuls) kang kong (water spinach), cut into 5–6cm lengths
Steamed jasmine rice, extra lime wedges, Thai basil leaves + finely sliced chilli, to serve

Curry paste

1 small red onion or shallot, roughly chopped
3 cloves garlic, peeled
1 tablespoon finely grated ginger
1 long green chilli, roughly chopped
1 stalk lemongrass, white part only, finely sliced
Roots of 4–5 coriander plants, roughly chopped
1 teaspoon ground coriander
½ teaspoon ground turmeric
½ teaspoon fine sea salt

+ To make curry paste, place all ingredients into a small food processor and blend until a fine paste forms. You may need to stop and scrape the sides down a few times to assist blending.

+ To make curry, shallow-fry tempeh in a little coconut oil over medium-high heat until golden and crisp on each side, then remove from pan and set aside. Scrape out any crispy bits which have stuck to the bottom of the pan, then add 1 tablespoon coconut oil, along with curry paste and fry, stirring often, for 4–5 minutes. Add coconut milk and cook for a further 2–3 minutes until fragrant. Pour in 125ml (½ cup) water, and add kaffir lime leaves, palm sugar and soy sauce. Bring to the boil, then reduce heat to low and simmer for 10 minutes (adding more water as needed to form a sauce). Return tempeh to the pan and stir well to coat in sauce, simmering for 5 minutes to warm through. Remove from heat and stir in lime juice, to taste.

+ Heat another large frying pan or wok over high heat. Add a little coconut or olive oil, along with garlic and chilli. Stir-fry for 20–30 seconds. Add chopped kang kong and stir-fry until just starting to wilt. Add a good splash of soy sauce and mix well.

+ Serve curry with steamed jasmine rice and chilli kang kong, with extra lime wedges, Thai basil leaves and finely sliced red chilli on the side.

NOTE: You can prepare the curry paste in advance, as it will store in the fridge for up to 1 week, or can be frozen in ice-cube trays, then transferred to zip-lock bags, where it will store for 2–3 months.

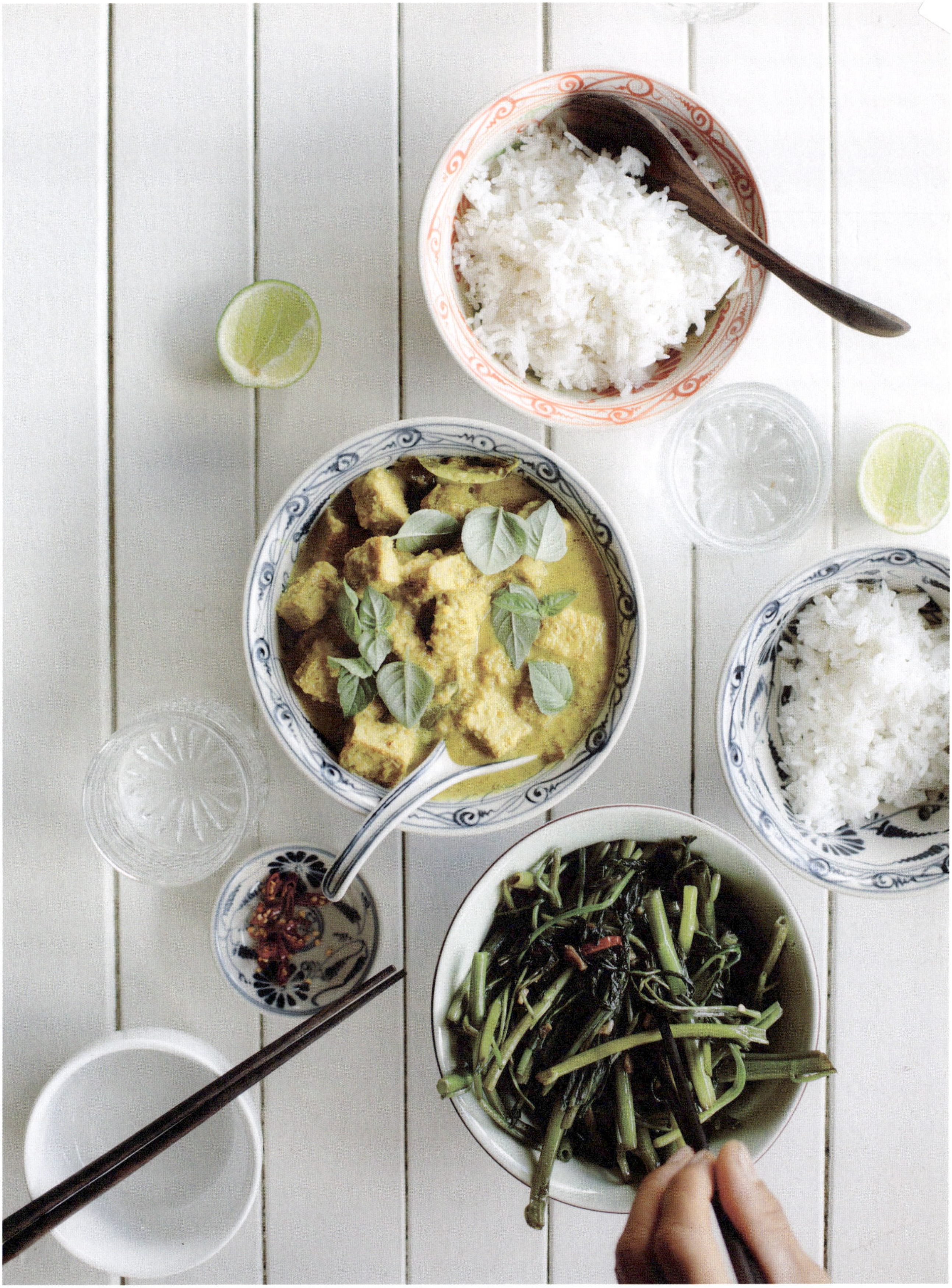

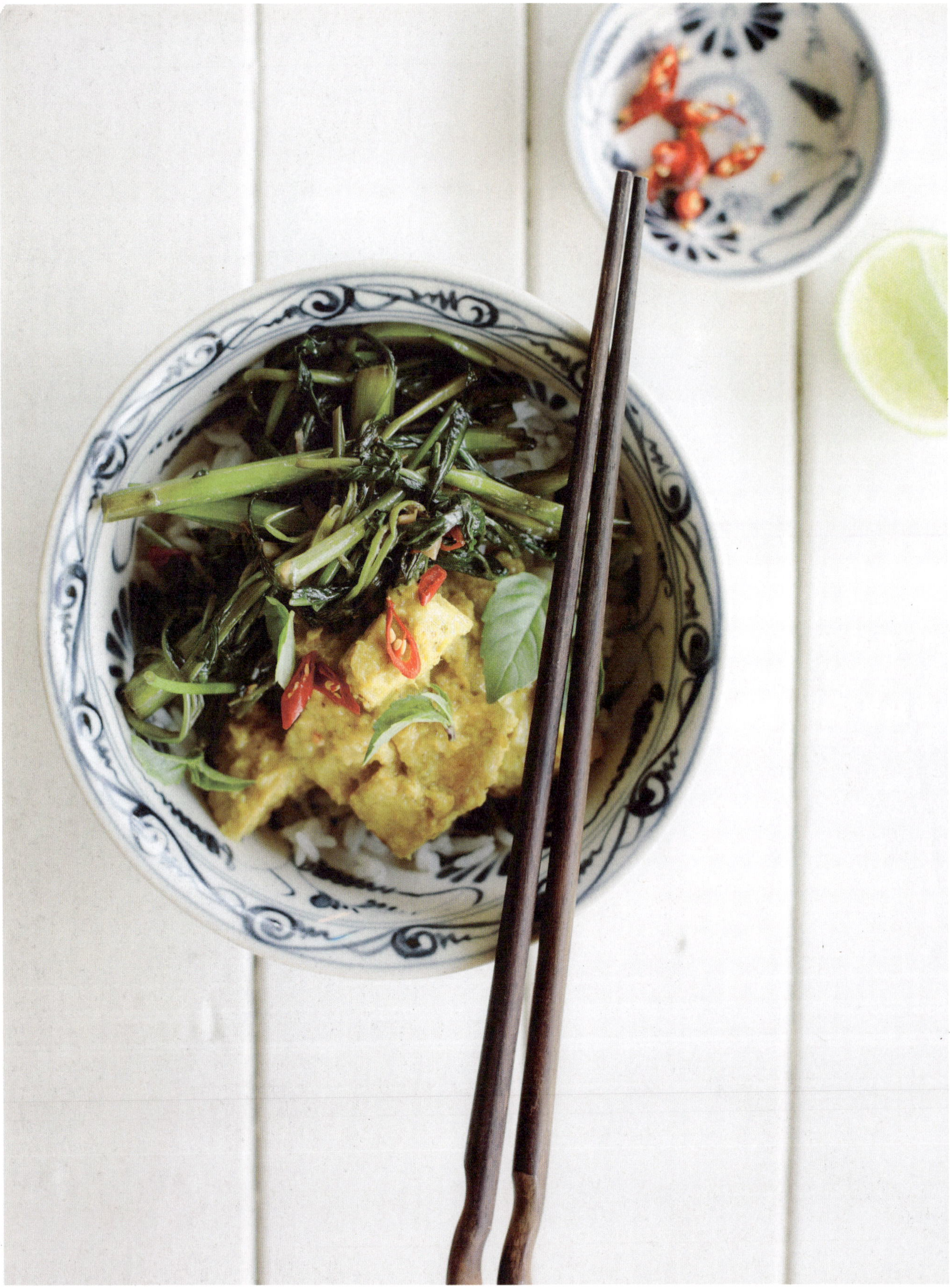

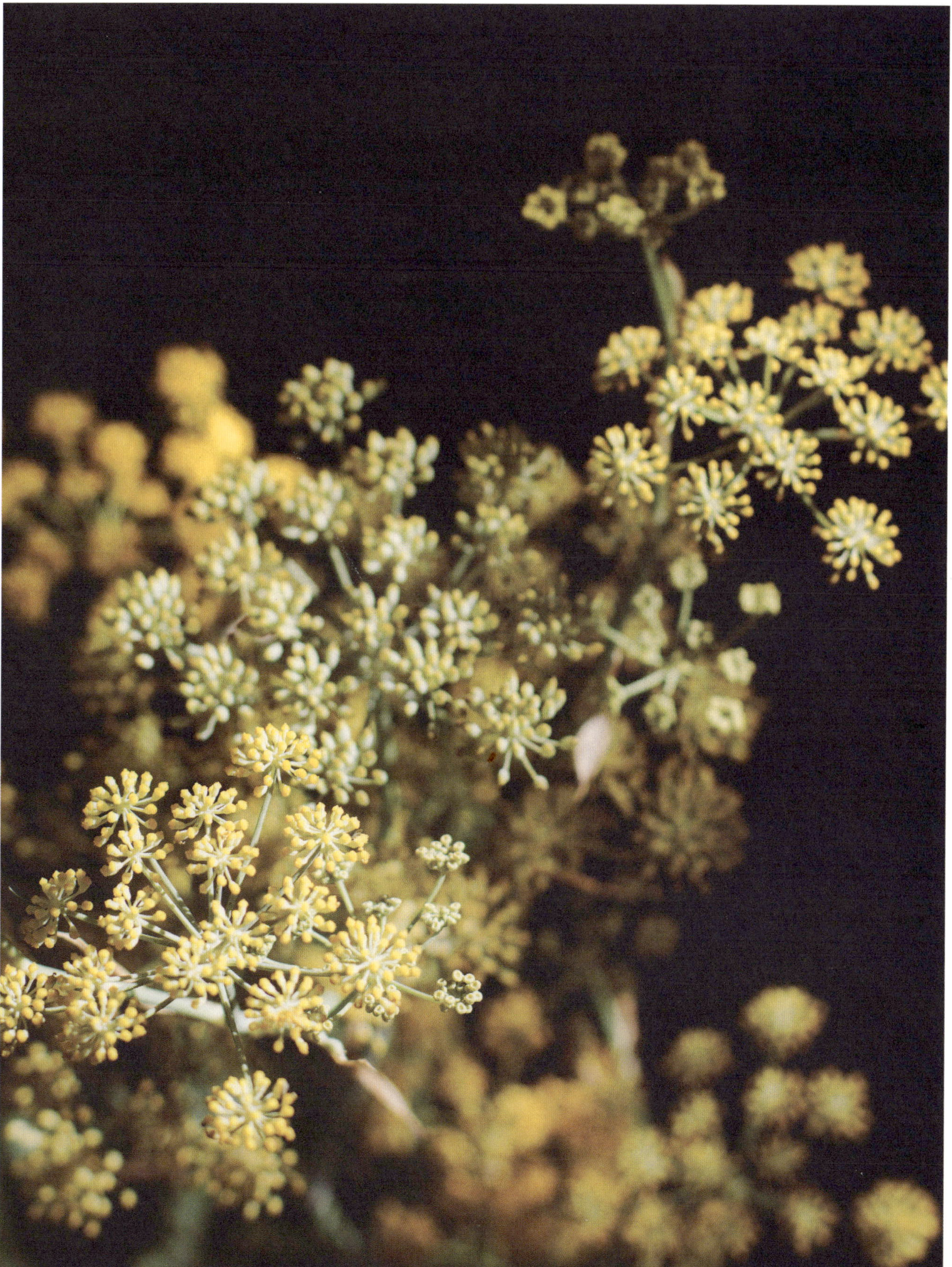

PICKLED BABY BEETS

MAKES 1 LARGE JAR | GLUTEN-FREE | VEGAN

Growing up we hardly ever had store-bought tinned beetroot at home; mostly we ate beets from our garden, which my mum would boil in her trusty little cast-iron pot. I liked them, don't get me wrong (homegrown, organic, cooked with love, how could I not?!), but there's something about the flavour of tinned beets that I've always been a sucker for. Spiced vinegary anything and I'm a happy girl, so nowadays I make my own! Large beetroots can be used if baby are unavailable, you'll just need to adjust the cooking time and then cut them into wedges once peeled. I love using golden baby beets if I come across them at the markets, but regular beets are perfect too.

- 1 bunch (approx. 12–14) baby beetroot (golden if available)
- 250ml (1 cup) apple cider vinegar
- 50g (¼ cup) unrefined raw sugar or brown rice syrup
- ½ teaspoon whole black peppercorns
- ¼ teaspoon fine sea salt
- 2 whole cloves
- 1 fresh or dried bay leaf

+ Trim leaves off beets, leaving about 2–3cm of stem on each one. Place beets in a saucepan, cover with plenty of cold water, bring to the boil, then simmer for 20–30 minutes, or until fork-tender. The cooking time will vary depending on the size of your beets. Drain off water and set aside until cool enough to handle. Peel and place into a large sterilised glass jar (see NOTE, page 22).

+ Place vinegar, 125ml (½ cup) water, sugar, peppercorns, salt, cloves and bay leaf into a small saucepan, bring to the boil and simmer for 2 minutes. Remove pan from the heat and allow to cool for 5 minutes before pouring the pickling liquid over beets. Cool, screw on lid, then refrigerate for 1–2 weeks to allow the flavours to develop before eating. These beets will store in the fridge for up to 2–3 months.

NOTE: Instead of throwing out the tender leaves of your trimmed beetroot, they can be eaten in salad; sautéed in a little olive oil or butter, with garlic, salt and pepper; or composted or fed to your worm farm.

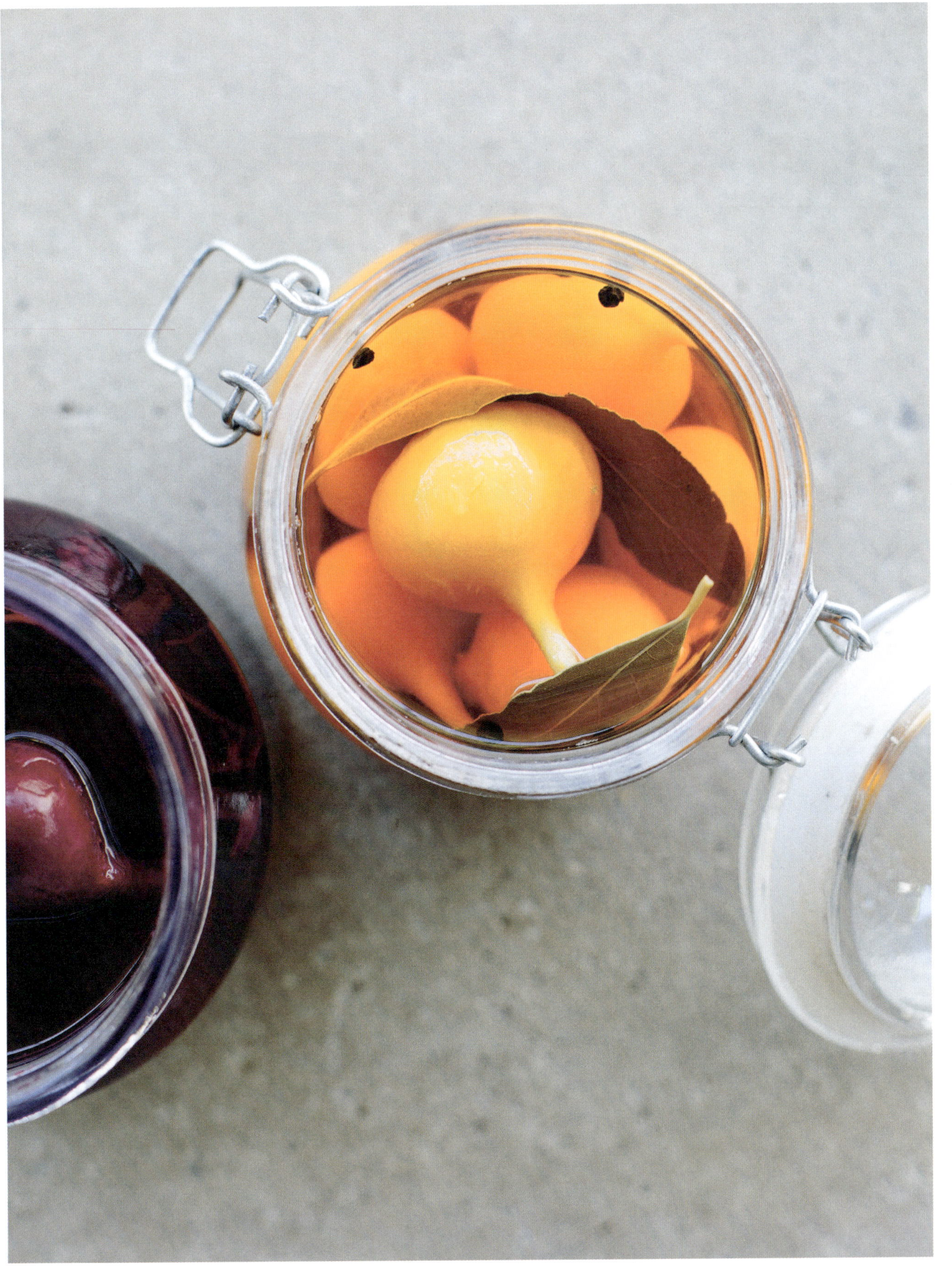

PICKLED BEETROOT, LENTIL + FETA SALAD

SERVES 4 | GLUTEN-FREE

This hearty salad is all about celebrating those beautiful homemade pickled beets (page 144). Other than the addition of a little cooked lentils for protein, and capers, parsley and lemon, not much else needs to be done to these flavour-packed little beets to create something special. French-style Puy lentils can be used in place of beluga if unavailable.

- 200g (1 cup) beluga black lentils
- 4 cloves garlic
- 2 fresh or dried bay leaves
- Juice of 1 lemon
- 2 tablespoons capers, roughly chopped
- Small handful of flat-leaf parsley, roughly chopped
- Good glug of extra-virgin olive oil
- Large handful baby beetroot leaves and/or rocket
- 1 quantity pickled baby beets (page 144), sliced in half if large
- 80–100g soft Danish-style feta cheese, to serve

+ Rinse and drain lentils. Place in a saucepan with whole garlic cloves, bay leaves and enough cold water to cover by about 5cm. Bring to the boil, then reduce to a simmer and cook for 12–15 minutes or until just tender but not mushy. Drain well, compost bay leaves, and use a fork to mash garlic cloves on the side of the pan before stirring into lentils. Transfer to a large bowl and set aside to cool to room temperature.

+ When lentils have cooled, stir through lemon juice, capers, parsley and olive oil and season well with fine sea salt and freshly ground black pepper. Add baby beetroot leaves and/or rocket. Spoon into four bowls, top with baby beets and a crumbling of feta.

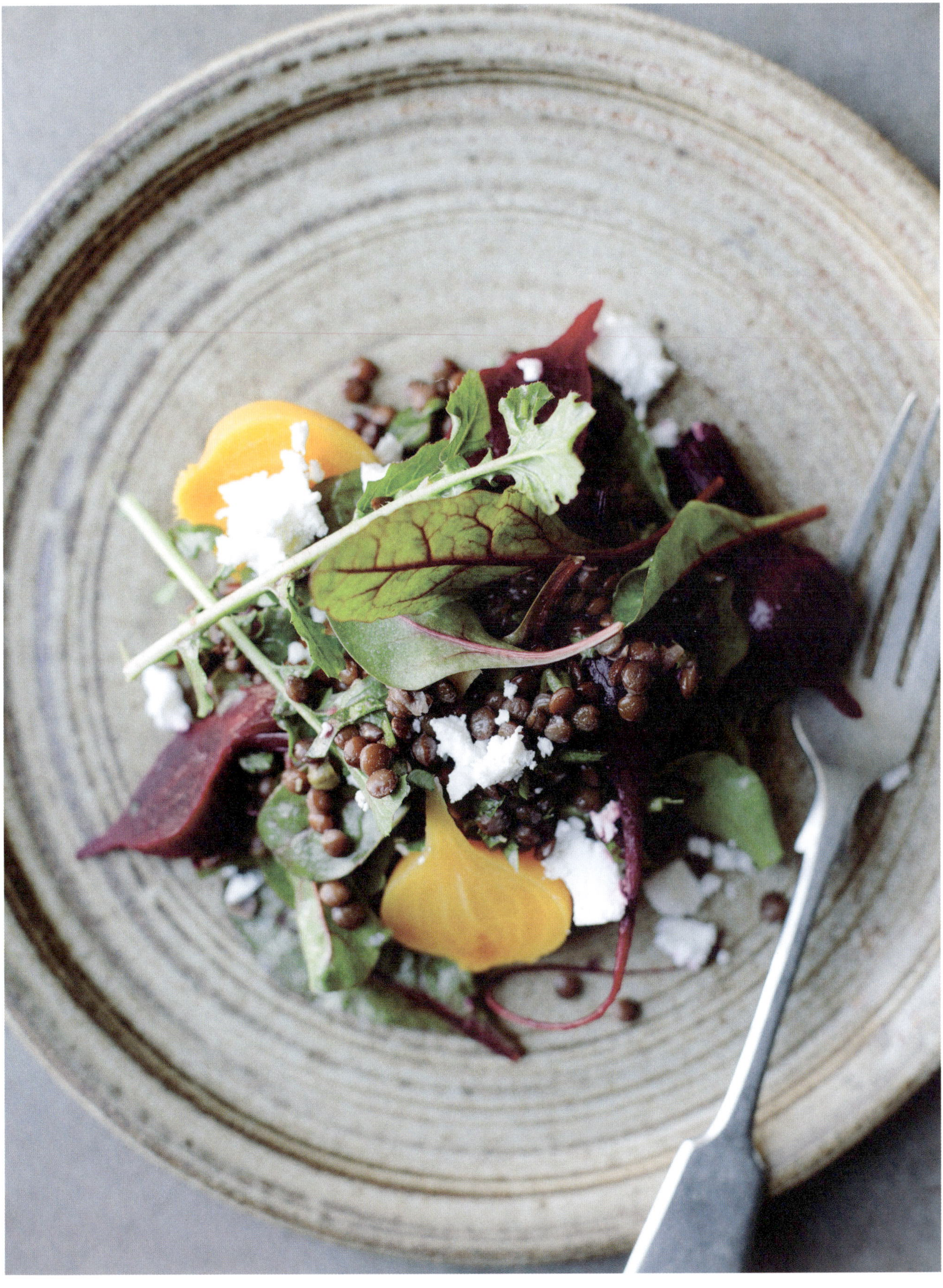

RAINBOW CARROT SALAD W/ MINT MOJO + TURMERIC PEPITAS

SERVES 4–6 AS PART OF A MEAL | GLUTEN-FREE | VEGAN

Antioxidant-rich colourful carrots were around long before the Dutch developed the common orange carrot we all know and love. It's lucky for us, then, that in recent years more and more growers are turning back time and planting heirloom varieties of carrots in (nearly) every shade of the rainbow, offering us more goodness than the orange carrot alone could ever dream of. I've purposely made twice as many turmeric pepitas as you'll need for this recipe, you'll soon realise they're a handy thing to have at hand to spruce up all manner of salads, vegetable stews, curries and rice dishes. They're also really good to just snack on straight up. If you can't get your hands on multi-coloured heirloom carrots, regular orange ones will do. Or use purple if available.

1 bunch (approx. 350g) heirloom baby carrots, peeled + shaved into long strips with a vegetable peeler

Turmeric pepitas

135g (1 cup) pepitas (pumpkin seeds)

2 teaspoons extra-virgin olive oil

1 teaspoon gluten-free soy sauce

1½ teaspoons ground turmeric

Mint mojo

1 cup packed mint leaves + extra, to serve

2 cloves garlic

1 teaspoon whole cumin seeds, lightly toasted + roughly ground

½ teaspoon fine sea salt

2 tablespoons lime juice

3 tablespoons extra-virgin olive oil

+ To make toasted pepitas, roast pepitas in a dry frying pan over medium-high heat, stirring often until light golden in places. Add olive oil and soy sauce and stir well to evenly coat. Continue to cook for a further 30–60 seconds, while stirring, until seeds are dry and deep golden. Add turmeric, stir well and cook for 10 seconds more before removing from heat and setting aside to cool.

+ To make mint mojo, place mint, garlic, cumin and salt in a small food processor, and pulse to roughly chop. Add lime juice and olive oil and pulse until mint is finely chopped.

+ Place shaved carrots into a bowl, drizzle over mint mojo and scatter with turmeric pepitas and mint leaves. Serve immediately. Any leftover pepitas will store, airtight, for 1 week.

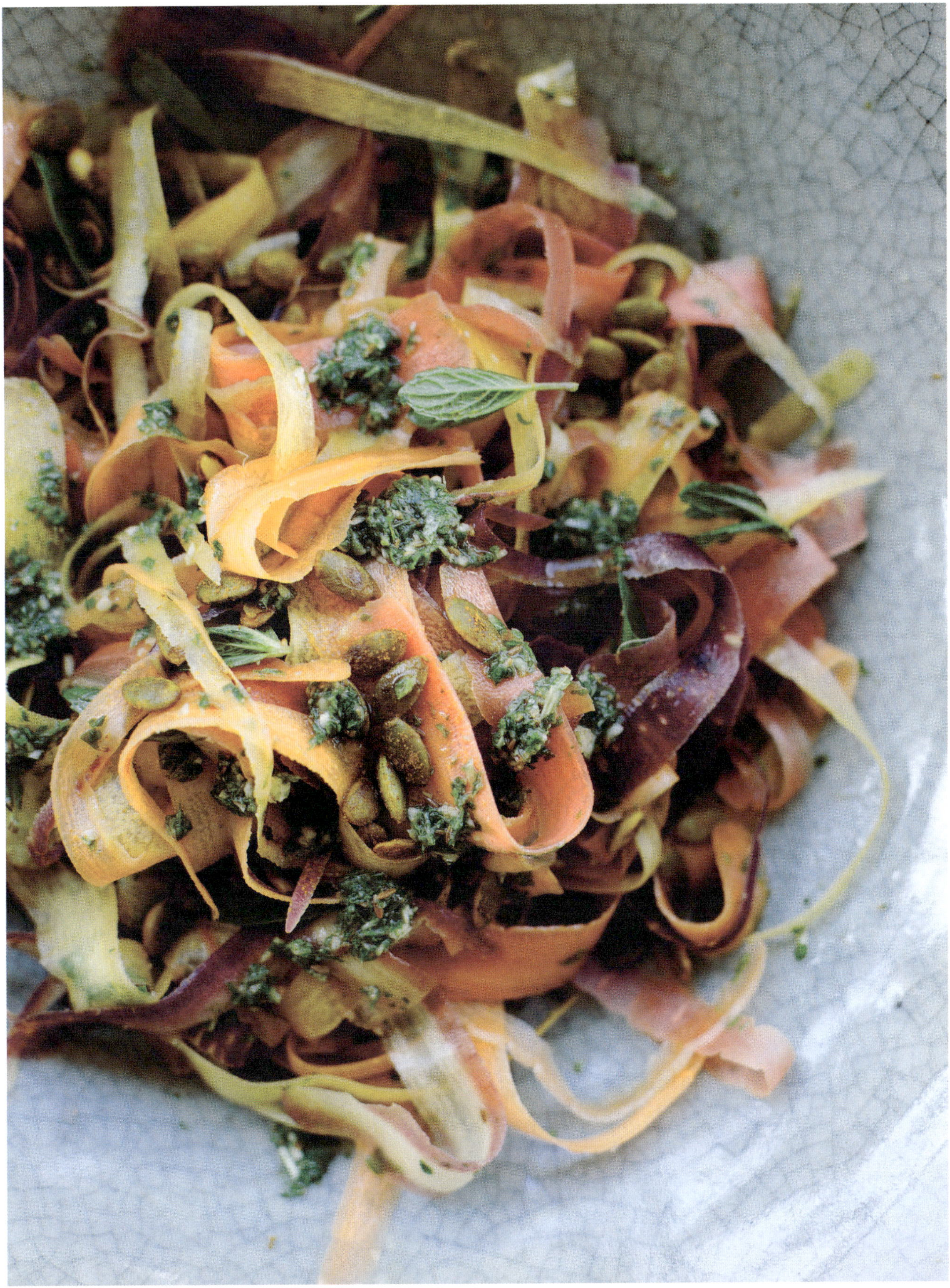

BUCKWHEAT NOODLES W/ CARROT + GINGER BROTH

SERVES 4 | GLUTEN-FREE

This is hands-down one of my favourite recipes in this book. The gingery broth is both warming and light and the silky smooth texture is the perfect sidekick to nutty, comforting homemade buckwheat noodles (see NOTE). Karengo is a beautiful purple wild New Zealand nori harvested off the coast of the South Island; it's rich in vegetable protein, fibre and a variety of vitamins and minerals. Dulse flakes could be used in place if karengo is not available. If you want to bump up the protein, slices of (gluten-free) soy-grilled tofu make a welcome addition.

1 bunch (approx. 15) baby carrots, topped (I sometimes leave approx. 1cm green on)
Olive oil, to drizzle
1.5 litres (6 cups) vegetable stock (page 242)
2 carrots, peeled + cut into bite-sized chunks
2 teaspoons finely grated ginger
2 cloves garlic, peeled
2 teaspoons gluten-free soy sauce
2 teaspoons mirin (or 1 teaspoon unrefined raw sugar)
½–1 teaspoon rice vinegar, to taste
Lightly toasted sesame seeds, finely sliced spring onions + finely chopped dried karengo fronds, to serve

Buckwheat noodles
70g (½ cup) buckwheat flour
45g (⅓ cup) fine brown rice flour
25g (¼ cup) tapioca flour
1 teaspoon psyllium husks
¼ teaspoon fine sea salt
1 large free-range egg, lightly whisked
2 large free-range egg yolks
1 tablespoon extra-virgin olive oil

+ Preheat oven to 200°C (400°F). To make noodles, place flours, psyllium husks and salt in a medium bowl, and whisk to combine. Make a well in the centre, add whole egg and yolks, olive oil and 1 tablespoon water. Using your fingers mix eggs together, slowly incorporating a little flour as you go until the mixture forms into one mass. Turn out onto a lightly rice-floured bench and knead a few times to bring together into a smooth dough. Don't be tempted to add extra flour, the dough should remain ever-so-slightly tacky to the touch. Cover and set aside on the bench for 20 minutes.

+ Cut baby carrots into random bite-sized lengths, place on an oven tray, drizzle with olive oil, and season with fine sea salt and freshly ground black pepper. Roast for 30–35 minutes, turning once or twice during cooking, until tender and golden.

+ While baby carrots are roasting, make broth. Place vegetable stock, carrot, ginger, garlic, soy sauce, mirin or sugar and 1 teaspoon of salt in a large saucepan. Bring to the boil, then reduce and simmer, partially covered with a lid, for 20 minutes. Remove from heat and blend until super-smooth. You can use a stick blender, but for the smoothest results use an upright blender. Add rice vinegar, to taste. You don't want to actually taste the vinegar, you're just after the slight lift it brings. Check seasoning and adjust salt if needed. Return to pan, cover and keep warm.

+ Divide noodle dough in two, keeping one half covered while you roll out the other on a sheet of rice-floured baking paper until approx. 2–3mm thick. Re-flour the paper as needed. Cut into 3mm-wide noodles and set aside while you repeat with remaining dough. (Alternatively if you have a pasta machine, use this to roll out dough to the thinnest setting, then cut noodles using the spaghetti setting.) Bring a large saucepan of lightly salted water to the boil. Add noodles, give them a stir to stop them from clumping together and cook for 3–4 minutes until tender. Drain.

+ Bring broth back up to the boil. Divide buckwheat noodles among bowls, top with roasted carrots and pour over piping-hot broth. Scatter with toasted sesame seeds, spring onions and karengo. Serve immediately.

NOTE: If the idea of making your own noodles seems just a tad too labour intensive, store-bought soba noodles can be used in place of homemade. If you're gluten-free just make sure you source 100% buckwheat soba, as regular soba noodles are made from mostly wheat flour. Rice noodles are also great.

LEEK + POTATO FRITTATA

SERVES 4–6 AS PART OF A MEAL | GLUTEN-FREE | DAIRY-FREE

Leek, potato and ground coriander are favourite flavours from one of my mum's soups. I've borrowed them for this super-simple, quick and easy frittata. Here I've added fresh coriander as well, to give a little added boost of herbaceous, citrusy flavour and colour. You can skip the step where I fry off the potato slices until golden if you're in a hurry, however, I really love the added flavour this creates, so I urge you to do it if you can. Frittatas are also a great way to use up leftover cooked potatoes hanging around in your fridge.

- 500g (4 medium) potatoes, scrubbed
- 4 tablespoons extra-virgin olive oil
- 1 large leek, thinly sliced
- 3 cloves garlic, roughly chopped
- 1½ teaspoons ground coriander
- 6 large free-range eggs, lightly whisked
- Handful of coriander leaves, roughly chopped
- Rocket leaves, to serve, optional

+ Place potatoes in a saucepan, cover with cold water, add a good pinch of salt, bring to the boil and cook for 10 minutes or until just tender (keeping in mind that they will get cooked further). Drain and set aside for 5 minutes before slicing into 1cm rounds.

+ Preheat oven to 200ºC (400ºF). Heat a large ovenproof frying pan (cast-iron or stainless steel is perfect), add 3 tablespoons of the olive oil and fry potato slices on both sides until golden; you'll need to do this in a couple of batches. Remove potato from the pan, add remaining tablespoon of olive oil along with sliced leek and garlic. Cook, while stirring, for 3–4 minutes or until lovely and tender. Add ground coriander, a little fine sea salt and freshly ground black pepper and continue to cook for a further 30–60 seconds. Remove from heat and return potato to the pan, arranging slices in a flat layer or alternating the leek mixture and potato slices. (Alternatively, if you don't own an ovenproof frying pan, arrange cooked potato and leek in an ovenproof dish, pour over egg mixture and bake.)

+ Season eggs with a good pinch of salt and pepper, stir through coriander leaves, then pour over leek and potato. Cook on the stovetop for 2 minutes until just starting to set around the edges, then transfer to the oven and cook for a further 15–20 minutes or until eggs are puffed and set in the centre. Remove from oven, slice into wedges and serve hot or at room temperature. Serve scattered with rocket leaves, if desired, or with a salad for a light meal.

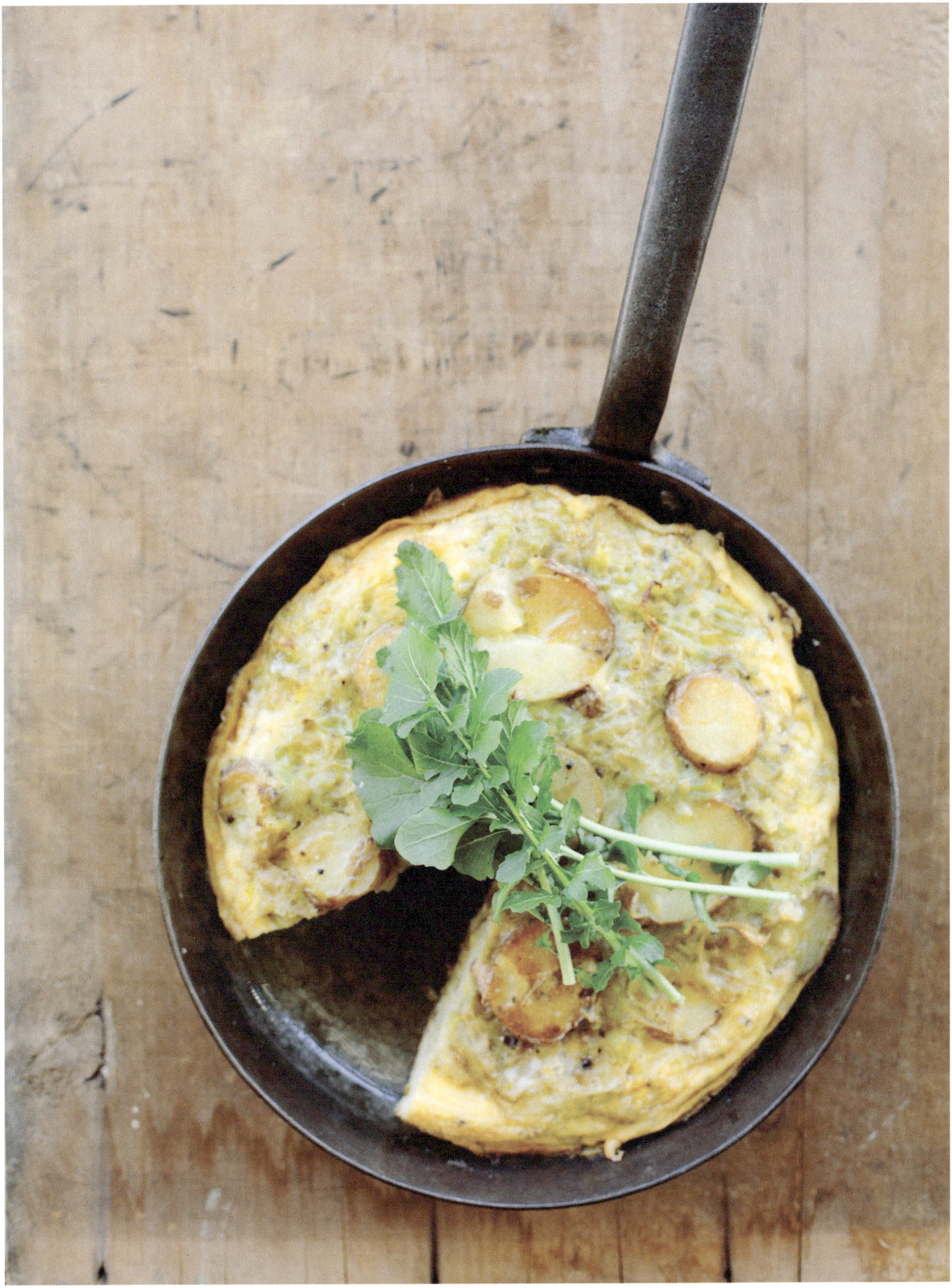

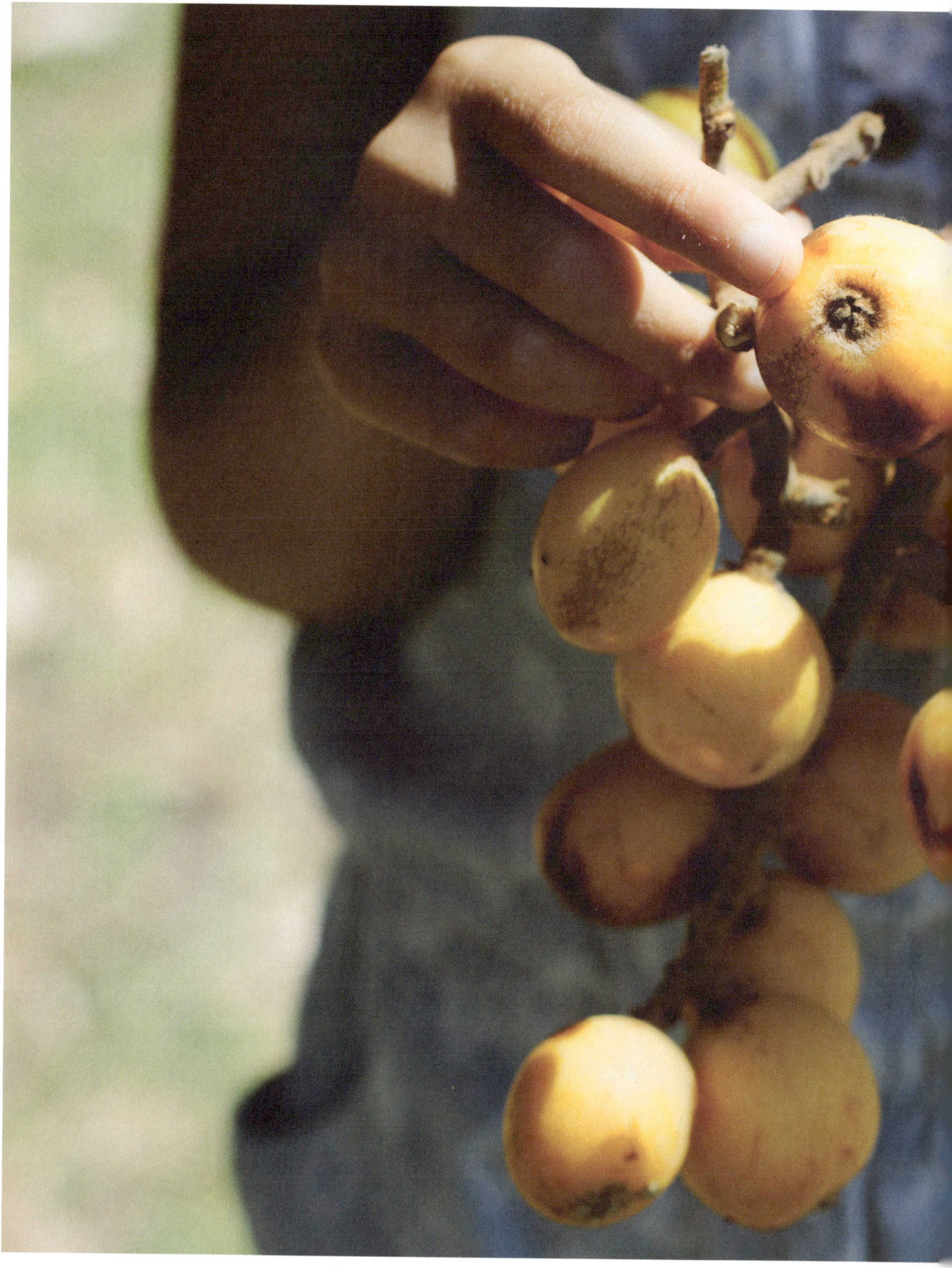

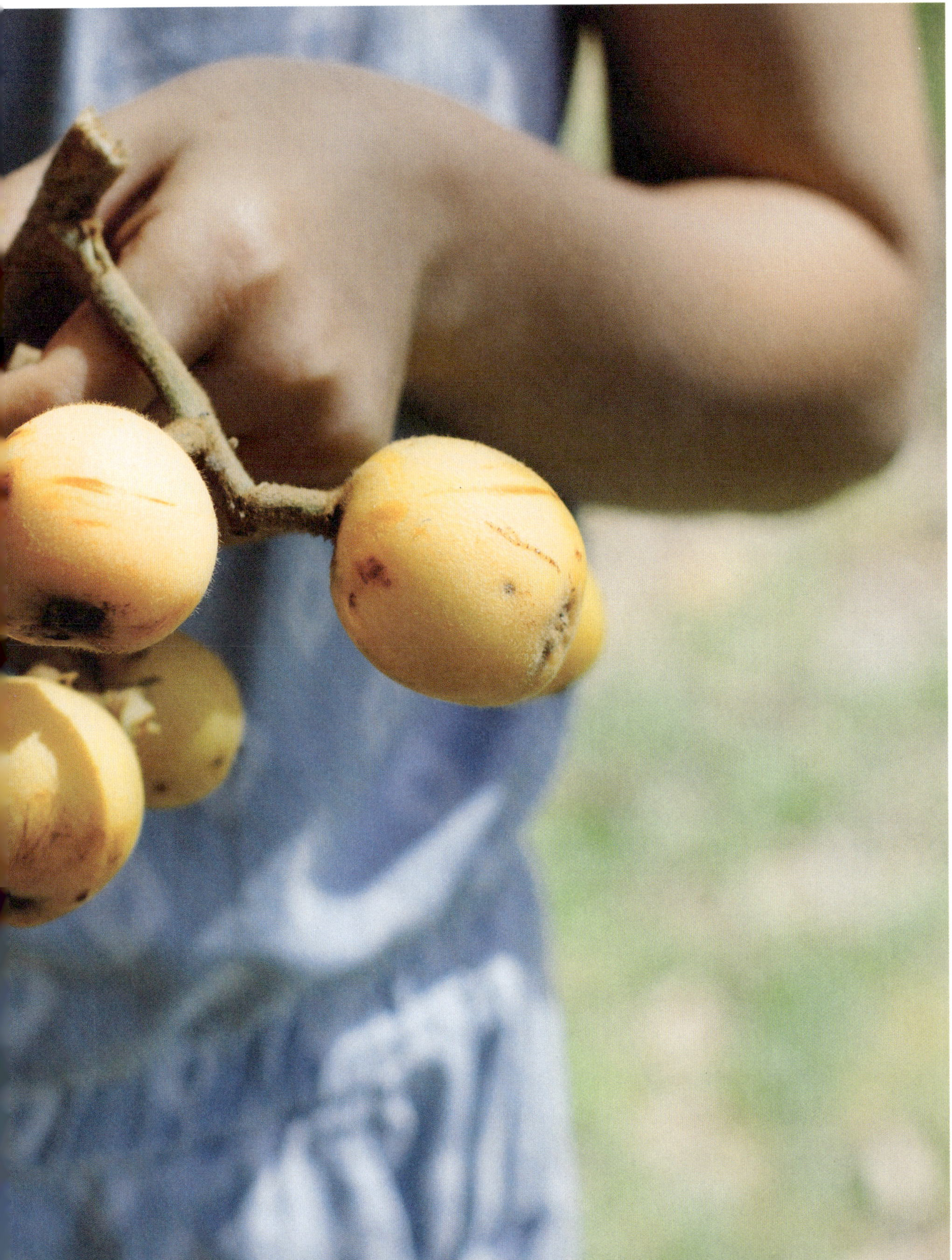

COCONUT PIKELETS W/ LEMON CURD

MAKES 16 PIKELETS | GLUTEN-FREE | DAIRY-FREE

I started making these pikelets a few years back when I wanted a high-protein after-school snack for the kids, but my flour jars were near empty. The desiccated coconut and arrowroot fill the role of flour and the end results are light, fluffy and, of course, coconutty! We often just eat them as is, or with a little pat of butter, but if my kids are lucky they'll also get this tart honey-sweetened lemon curd to smear on top. You can also cook them up as larger pancakes and serve with the usual trimmings: maple syrup and lemon juice. Please note, you must use desiccated coconut here, not coconut flour (which has been stripped of all its fat and moisture).

120g (1½ cups) desiccated coconut

25g (6 tablespoons) arrowroot or tapioca flour

1 teaspoon gluten-free baking powder

4 large free-range eggs

80ml (⅓ cup) coconut, rice or almond milk

Virgin coconut oil, to pan-fry

Fresh berries, to serve, optional

Lemon curd

2 large free-range eggs, lightly beaten

Finely grated zest of 1 lemon

125ml (½ cup) lemon juice

80ml (⅓ cup) honey

3 tablespoons virgin coconut oil

Good pinch of fine sea salt

+ To make lemon curd, combine all ingredients in a saucepan. Place over a low–medium heat, and stir continuously with a wooden spoon to melt the coconut oil, if solid. Once melted, reduce heat to low and cook for 6–8 minutes, stirring constantly until the mixture has thickened enough to coat the back of the spoon. Don't let the mixture ever come near boiling point or you'll end up with scrambled eggs. (Alternatively, if this chef-style shortcut scares you, put all curd ingredients in a heatproof bowl set over a saucepan of boiling water and cook, stirring occasionally, for 20 minutes or until lovely and thick.) Strain through a fine sieve, discarding the zest. Transfer to a clean jar and cool before sealing and chilling in the fridge to firm up further. Use within a week.

+ To make pikelets, place coconut, arrowroot or tapioca flour and baking powder in the bowl of a small food processor and blend until finely ground. Add eggs, milk and a small pinch of salt, then pulse a few times to incorporate.

+ Heat a large heavy-based frying pan over medium heat. Add a little coconut oil to lightly cover the base. Drop spoonfuls of batter into the pan and cook until bubbles start to show on the surface and the underside is golden. Flip over and cook for a further minute or so. You'll see the centre of each pikelet puff up a little when cooked through. Remove from pan and repeat with remaining batter. Serve pikelets with a dollop of lemon curd on top, and berries, if desired.

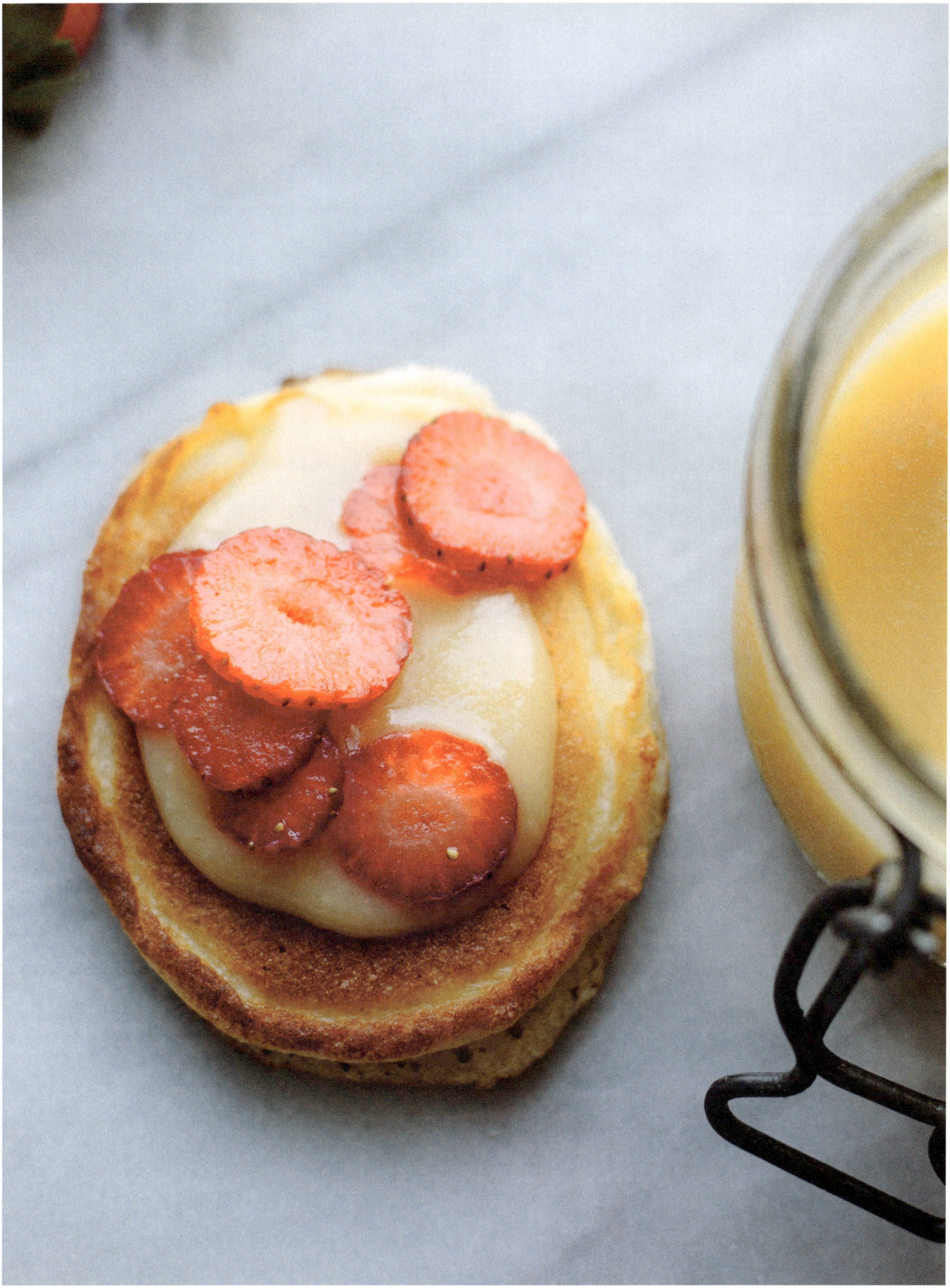

BEETROOT CHOCOLATE CAKES

MAKES 12 | GLUTEN-FREE | DAIRY-FREE

These are my son's favourite chocolate cakes; just please don't tell him they contain beetroot! He still hasn't forgiven me for adding beetroot to our chocolate shakes years ago, so I'm happy for him to never know the secret ingredient in these cakes! Although to be fair, I don't know who could say no to these light, fluffy little numbers, beetroot or no beetroot. You can sprinkle your cakes with finely chopped chocolate or cacao nibs instead of the freeze-dried raspberries if preferred. They're also delicious topped with the dairy-free chocolate icing found on page 60 instead of the chocolate coconut cream if preferred. You'll need to place the tin of coconut milk in the fridge the night before to chill (see NOTE, page 172).

- 125ml (½ cup) virgin coconut oil, macadamia nut or olive oil
- 150g (¾ cup) muscovado sugar
- 60g dark chocolate, roughly chopped
- 100g (½ cup) puréed cooked beetroot (see NOTE)
- 1 teaspoon vanilla extract
- 3 large free-range eggs, at room temperature
- 70g (½ cup) fine brown rice flour
- 60g (½ cup) quinoa flour
- 30g (¼ cup) arrowroot or gluten-free organic cornflour (starch)
- 3 tablespoons cocoa powder
- 2 teaspoons gluten-free baking powder
- 60ml (¼ cup) coconut, almond or rice milk

Whipped chocolate coconut cream
- 2 x 400ml tins coconut milk, refrigerated overnight
- 15g (¼ cup) cocoa powder
- 2–4 tablespoons pure icing sugar or pure maple syrup, to taste
- 1 teaspoon vanilla extract
- Freeze-dried raspberries, to serve, optional

+ Preheat oven to 180°C (350°F). Line a 12-hole 80ml (⅓ cup) muffin tin with paper cases. Combine oil, sugar and chocolate in a medium saucepan. Melt over low heat until just combined. Remove from heat and stir through beet purée, vanilla and eggs, one at a time. Sift over flours, cocoa, baking powder and a good pinch of salt, then stir until three-quarters combined, then add milk and stir until just combined. Divide between paper cases and cook for 20 minutes or until a skewer inserted into the centre of the cakes comes out clean. Remove from oven and set aside for 5 minutes, before transferring to a wire rack to cool completely.

+ To make icing, open tins of chilled coconut milk carefully, scoop off the top thick layer and place in a bowl (reserve coconut water left in the bottom of tins for another use, such as in smoothies, porridge, etc). Sift over cocoa powder and icing sugar or maple syrup, add vanilla and beat with electric beaters until thick and smooth. Ice cooled cakes and top with freeze-dried raspberries if desired.

NOTE: You will need approx. 1 medium beetroot for this recipe, either roasted or boiled until tender, then peeled and puréed until smooth. To avoid colour loss, make sure you don't peel your beetroot before cooking, and leave 2–3cm of stems on for this same reason.

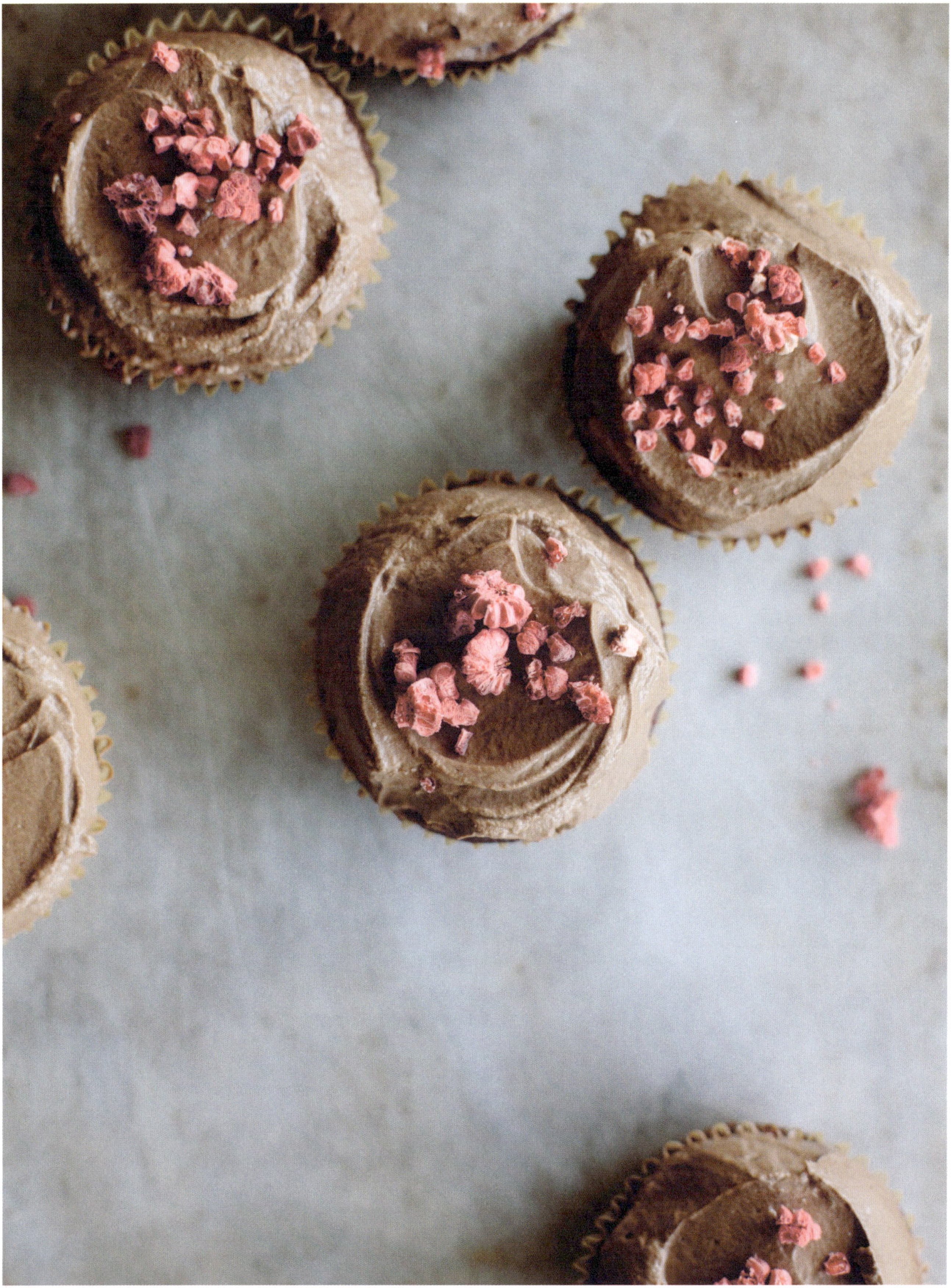

RHUBARB + ROSEMARY TARTS

MAKES 6 | GLUTEN-FREE

If you follow my blog or any of my social media channels you'll know that I have a bit of a soft spot for mini fruit tarts (aka crostata or galette). While you can absolutely make this recipe into one large tart, I find it's much easier to handle the gluten-free pastry when you make the tarts small. Also, they're much cuter and who doesn't love a single-portion tart? The pastry can be prepared in advance and stored in the fridge for up to 2–3 days, or frozen for 1–2 months. I like the tartness of the rhubarb to shine through, so I use less maple. However, if you like things a tad sweeter, add the other tablespoon.

- 500g (6–8 skinny stems) rhubarb, ends trimmed + cut into 5mm diagonal slices
- 3–4 tablespoons pure maple syrup or unrefined raw sugar
- 2 teaspoons gluten-free organic cornflour (starch)
- 1 teaspoon finely chopped rosemary
- 1 teaspoon finely grated orange zest
- 3 teaspoons ground almonds

Pastry
- 140g (1 cup) fine brown rice flour
- 80g (¾ cup) ground almonds
- 35g (¼ cup) buckwheat flour
- 25g (¼ cup) tapioca flour or gluten-free organic cornflour (starch)
- 50g (¼ cup) firmly packed blended unrefined raw sugar (page 235)
- 125g cold butter, cut into 1cm cubes
- 1 large free-range egg, lightly beaten

+ To make pastry, place brown rice flour, ground almonds, buckwheat flour, tapioca flour and blended raw sugar in the bowl of the food processor and pulse a few times to evenly distribute the flours. Add butter cubes and pulse until mixture resembles fine breadcrumbs. Add egg and pulse to just incorporate. Take a little piece of the mixture between your fingers and give it a little pinch. It should hold together well, if it doesn't, add 1 teaspoon iced water at a time until it does. You should only need 1–2 teaspoons at the absolute maximum – too much liquid and you will end up with rubbery pastry. More often than not I find I don't need to add any water at all. Turn out mixture onto a lightly rice-floured bench and use your hands to bring it all together to form a soft dough. Form into a flat disc, place in a zip-lock bag and chill for 30 minutes.

+ Combine rhubarb with maple syrup or sugar, cornflour, rosemary and orange zest in a bowl. Mix well. Preheat oven to 180ºC (350ºF). Grease a large baking tray or line with baking paper.

+ Divide pastry into six equal portions, rolling each into a ball. Roll out pastry on a sheet of lightly rice-floured baking paper into a circle, about 3mm thick. Transfer to the tray carefully. Spread ½ teaspoon of ground almonds in the centre of the pastry, leaving a 2cm border around the edge. Arrange a sixth of the rhubarb filling in the centre (it will seem like a lot of filling, but it cooks down), pull up the sides of the pastry in a rustic fashion, enclosing most of the filling. Repeat with remaining ingredients. Brush pastry with a little milk (I use rice milk) and bake for 30–35 minutes, or until lovely and golden. Remove from oven and serve either hot or at room temperature. These are best eaten within an hour or two of baking, before the pastry softens too much. You can scatter with rosemary flowers before serving, if you have them.

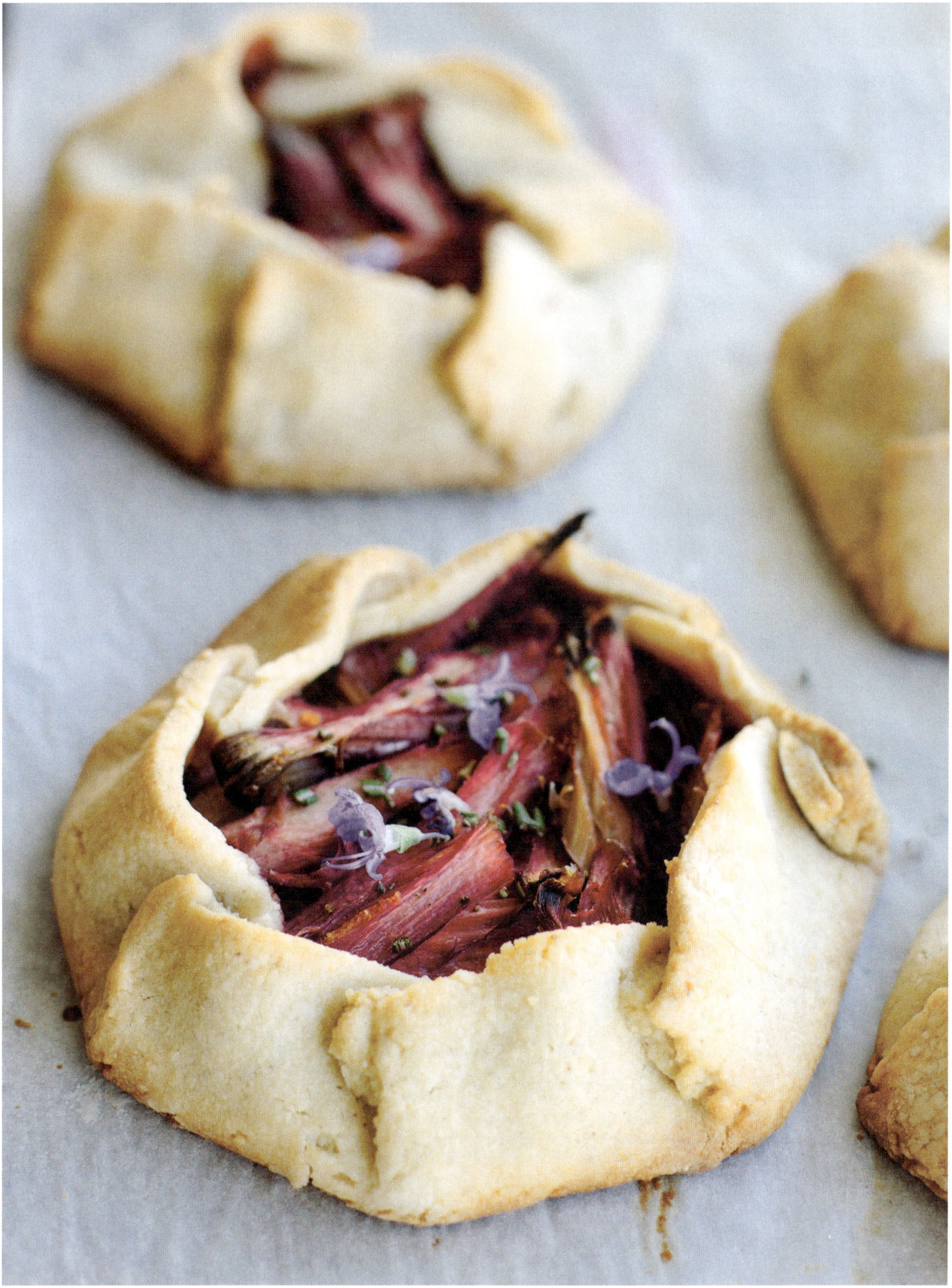

BANANA CAKE w/ LEMON COCONUT ICING

SERVES 10–12 | GLUTEN-FREE

Eating this cake takes me straight back to my childhood and time spent at my nana's house. Unlike the carob icing my mum always uses to ice her banana cakes, Nana would always ice hers with lemon icing and, from faint memory, she often added coconut too. So many other gluten-free cakes are best eaten on the day of baking before they dry out, but this one actually improves with time, getting more and more moreish as the days go by.

115g soft butter

100g (½ cup firmly packed) muscovado or brown sugar

100g (½ cup) firmly packed unrefined raw sugar (see page 235)

1 teaspoon vanilla extract

2 large free-range eggs, at room temperature

1½ cups mashed banana (from approx. 3 large over-ripe bananas)

80ml (½ cup) natural plain yoghurt

60g (½ cup) quinoa flour

70g (½ cup) fine brown rice flour

50g (½ cup) gluten-free organic cornflour (starch)

3 teaspoons gluten-free baking powder

½ teaspoon fine sea salt

110g (1 cup) ground almonds

Lemon coconut icing

125g (1 cup) pure or golden icing sugar

45g (½ cup) shredded coconut

2 teaspoons finely grated lemon zest

3 tablespoons lemon juice

+ Preheat oven to 180ºC (350ºF). Grease a 23cm cake tin and line with baking paper. Cream butter and sugars until light and fluffy. Add vanilla and beat in eggs, one at a time, until well incorporated. Stir through mashed banana and yoghurt (the mixture will curdle at this stage, that's okay). Sift over dry ingredients, tipping back any bits of ground almonds left in the sieve into the bowl, and mix until a smooth batter forms. Spoon mixture into prepared tin and bake for 45–55 minutes or until a skewer inserted into the centre of the cake comes out clean. Remove cake from oven and set aside to cool for 10 minutes in tin, before turning out onto a wire rack to cool completely.

+ To make icing, combine icing sugar, coconut, lemon zest and juice in a small bowl and mix well. Pour over cooled cake, spreading out a little to cover the top.

+ This cake will happily keep, airtight, for 2–3 days.

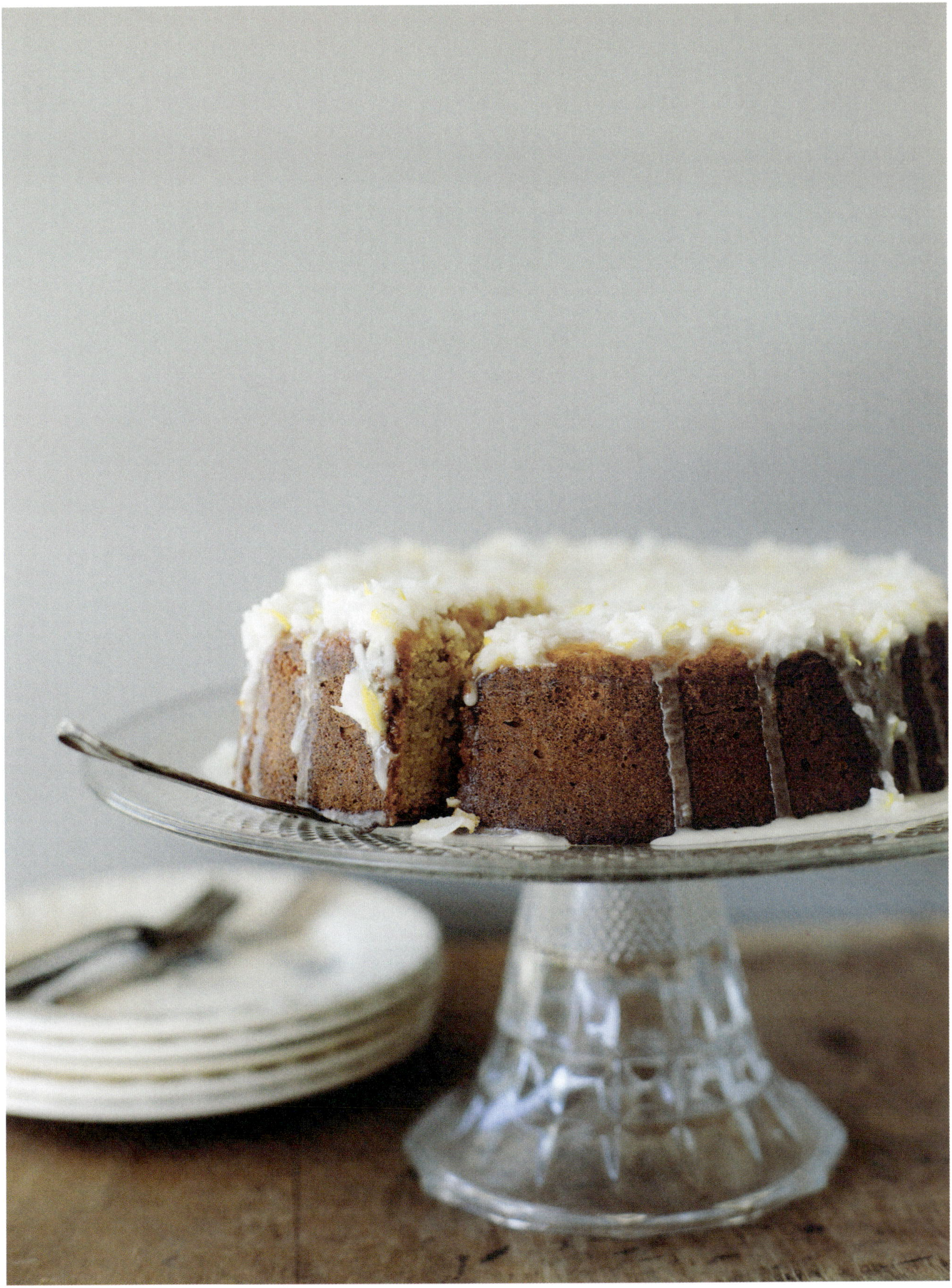

RHUBARB, HIBISCUS + ORANGE SORBET

SERVES 4–6 | GLUTEN-FREE | VEGAN

Some would argue that in addition to the tang of rhubarb in this sorbet there IS another slightly different twang of hibiscus also present. It's there faintly if you go searching for it, no doubt, but to be honest, it's the beautiful vibrant hue hibiscus exudes which is the real reason why I like to add it to recipes such as this sorbet! The added colour is especially helpful if your homegrown rhubarb, like ours, is always more on the greener side of things, than pink. You can find dried hibiscus flowers at health food and specialty food stores. Or use hibiscus tea bags from the supermarket. Chopping the rhubarb on an angle makes it easier to cut through the stringy bits.

- 500g (approx. 4–5 large stems) rhubarb, ends trimmed + finely chopped on an angle
- 1 tablespoon dried hibiscus flowers (or 2 tea bags)
- 150g (¾ cup) unrefined raw sugar
- 2 teaspoons finely grated orange zest
- Good pinch of fine sea salt
- 3 tablespoons lemon juice

+ Place rhubarb in a large saucepan. Combine 375ml (1½ cups) boiling water and hibiscus flowers or tea bags in a bowl or jug and set aside for 5 minutes to steep. Strain, add brewed tea to rhubarb and compost hibiscus. Add sugar, orange zest and salt. Cover and bring to the boil, stirring every now and then to ensure the sugar melts. Reduce heat and simmer with lid partially on (watch out for overflowing!) for 5–8 minutes or until rhubarb is really tender and broken down. Remove from heat, add lemon juice and set aside for 5 minutes to cool. Either using a stick blender or an upright blender, blend until completely smooth. Set aside until cold, then chill in the fridge for at least 2 hours. Churn in an ice cream machine for 20–25 minutes until done. Transfer to a lidded container and freeze for a further 2–3 hours until set to your liking. This sorbet will keep for 4–5 days in the fridge. If it's set too hard, leave out on the bench for 10–15 minutes to soften before serving.

+ If you don't own an ice cream churn, simply place the sorbet mixture into a shallow dish (a loaf tin is perfect) and freeze for 1 hour until the edges are starting to freeze. Beat with an electric beater or whisk, return to the freezer and repeat a further 2–3 times before returning to the freezer for 2 hours. This won't give the exact same results as a churn, but the sorbet is still delicious nonetheless.

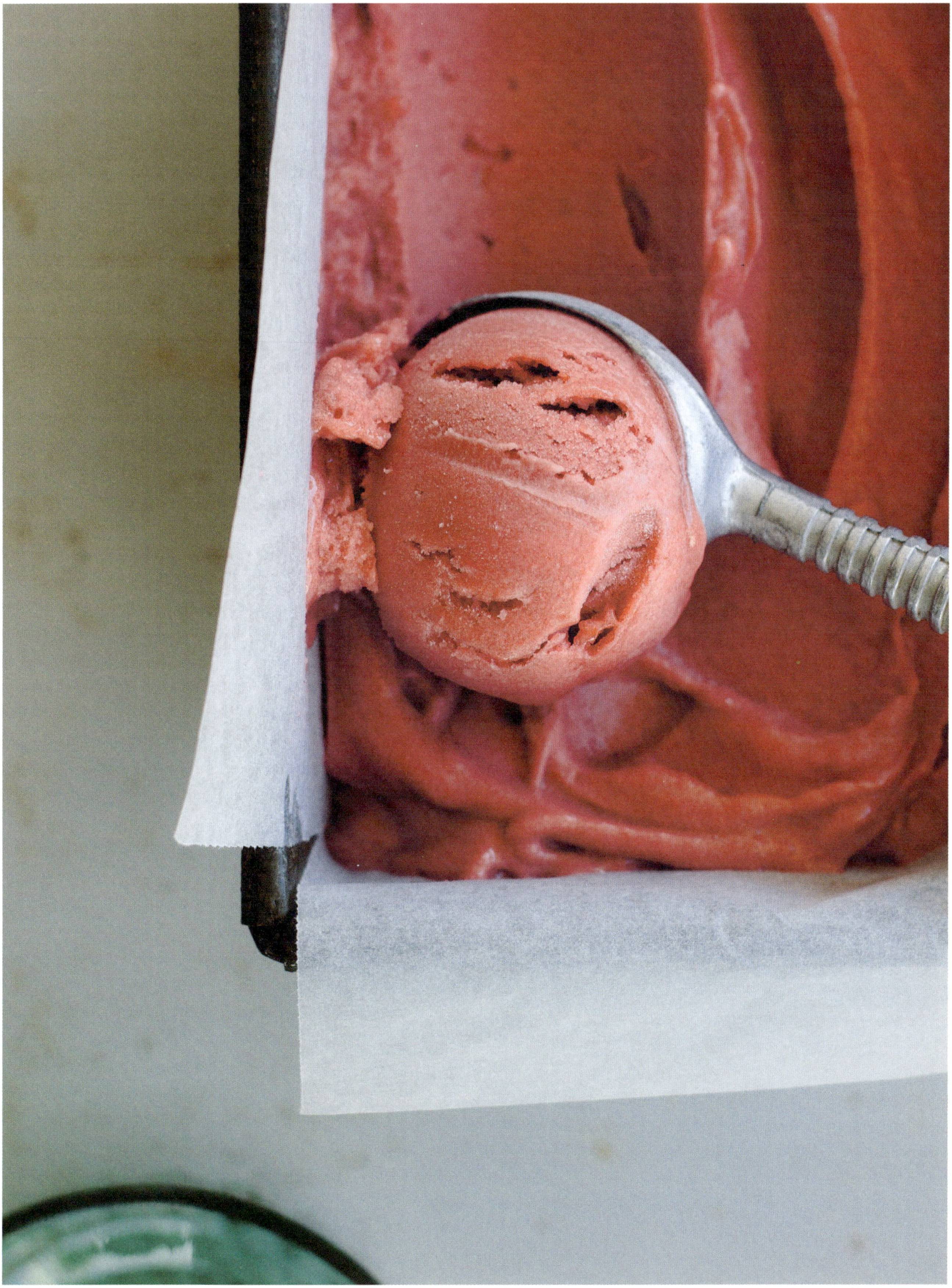

RHUBARB, STRAWBERRY + GINGER MUFFINS

MAKES 8 | GLUTEN-FREE | DAIRY-FREE

Strawberry, rhubarb and ginger pair perfectly in these tasty fruit-packed muffins. I like to go pretty heavy on the ginger front, but you can always leave the crystallised ginger out if you'd like a gentler ginger hit. This is a great base muffin recipe to sub in whatever seasonal fruit you have at hand. In summer I make a peach and passionfruit version, and in winter, pear and dark chocolate always goes down a treat.

- 75g (⅔ cup) ground almonds
- 70g (½ cup) fine brown rice flour
- 40g (¼ cup) potato flour
- Pinch of fine sea salt
- 2 teaspoons gluten-free baking powder
- 65g (⅓ cup) unrefined raw sugar
- Finely grated zest of 1 lemon
- 1 tablespoon finely grated ginger
- 1 tablespoon finely chopped crystallised ginger, optional
- 125ml (½ cup) coconut or almond milk
- 2 tablespoons virgin coconut or olive oil
- 1 large free-range egg
- 1 teaspoon vanilla extract
- 250g punnet strawberries, hulled + roughly chopped
- 1 cup thinly sliced rhubarb (from 2 stalks)

+ Preheat oven to 180ºC (350ºF). Line an 8-hole 80ml (⅓ cup) muffin tin with paper cases. Place ground almonds in a medium bowl and sift over rice flour, potato flour, salt and baking powder. Add sugar, zest, grated and crystallised ginger and whisk to combine. In another bowl combine milk, oil, egg and vanilla, whisking well.

+ Stir strawberries and rhubarb through dry ingredients, reserving a handful to put on top. Add wet ingredients and stir until just combined. Spoon into paper cases, top with a few slices of strawberry and rhubarb and cook for 30–35 minutes or until a skewer inserted in the centre of the muffins comes out clean. Remove from oven and set aside for 5 minutes before transferring to a wire rack to cool. Best eaten on the day of baking, however, any leftovers will store, airtight, for 2–3 days or can be frozen for up to 2 months.

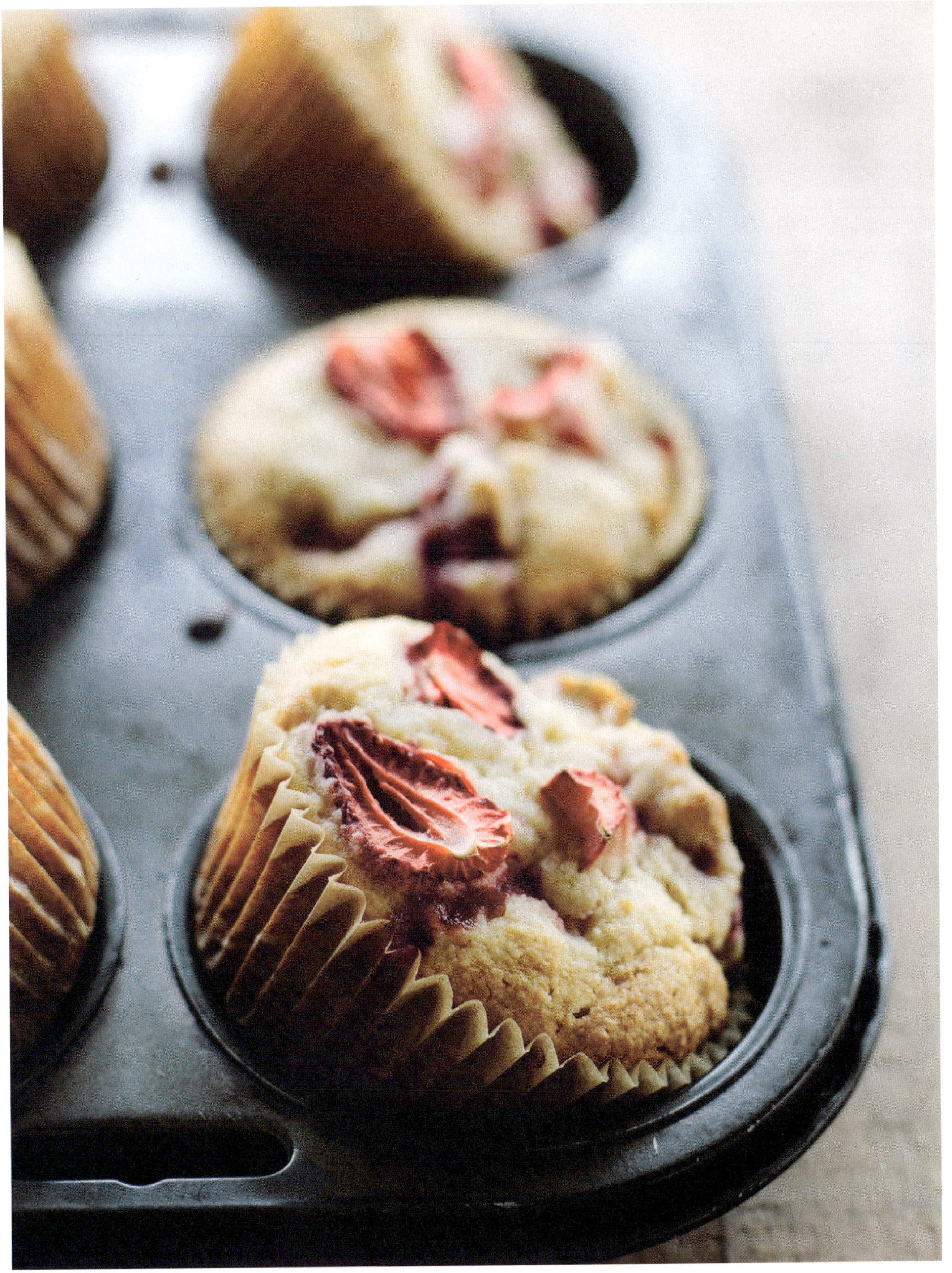

PINK GRAPEFRUIT + ROSEMARY POPSICLES

MAKES 6 | GLUTEN-FREE | VEGAN

I first shared this recipe on my site a few years back, and these popsicles have since become one of the most requested from my kids as the weather starts to warm up. They're sweet, sour and herbaceous all at once, and also mildly addictive! Regular grapefruit juice could be used, however, the resulting popsicles will be slightly sourer than those made using pink grapefruit juice.

- 185ml (1½ cups) freshly squeezed pink grapefruit juice (from 2 large grapefruit)
- 100g (½ cup) brown rice syrup or unrefined raw sugar
- 2 teaspoons roughly chopped rosemary leaves

+ Pour grapefruit juice into a large jug and set aside. Combine brown rice syrup or sugar, 60ml (¼ cup) water and rosemary in a small saucepan. Heat over medium heat, stirring until the sugar dissolves. Boil for 30 seconds, then remove from heat and set aside to infuse and cool for 30 minutes. Strain rosemary syrup over grapefruit juice, squeezing the rosemary with your hands to extract as much of its flavour as you can. Whisk to combine.

+ Pour into popsicle moulds, pop on the top and freeze overnight. Alternatively, if you are using wooden sticks, freeze the popsicles for 1 hour until partially frozen before inserting wooden sticks and returning to the freezer overnight.

+ Run moulds under warm water to help release the popsicles.

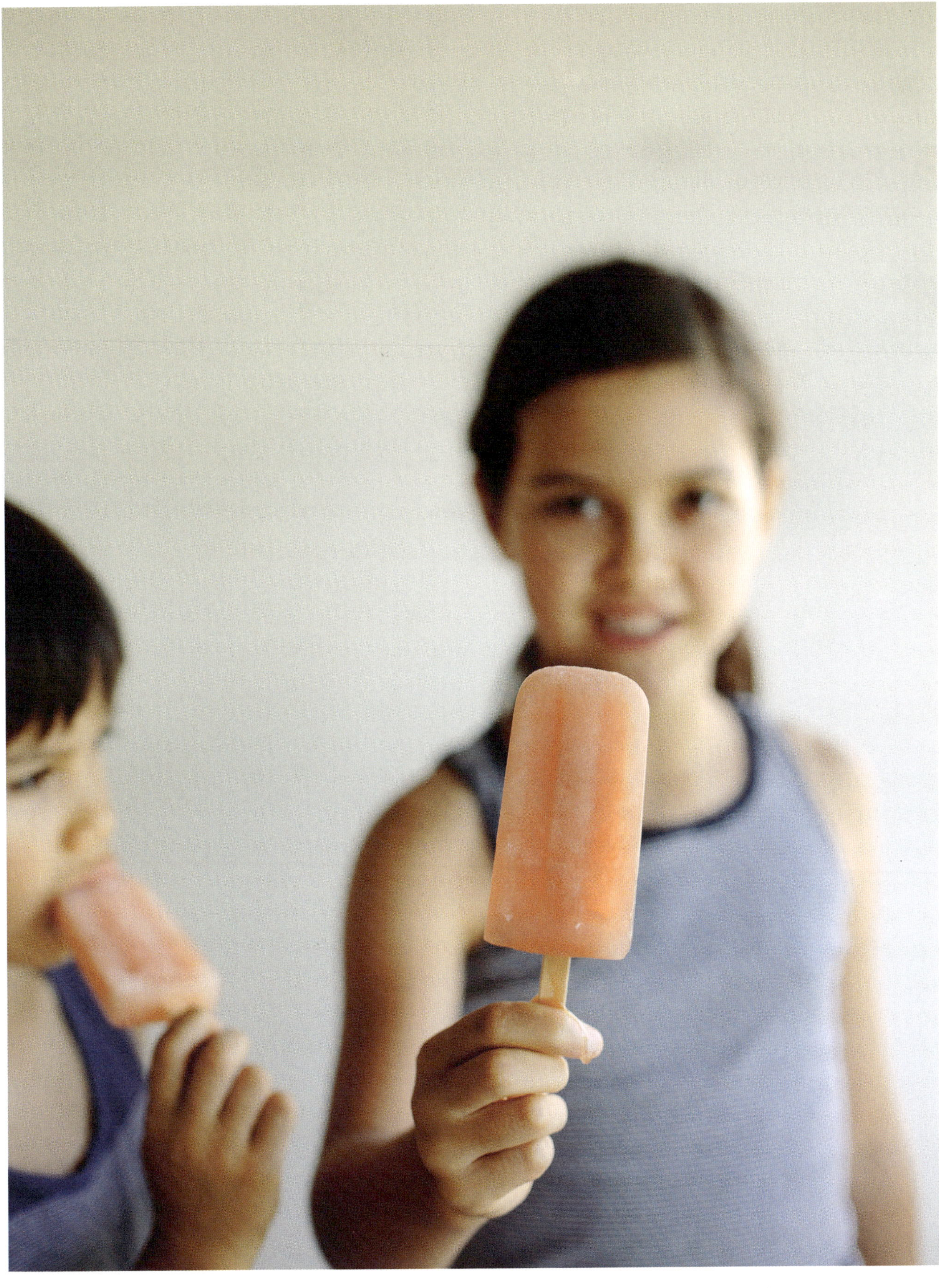

STRAWBERRY AVOCADO SHAKE

SERVES 3–4 | GLUTEN-FREE | VEGAN

We are a house of shake-loving humans. So much so that on a recent trip to Vietnam to visit my husband's family, getting our daily fix of icy fruit shake was the first priority every morning. I laughed at the sign saying 'no sugar' at the shake shop set up down a dingy alleyway; it only took a few minutes to see spoonfuls of white sugar and a generous drizzle of sweetened condensed milk going into the mix to know they'd got their marketing somewhat mixed up! When on holiday, who cares though, right? But at home we try to keep things as healthy as possible which is why I came up with this delicious combo. I use locally grown strawberries which I trim and freeze to give a lovely icy texture to the shake. However, you can use fresh strawberries and just add a handful of ice if preferred. Using homemade almond milk in a recipe as simple as this really makes a huge difference.

750ml (3 cups) almond milk (preferably homemade, see page 240)

approx. 2 x 250g punnets (3 cups) frozen strawberries + extra sliced ones, to serve

Flesh of 1 ripe avocado

2 tablespoons brown rice or pure maple syrup, or to taste

+ Place everything in your blender and blend until smooth. Serve immediately topped with extra slices of fresh strawberries, if you like.

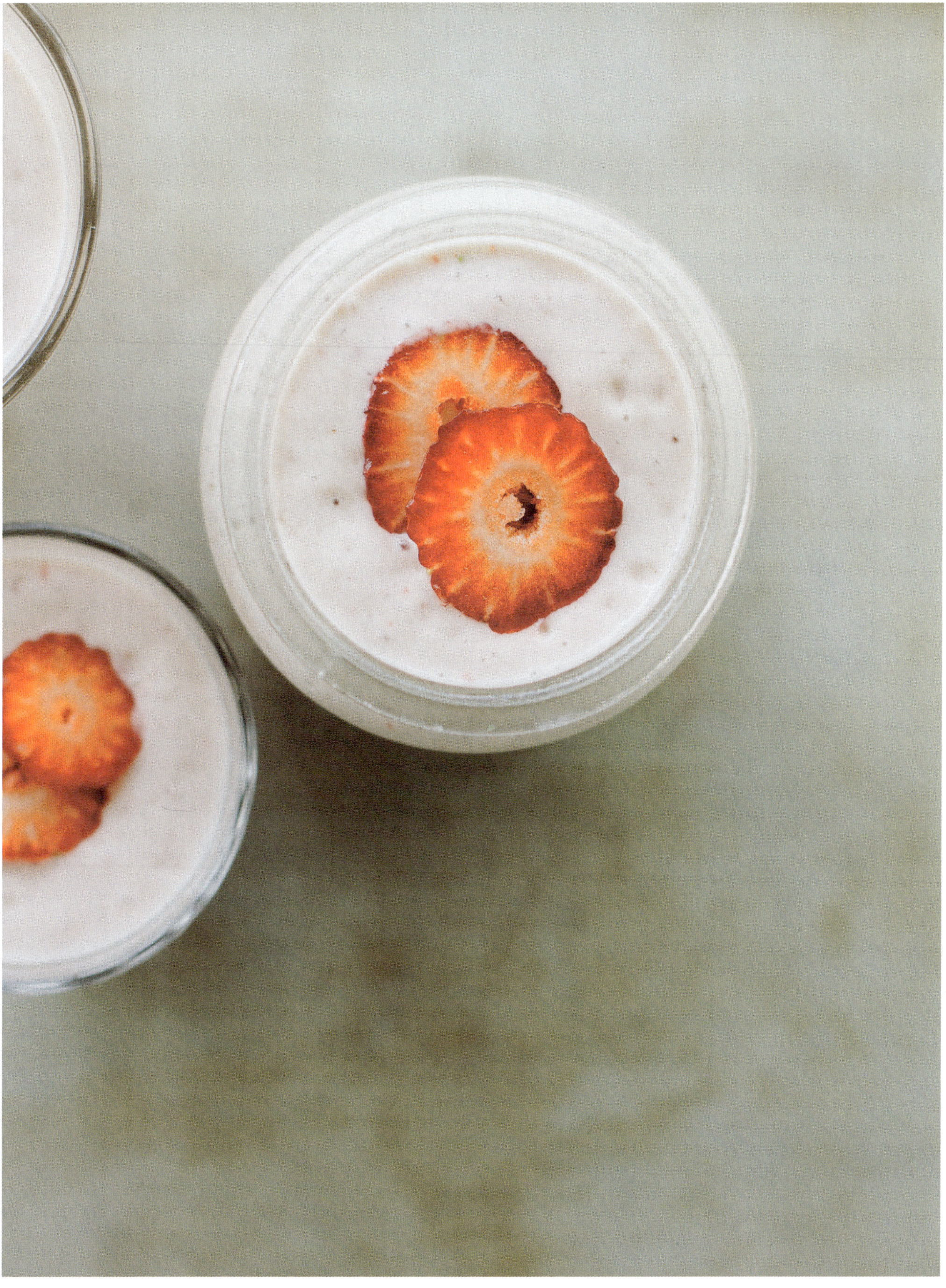

LITTLE RAW CARROT CAKES w/ WHIPPED ORANGE MAPLE CREAM

MAKES 6 | GLUTEN-FREE | VEGAN

Yes raw treats are so incredibly on trend, however, that's not why I love these little cakes. They're super-quick to make, use readily available ingredients and, believe it or not, they actually taste just like carrot cake! All the flavours you'd expect are there: carrot, walnut, cinnamon, ginger, orange, and the whipped coconut cream is a lovely, lighter alternative to traditional cream cheese icing. You'll need to start the recipe a day ahead to give the cakes time to firm up in the fridge and to chill the coconut milk. If you own a food processor then these take mere minutes to prepare.

- 2 medium carrots, peeled, ends trimmed + coarsely grated
- 140g (1 cup) walnuts, whole or pieces
- 45g (½ cup) shredded or desiccated coconut
- 1 cup pitted dried dates, soaked for 20 minutes in warm water + drained well
- 3 tablespoons virgin coconut oil, melted if solid
- 1 teaspoon ground cinnamon + extra to serve, optional
- ½ teaspoon ground ginger
- Finely grated zest of ½ orange (reserve the other half an orange as you'll need it for the cream)
- Pinch of fine sea salt

Orange maple cream
- 400ml tin good-quality coconut milk, refrigerated overnight (see NOTE)
- 1–2 tablespoons pure maple syrup
- Finely grated zest of ½ orange + extra to serve, optional
- Pinch of fine sea salt

Day 1

+ Line a 6-hole 80ml (⅓ cup) muffin tin with cling film. Place tin of coconut milk in the fridge overnight.

+ To make cake mixture, place all ingredients in a food processor and blend on high until everything is finely chopped and almost paste-like. I leave mine a little bit chunky for added texture. Alternatively, if you don't own a food processor, simply finely chop the grated carrot, walnuts and dates and mix them all together with the remaining ingredients, using your hands to almost mash the mixture together, forming a rough paste. Evenly divide mixture between each hole. Press firmly to pack it down, cover and refrigerate overnight.

Day 2

+ To make cream, carefully open tin of coconut milk, scoop off the thick cream that's settled on top and place it in a bowl, leaving behind the thin watery liquid at the bottom (this is great to add to porridge or smoothies, so don't waste it!) Use a whisk or electric beater to beat cream until thick and billowy. Add maple syrup, orange zest and salt, and whisk to combine.

+ Top cakes with a dollop of orange maple cream, a dusting of cinnamon and some extra orange zest, if you like and serve immediately. Un-iced cakes can be stored happily in the fridge, covered, for 4–5 days.

NOTE: Now, not all coconut milks will set hard in the fridge, which is what you're after when using it to whip. I always pick up the tins of coconut milk in the shop and give them a little shake, if you don't feel too much movement or hear much sloshing about then this is usually an indication that it's a good one to use.

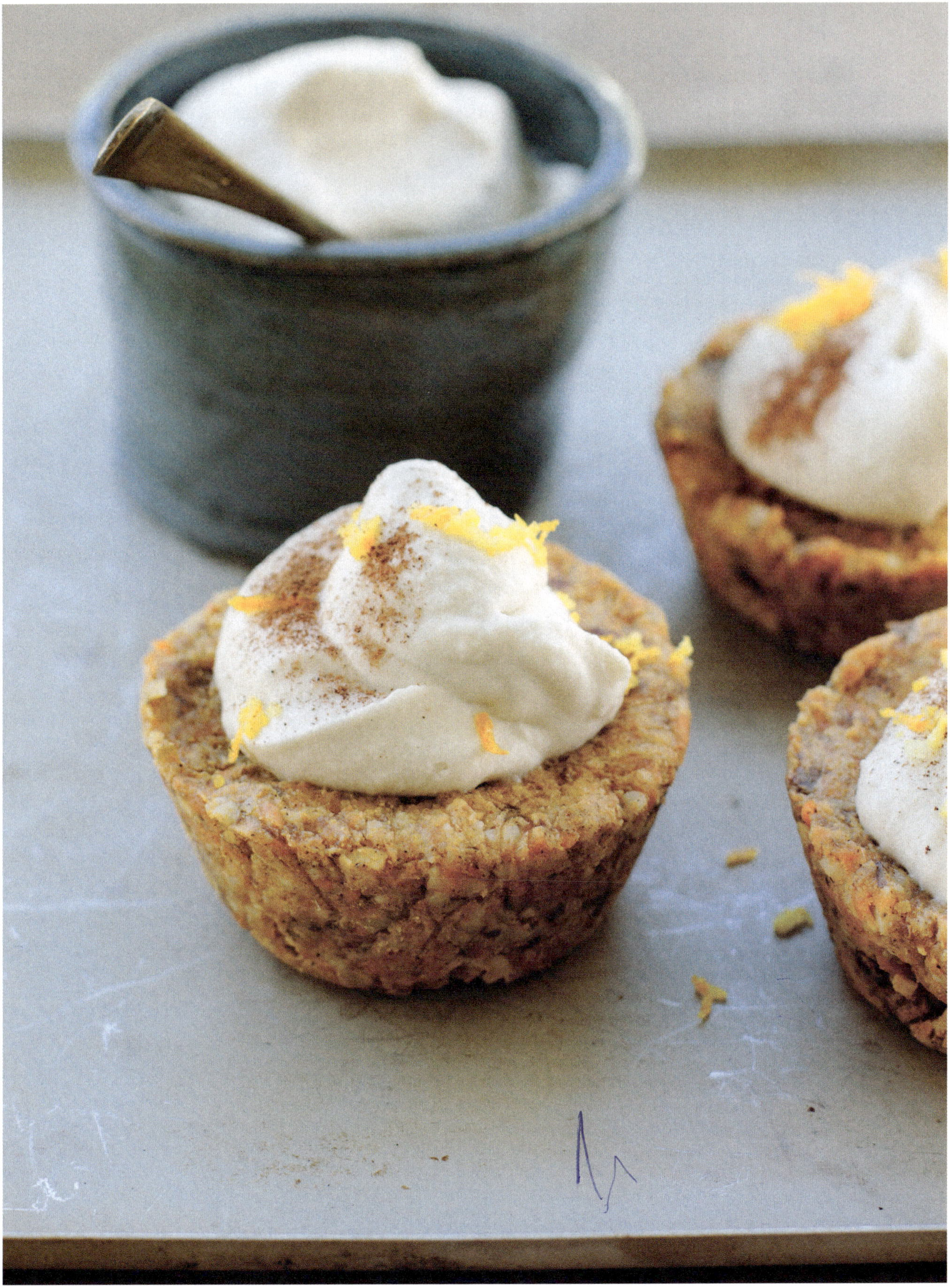

OLIVE OIL + CHOCOLATE CHUNK ICE CREAM

SERVES 3–4 | GLUTEN-FREE | DAIRY-FREE

If you're new to olive oil ice cream you're in for a lovely surprise! The texture olive oil gives to any ice cream, but more so dairy-free versions which can easily turn icy, is truly beautiful. Silky smooth, every-so-slightly grassy and flecked generously with chunks of dark chocolate, this is one treat which never lasts long in our house. I use a good-quality extra-virgin olive oil, but you can use a slightly mellower-flavoured one if preferred. You could try a lovely raw chocolate like Loving Earth's dark chocolate here, but feel free to use whichever dark dairy-free chocolate you can get your hands on. For a change I sometimes melt the chocolate, and drizzle it into the churn while it's still going to create random flecks of chocolate.

250ml (1 cup) almond milk (preferably homemade, see page 240)
250ml (1 cup) coconut milk
4 large free-range egg yolks
100g (½ cup) unrefined raw sugar
Good pinch of fine sea salt
60ml (¼ cup) extra-virgin olive oil
30g dark chocolate, roughly chopped

+ Combine almond and coconut milk in a medium saucepan over medium-high heat. Bring slowly up to just below boiling point, stirring occasionally to prevent milk from catching on the bottom.

+ In a large heatproof bowl, whisk egg yolks, sugar and salt until thick and pale. When the milk has nearly come up to boiling point, pour a little over the yolks while whisking constantly, then whisk in the rest. Pour the whole lot back into the pan, turn heat down to medium and return to heat. Cook, while stirring constantly with a wooden spoon, for 5–6 minutes or until mixture thickens and coats the back of your spoon.

+ Remove from heat and strain through a fine sieve set over a clean bowl. Whisk in olive oil in a steady stream, then set aside until cool, stirring occasionally to prevent a skin forming on the surface (see NOTE). When the mixture is cool, cover and place in the fridge to chill for a few hours or overnight. If you've used an ice bath, it should be good to churn right away.

+ Churn the ice cream for 20–25 minutes until nearly frozen, stir through chopped chocolate and transfer to a lidded container. Freeze for a further 2–3 hours until set to your liking. This ice cream will keep for 4–5 days in the freezer. Leave out on the bench for 10–15 minutes to soften before eating if it's too hard.

+ If you don't own an ice cream churn, simply place custard mixture in a shallow dish (a loaf tin is perfect) and freeze for 1 hour, until the edges are starting to freeze. Beat with an electric beater or whisk, return to the freezer and repeat a further 2–3 times before stirring through roughly chopped chocolate and returning to the freezer for 2 hours. This won't give the exact same results as a churn would, but it still tastes delicious nonetheless.

NOTE: To speed up the cooling process of the custard you can place the bowl of custard into another larger bowl filled with ice and stir until cold.

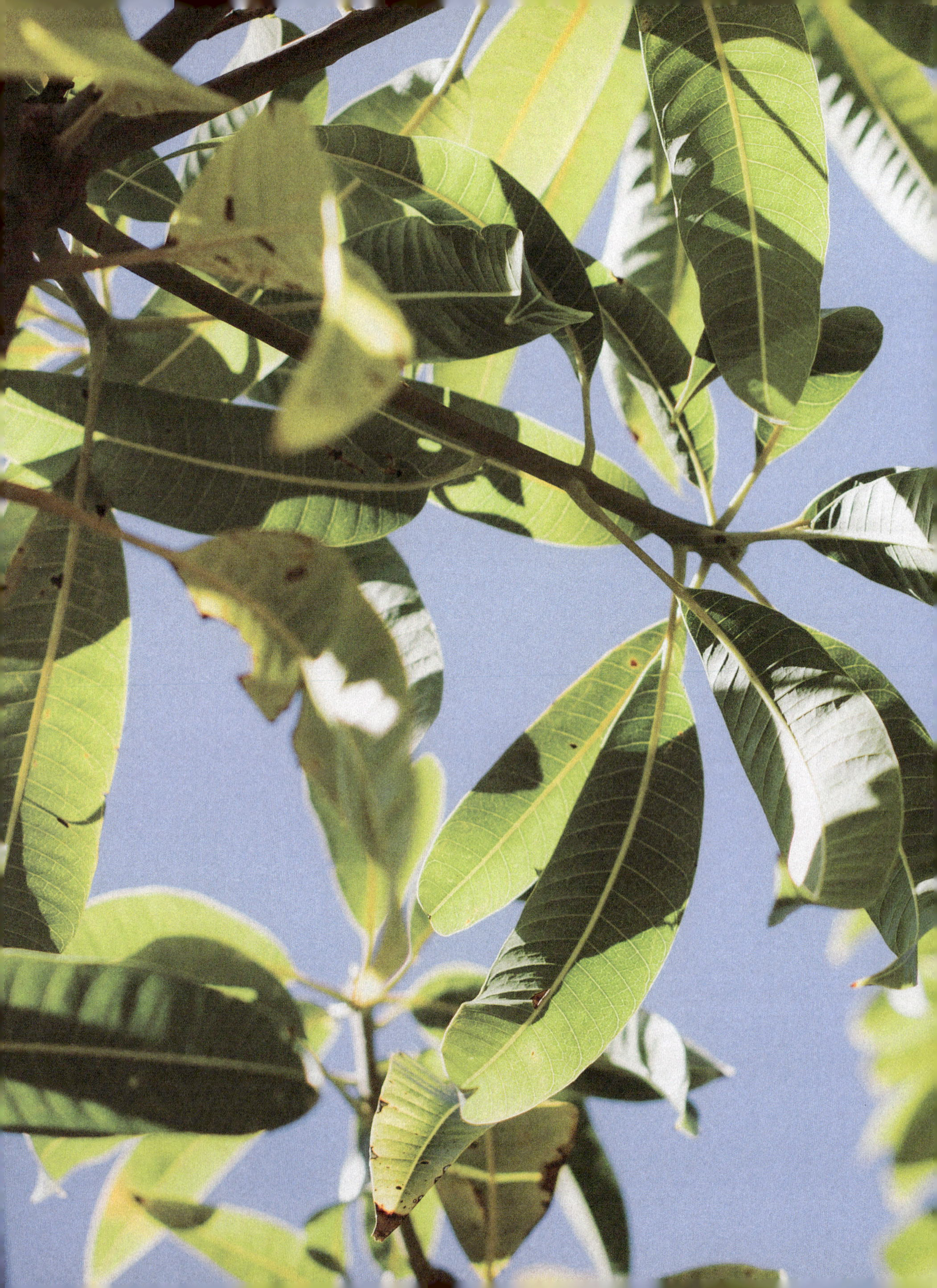

SUMMER

sweetcorn + green beans + courgette/zucchini + radish + apricot + cucumber + chilli + peach + new potato + tomato + snow pea + lettuce + eggplant + celery + cherry + carrot + capsicum + plum + grapes + pineapple + mango + avocado + banana + blackberries + blueberries + boysenberries + strawberries + raspberries + watermelon + honeydew + currants + lychee + nectarine + passionfruit + butter beans + beetroot + eggplant + leek + lettuce + daikon + sugar-snap peas + silverbeet + squash + rambutan + watercress + rockmelon + okra

ZA'ATAR ROASTED CARROT + CHICKPEAS W/ PICKLED CHILLI, RADISH + YOGHURT

SERVES 4 AS A STARTER OR MORE AS PART OF A MEAL – ALTHOUGH TO BE HONEST, I COULD EAT THIS WHOLE SERVE SOLO... | GLUTEN-FREE

If you have a large overgrown thyme plant in your backyard, you can dry your own really easily to use in the za'atar (see NOTE). I dry fresh thyme periodically to keep my plant from running wild, but also because I prefer the vibrant flavour you get from home dried over store-bought. In spring and summer my parsley is usually going to seed, so I make the most of the little flowers and use them to garnish dishes such as this. Regular carrots can be used if baby ones are not available.

- 135g (¾ cup) dried chickpeas, soaked overnight in cold water, or 400g tin cooked chickpeas, rinsed, or 1½ cups cooked chickpeas
- 1 bunch (approx. 10) baby carrots, ends trimmed + sliced into 1cm rounds
- 2 tablespoons extra-virgin olive oil
- 6–8 small radishes, finely sliced (use a mandolin if you have one)
- 1 pickled chilli (page 180), finely sliced or chopped
- Natural plain yoghurt, to serve
- Fresh herbs or flowers, to serve, optional

Za'atar
- 1 tablespoon dried thyme
- 1 teaspoon sumac
- ¼ teaspoon flaky sea salt, lightly crushed
- 2 teaspoons lightly toasted sesame seeds (page 238)

+ Drain and rinse chickpeas, put in a saucepan and cover with cold water. Bring to the boil, skimming off any foam that rises to the surface. Reduce to a simmer and cook for 25–35 minutes or until tender but not falling apart. Drain well and allow to steam dry while you preheat oven to 200ºC (400ºF).

+ To make za'atar, pound thyme in a mortar and pestle until finely ground, stir through sumac, salt and sesame seeds.

+ Place carrots on a large oven tray, along with drained chickpeas, sprinkle over 1 tablespoon za'atar (reserving the rest to sprinkle over later), olive oil and season well with fine sea salt and freshly ground black pepper. Mix, then roast for 25–30 minutes, giving it all a good stir a couple of times during cooking, until carrots are tender and golden and some chickpeas have crisped up (it doesn't matter if some still remain soft). Remove from oven.

+ To plate up, divide carrot and chickpea mixture between bowls, scatter with sliced radishes, sliced pickled chilli, dollop a few spoons of yoghurt on each plate, dust with reserved za'atar, scatter over fresh herbs or flowers, and serve.

NOTE: To dry your own thyme just snip off a handful of stems, tie together and hang them upside down in an airy spot for about a week to dry naturally. Alternatively you can lay the stems out on a tray and bake in a 150ºC (300ºF) oven for around 10 minutes, or until the leaves are dry and crumbly, before cooling and stripping the leaves from the stalks. Or if it's a particularly hot and dry day, you can also dry them out in the sun.

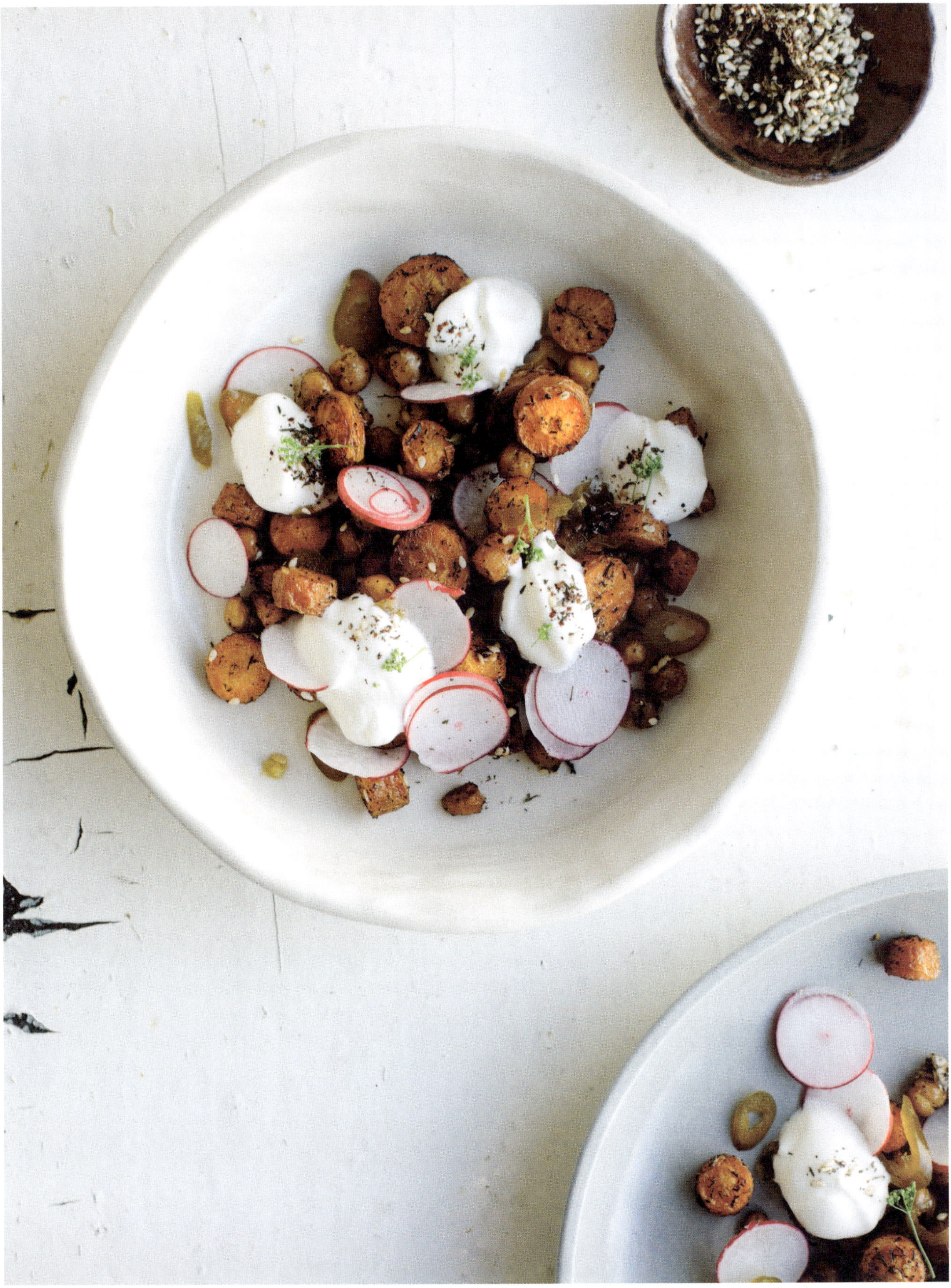

PICKLED CHILLIES

MAKES 1 LARGE JAR | GLUTEN-FREE | VEGAN

Pickling chillies is a great way to make use of a bumper crop, or to simply stockpile some of summer's bounty for later in the year when fresh chillies can be hard to come by (unless you freeze them! See my tip on page 184). It's also the main reason I grow jalapeños! They are the best chillies to pickle if you have them, but the more common long green variety also work great too. I prefer to use green chillies, but you can use red or yellow, however, just note that they don't hold their bold colour once pickled. I often slice up pickled chillies to add to tacos, pizza and egg dishes, and they're also lovely finely diced and added to dressings (page 20, Roasted kumara salad) or to add a little excitement to dishes such as the Za'atar roasted carrot and chickpeas (page 178).

250g (approx. 10–12) whole green chillies
375ml (1½ cups) water
375ml (1½ cups) apple cider vinegar
2 tablespoons unrefined raw sugar
2 tablespoons fine sea salt
2 fresh or dried bay leaves
1 tablespoon whole coriander seeds
1 tablespoon whole black peppercorns
2 cloves garlic, peeled

+ Prick each chilli about 5–8 times with a sharp knife and pack into a sterilised 1 litre glass jar (see NOTE, page 22). Combine remaining ingredients in a saucepan and bring to the boil. Reduce heat and simmer for 5 minutes. Pour hot liquid over chillies, screw on lid and cool. Store in a cool, dark place for at least 1 week before using. They'll keep in the pantry unopened, or in the fridge for approx. 4–6 months once opened.

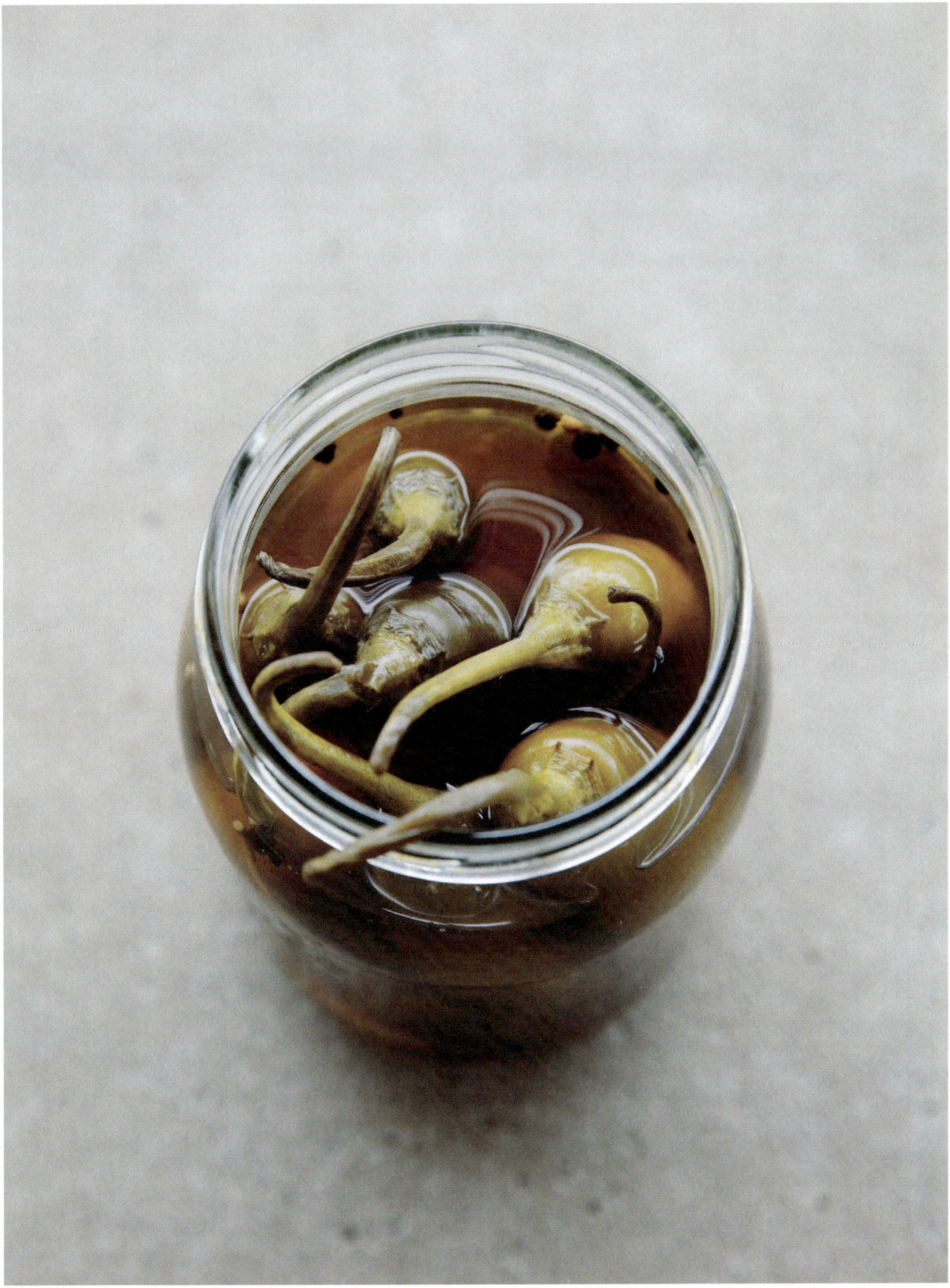

ZUCCHINI, FETA + MINT FRITTERS

MAKES AROUND 16 MEDIUM FRITTERS | GLUTEN-FREE | DAIRY-FREE OPTION

I remember absolutely falling in love with an eggy zucchini slice my Granddad made. When I asked him how he'd made it, he shared an important little zucchini tip, which I still use today. After grating the zucchini it's important to get as much moisture out of it as possible otherwise your fritters (or in Granddad's case, his slice) will end up soggy (see NOTE). To make this recipe dairy-free, simply omit the feta. If you can't eat corn, replace the cornflour with arrowroot.

3 cups grated zucchini (from approx. 3 small zucchini)
55g (½ cup) chickpea (chana or besan) flour
2 tablespoons gluten-free organic cornflour (starch)
1 teaspoon gluten-free baking powder
2 large free-range eggs
Finely grated zest of 1 small lemon
½ cup loosely packed mint, roughly chopped
50g feta cheese, crumbled
Extra-virgin olive oil, to shallow-fry
Lemon wedges, to serve, optional

+ Squeeze out as much liquid as you can from grated zucchini (see NOTE).

+ Sift chickpea flour, cornflour and baking powder into a medium bowl. Whisk 60ml (¼ cup) cold water and eggs together in a small bowl, then add to flours, mixing to form a smooth batter. Add lemon zest, chopped mint, crumbled feta and grated zucchini. Season with a little fine sea salt and freshly ground black pepper, then mix to combine.

+ Heat a heavy-based frying pan over medium-high heat. Add a little olive oil to cover the base of the pan. Spoon heaped tablespoonfuls of mixture into the pan, without over-crowding. Cook for approx. 2 minutes until lightly golden brown on the base, then flip over and continue to cook for a further few minutes until cooked through. Remove from pan and place on a plate lined with paper towels. Repeat with remaining fritter mixture. Serve immediately with a squeeze of fresh lemon juice.

NOTE: I find the easiest way to get the excess moisture out of your zucchini is to place it all into a clean tea towel, wrap it up and squeeze as hard as you can until the dripping stops.

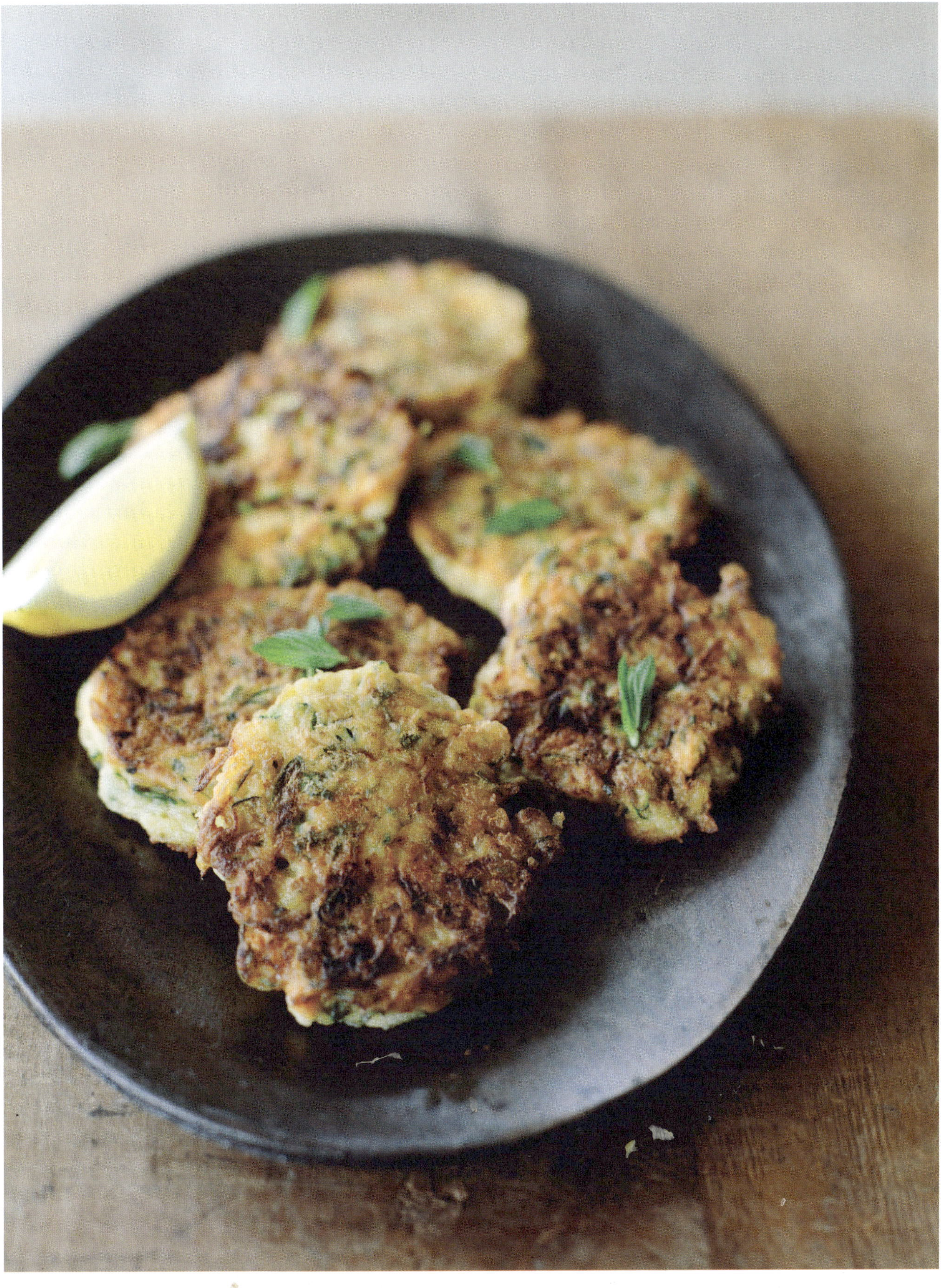

SRIRACHA

MAKES 250ML | GLUTEN-FREE | VEGAN

I'm a total chilli freak and for as long as I can remember I've loved adding a little heat to my meals. Back when I was younger it was usually in the form of sweet chilli sauce, but as I got older and more brave I started growing my own plants and progressed to using fresh chillies in everything. Anyone who grows their own will know how many just one little plant can produce (which always makes me question why they are so expensive to buy from the store?!) So to preserve my haul for later use I long ago adopted my chilli-fiend mother-in-law's way of storing them, by simply popping them into zip-lock bags and freezing. They can be used straight from frozen and at the end of summer our freezer is chocka block with bags of chillies of every kind.

A few years back I also started making my own raw, fermented sriracha and now I've always got a bottle or two in the fridge to appease my chilli-loving tendencies. Use mild chillies, don't be tempted to use a hotter variety such as bird's-eye, unless you want to blow your head off.

---

15 (approx. 300g) long red chillies, stems removed + roughly chopped
2 cloves garlic
2 tablespoons unrefined raw sugar
1½ teaspoons fine sea salt
60ml (¼ cup) apple cider vinegar

+ Place chillies in a small food processor, along with garlic, sugar, salt and 2 tablespoons water and blend until a fine paste forms. Transfer mixture to a clean glass jar, screw lid on loosely and leave in a warm place out of direct sunlight for 3–5 days (Three if you live somewhere hot, 5 if your climate is cooler). After 3–5 days you will notice little pockets of air in the mixture, this is what you are after.

+ Transfer mixture to a blender along with vinegar, and blend to a smooth paste. Pass through a sieve set over a bowl, and do your best to extract as much of the liquid as you can using the back of a metal spoon. Discard solids collected in the sieve and pour the chilli sauce into a sterilised glass jar (see NOTE, page 22). Refrigerate and use within a few months.

+ I really like the consistency of this raw, but you can also reduce the sauce by simmering in a saucepan approx. 8–10 minutes or until the desired consistency is achieved (but just know that some of the good enzymes you have created during fermentation will be destroyed).

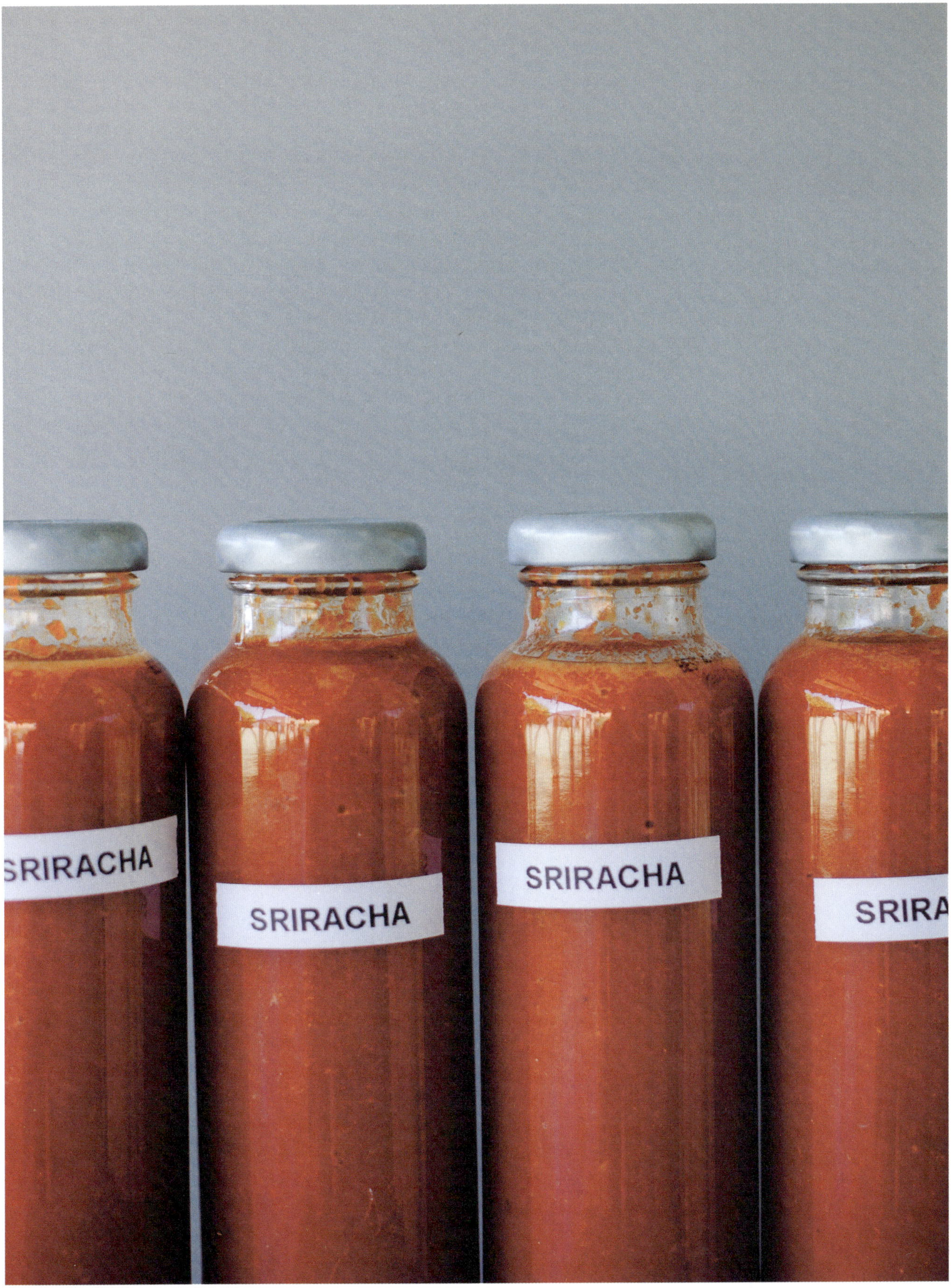
SRIRACHA
SRIRACHA
SRIRACHA

SWEETCORN SOUP W/ ROASTED CHERRY TOMATOES + CRISPY TORTILLAS

SERVES 3–4 | GLUTEN-FREE | VEGAN

It was summer's produce that I looked forward to the most from my parent's vegetable garden, with freshly picked sweetcorn right at the top of the list. Straight from the plant, the flesh is so tender and juicy that we kids would just sit down in the middle of the rows and dig right in. I still to this day love eating raw corn and am often found picking the few outer rows off each cob before cooking – I just can't help myself! But as much as I love corn raw, I also love it cooked and this soup is a celebration of the simple beauty of summer produce. The little additions of sweet roasted tomatoes and crispy tortillas provide texture, but also a boost of colour and flavour, however, I'm more than happy to have a mug full of sweetcorn soup on its own too.

250g punnet cherry tomatoes, sliced in half
Extra-virgin olive oil, to drizzle
Handful of oregano leaves (or a sprinkling of dried)
3 tablespoons extra-virgin olive oil
1 large onion, finely diced
1 celery stalk, finely diced
½ teaspoon ground cumin
5 cloves garlic, crushed
3 corn cobs, kernels shaved off + cobs reserved
1 fresh or dried bay leaf
2 white corn tortillas homemade (page 204) or store-bought
Extra-virgin olive oil, for cooking

+ Preheat oven to 180ºC (350ºF). Lay tomatoes on an oven tray in a single layer. Drizzle with olive oil, season well with fine sea salt and freshly ground black pepper and scatter with oregano. Roast for 25–30 minutes, or until tender and semi-dried. Remove from oven and set aside.

+ To make soup, heat olive oil in a large saucepan over medium-high heat. Add onion and celery and cook for 5 minutes until golden and tender. Add cumin, garlic and corn kernels and cook for a further 2–3 minutes. Add 1 litre (4 cups) cold water, reserved corn cobs, bay leaf and a generous pinch or two of fine sea salt. Cover with a lid and bring to the boil. Reduce to a simmer, leaving lid ajar, and cook for 20–25 minutes.

+ While soup is cooking, finely shred tortillas with a sharp knife or kitchen scissors. Heat enough olive oil to just cover the base of a small frying pan and cook shredded tortillas, stirring often until golden and crispy. Remove from pan and transfer to a paper-towel-lined plate. Sprinkle with fine sea salt.

+ Remove soup from heat, compost corn cobs and bay leaf, and purée soup in a blender until smooth and creamy. Adjust seasoning if needed. Serve soup topped with a good spoonful of roasted tomatoes and a handful of crispy tortillas.

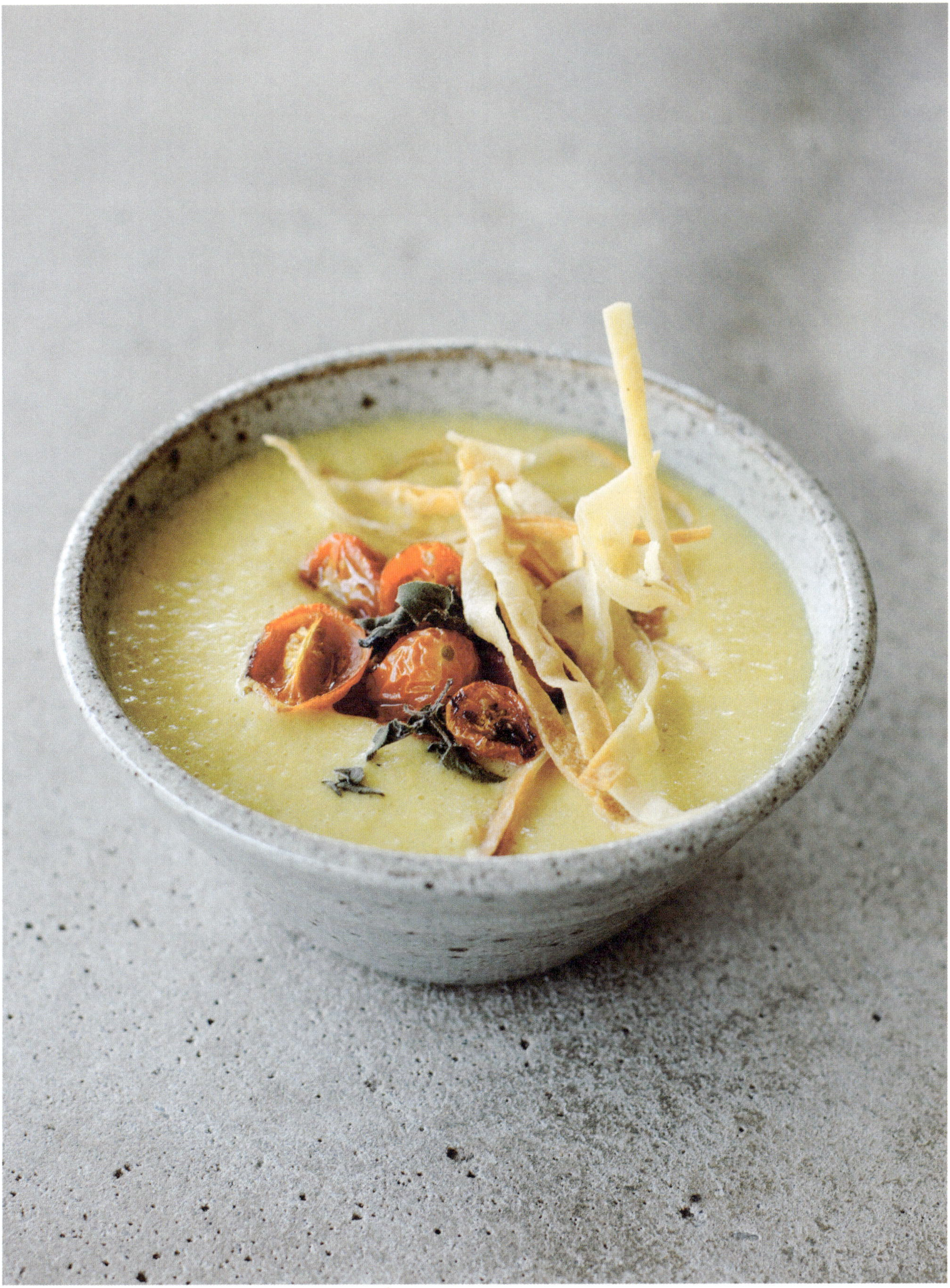

SPICY TOFU NOODLES

SERVES 4 | GLUTEN-FREE | VEGAN

Loosely based on the Burmese spicy chicken noodle dish shan khaut swe, this somewhat strange combination of ingredients has found a loyal following among the readers of my blog. You can find fermented tofu at your local Asian grocer in small jars, often with added chilli. It stores indefinitely in the fridge once opened and adds a beautiful depth of flavour to vegetarian Asian dishes in place of shrimp paste or fish sauce. If you're hardcore like my mother-in-law, you can also just eat it as is, with rice.

- 3 tablespoons olive or peanut oil
- 1 onion, finely diced
- 4 cloves garlic, finely chopped
- 2 teaspoons finely grated ginger
- 3 large tomatoes, finely chopped
- 2 tablespoons tomato paste
- ½ teaspoon ground turmeric
- ½–1 teaspoon chilli powder
- 300g firm tofu, crumbled into small bite-sized pieces
- 3 tablespoons gluten-free soy sauce or tamari
- 1 tablespoon fermented tofu
- 1 teaspoon unrefined raw sugar
- 400g packet rice noodles, cooked according to packet instructions
- Chopped roasted peanuts + finely sliced spring onion, to serve

+ Heat oil in a large frying pan over medium-high heat. Add onion, garlic and ginger and cook for 2–3 minutes, stirring, until tender and golden. Add tomatoes, tomato paste, turmeric and chilli, then stir well. Cook for 2–3 minutes or until tomatoes start to break down, add 125ml (½ cup) water and continue to cook for 10 minutes. Stir in tofu, soy sauce, fermented tofu and sugar. Add another 60–125ml (¼–½ cup) water if the mixture is looking a tad dry and season well with fine sea salt. Cook for a further 5 minutes, stirring well to dissolve the fermented tofu throughout the dish.

+ Serve tofu hot or at room temperature, over cooked rice noodles and scatter with peanuts and sliced spring onions. Any leftovers are just as good cold.

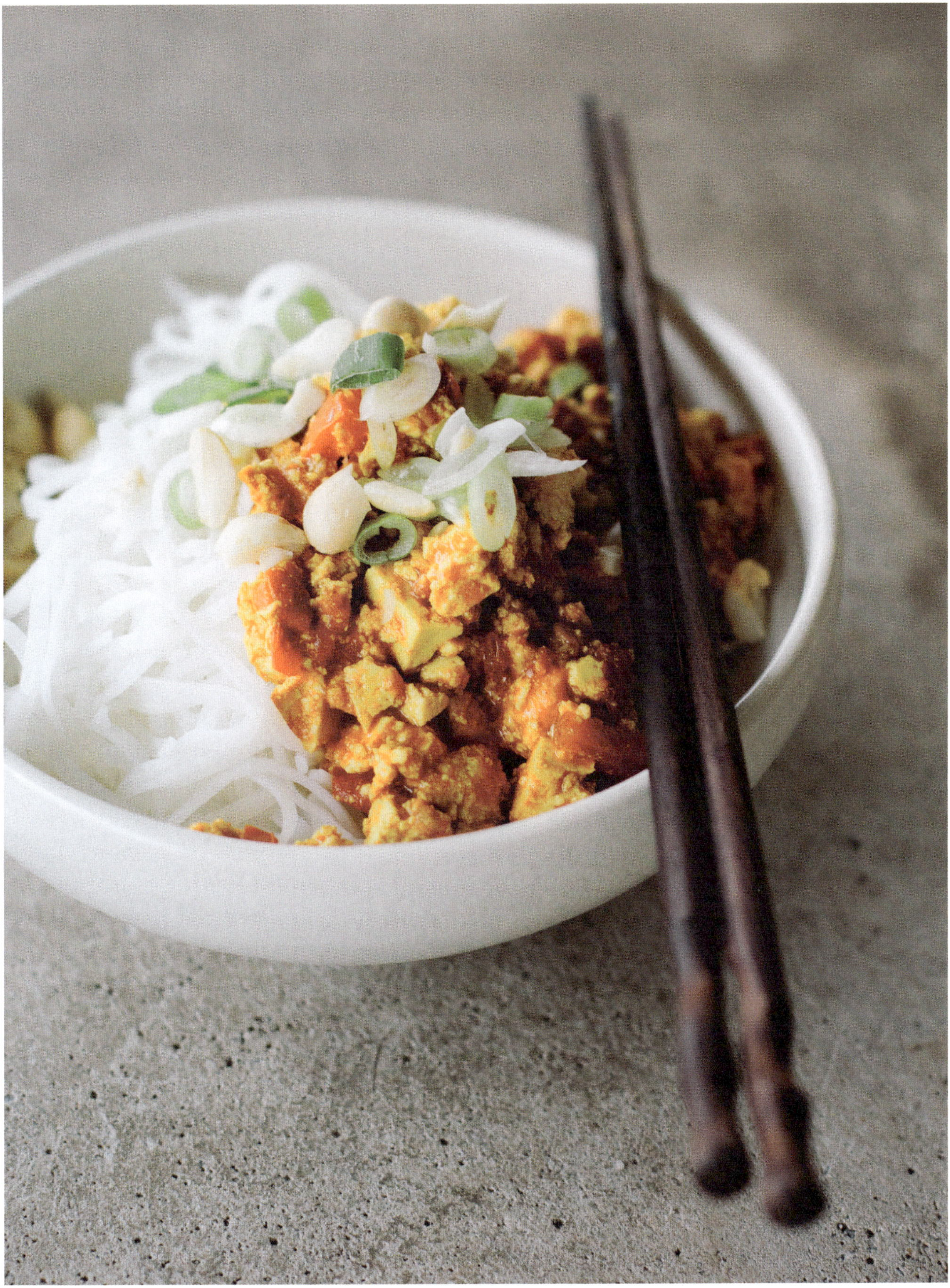

POTATO SALAD W/ THYME + MUSTARD RED WINE VINAIGRETTE

SERVES 6–8 AS PART OF A MEAL | GLUTEN-FREE | DAIRY-FREE | VEGAN OPTION

This recipe was inspired by a simple potato salad we served at a café where I used to work in the years before having kids. Liz and Rick, good friends of just about everyone in Raglan, grow the most amazing heirloom Maori potatoes, in shades of pink and purple. And it was these beauties that we'd boil and dress simply with a thyme and mustard red wine vinaigrette. During my first pregnancy, while still working in the kitchen, it was this mustard-heavy potato salad that I craved the most. Nowadays I love to add lightly cooked beans, radishes and boiled eggs to make things a little more substantial, but if you don't eat eggs, simply leave them out.

800g new season baby potatoes, scrubbed clean

Handful of mint leaves

Few good pinches of fine sea salt

250g (2 big handfuls) green beans, ends trimmed

6–8 small radishes, finely sliced (with a mandolin if you have one)

A handful of dill or flat-leaf parsley leaves, roughly torn

Boiled eggs, to serve, optional

Thyme + mustard red wine vinaigrette

1 tablespoon extra-virgin olive oil

¼ medium onion, finely diced

1 clove garlic, crushed

2 teaspoons finely chopped thyme

3 teaspoons honey or brown rice syrup

1 teaspoon Dijon mustard

3 tablespoons red wine vinegar

90ml (6 tablespoons) extra-virgin olive oil

2 tablespoons wholegrain mustard

+ Place potatoes and mint in a large saucepan, cover with cold water and add salt. Cover with a lid, bring to the boil, reduce heat and simmer for 15–20 minutes or until tender (this time will vary depending on the size and freshness of your spuds, so check after 10 minutes).

+ Bring another saucepan of water to the boil and cook beans for 2–3 minutes until just tender. Drain and plunge into a bowlful of cold or iced water to stop them from cooking further. Drain well and cut in half on a slight diagonal. Set aside.

+ To make dressing, heat 1 tablespoon olive oil in a small frying pan over medium-high heat, sauté onion for 3–4 minutes until golden and tender. Add garlic and thyme and cook for a further 2–3 minutes. Remove from heat and transfer to a small food processor, along with honey or brown rice syrup, Dijon mustard and red wine vinegar. Blend on high for 1 minute, then add olive oil in a steady stream with the motor still running and blend until a smooth-ish dressing forms. Stir through wholegrain mustard and season well with fine sea salt and freshly ground black pepper.

+ Drain potatoes, leave whole if they are small enough to eat in 1–2 mouthfuls, otherwise cut in half. Place in a large bowl along with enough dressing to generously coat the potatoes (any leftover dressing will store in a glass jar for 1 week). Set salad aside to cool for 20–30 minutes before stirring through green beans, radish and chopped dill or parsley, adding a touch more dressing if desired. Serve with boiled eggs.

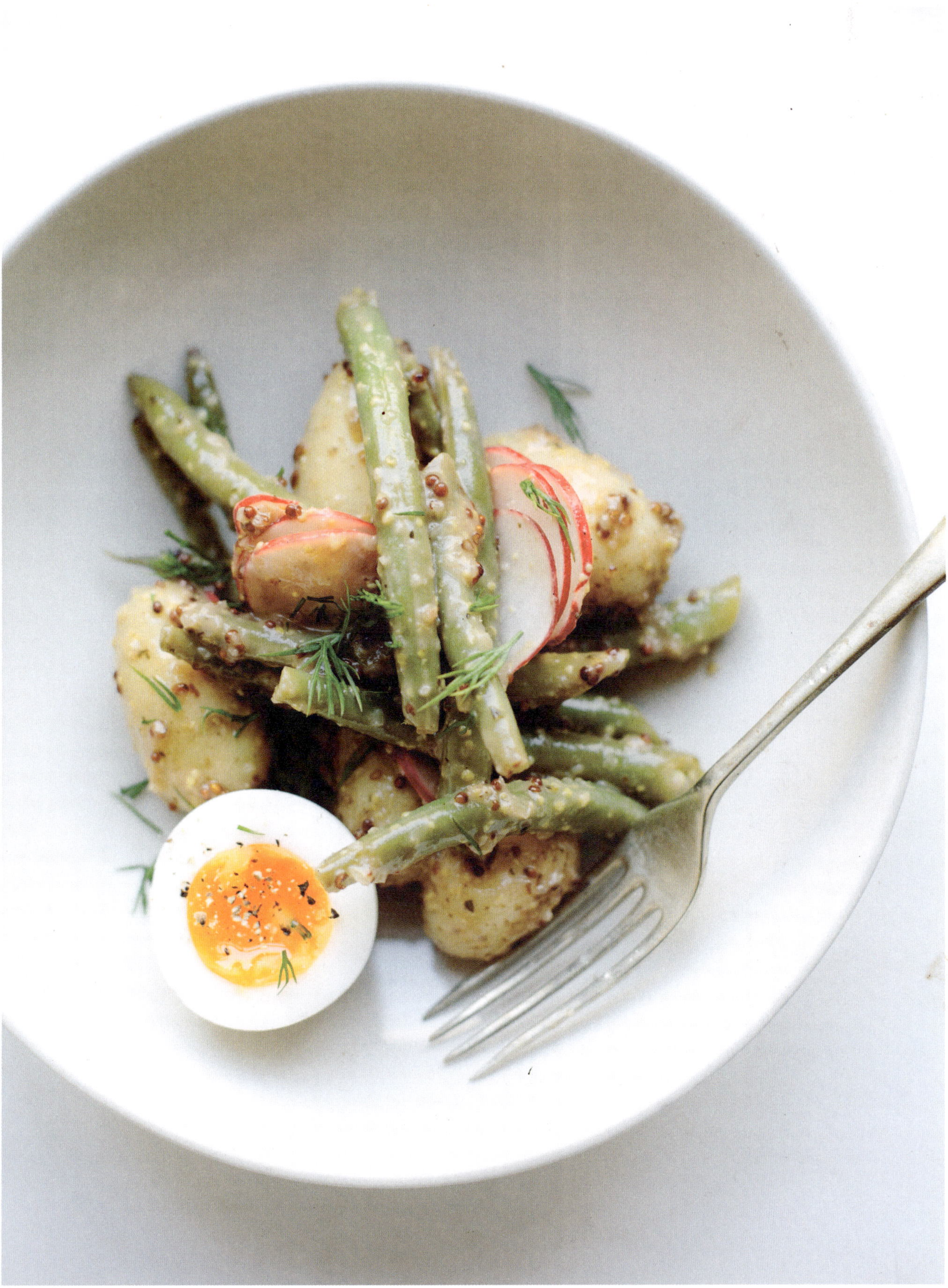

CHARRED CORN + RED RICE SALAD

SERVES 4 OR MORE AS PART OF A MEAL | GLUTEN-FREE | VEGAN OPTION

Charring corn produces a really great texture – almost chewy – as most of the water content gets evaporated. Red rice is a beautiful nutty rice native to Thailand, Bhutan, Tibet and Southern India which is thankfully becoming more and more readily available at supermarkets and health food stores. It has a lovely chewy texture and nutritional profile similar to that of brown rice, but its deep-red antioxidant-rich colour is what makes it truly special. For a vegan option, omit the feta.

- 185g (1 cup) red rice (see NOTE)
- 1 tablespoon extra-virgin olive oil
- 2 cobs corn, kernels shaved off with a sharp knife
- 2 cloves garlic, finely chopped
- 2 spring onions, finely chopped
- Crumbled feta cheese + lime wedges, to serve, optional

Coriander dressing
- 1 cup roughly chopped coriander leaves + tender stems (from 1 small bunch)
- 1 teaspoon cumin seeds, lightly toasted + roughly ground
- 1 long green chilli, deseeded (leave a few seeds in if you like heat)
- Juice of 2 limes
- 3–4 tablespoons extra-virgin olive oil
- ½ teaspoon fine sea salt

+ Rinse rice well, then place in the bowl of a rice cooker, along with 500ml (2 cups) water and cook according to the manufacturer's instructions. Alternatively, place rinsed rice in a saucepan, add water and bring to the boil. Reduce heat to lowest setting, cover with a lid and simmer for 35 minutes. Remove from heat and stand, covered, for a further 10 minutes before fluffing up with a fork. Set aside to cool to room temperature.

+ Heat olive oil in a large heavy-based frying pan over medium-high heat. Add corn kernels and cook, stirring often, for a good 10 minutes, until slightly charred in places. You will find that after about 5 minutes the corn will start to splatter and pop. Take care and if you have a splatter screen I suggest you use it, or a lid, to prevent the kernels from exploding in your face! When corn is looking charred and somewhat dry, add garlic and cook for a further 30 seconds before removing from heat. Set aside.

+ To make dressing, combine all ingredients in a small food processor and blend on high until coriander and chilli are finely chopped.

+ Combine cooled rice with charred corn, spring onions and about half the dressing. Mix well and add a little more dressing if desired. If preparing ahead of time, reserve leftover dressing to stir through right before serving (the rice will absorb a lot of the dressing over time). Scatter with feta and serve with lime wedges, if using. Any leftover dressing will store in the fridge for 1–2 days.

NOTE: When cooking rice, I usually rinse it, combine with the stated amount of water, cover and leave to soak overnight on the bench, and then cook it the next day. Unlike most other grains, there's no need to change the water before cooking. Soaking makes the rice easier to digest, however, it's not an absolute must if you are in a hurry or forget.

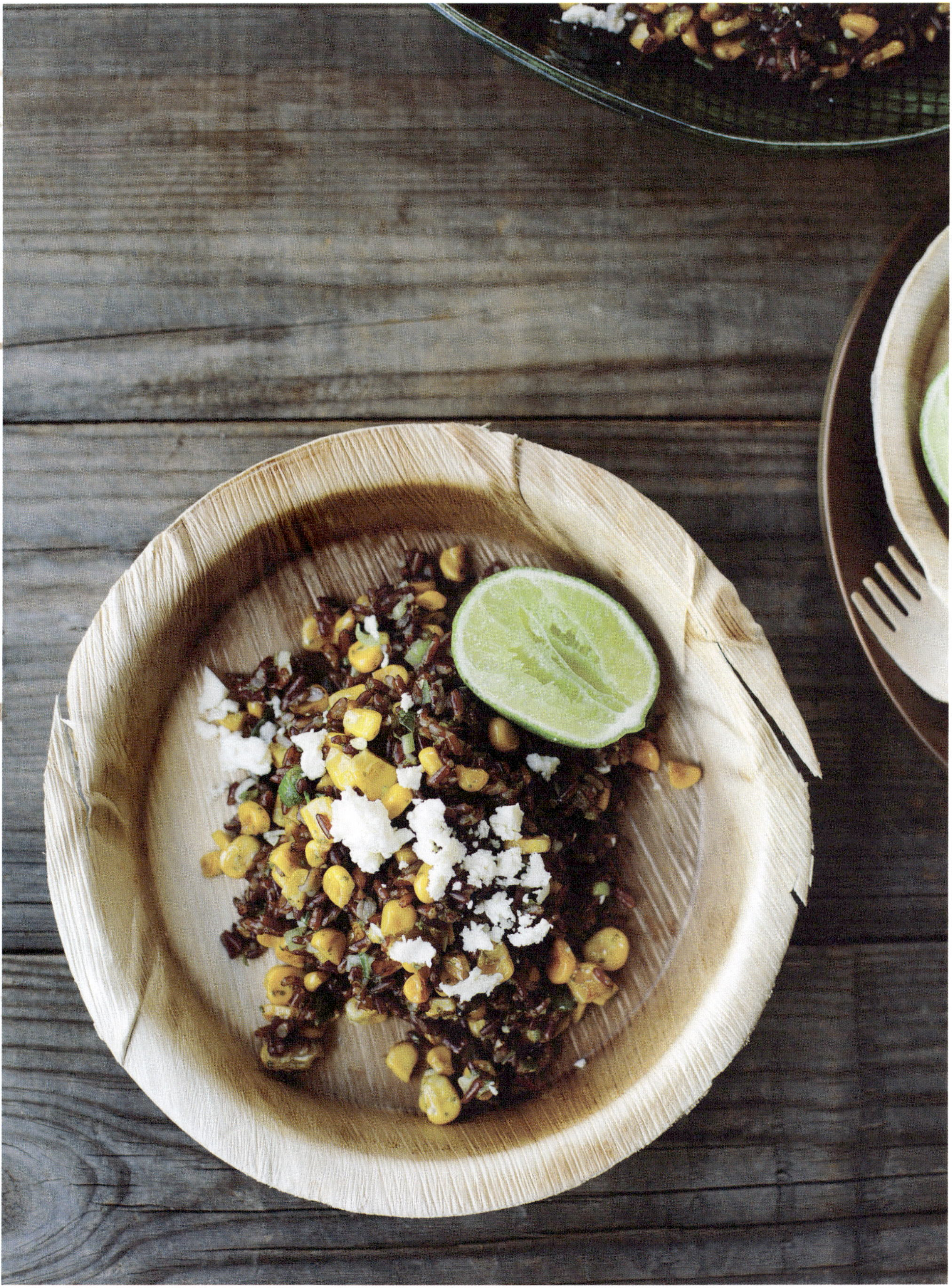

BLACK PEPPER TOFU w/ CUCUMBER PICKLE

SERVES 4 | GLUTEN-FREE | VEGAN

During our last trip to Vietnam a few years back, I fell in love with a black pepper tofu dish served at a little restaurant in Saigon. It came to the table in a piping-hot cast-iron dish, straight from the oven. The tofu pieces, rich with soy sauce and black pepper, were surrounded by stems of fresh green peppercorns, which popped in your mouth like a little firecracker of heat and flavour. As soon as we got home I started playing around with the ingredients, taming the black pepper just a tad so my kids would eat this dish as well. The hum of black pepper is most definitely the star and the reason why I love this dish so much, but should you be a little less tolerant of heat, I suggest you start with 1 teaspoon of black pepper and go from there. The quick little cucumber pickle not only looks great on the plate, but adds some refreshing relief from all that pepper. I love the texture you get from dusting the tofu in potato flour, but gluten-free cornflour can be used in place.

- 150ml apple cider or rice vinegar
- 75g (⅓ cup) unrefined raw sugar
- 1½ teaspoons fine sea salt
- 1 large telegraph cucumber
- 300g firm tofu, patted dry + cut into 1cm dice
- 1 tablespoon potato flour
- 2–3 tablespoons virgin coconut oil or extra-virgin olive oil
- 2 shallots (or 1 medium onion), thinly sliced
- 4 cloves garlic, finely chopped
- 2 teaspoons coarsely ground black peppercorns
- 2 tablespoons gluten-free soy sauce
- 1 teaspoon pure maple syrup or unrefined raw sugar
- 1 spring onion, finely sliced
- Steamed jasmine rice, to serve

+ To make cucumber pickle, combine vinegar, 300ml water, sugar and salt in a medium saucepan. Bring to the boil, stirring to dissolve sugar. Boil uncovered for 5 minutes, then remove from heat and set aside until cold. Trim ends of cucumber and slice into 10cm lengths. Finely shred using a mandolin or use a sharp knife to julienne, avoiding the very seedy bit in the centre (eat this!). Once pickling liquor is cool, pour over cucumber and set aside while you prepare the rest of the meal. While this pickle can be eaten immediately, the flavours are much better if made in advance. It will store in a glass jar in the fridge for up to 3 days.

+ Heat a large frying pan over medium-high heat. Combine tofu pieces with potato flour and mix well with your hands to evenly coat each piece. Add 2 tablespoons of the oil to the pan and fry tofu for a good 8–10 minutes, allowing each side to go golden and crisp. You may find you need to cook the tofu in batches if you have a smaller pan. Transfer tofu to a paper-towel-lined plate, add a touch more oil to the pan and sauté shallots for 1–2 minutes until tender and golden. Add garlic and pepper, and tofu back to the pan. Stir everything well to combine and cook for a further 1–2 minutes. Add soy sauce and maple syrup or sugar, then stir well. Remove from heat and stir through sliced spring onions. Serve tofu over steamed jasmine rice with a bowl of cucumber pickle for people to help themselves.

NOTE: If you eat all of the cucumber pickle in one go, save the pickling liquor, add some more finely sliced cucumber and store it in the fridge for up to 3 days. It's great added to salads, sandwiches or any kind of stir-fry.

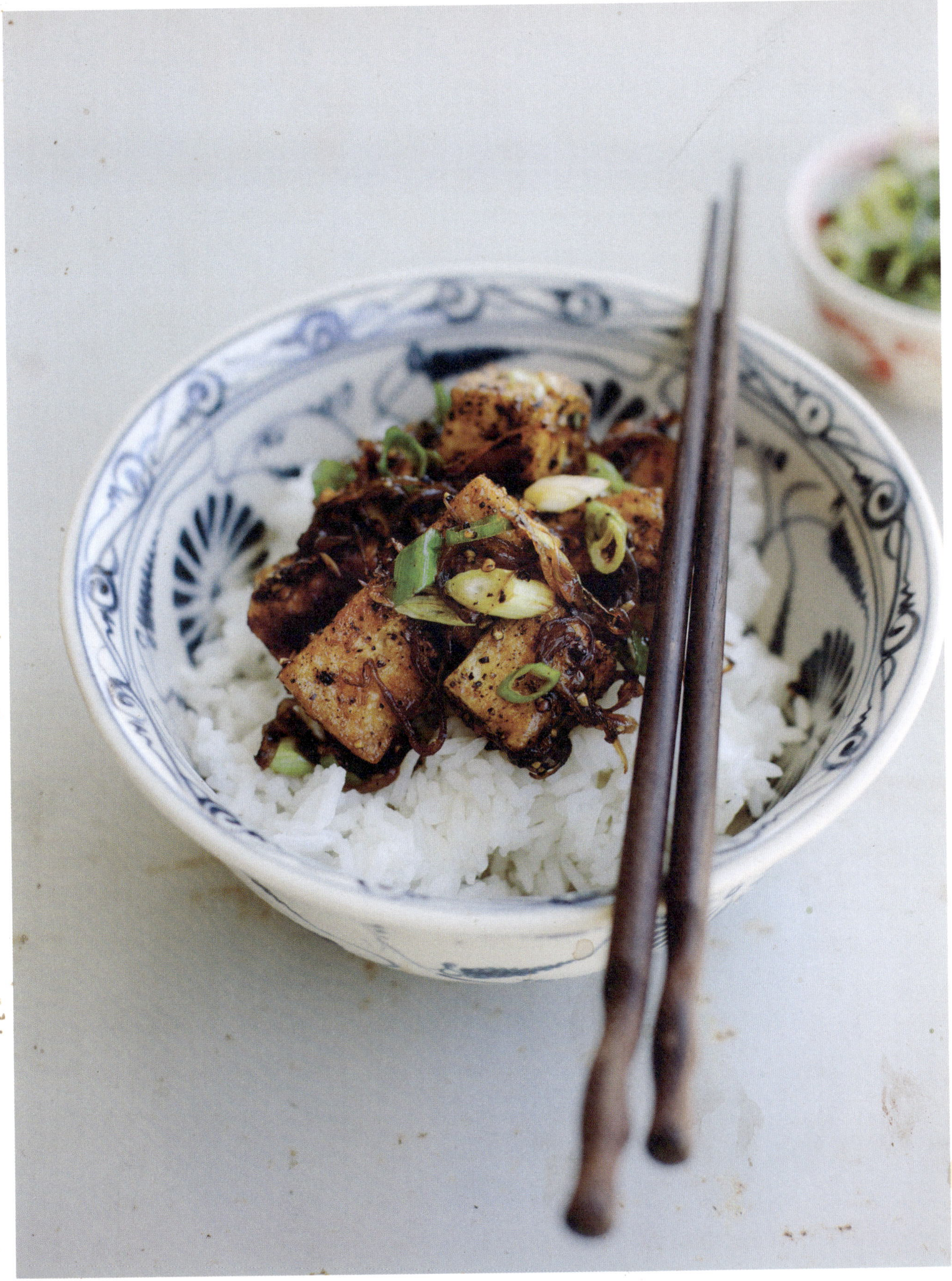

TOMATO + CHICKPEA SALAD W/ GREEN OLIVE DRESSING

SERVES 4 OR MORE AS PART OF A MEAL | GLUTEN-FREE | VEGAN OPTION

This simple salad is the one you want to make in the height of summer, when sun-kissed tomatoes in varying shapes, colours and sizes are abundant and beautiful. Whenever I eat tomatoes and chives together I'm reminded of the sandwiches my mum would always make us in the summer holidays, using just picked still-warm-from-the-sun homegrown tomatoes and freshly snipped chives. Fresh marjoram or oregano can be used in place of basil, or simply add a few more chives. When buying whole green olives, just make sure that they don't contain any food colouring, as I've noticed a few sneaky brands do. Allow time for overnight soaking, if using dried chickpeas. For a vegan option, use raw sugar in the dressing, not honey.

- 135g (¾ cup) dried chickpeas, soaked overnight in cold water, or 400g tin cooked chickpeas, rinsed, or 1½ cups cooked chickpeas
- 800g mixed tomatoes, chopped into bite-sized pieces or kept whole if small
- 2 tablespoons finely chopped chives
- Small handful of basil leaves, finely chopped

Green olive dressing

- 160g (1 cup) whole green olives
- 1 teaspoon Dijon mustard
- 1 teaspoon honey or unrefined raw sugar
- 3 tablespoons apple cider vinegar
- 4 tablespoons extra-virgin olive oil

+ Drain and rinse chickpeas, put in a saucepan and cover with cold water. Bring to the boil, skimming off any foam that rises to the surface. Reduce to a simmer and cook for 25–35 minutes or until tender but not falling apart. Drain well and set aside to cool to room temperature before using.

+ Place tomatoes, chickpeas, chives and basil in a large bowl.

+ To make dressing, cut flesh from the green olives using a small knife, compost pips, and finely chop olives. Place mustard and honey or sugar in a medium bowl, whisk to combine before adding in vinegar and whisking well. Continue to whisk while drizzling olive oil in a steady stream to form a lovely emulsified dressing. Stir through chopped olives and season with fine sea salt and freshly ground black pepper. Stir dressing through tomatoes and chickpeas, taste and adjust seasoning if needed. Serve immediately.

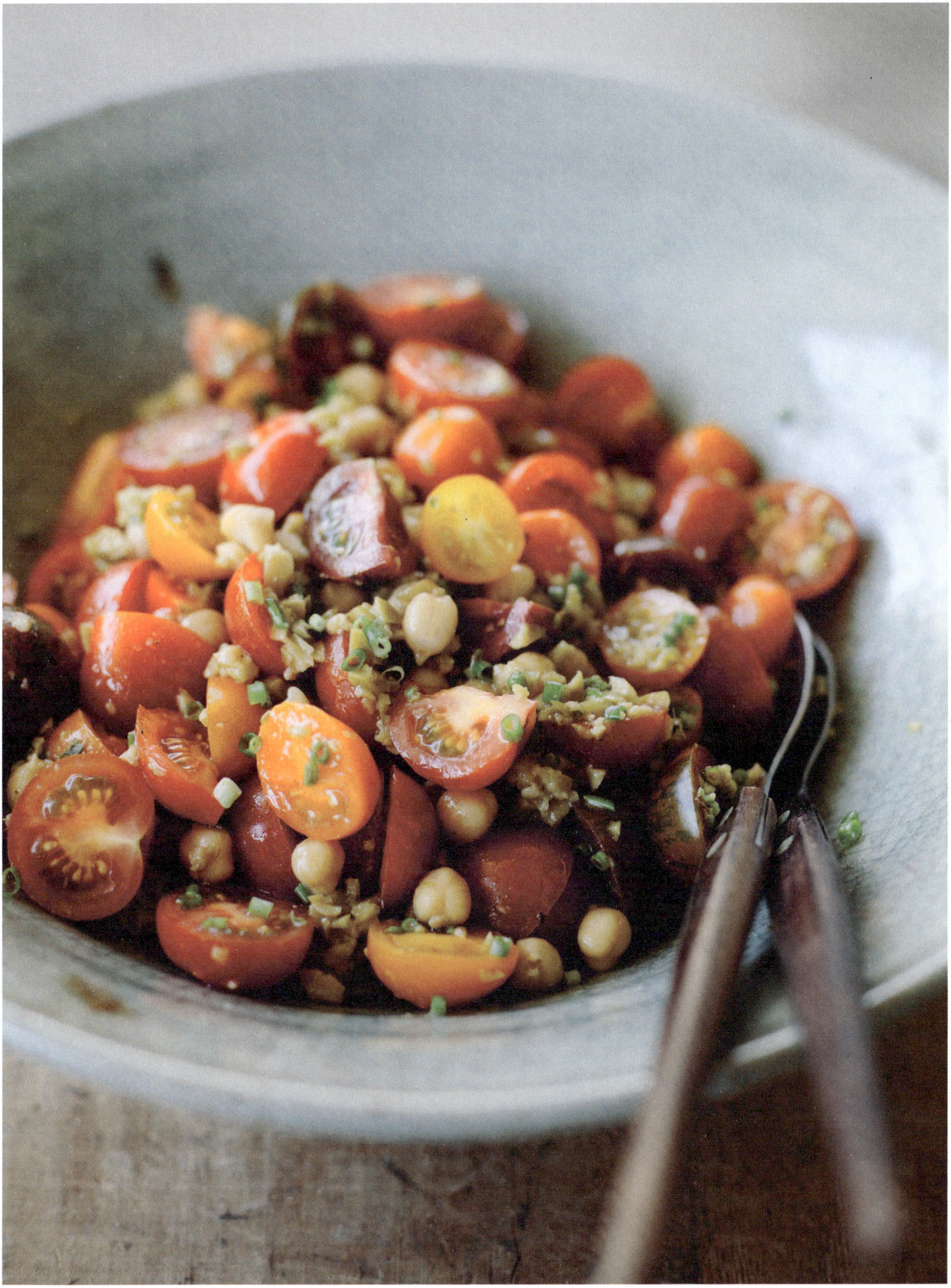

GRILLED HALOUMI W/ ROASTED GRAPE DRESSING

SERVES 4 AS AN ENTRÉE OR AS PART OF A MEAL | GLUTEN-FREE

I'm a huge fan of roasting, well, everything! But one of my all-time favourite things to roast would have to be grapes. While they roast they release their sticky sweet juices which meld with the olive oil to produce the perfect dressing for the teeth-squeaking pieces of golden grilled haloumi. This dish often doesn't even make its way out of our kitchen, as my daughter and I stand at the bench stuffing our faces the moment it's cooked. Of course, it's always nice to sit down when you eat, but make sure you have the dressing all prepared before grilling the haloumi, so you can eat it while still hot from the pan.

- 2 tablespoons natural sultanas or raisins, roughly chopped
- 1 tablespoon red wine vinegar
- 300g (approx. 2 cups) red seedless grapes
- 4 tablespoons extra-virgin olive oil
- 1 tablespoon finely chopped thyme
- 180g packet haloumi, sliced into 1cm pieces (aim for around 12 slices)

+ Preheat oven to 180ºC (350ºF). Combine chopped sultanas and vinegar in a medium bowl (big enough to contain the grapes once roasted) and set aside for 20–30 minutes. Place grapes in a 2 litre ovenproof dish or lipped oven tray, drizzle with 2 tablespoons of the olive oil, scatter over thyme, and season well with fine sea salt and freshly ground black pepper. Roast for 20–25 minutes or until grapes are tender and have released some of their juices. Remove from oven and pour grapes and their juices over soaked sultanas. Mix well to combine, taste and adjust seasoning.

+ Heat remaining 2 tablespoons of olive oil in a large frying pan over medium-high heat and pan-fry haloumi slices until golden on both sides. Transfer three slices to each plate, top with a generous spoonful or two of the roasted grape dressing and serve immediately.

NOTE: If you find yourself with an abundance of grapes, another lovely way to enjoy them is frozen. Eaten straight from the freezer they're like nature's little sorbet bombs!

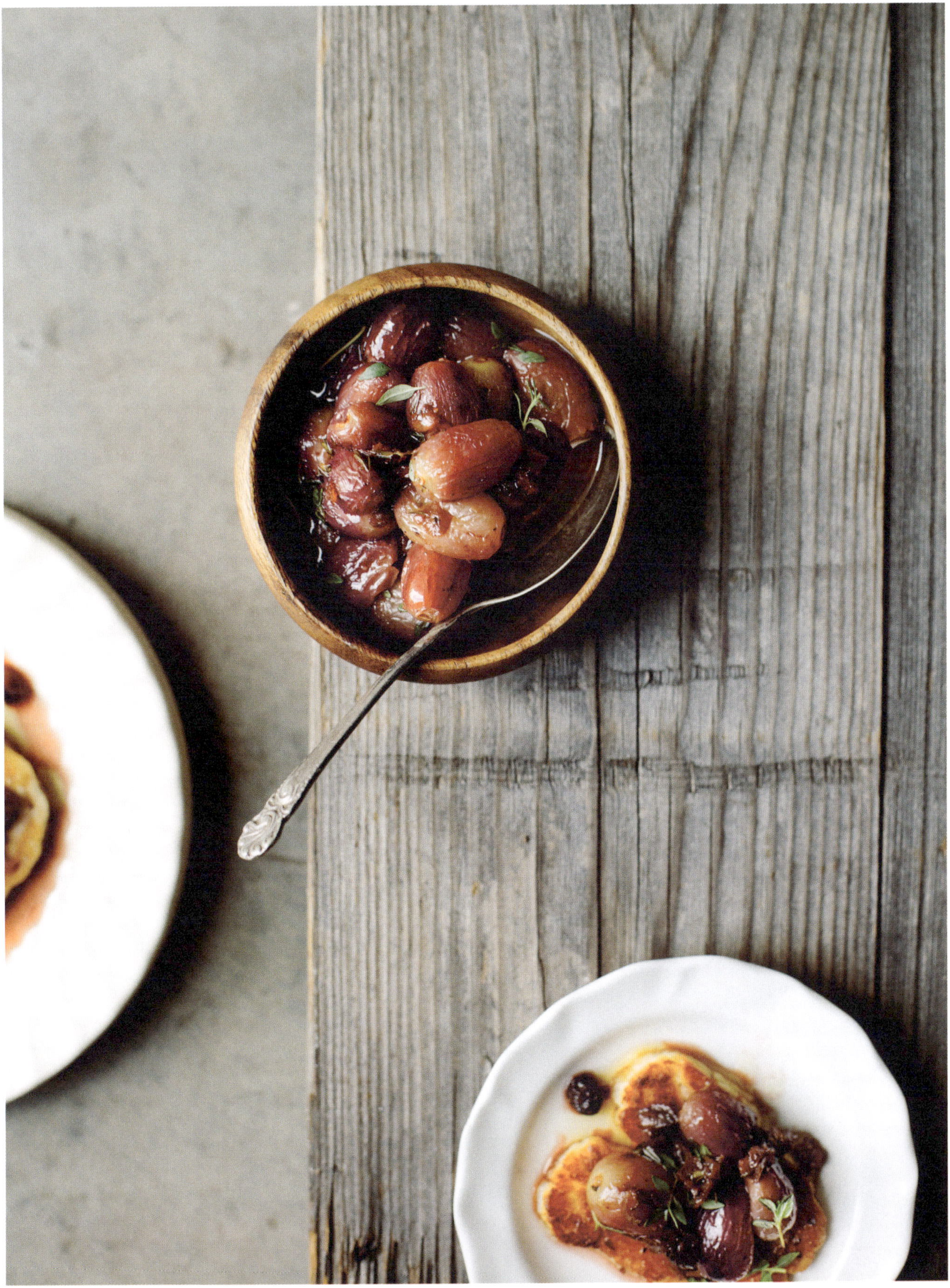

RICE NOODLE SALAD w/ PICKLED VEGETABLES + 5-SPICE DRESSING

MAKES ENOUGH FOR 2 LARGE SERVINGS OR MORE AS A SIDE | GLUTEN-FREE | VEGAN

I prefer to use fresh herbs such as mint, basil and coriander with reckless abandon, throwing huge handfuls of each into my salads, often using them in place of lettuce. I think I've always done this, but I also know marrying into a Vietnamese family has helped this little obsession along quite nicely too; it's not an uncommon sight at my mother-in-law's house to see humongous platters of fresh herbs and salad greens served up with every feast we have. If you have a mandolin or any sort of vegetable shredder, it will come in handy with this salad. We have loads of Thai basil growing in our garden all year round, but if you can't get your hands on it, regular sweet basil is fine. Add grilled tofu for extra protein.

- 2 small carrots, peeled and finely shredded
- 1 small Lebanese cucumber, finely shredded
- 1 teaspoon fine sea salt
- 125ml (½ cup) rice vinegar
- 2 tablespoons brown rice syrup or unrefined raw sugar
- 150g thin rice noodles
- 1 cup finely shredded cabbage
- ½ cup Thai basil leaves (or sweet basil), roughly torn
- ½ cup coriander leaves, roughly torn
- ½ cup mint leaves, roughly torn
- 2 tablespoons finely chopped chives
- 2 teaspoons lightly toasted sesame seeds

5-spice dressing
- 1 tablespoon gluten-free soy sauce
- 1 tablespoon Chinese black (rice) vinegar (see NOTE)
- ½ teaspoon pure sesame oil
- ½ teaspoon Chinese 5-spice
- 1 bird's-eye chilli, finely chopped (deseeded if you aren't a fan of hot)

+ To make pickled veg, place shredded carrots and cucumber in separate bowls. Sprinkle ½ teaspoon of the salt over each and mix well to evenly distribute. Set aside for 20–30 minutes. Meanwhile combine rice vinegar and brown rice syrup or sugar in a small saucepan and bring to the boil. Reduce heat and simmer for 4–5 minutes or until reduced by half, thickened and slightly syrupy. Remove from heat and set aside to cool. Squeeze excess liquid from carrot and cucumber and combine vegetables in a small bowl with cooled vinegar syrup.

+ To make salad, cook rice noodles in a saucepan of boiling salted water for 2–4 minutes or until just tender. Drain in a sieve and run under cold water to prevent them from cooking any further. Drain well and place in a large bowl along with shredded cabbage, herbs and sesame seeds.

+ To make dressing, combine ingredients in a small bowl.

+ Drain pickled vegetables (you can reuse the syrup for more pickled vegetables if you like, see NOTE on page 194) and add to salad. Pour over dressing and serve immediately.

NOTE: You can find rice vinegar and black vinegar (also made from rice) at your local Asian grocers. Just make sure you check the ingredients of the black vinegar if you are sensitive to gluten as some brands contain barley. Use extra white rice vinegar if you can't find black. Balsamic vinegar is also a pretty good substitute.

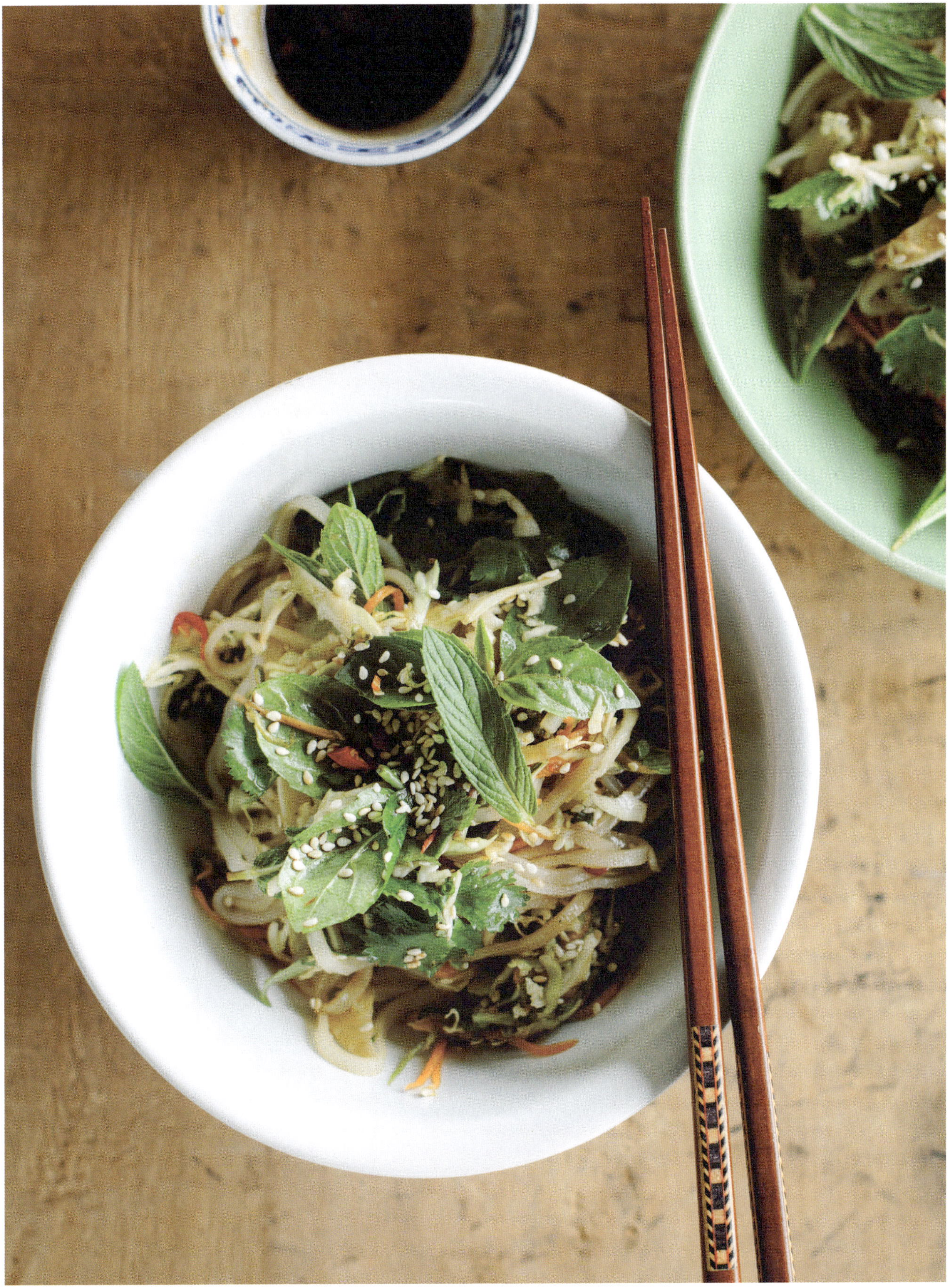

CHICKPEA 'POLENTA' W/ TOMATO ZUCCHINI STEW

SERVES 4 | GLUTEN-FREE | VEGAN

If you've only ever thought of making polenta out of corn, think again. Versions of this dish appear across the globe with differing names: panisse in France, panelle in Italy and in Burma they do a similar thing called shan tofu. It's magical stuff. This polenta makes the perfect protein-rich accompaniment to one of my childhood favourites: Mum's tomato and zucchini stew. For gardeners, the zucchini is possibly as loved as it is loathed. One little plant can produce an astounding number of zucchini, so much so that it feels like if you look away for one second what was a baby zucchini has now turned into a whopping big marrow, right before your eyes. Coming up with inventive ways to use up this humble vegetable is the pursuit of many a kitchen gardener, and I gotta say this stew is the best way to get through a good few zucchini with minimal effort. It's just as nice served stirred through pasta or alongside mashed potato, corn cobs and salad. You'll need to start this recipe the night before, or the morning of, to allow time for the polenta to set in the fridge.

Extra-virgin olive oil, to grease
110g (1 cup) chickpea (chana or besan) flour
1 teaspoon fine sea salt
3 tablespoons extra-virgin olive oil
4 cloves garlic, roughly chopped
3 medium (approx. 700g) zucchini, sliced into thin rounds
8 medium (approx. 700g) ripe tomatoes, cored + finely diced
Pinch of unrefined raw sugar
Rocket or other salad greens, to serve

+ Grease a 2 litre glass or ceramic ovenproof dish with plenty of extra-virgin olive oil. You'll just be using this dish to set the polenta in, so you can really use anything – a deep plate or cake tin will even do if that's all you have. To make polenta, combine chickpea flour and salt in a bowl, whisk in 250ml (1 cup) cold water to form a smooth paste. Pass through a fine sieve to remove any small lumps, then set aside. Bring 500ml (2 cups) water to the boil, pour in chickpea paste, whisking continuously to prevent lumps from forming. Reduce heat to a simmer and cook, stirring continuously, for 5 minutes. Transfer mixture to oiled dish, smoothing off the top as you do. Set aside until cold, then cover and refrigerate for at least 4 hours or overnight.

+ To make stew, heat olive oil in a large frying pan over medium-high heat. Add garlic and cook for 20 seconds until fragrant. Add zucchini, tomatoes, sugar and plenty of fine sea salt and freshly ground black pepper. Give it all a good mix, reduce heat slightly, cover with a lid and cook for 5–8 minutes, stirring occasionally, until tomatoes release their juices and zucchini is tender. Remove lid and continue to cook for a further 8–10 minutes, stirring often, until tomatoes have reduced to a lovely sauce. You can add a touch of water if your tomatoes aren't very juicy and the mixture seems a little dry. Have a taste and adjust seasoning if needed.

+ Remove polenta from the fridge, turn out onto a chopping board and cut into 1cm slices. Heat a few good glugs of olive oil in a large frying pan over medium-high heat and fry polenta slices in batches until golden and crispy on both sides.

+ Serve zucchini and tomato stew topped with slices of crispy polenta and with some salad greens on the side.

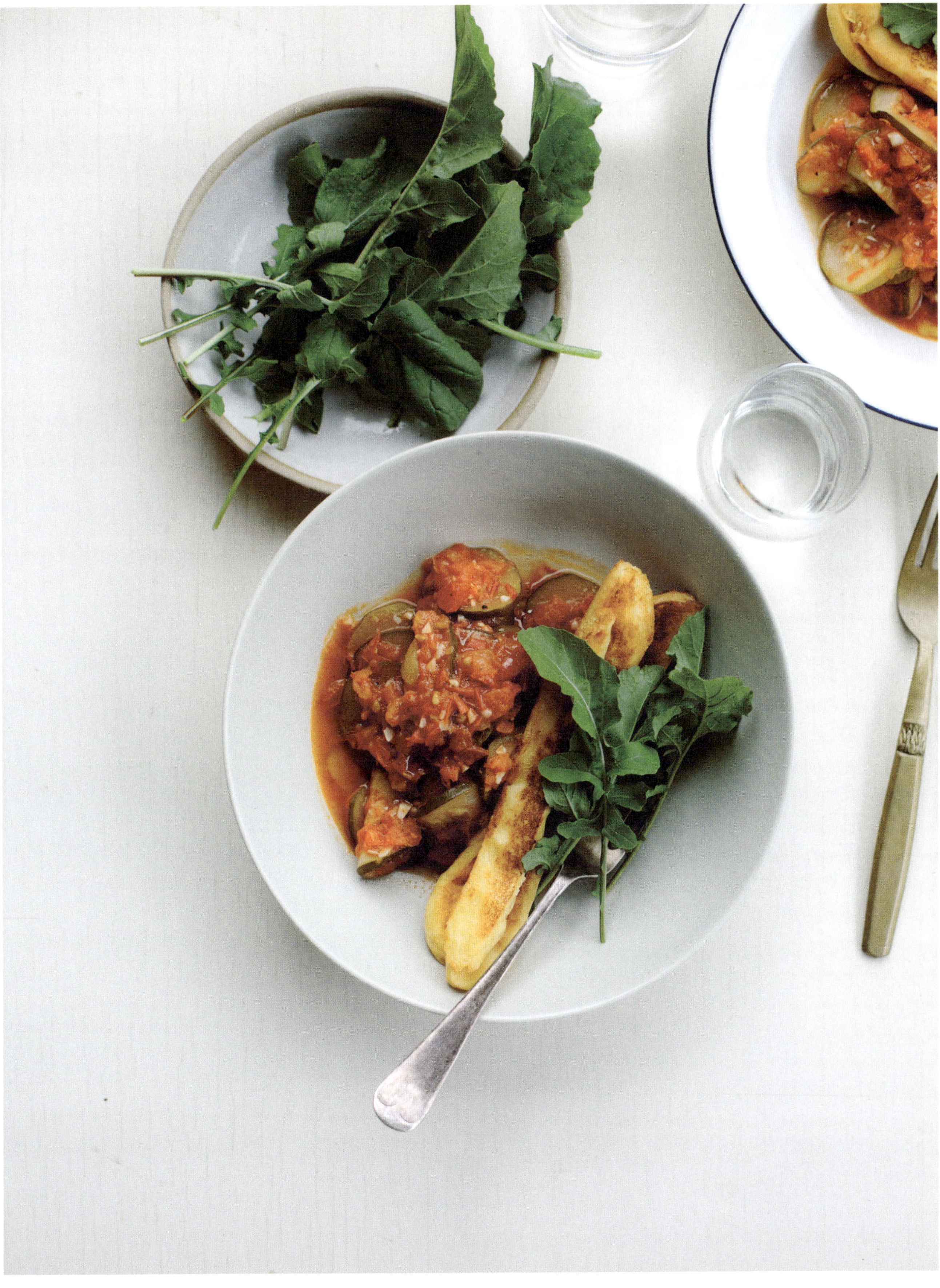

SMOKEY TEMPEH TACOS w/ APPLE RADISH SLAW

SERVES 4 (MAKES APPROX. 10 TACOS) | GLUTEN-FREE | VEGAN

There is something incredibly joyous about eating tacos. Maybe it's the fact that you get to eat like a child again, making a mess without a care in the world. Or maybe it's because you can jam so many different flavours, textures and colours into one mouthful. For these tacos, I slow braise strips of tempeh with tomato, a ton of spices and chipotle before serving with freshly made tortillas and a vibrant crunchy slaw. You'll find chipotle in adobo sauce at some supermarkets or specialty stores. To speed things up, you can use store-bought white corn tortillas, no worries.

1½ teaspoons fennel seeds
1 teaspoon whole black peppercorns
1 teaspoon coriander seeds
1 teaspoon cumin seeds
1½ teaspoons smoked paprika
375ml (1½ cups) tomato passata (purée)
1–2 chipotle chillies in adobo sauce, to taste
1 clove garlic
1 tablespoon apple cider vinegar
1 teaspoon Dijon mustard
1 teaspoon unrefined raw sugar
300g block tempeh, cut into 10 thick slices
2 cups masa harina or masa lista (white corn flour)
Flesh of 2 ripe avocados
Juice of 1 lime

Apple radish slaw

¼ small white cabbage, finely shredded
4 radishes, finely shredded
2 spring onions, sliced
Large handful each of coriander + mint leaves, roughly torn
1 green apple, cored + finely shredded (skin on)
Juice of 1 lime + extra lime wedges, to serve
Extra-virgin olive oil

+ Preheat oven to 180ºC (350ºF). Dry roast whole spices in a frying pan over medium heat until fragrant. Add smoked paprika and cook, while stirring, for a further 10 seconds. Remove from heat and finely grind in a mortar and pestle or electric spice grinder. Transfer to a blender, add passata, chipotle, garlic, vinegar, mustard, sugar and one teaspoon of fine sea salt, and blend on high until smooth. Arrange tempeh slices snugly in a 2 litre ovenproof dish and pour over tomato sauce, making sure tempeh slices are thoroughly coated in sauce. Cover the dish with a lid or tinfoil and bake for 1 hour, turning tempeh once during cooking. Remove from oven and keep warm.

+ While tempeh is cooking, prepare slaw ingredients. Combine shredded cabbage, radish, spring onion and herbs in a large bowl. Place apple in a separate small bowl and squeeze over lime juice. When ready to serve, add apple and lime juice to salad ingredients along with a good glug of olive oil. Season well with fine sea salt and freshly ground black pepper.

+ To prepare tortillas, combine masa and 310ml (1¼ cups) hot water in a bowl along with a good pinch of salt and mix to form a soft dough. If the dough is feeling a little dry, add a little more water and knead in. Turn out onto your bench and knead for 1–2 minutes until the mixture comes together in a smooth, soft dough (it shouldn't be sticking to your hands too much, so add a touch more masa if it is). Place dough back into the bowl, cover with a tea towel and set aside for at least 20 minutes.

+ Divide tortilla dough into 10 pieces. Roll each into a ball, then, one at a time, roll out each ball between 2 sheets of baking paper to approx. 3mm thick, or use a tortilla press if you own one. Cook tortillas in a hot unoiled heavy-based frying pan over high heat for 1–2 minutes on each side until lightly browned and cooked through. Wrap cooked tortillas in a clean tea towel to keep them warm.

+ Mash avocados with lime juice and plenty of salt and pepper. To serve tacos, smear a little avocado on each tortilla, top with a piece of tempeh along with some sauce. Add a good handful of slaw and eat immediately. Serve with extra lime wedges to squeeze over, if desired.

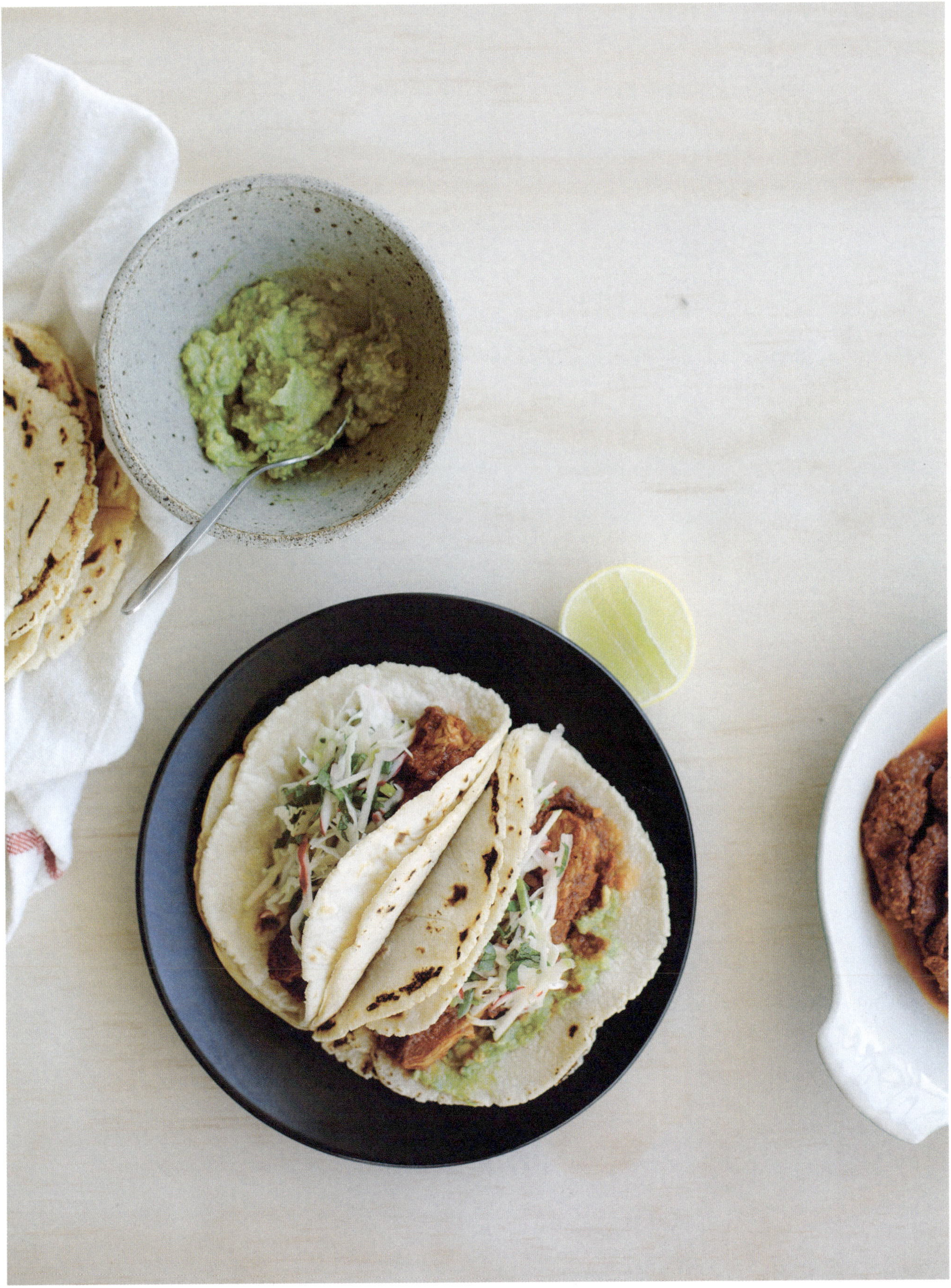

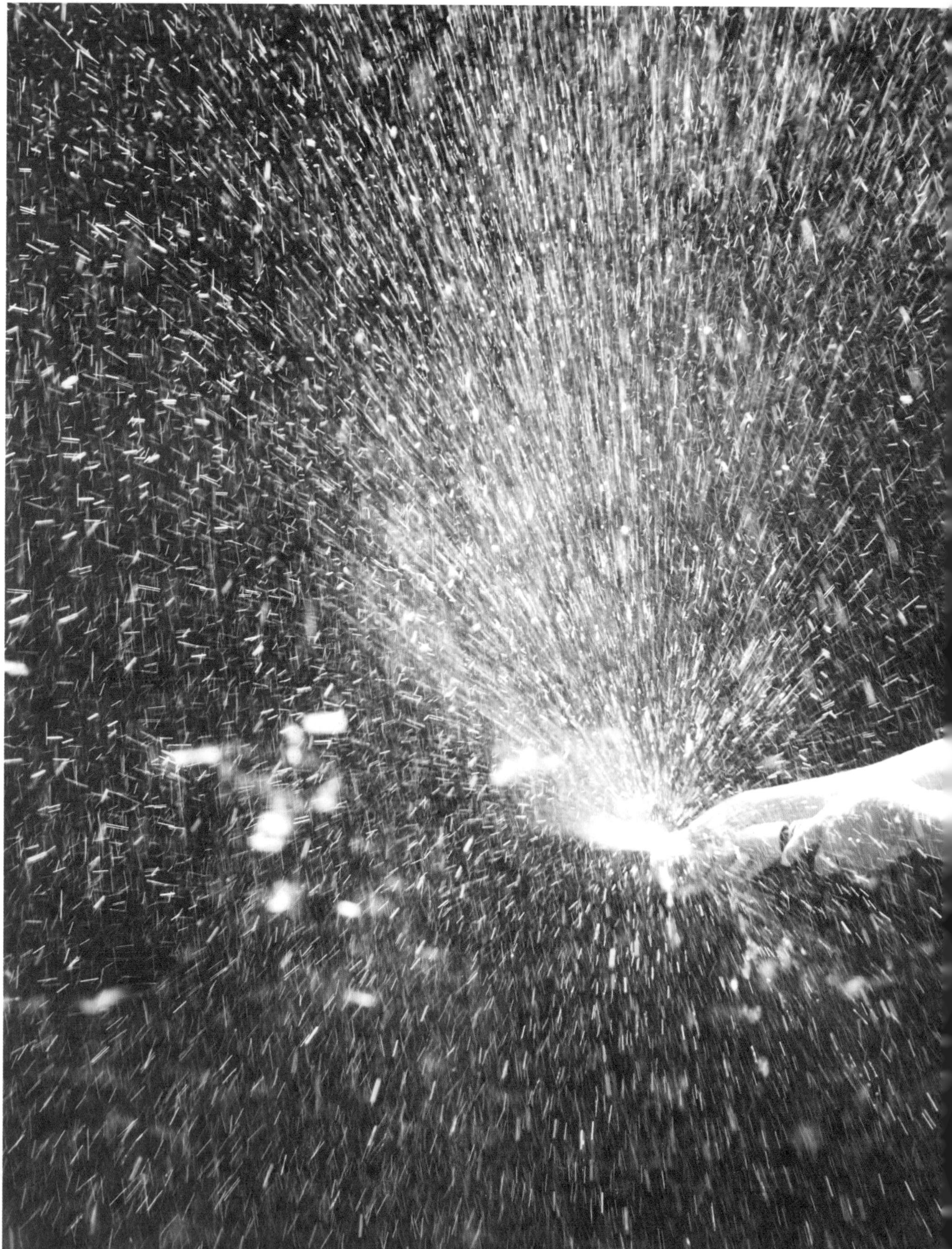

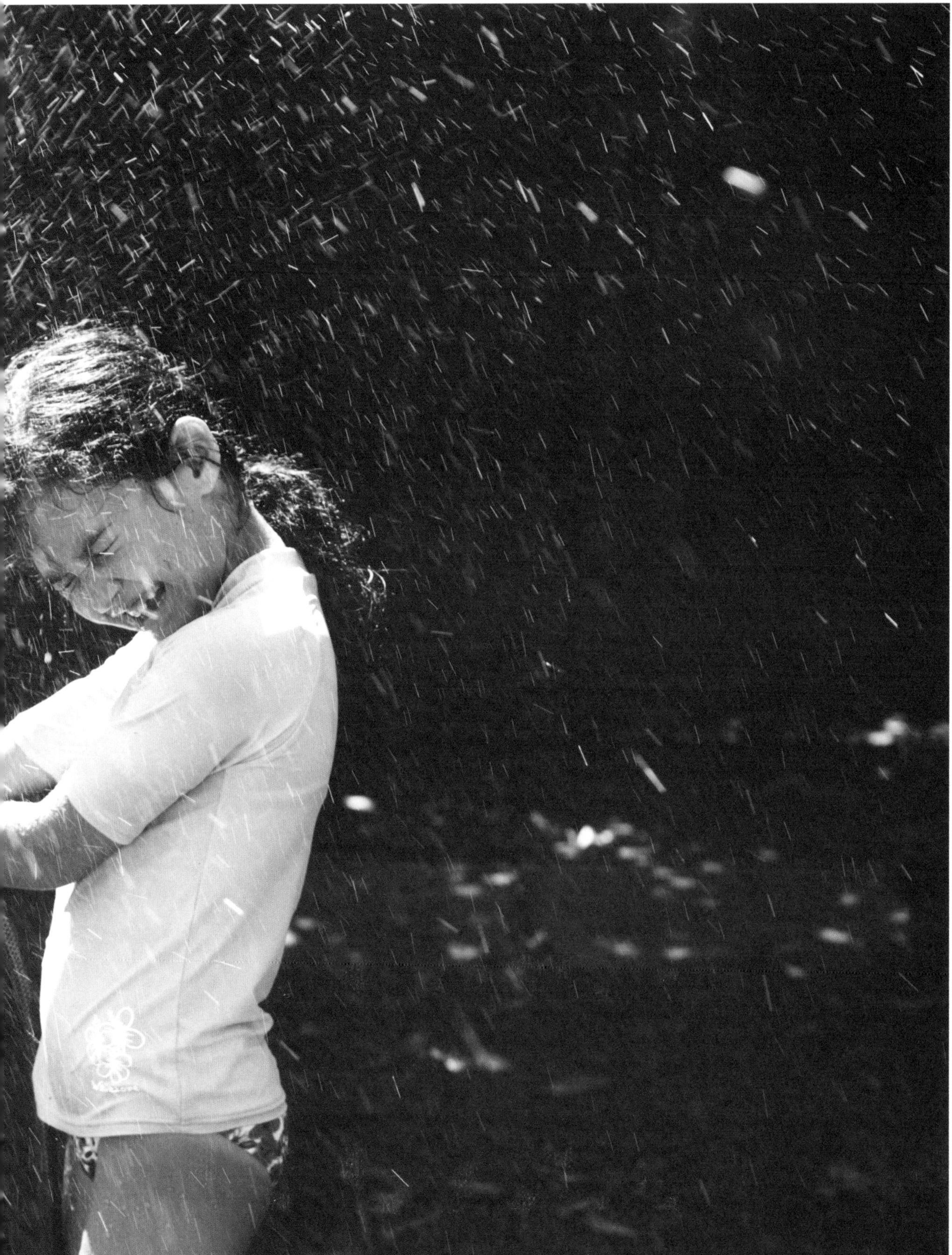

LABNEH W/ APRICOT PURÉE + SALTED NUTS

SERVES 4 | GLUTEN-FREE

Labneh is one of those things that I could happily eat on a daily basis. If you're a fan of Greek-style yoghurt, labneh's thick creaminess will quickly have you under its spell too! The orange blossom water adds a lovely floral note, however, you could also add ½ teaspoon finely grated orange zest to the apricots when cooking in its place. The salted nuts will store for up to a week in a glass jar, if you feel like doubling up that part of the recipe. They're lovely to just snack on!

1 litre (4 cups) natural plain yoghurt (see NOTE)
Pinch of fine sea salt
4 large apricots, sliced
1 tablespoon brown rice syrup, honey or unrefined raw sugar
¼–½ teaspoon orange blossom water, to taste, optional
70g (½ cup) slivered almonds
40g (¼ cup) pistachio nuts, roughly chopped
2 tablespoons brown rice syrup or unrefined raw sugar
Good big pinch of fine sea salt

+ Combine yoghurt with a pinch of fine sea salt. Spoon into a clean square of cheesecloth. Pull up all four corners of the cloth and tie. Hang it from a wooden spoon that is resting over a bowl or large plastic container (to collect the dripping whey; see NOTE, page 44). Leave in the fridge overnight (see NOTE for a speedy version). Check the drip tray occasionally to make sure it's not overflowing during the first hour or so.

+ Place sliced apricots in a saucepan, along with sweetener of your choice. Cover and cook over medium heat for 5 minutes, or until just tender. Remove from heat and purée using a stick blender or transfer to an upright blender or food processor and blend until smooth. Add orange blossom water to taste, just a little to start with then going from there (a little goes a long way!) Set aside to cool, then chill until needed. This stage can be done the night before when you strain the yoghurt, and any leftover apricot purée will happily store in a glass jar for 3–4 days.

+ Toast almonds and pistachios in a dry frying pan for 3–4 minutes, or until golden. Add brown rice syrup and salt and cook for a further 30–45 seconds, stirring continuously, until lovely and golden. Immediately transfer to a plate and set aside to cool. Break into chunks. This can also be done the night before and stored in an airtight glass jar.

+ To serve, remove labneh from the cloth and divide between bowls, top with a generous dollop or two of apricot purée and scatter over salted nuts.

NOTE: I use homemade plain yoghurt (page 239) which makes it so much cheaper, however, a natural unsweetened store-bought yoghurt is perfectly fine too. To speed things up even further, use store-bought natural Greek yoghurt and strain for 2–4 hours, instead of overnight.

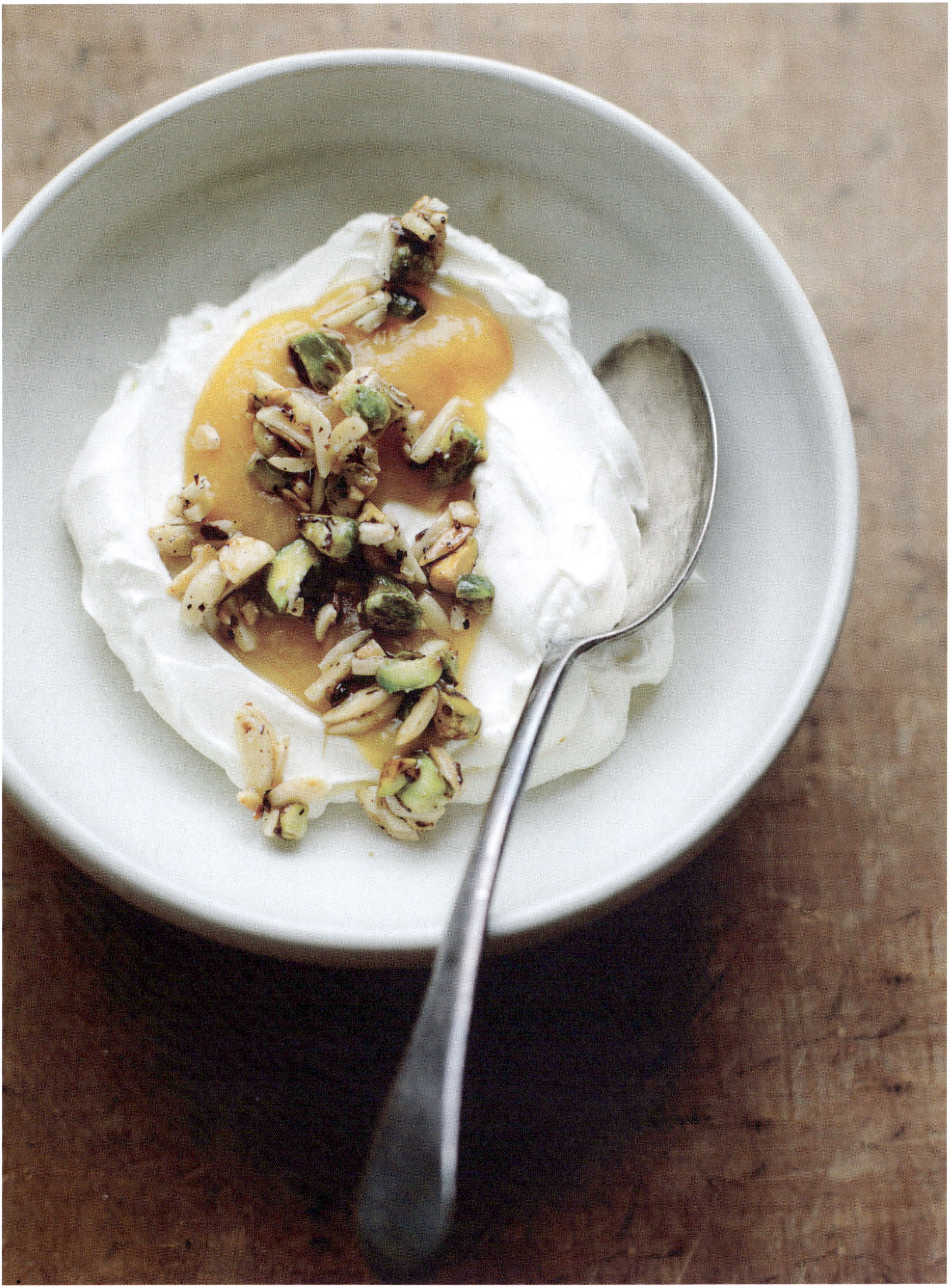

SUNSHINE SMOOTHIE

SERVES 2, EASILY DOUBLED | GLUTEN-FREE | VEGAN OPTION

We drink smoothies most days during summer. Nothing beats them as a late afternoon pick-me-up or cool down, especially if you make them thick and ice-creamy like this one. The trick is to use frozen fruit, in this case banana and mango, which together make the best creamy smoothie out. Adding some kind of fat helps to lessen the blood sugar spike some people experience from fruit-based smoothies, while the ginger adds a lovely kick alongside that little burst of turmeric sunshine. Use freshly grated turmeric if you can get your hands on it. Adding a little bee pollen to your smoothies is a great way to get a natural dose of minerals, vitamins and protein, in place of the commercially made protein powders which seem to be all the rage at the moment. Omit, for vegan option.

- 2 ripe bananas, cut into chunks
- Flesh of 1 large mango, cut into chunks
- 2 cups (500ml) almond (preferably homemade page 241) or coconut milk, or a combination
- 1 teaspoon finely grated ginger
- 1 teaspoon ground turmeric
- Pinch of fine sea salt
- 1 tablespoon virgin coconut oil, melted if solid
- Bee pollen, to dust, optional

+ Place banana chunks on a tray with chunks of mango and freeze for 4–5 hours or overnight.

+ To be kind on your blender (even high-powered ones), and to avoid your motor burning out, it pays to remove the frozen fruit from the freezer and allow it to slightly defrost for 5 minutes. Place all ingredients except coconut oil and bee pollen in your blender and blend on high until smooth, thick and ice-creamy. With the blender still going, drizzle in coconut oil and continue to blend for a few more seconds (adding the coconut oil last prevents it from freezing in clumps on contact with the frozen fruit). Serve immediately scattered with bee pollen, if desired. I sometimes swirl a little blended mango purée on the top for a pretty effect and scatter with edible flowers (such as rosemary), however, this is completely up to you.

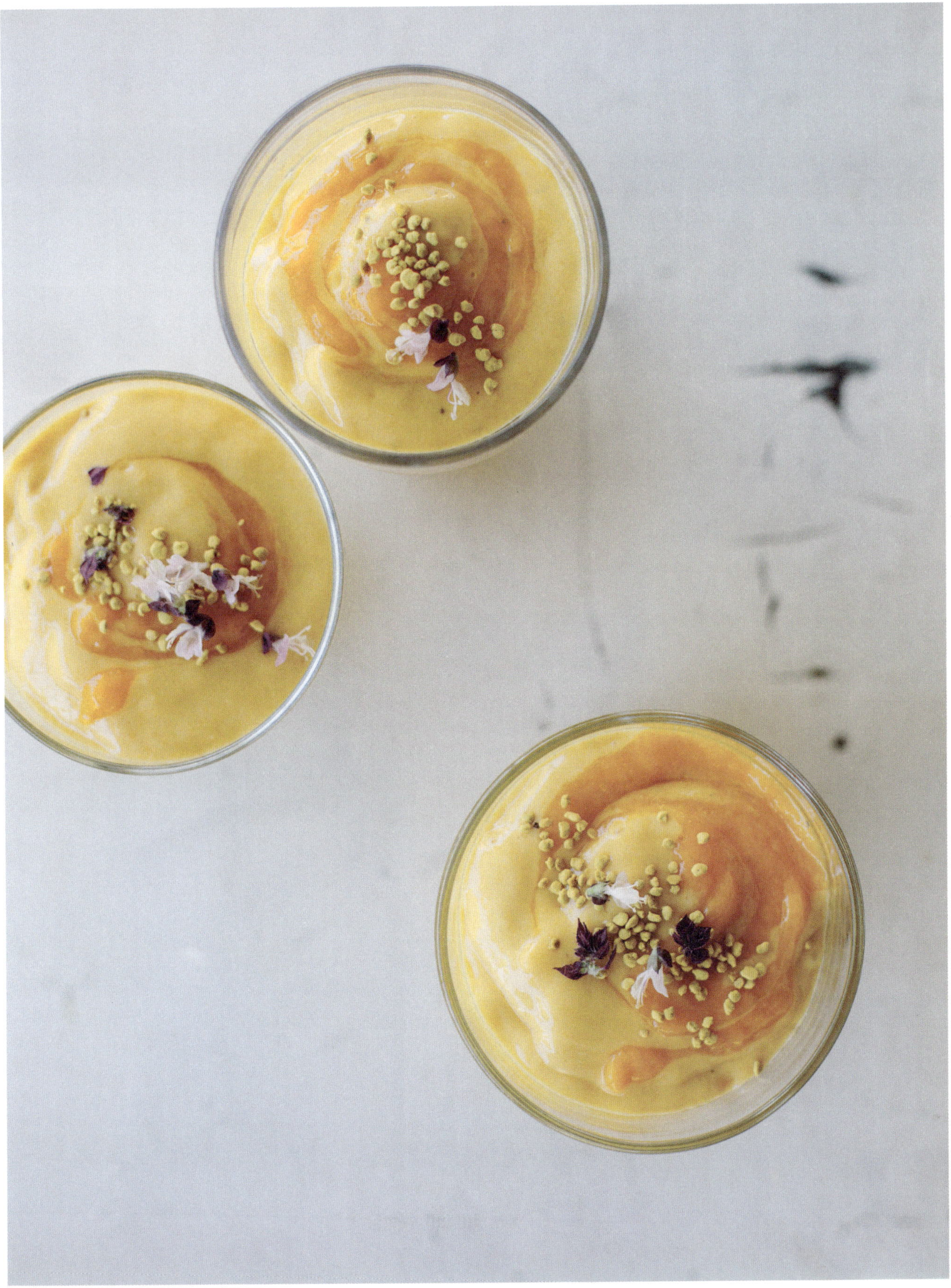

Raspberry, Apricot + Orange Popsicles

MAKES 8 | GLUTEN-FREE | VEGAN

Soaked cashews are the secret to lovely creamy dairy-free popsicles. As much as I love fresh apricots, there's something truly special about them once cooked. Their flavour and colour deepens and they become one of my favourite summertime treats when eaten with a little homemade yoghurt (page 239) or labneh (page 240), added to crumbles or in popsicles such as these. If using frozen berries, make sure you know their country of origin and make a special effort to buy locally grown berries, always. If frozen, allow them to defrost a little before using in this recipe. Honey can be used in place of maple syrup, if desired. Start the night before to allow time for the cashews to soak.

- 6 large (approx. 500g) apricots, sliced
- Juice of 1 orange
- 125g (1 cup) fresh or locally grown frozen raspberries
- 4–5 tablespoons pure maple syrup
- 60g (½ cup) raw cashews, soaked overnight in cold water, drained + rinsed
- 1 teaspoon finely grated orange zest
- Small pinch of fine sea salt

+ Place apricots and orange juice in a medium saucepan, cover with a lid and bring to the boil. Reduce to a simmer and cook for 5 minutes. Remove lid and cook for a further 8–10 minutes, stirring often to prevent the bottom from catching, until thick and pulpy. Remove from heat and set aside to cool.

+ Combine raspberries and 1–2 tablespoons of the maple syrup in a small bowl and lightly crush with a fork to form a rough paste. Divide evenly between 8 popsicle moulds and set aside.

+ Transfer cooled apricots to a blender, along with soaked cashews, 3 tablespoons maple syrup, orange zest and salt. Blend until smooth. Pour into moulds (it's a thick mixture, so you may need a spoon to help), then using a knife, marble raspberries through apricot mixture slightly. Insert wooden sticks and freeze for at least 4 hours or overnight. Run moulds under warm water to help release the popsicles.

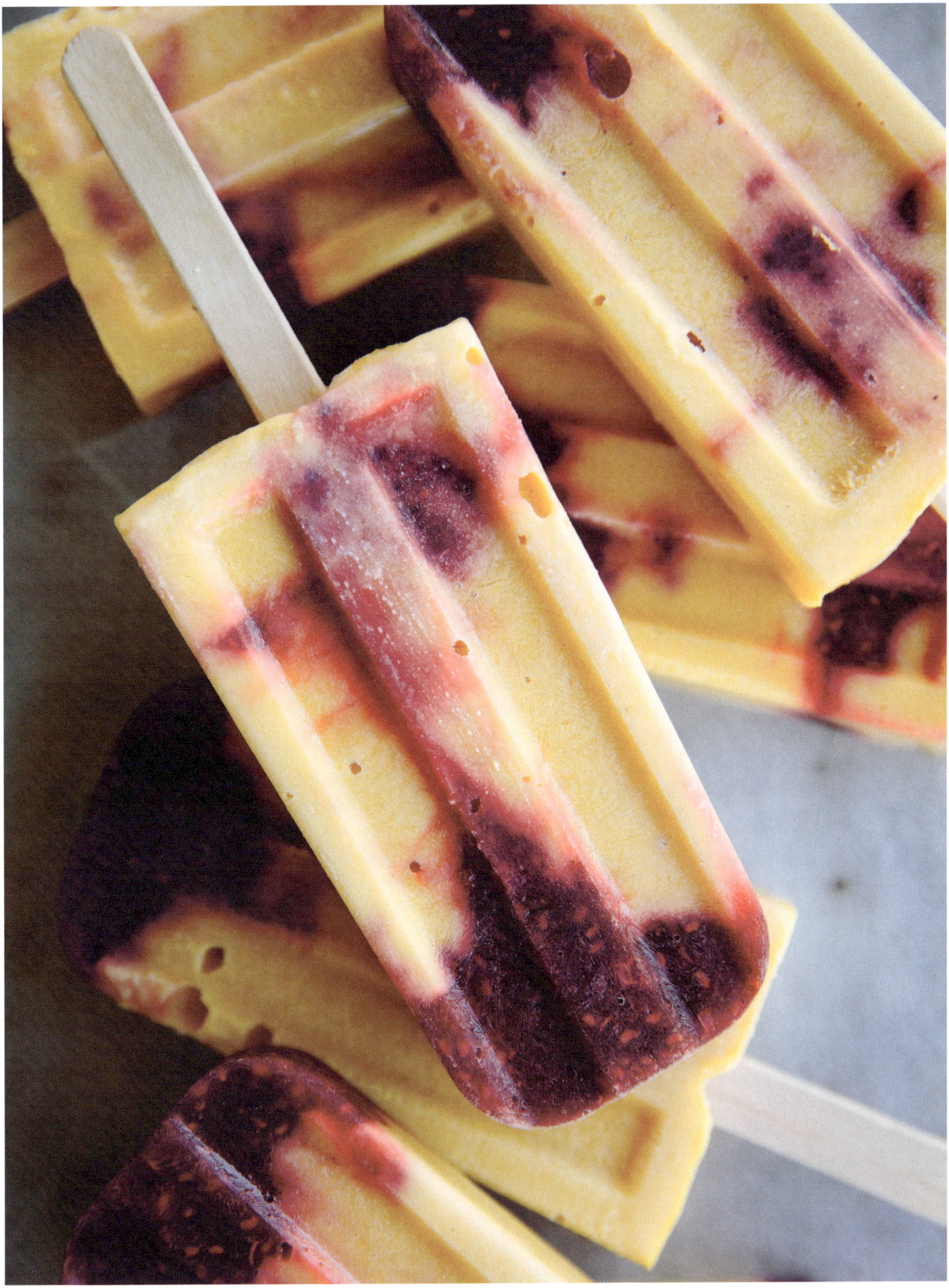

FLOURLESS BANANA, CHERRY + CHOCOLATE MUFFINS

MAKES 8 | GLUTEN-FREE | DAIRY-FREE

This is another great muffin recipe to add to your repertoire. Using easily found ingredients and with the most beautiful texture, thanks to its flourless nature, these just-sweet muffins are as good to have for breakfast (omit chocolate and make the night before for an on-the-run option) as they are for a snack or afternoon tea. The little pops of cherry are lovely, however, the muffins are also just as good made without, or substitute with strawberries, raspberries, blueberries or a combo of all three.

- 1 cup mashed over-ripe bananas (approx. 2 large bananas)
- 2 large free-range eggs
- 3 tablespoons olive oil or virgin coconut oil, melted if solid
- 2 tablespoons pure maple syrup or unrefined raw sugar
- 1 teaspoon vanilla extract
- Good pinch of fine sea salt
- 110g (1 cup) ground almonds
- 20g (¼ cup) desiccated coconut
- ½ teaspoon gluten-free baking powder
- 100g (a handful) cherries, halved and pips removed
- 50g dark chocolate, roughly chopped

+ Preheat oven to 170ºC (335ºF). Line an 8-hole ⅓ cup (80ml) muffin tin with paper cases. Whisk together mashed banana, eggs, oil, maple syrup or sugar, vanilla extract and salt.

+ In a medium bowl, whisk ground almonds, desiccated coconut and baking powder together to evenly distribute before adding to wet mixture and mixing well. Fold through cherries (saving a few pieces for the top, if desired) and two-thirds of the dark chocolate. Spoon mixture into paper cases, top with a few of the reserved cherries if you have them and scatter with remaining chocolate. Bake for 35–40 minutes or until a skewer inserted into the centre of the muffins comes out clean. Remove from oven, set aside for 5 minutes before transferring to a wire rack to cool. Best eaten on the day of baking, however, the muffins will store, airtight, for 2–3 days or longer in the fridge. They also freeze well.

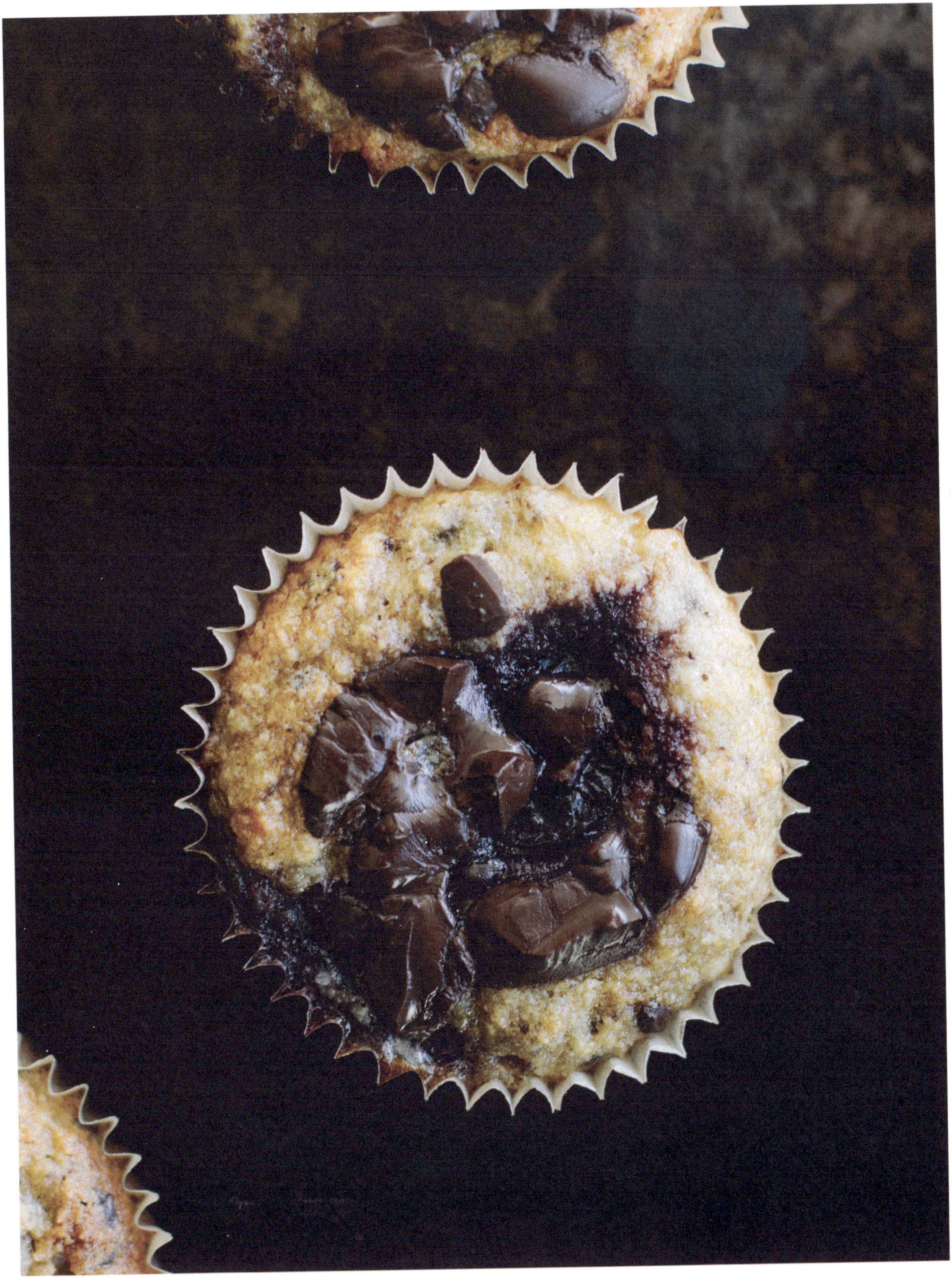

NECTARINE HONEY CAKES

MAKES 9 | GLUTEN-FREE

There are certain times when honey's beautiful floral tones definitely make baked goods sing. I've used slices of nectarine on top of these tender little honey-scented cakes, but you could also use slices of peach, apricot or plums (see NOTE). A few fresh berries pressed into the batter before baking would also be lovely.

75g butter, diced
60ml (¼ cup) honey
80g (¾ cup) ground almonds
45g (¼ cup) fine brown rice flour
2 tablespoons arrowroot or gluten-free organic cornflour (starch)
1½ teaspoons gluten-free baking powder
Finely grated zest of 1 small lemon
60ml (¼ cup) almond, rice or coconut milk
1 large free-range egg
1 teaspoon vanilla extract
1 medium nectarine, thinly sliced

+ Preheat oven to 160ºC (320ºF). Grease a 9-hole friand tin generously with melted butter. Place butter and honey into a small saucepan over low heat, stirring often until butter has just melted, remove from heat and set aside to cool for 5 minutes.

+ Place ground almonds in a medium bowl and sift over brown rice flour, arrowroot or cornflour and baking powder. Add lemon zest and whisk well to evenly distribute flours. Whisk milk, egg and vanilla in a separate bowl. Add to dry ingredients along with melted butter and honey. Whisk to form a smooth batter. Pour ¼ cup batter into each friand hole, top with a couple of slices of nectarine. Bake for 15–20 minutes or until golden and a skewer inserted into the centre comes out clean. Remove from oven and set aside for 5 minutes. Run a thin knife around the perimeter of each cake, then gently remove and transfer to a wire rack to cool further. Best eaten on the day of baking, however, they will store, airtight, for 3 days.

NOTE: During the summer months when stonefruits are cheap and plentiful, I buy in bulk, slice, lay out on a tray, freeze then transfer to zip-lock bags. I then use the slices in smoothies. Or I lightly stew and freeze in containers for later use in pies, tarts and crumbles – there's nothing like pulling out a container of summer fruit to make a crumble in the midst of winter!

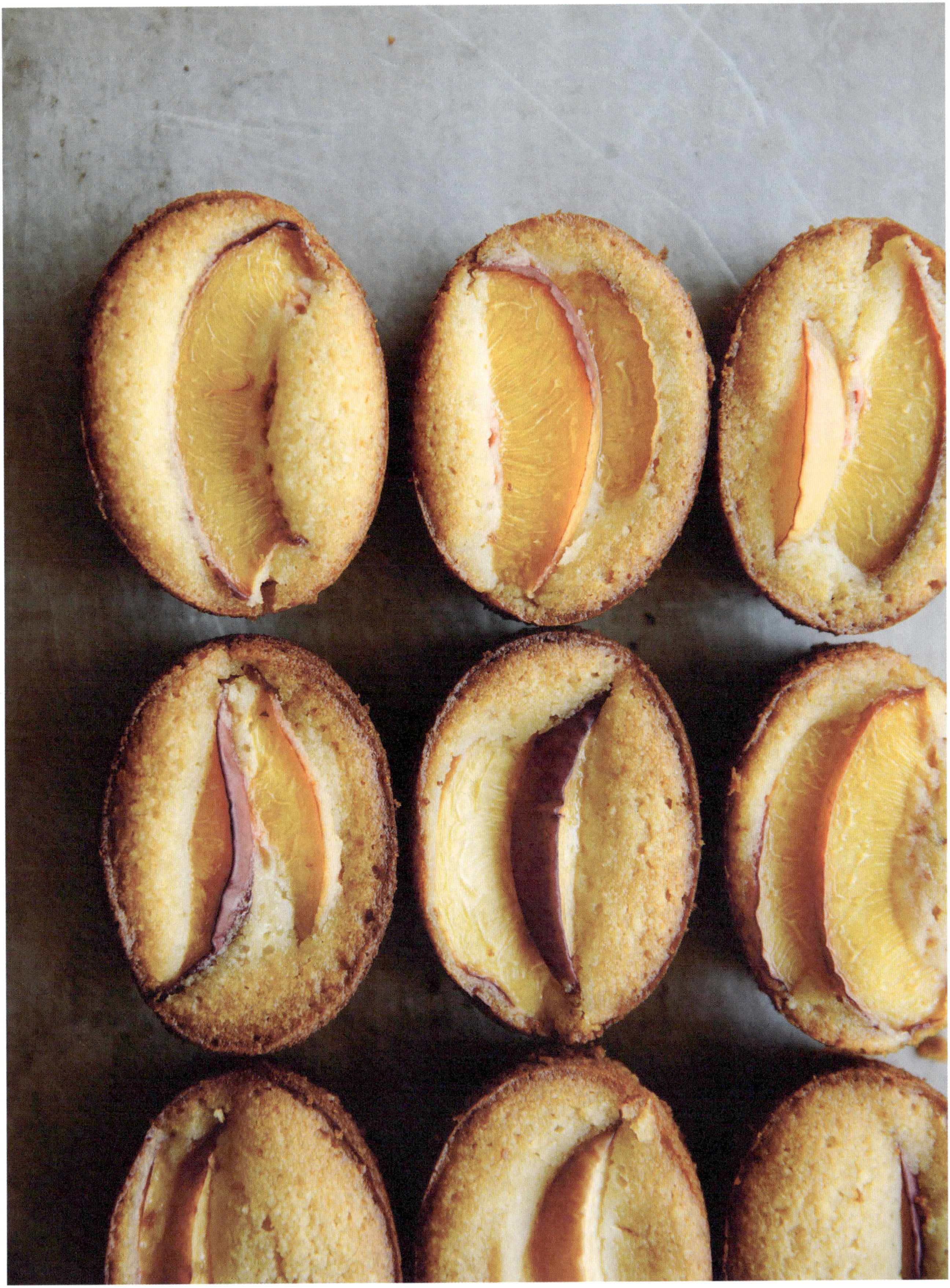

ROASTED STRAWBERRY, ORANGE + PINK PEPPERCORN POPSICLES

MAKES 4 | GLUTEN-FREE | VEGAN OPTION

At our local farmers markets there's a family-run stall selling the most beautiful strawberries and, come peak season, you're able to pick up huge boxes of their seconds for a ridiculously cheap price. We buy a box every week, wash and hull them before freezing on trays and transferring to zip-lock bags. Throughout the year, we then have locally grown berries to use in baking, smoothies and desserts. It's around this time that I also make loads of homemade popsicles, often strawberry-based ones in an attempt to use up a few of the hundreds! Use 1 teaspoon of pink peppercorns if you're a little unsure, but go the full two if you're feeling brave, the little kick they add is beautiful. If you can't find pink peppercorns sold separately, buy a packet of mixed peppercorns and just pick the pink ones out. I find tasks like these strangely therapeutic.

- 500g strawberries, hulled
- 3 tablespoons pure maple syrup, or unrefined raw sugar, brown rice syrup or honey
- 1 tablespoon extra-virgin olive oil
- Finely grated zest of 1 orange
- 1–2 teaspoons pink peppercorns, finely ground
- Good pinch of fine sea salt

+ Preheat oven to 200ºC (400ºF). Combine all ingredients in a medium bowl, transfer to a lipped baking tray or ovenproof dish and roast for 25 minutes or until strawberries are tender and their juices have been released. Remove from oven and cool.

+ Transfer berries and their juices to a blender and blend until smooth. Spoon into popsicle moulds, snap on lids and freeze. If using wooden sticks, freeze popsicles for an hour until partially frozen before inserting sticks. Freeze for 4 hours or overnight. Run moulds briefly under warm water to help release the popsicles.

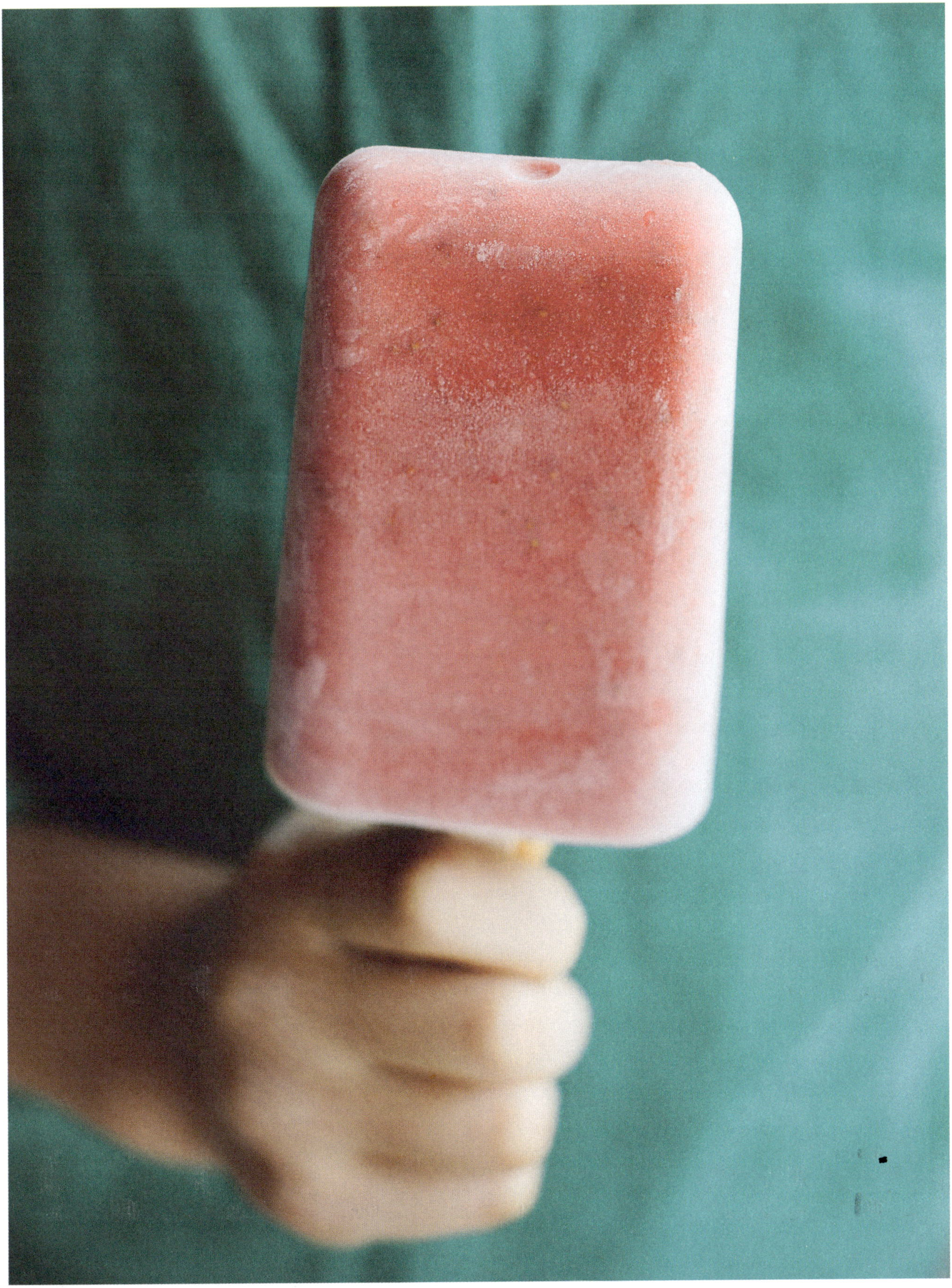

Raspberry + Peach Crumble Cake

SERVES 8–10 | GLUTEN-FREE

The combination of sweet juicy peaches and tart fresh raspberries has long been a classic, and with good reason. Here I scatter them both over buttery almond cake mixture before topping with crumble and baking until golden. I'm a sucker for this summery combination, but you can use any seasonal fruits you have at hand. Sliced rhubarb, apricots or blueberries, or a combination of all three (!) also works perfectly. Or do a winter version later in the year, with thinly sliced apples or pears and add a little cinnamon and ginger to the batter.

Crumble topping
- 45g (¼ cup) fine brown rice flour
- 25g (¼ cup) ground almonds
- 25g chilled butter, finely diced
- 2 tablespoons light muscovado or soft brown sugar
- 25g (⅓ cup) sliced almonds

Cake
- 125g softened butter
- 200g (1 cup) firmly packed blended unrefined raw sugar (page 235)
- 1 teaspoon vanilla extract
- Finely grated zest of 1 lemon
- 2 large free-range eggs, at room temperature
- 110g (1 cup) ground almonds
- 105g (¾ cup) fine brown rice flour
- 15g (2 tablespoons) gluten-free organic cornflour (starch) or arrowroot
- 1½ teaspoons gluten-free baking powder
- 2 tablespoons almond, rice or coconut milk
- 1 large peach, thinly sliced
- 125g (1 cup) fresh or locally grown frozen raspberries

+ Preheat oven to 170ºC (335ºF). Grease a 23cm springform cake tin and line the base and sides with baking paper.

+ To make crumble topping, combine brown rice flour and ground almonds in a bowl. Add butter, then, using your hands, rub butter in until the mixture resembles fine breadcrumbs. Stir through sugar and almonds. Set aside.

+ To make cake, cream butter, sugar and vanilla in a large bowl until light and fluffy using an electric beater or wooden spoon. Add lemon zest and eggs, one at a time, beating well after each addition. Add ground almonds, sift over brown rice flour, cornflour or arrowroot and baking powder and gently fold in along with milk. Transfer to prepared cake tin, top with peach slices and raspberries. Squeeze crumble mixture in your hands to form clumps before scattering over the cake. Bake for 55–65 minutes or until a skewer inserted into the centre comes out clean. Remove from oven and set aside to cool in tin. Best eaten on the day of baking, however, the cake will store, airtight, for up to 2–3 days.

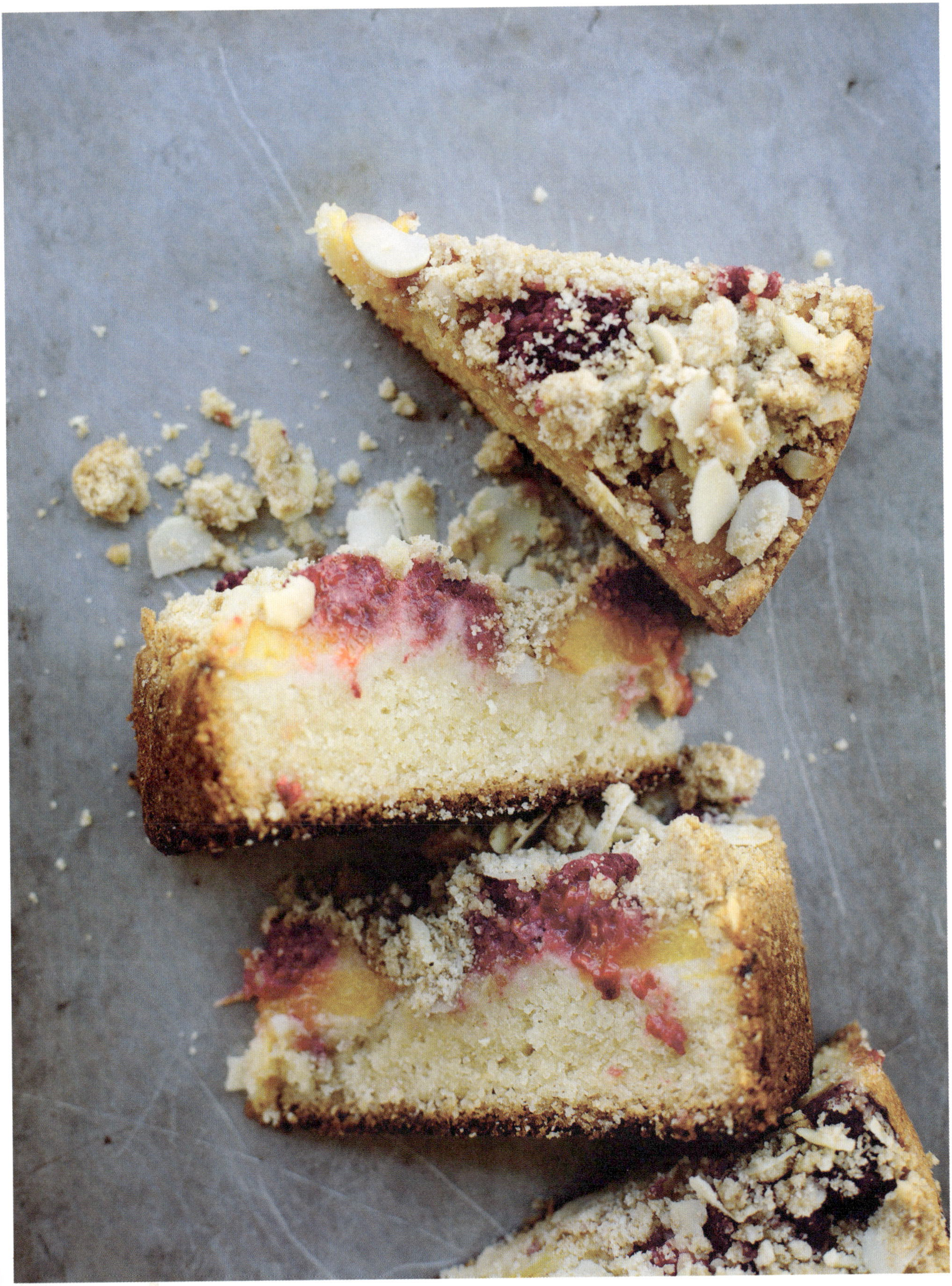

MANGO, LIME + COCONUT CAKE

SERVES 8–10 | GLUTEN-FREE | DAIRY-FREE

Juicy mangoes, coconut and lime come together in this quintessential summer cake. Having lived in Western Australia for the past five years, we have been totally spoilt with two huge Kensington mango trees in our backyard. At the start of the season, we'd feast on green mango dipped in chilli salt or made into green mango salad (one of my favourite things on earth). Come mid-summer we'd eat beautiful organic sun-ripened mangoes straight from the tree. When we'd had our fix, it was my cue to get creative in the kitchen where I'd use mango in jellies, sorbets, ice cream, popsicles, curds, smoothies and cakes such as this.

Cheeks of 2 ripe mangoes

200g (1 cup) firmly packed blended unrefined raw sugar (page 235)

4 large free-range eggs, at room temperature

Pinch of fine sea salt

125ml (½ cup) virgin coconut oil, melted if solid

1 teaspoon vanilla extract

Finely grated zest of 1 lime + extra to serve, optional

35g (⅓ cup) desiccated coconut

140g (1 cup) fine brown rice flour

2 teaspoons gluten-free baking powder

80ml (⅓ cup) coconut milk

+ Preheat oven to 180ºC (350ºF). Grease and line the base of a 23cm springform cake tin. Slice each mango cheek in half to produce two flat pieces about 1cm thick. Arrange slices in prepared tin to cover the base as much as you can.

+ Beat sugar, eggs and salt for 8–10 minutes using an electric beater or whisk, until thick and fluffy. Gradually drizzle in oil and vanilla with the beaters still running (you may need someone else to help you pour if you're whisking by hand). Add lime zest and coconut and sift over flour and baking powder. Using a large metal spoon, gently fold in flour until batter is about three-quarters combined, doing your best not to knock out all that beautiful air in the mixture. Pour in coconut milk and continue to fold in, until just combined. Gently scoop batter over mango slices.

+ Bake for 40–45 minutes, or until a skewer inserted into the centre comes out clean. Remove from oven and set aside to cool in tin for 5 minutes, before transferring cake to a wire rack to cool further. Scatter the top with a little extra lime zest to serve, if you like. Best eaten on the day of baking, however, the cake will store, airtight, for 2–3 days.

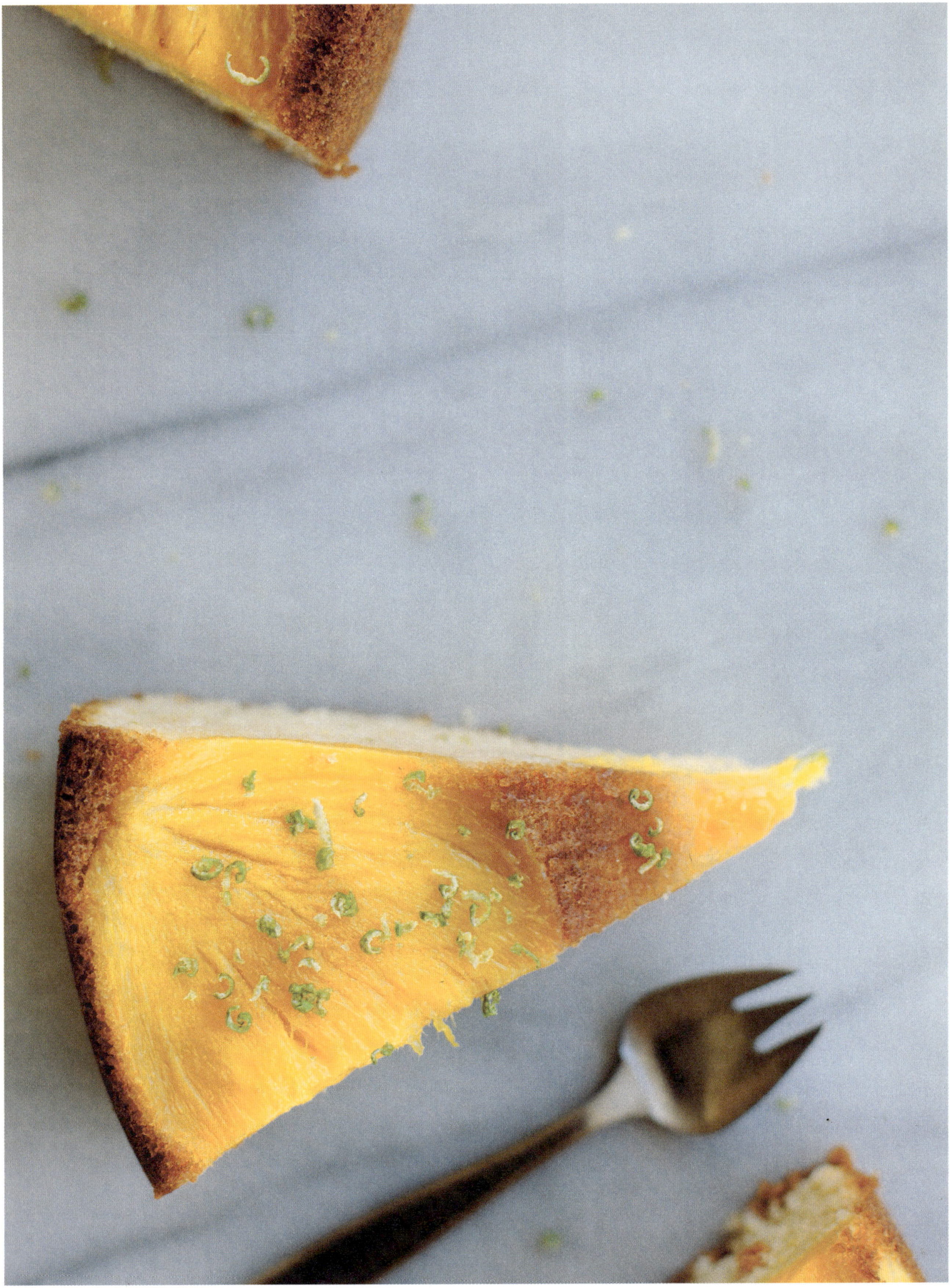

DARK CHOCOLATE, PISTACHIO HALVA ICE CREAM BITES

MAKES 10 | GLUTEN-FREE | VEGAN OPTION

Made of whole, real ingredients, these ice cream bites are a firm favourite in our house during the hot summer months. Packed with calcium-rich tahini, their flavour is reminiscent of the sesame halva found throughout the Middle East. I prefer the less-aggressive bitterness of hulled tahini in this recipe, but you'll be treated with more nutrients if you go for unhulled. You could even use black tahini if it's available, which will give your bites a somewhat strange grey colour, but what a great talking point, no? Start this recipe the night before, to allow time for the cashews to soak.

60g (½ cup) cashews, soaked overnight in cold water, drained + rinsed

60ml (¼ cup) virgin coconut oil, melted if solid

60ml (¼ cup) tahini

60ml (¼ cup) almond, coconut or rice milk

60ml (¼ cup) brown rice syrup, pure maple syrup or honey

1 teaspoon vanilla extract

Good pinch of fine sea salt

2 tablespoons roughly chopped pistachio nuts

Chocolate coating

3 tablespoons virgin coconut oil

3 tablespoons cacao or cocoa powder

2 tablespoons pure maple syrup

+ Place drained cashews, coconut oil, tahini, milk, sweetener, vanilla and salt into a blender and blend until smooth. You may need to stop and scrape down the sides a few times if you don't own a high-powered blender. Half-fill 10 x 2 tablespoon-capacity silicone cupcake moulds or mini paper cupcake cases with mixture, sprinkle with half the pistachio nuts, then top with remaining tahini mixture. Pop into the freezer for 4 hours or overnight. Remove ice cream bites from moulds or cases, place onto a tray and return to the freezer while you make the chocolate coating.

+ To make coating, place coconut oil, cacao or cocoa powder, and maple syrup in a heatproof bowl set over a saucepan of boiling water, stirring until melted and smooth. Pour into a small bowl and set aside for 10 minutes to thicken up slightly before dipping each ice cream bite into the chocolate to coat evenly. Return to tray, scatter with pistachios and repeat with remaining bites. Pop back in the freezer for 5 minutes to set. If you find you have excess chocolate, pour into moulds and freeze until set. Serve ice cream bites straight from the freezer. The bites will store in an airtight container in the freezer for 3–4 weeks. Although, they don't even last 1 week in our house…

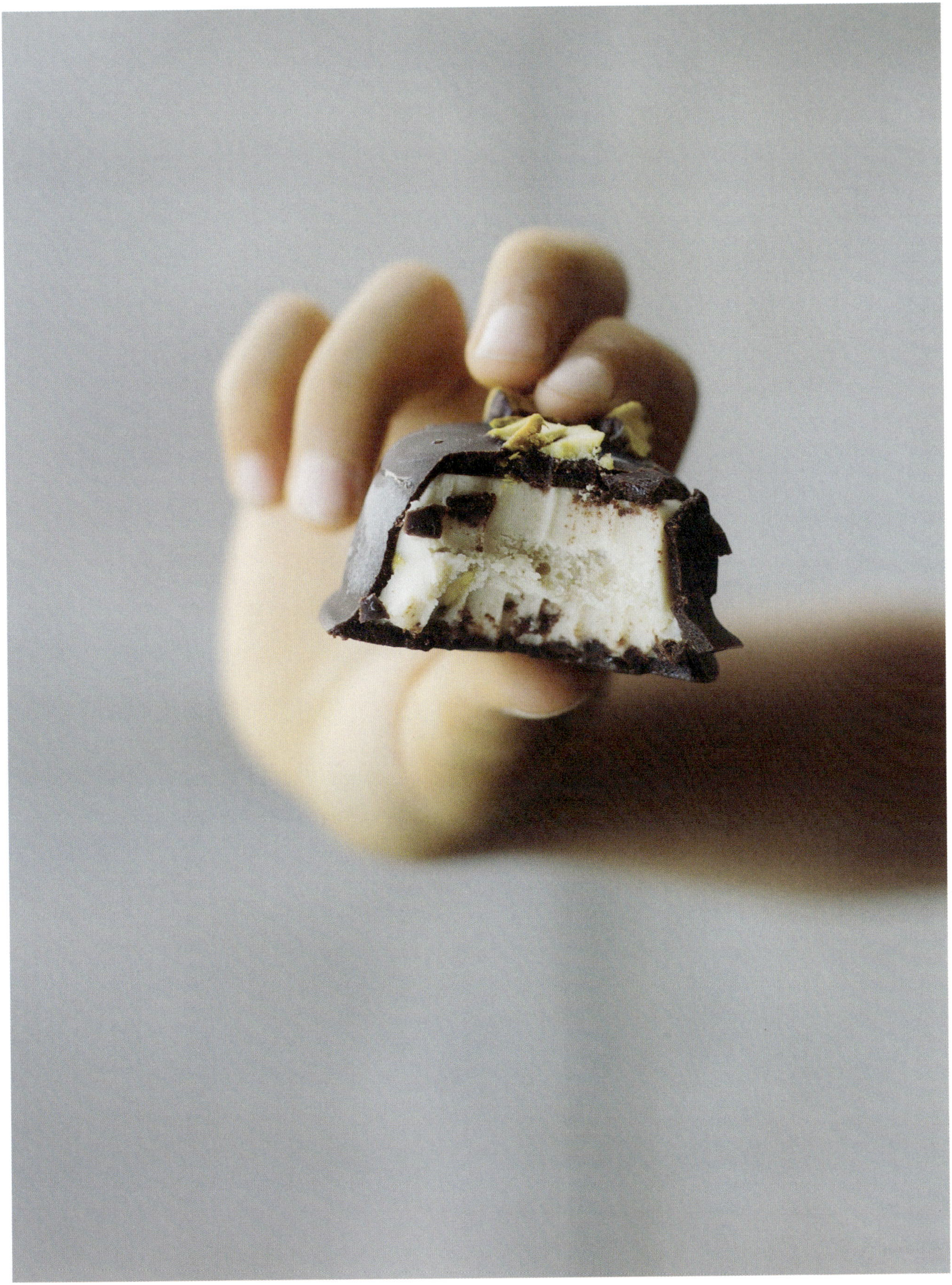

DARK CHOCOLATE CINNAMON ICE CREAM

SERVES 4 | GLUTEN-FREE | DAIRY-FREE

This ice cream is lusciously rich, smooth and silky thanks to the traditional egg-custard base. I sometimes find that egg-custard made with coconut milk tastes a little, well, eggy. So to counteract this I tend to add bold flavourings such as chocolate or spice. Here I've gone for both! Go full fat with the coconut cream; it's the fat which gives the creaminess to this dairy-free ice cream and if you took one look at the ingredients list of most 'lite' coconut milks I think you'd agree that going full fat is the better choice (see page 240).

600ml coconut milk

100g dark chocolate, chopped into small chunks

1 teaspoon ground cinnamon

1 teaspoon vanilla bean paste or vanilla extract

4 large free-range egg yolks

100g (½ cup) firmly packed blended unrefined raw sugar (page 235)

Good pinch of fine sea salt

+ Place coconut milk, chocolate, cinnamon and vanilla into a medium saucepan over medium-high heat. Slowly bring up to near boiling point, stirring constantly to melt the chocolate (give it a good mix with a whisk if the chocolate is having a hard time combining to form a smooth, even sauce).

+ In a large glass bowl, whisk egg yolks, sugar and salt until thick and pale. Pour hot chocolate mixture over yolks, whisking constantly. Quickly rinse out pan and pour the whole lot back in. Turn heat down to medium and return pan to heat. Cook, stirring constantly with a wooden spoon, for 5–6 minutes or until the mixture thickens and coats the back of your spoon.

+ Remove from heat and strain chocolate custard through a fine sieve placed over a clean bowl. Set aside until cool, stirring occasionally to prevent a skin forming on the surface. Or if you have loads of ice you can always speed up this process by placing the bowl of custard into another larger bowl filled with ice and stirring until cold. When the mixture is cool, cover and place in the fridge to chill for a few hours or overnight.

+ Churn ice cream in an ice cream maker for 20–25 minutes before transferring to a lidded container and freezing for a further 2–3 hours until set to your liking. The ice cream will keep for 4–5 days in the freezer. Leave out on the bench for 10–15 minutes to soften before eating if it has set too hard.

+ Alternatively, if you don't own an ice cream churn, simply place custard mixture into a shallow dish (a loaf tin is perfect) and freeze for 1 hour, until the edges are starting to freeze. Beat with a hand mixer or whisk, return to the freezer and repeat this a further 2–3 times before returning to the freezer for 2 hours. This won't give the exact same results as a churn would, but the ice cream is delicious nonetheless.

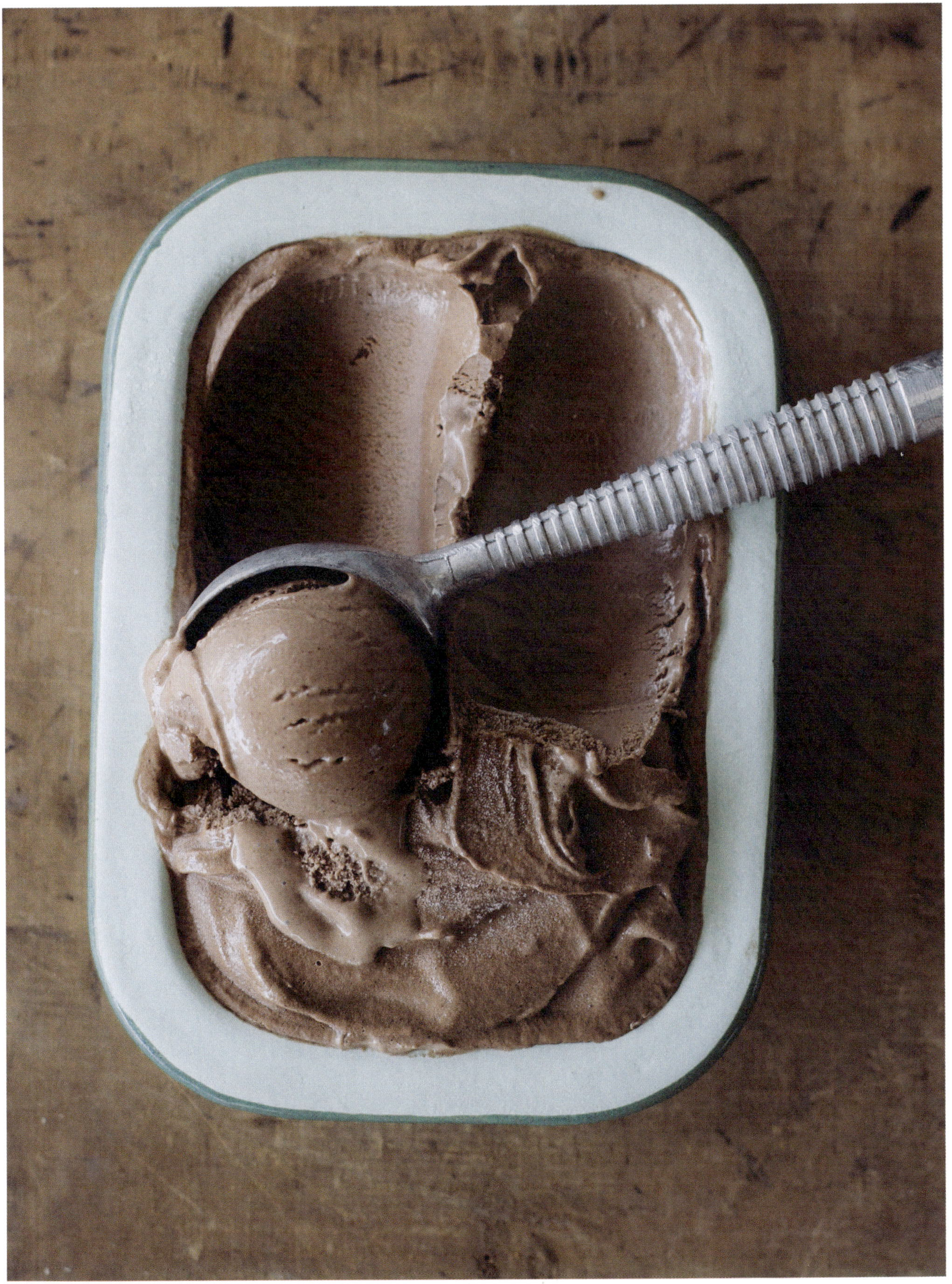

BLACKBERRY, APPLE + CINNAMON SLICE

MAKES APPROX. 15 SLICES | GLUTEN-FREE | DAIRY-FREE

This slice sits somewhere between a cake and baked oatmeal in texture, lovely and sturdy and filling too. It's the kind of thing I like to pack when we're having a day out, going on a road trip or flight, to keep those hunger pangs at bay. I use quinoa flakes for a 100% gluten-free slice, however, if you can eat oats by all means use them.

- 165g (2 cups) quinoa flakes
- 70g (½ cup) fine brown rice or quinoa flour
- 45g (½ cup) shredded coconut
- 2 teaspoons ground cinnamon
- 1 teaspoon gluten-free baking powder
- Good pinch of fine sea salt
- 80ml (⅓ cup) virgin coconut oil
- 125ml (½ cup) honey
- 3 large free-range eggs
- Finely grated zest of 1 lemon
- 125g (1 cup) fresh or locally grown frozen blackberries, (don't defrost frozen)
- 1 small apple, peeled, cored + finely diced

+ Preheat oven to 160ºC (320ºF). Grease and line a 28 x 18cm slice tin with baking paper, extending up and over the sides by roughly 2cm. Place dry ingredients in a large bowl, mixing well to combine. Heat coconut oil and honey in a small saucepan over medium heat, stirring until melted. Pour into dry ingredients and mix until just combined. Add eggs and zest and mix well. Fold through blackberries and apple at the last second, then transfer mixture to the slice tin, pressing down with the back of a spoon to even it out.

+ Bake for 20–25 minutes or until golden around the edges and firm to the touch in the centre. Remove from oven and set aside to cool in the tin before slicing. This slice will store, airtight, for 2–3 days, or in the fridge for longer.

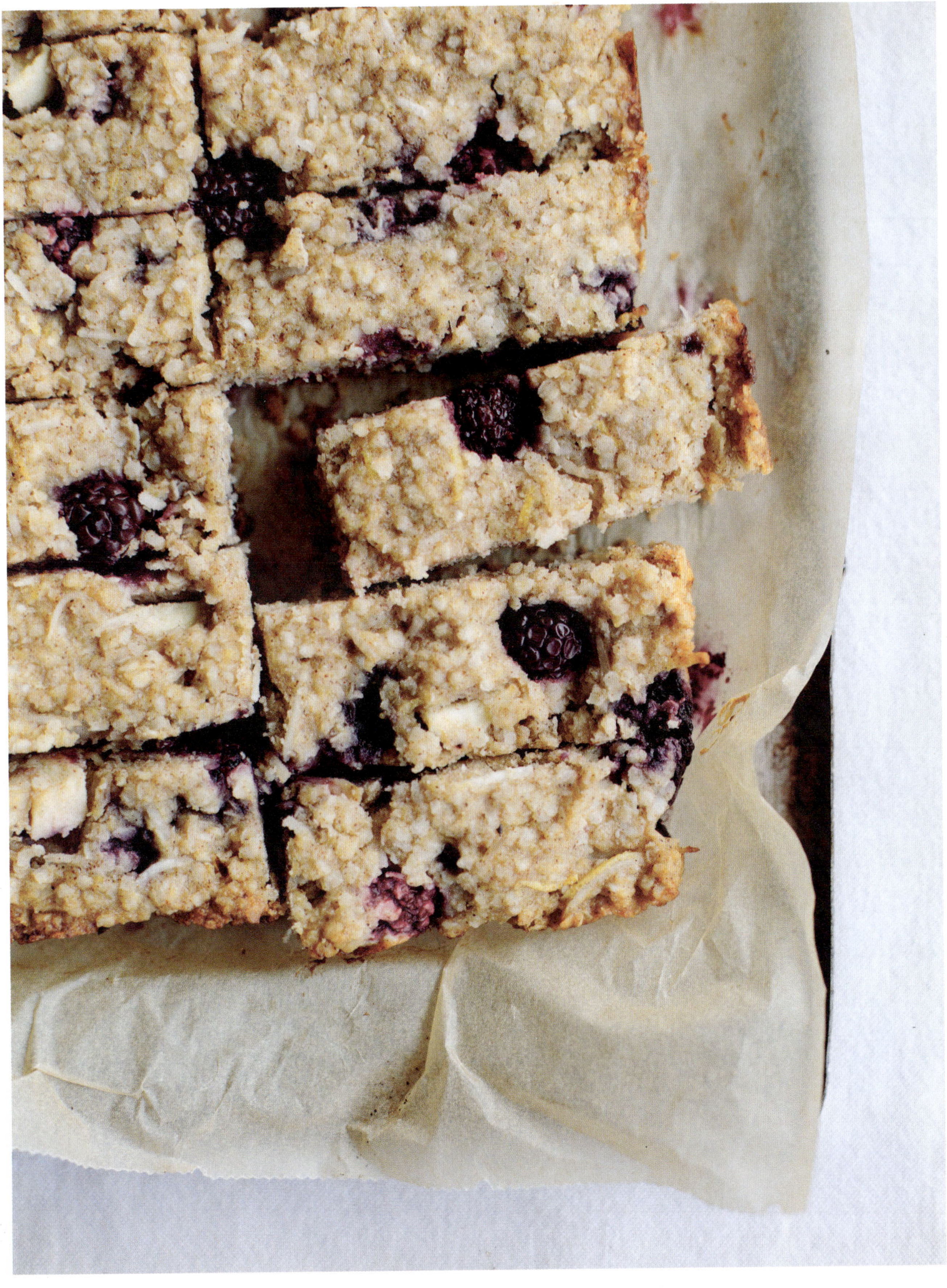

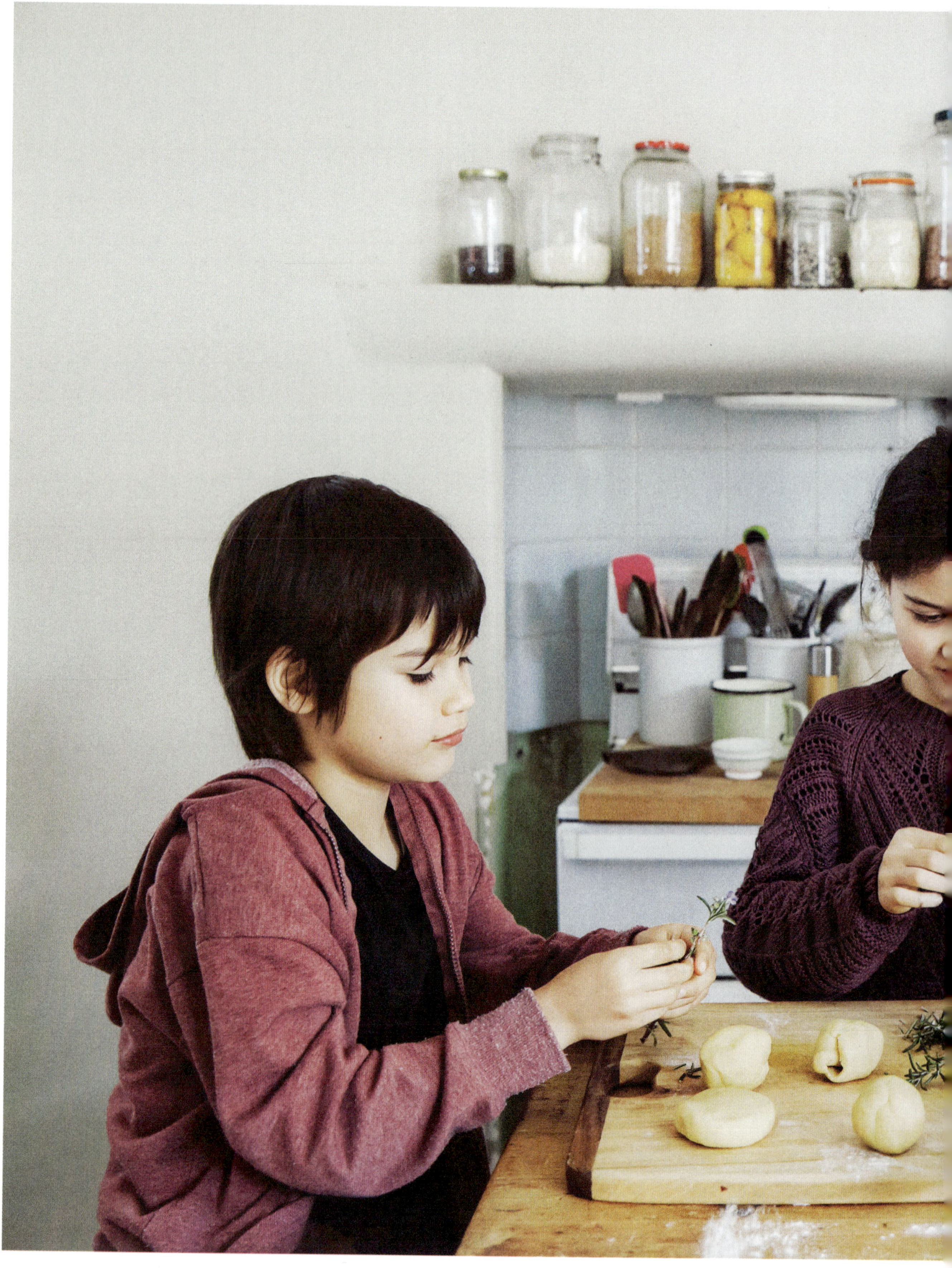

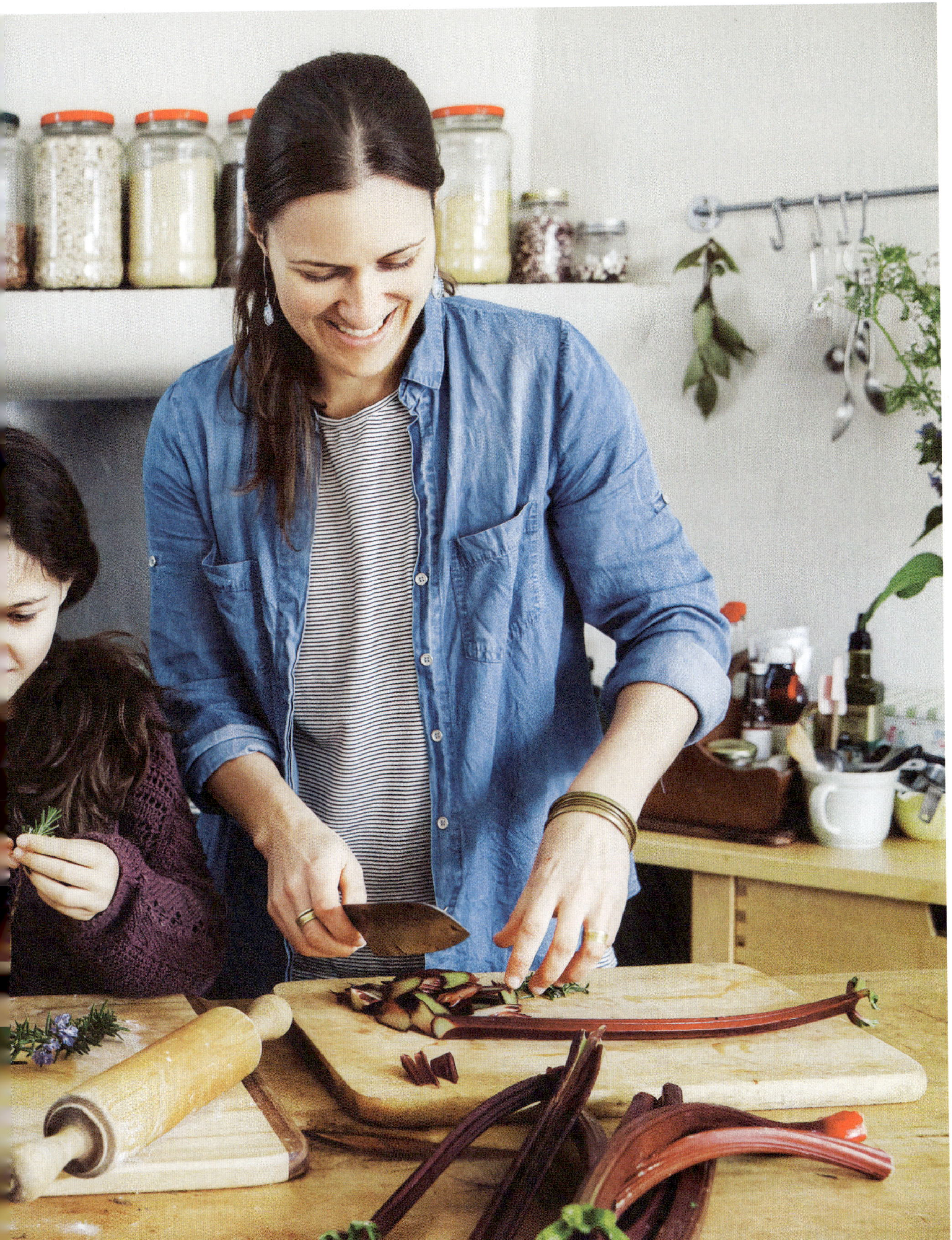

A WELL-STOCKED PANTRY

I don't know if it's from my years spent working in professional kitchens with store rooms full to the brim with all manner of ingredients, or from growing up in an isolated coastal town where grocery shopping was done once a week or fortnight, so stocking up was a necessity, but I really do love a well-stocked pantry. When you make food from scratch, it pays to have a good selection of whole food ingredients at hand, to avoid too many trips to the supermarket, where ready-made products may catch your eye! I love being able to whip up food simply from what I have at hand and, much to my husband's dismay when he tries to get something out of the booby-trapped pantry, our cupboards are nearly always full. Those of you who have my first cookbook will be familiar with the ingredients I like to use, but there's also a few extra little notes I've added in this time around.

flours

I keep a range of wholegrain gluten-free flours and starches at hand and, depending on the specifics of the recipe, I use a few of them in combination. By combining at least three different gluten-free flours, you will have a product with good texture and taste.

I usually go for one bulk flour (usually fine brown rice flour), a little wholegrain flour for goodness (such as buckwheat or quinoa) and a little starch (cornflour/ potato/tapioca) to bind and help keep things light. And I often add ground almonds or desiccated coconut to keep the moisture in and add texture.

fine brown rice flour

I use fine (super fine in the US) brown rice flour as my main bulk flour. It is made of finely ground brown rice, as the name suggests, and has a lovely mellow sweet flavour that works well in both sweet and savoury baking. When you rub a little between your fingers it should feel as smooth as wheat flour with no trace of grittiness. The more coarsely ground variety, while cheaper, leaves a gritty taste in your mouth and isn't suitable for sweet baking. Brown rice flour is less refined than white rice flour and contains more nutrients and vitamins. For years I have been saying that brown and white rice flours are interchangeable, but now I don't believe they are. Brown rice flour sucks up more moisture than white, so if you're using white you will need to add a little extra. You can buy fine brown rice flour from some health food stores in NZ, and in Australia you can also find it at selected supermarkets. Buy in small amounts and store in an airtight jar or container in your pantry or in the fridge during hot weather.

white rice flour

White rice flour is a super-fine flour made from finely ground white rice and can be bought very cheaply at your local Asian grocers (in 500g bags) and health food stores. I don't use white rice flour very often, except when cooking Asian dishes such as dumplings and sometimes in pasta, but I do use it often for dusting my benches for rolling out pastry. Make sure you buy 'rice flour' rather than 'glutinous rice flour' (sometimes known as 'sweet rice flour'), which is made from finely ground sticky white rice and is not suitable for use in my recipes.

buckwheat flour

Buckwheat flour is made from the gluten-free grain buckwheat. Although its name suggests it's part of the wheat family, it is actually a seed from a plant in the same family as rhubarb and sorrel. It has a nutty flavour and is extremely good for you, being high in protein, iron, zinc, B vitamins and selenium. By itself it has a tendency to become gluey in some recipes, but when paired with a lighter flour, such as brown rice flour, and a starch, like tapioca or cornflour, its somewhat strong flavour is mellowed perfectly. Buy in small amounts from health food stores and selected supermarkets and store in an airtight jar or container in the fridge. You can also find buckwheat flour at Indian stores labelled as kuttu ka atta or okhla flour – but be sure the shop has a high turnover as buckwheat flour can go rancid quite quickly.

quinoa flour

Quinoa flour is made from the nutrient-dense 'superfood' quinoa (pronounced keen-wa). It has a strong grassy flavour and is great in both sweet and savoury cooking. Because it is one of the more expensive and sometimes harder to find gluten-free flours, I have limited its use in this book to just a few recipes, but I do use it a lot in my day-to-day cooking. A little goes a long way and even just a touch added with cheaper flours can help to improve the texture of baked goods. You can find quinoa flour at health food stores but its price varies hugely, so shop around. Or, if you have access to a thermomix or flour mill, you can grind whole quinoa grains into a fine flour yourself. Buy in small amounts and store in an airtight jar or container in the fridge to prevent it turning rancid. I also use quinoa flakes as a 100% gluten-free alternative to oats in recipes such as my Blackberry, Apple + Cinnamon Slice (see page 228). You can track these down at your local health food store or at selected supermarkets.

potato flour (potato starch)

What most New Zealanders and Australians call potato flour is called potato starch in the rest of the world. The potato flour used in my recipes is made from just the starch of the potato, is very finely ground and looks a little like cornflour. It gives a lovely lightness to baked goods and also holds lots of moisture, which is always a good thing with any gluten-free baking. You can buy it at health food stores, some supermarkets and at most Asian grocers (where it is labelled 'potato starch'). Store in an airtight jar or container in your pantry.

cornflour

Cornflour is the finely ground endosperm of the corn kernel and is not to be confused with corn (maize) flour which is used in Mexican cooking. Because of the risk of GMO with all corn products, I like to buy organic cornflour from the health food store and always do a quick check to make sure it's gluten-free too. A lot of regular cornflour from the supermarket contains wheat. I use cornflour in all sorts of recipes: it's a great binder; gives a lovely lightness to baked goods; and is also great to thicken sauces and puddings. In some recipes it's totally fine to use tapioca flour or arrowroot instead of cornflour (for those of you who don't eat corn) and I sometimes suggest either one. However, there are times when the results just aren't the same. Store airtight in your pantry.

tapioca flour

Called flour but really more of a starch, tapioca flour is made from the root of the cassava plant. I use it as the starch component in some of my baking, however it can turn a little gummy in recipes with a lot of moisture. You can buy tapioca flour at health food stores, however I prefer to use the Erawan brand found at Asian grocers in 500g bags. I find it gives the best results when making dumplings in particular. In Australia some supermarkets also sell it in the Asian food section. Store airtight in your pantry. Most arrowroot you'll find at the supermarket is actually just tapioca flour, so use that if tapioca flour is hard to come by.

ground almonds

Also known as almond meal or almond flour, ground almonds are finely ground blanched almonds and are one of my favourite 'flours'. They add a lovely tender crumb and moisture to baked goods. Even just ¼ cup can take a gluten-free muffin from something good to something truly lovely. Ground almonds are also very high in protein and I add them to breakfast foods such as pancakes and muffins to keep us all full until lunch. Shop around, as there can be a huge difference in prices. I buy mine from the bulk bins of my local health food store at less than half the price of the supermarket. Buy in small amounts and store in an airtight jar or container in the fridge. Or double bag and freeze if you have bought in bulk. For a nut-free alternative to ground almonds, I'll often whizz up sunflower seeds until finely ground and use this instead.

chickpea flour

Also known as chana or besan flour, this is made from finely ground chickpeas (garbanzo beans). It has a somewhat strong flavour so is best for savoury dishes where its uses are endless! Its high protein content makes it perfect for use in savoury pastry, crepes and fritters. And when combined with water and cooked until thick, it can also be used as a polenta or tofu substitute (see page 202). It's very well priced and is easily found at your local Indian grocer or health food store. Store in an airtight jar or container in your pantry, or in your fridge in hot weather.

other gluten-free flours . . .

Above are the most common gluten-free flours that I use in this book. I do also use a few other flours in my day-to-day cooking and I think they're interesting to mention.

millet flour

Made from millet seeds that have been very finely ground to a fine powder, this is a high-protein flour with a sweet but slightly bitter flavour. I tend to use millet flour more in my savoury cooking, but there are a few sweet baked recipes where its flavour is complementary. You can buy millet flour for a reasonable price at health food stores and at Indian stores as bajri or bajra flour – but be sure the shop has a high turnover as millet flour can go rancid quite quickly. Buy in small amounts and store in an airtight jar or container in the fridge.

teff flour

Made from the highly nutritious teff grain from Eastern Africa, teff flour is thankfully becoming more and more available here in Australia and NZ although it is incredibly pricey. It gives a lovely soft crumb and colour to baked goods.

amaranth flour

Made from the tiny amaranth seed, amaranth flour has a strong flavour similar to that of quinoa.

sorghum flour

Made from finely ground sorghum grain, sorghum flour is also known as jowar in Indian grocers where it can sometimes be found.

coconut flour

Made as a by-product of coconut oil, coconut flour can be found at your local health food store and some supermarkets. It behaves like no other flour I know and needs way more liquid than regular flours to avoid producing dry products.

mesquite flour

More commonly known as mesquite powder, this is a wonderful ingredient and is made from the finely ground pods of the mesquite tree (not unlike carob). It has a sweet, chocolatey aroma and I love using even the tiniest amount in cakes and biscuits. It is very pricey, but a lovely thing to have around. It's nice added to smoothies, used to flavour maple syrup or added to raw sweet treats to add a boost of nutrients.

sweeteners

unrefined raw sugar

My go-to sugar is a golden unrefined cane sugar, which is similar in grain size to golden caster sugar, but contains more nutrients. Billington's brand is my favourite (although any raw sugars will do; I often use organic raw sugar as well) and is available in both NZ and Australia at health food stores and selected supermarkets. This is actually semi-refined, as the cane juice is cleaned before crystallising, but a much better alternative to highly refined white sugar. It's a step in the right direction if you are wanting a more wholefood diet but are not yet ready to use completely unrefined sugars such as rapadura and panela (which I haven't used in this book because of their high cost). Because the grain size of the golden unrefined raw sugar is smaller than regular raw sugar it's great to use for a lot of the baking I do. However, I find the grain a little too large to fully dissolve when creaming butter and sugar or adding sugar to beaten egg whites, so in this instance I always blend my sugar to create a much finer grain. To do this, simply place a couple of cups of sugar in a blender and blend on high for 30–45 seconds or until it's white and almost as powdery as icing sugar. Use immediately or store in an airtight jar or container. It does have a tendency to clump if stored for long periods once blended, so might need sifting or another quick blend before using. This is what I mean in recipes that list 'blended unrefined raw sugar'. This can also be used in place of pure icing sugar for dusting cakes.

muscovado sugar

Muscovado sugar is a semi-unrefined cane sugar that still contains the molasses in varying degrees and has more nutrients than regular soft brown sugar (which is really just refined white sugar with some of the molasses added to turn it brown). If you can't track down muscovado sugar, soft brown sugar is your next best choice. Muscovado comes in either light or dark and I tend to use light. It has a tendency to clump together so break up with your fingers. Store airtight in your pantry and do note that if left opened for long periods it can dry out, making it not great for baking, but still fine for using in recipes where it's added to warm liquids. Buy it at health food stores and selected supermarkets.

brown rice syrup

Sometimes referred to on the label as brown rice malt syrup, this is a sweet (but not in-your-face so) sticky syrup made from cooked brown rice flour or brown rice starch and enzymes. It's considered one of the most 'whole' natural sweeteners out there and is one of my favourites to use. It has the same consistency as honey but is not so sickly sweet. It can be found at health food stores in both NZ and Australia and at selected supermarkets in Australia for a very reasonable price. If you are coeliac or ultra-sensitive to gluten, make sure you source certified gluten-free brown rice syrup (or use honey), as some brands are made in factories where wheat is handled. Store airtight in the pantry.

maple syrup

I always buy 100% pure maple syrup; imitation maple syrup is mostly just cane sugar with flavours and colours added in. It's not the cheapest thing to buy in NZ and Australia, but its flavour is beautiful. Store in the fridge once opened.

honey

I buy local unrefined honey that has a beautiful floral sweet flavour. Store airtight in your pantry. Gently melt if solid.

dates

I often use dates to naturally sweeten baked goods and raw treats. I love eating medjool dates for a natural caramel hit, however, they can be pricey (especially in NZ), so I've only used the more readily available pitted dried dates in this book.

fats

butter

I grew up in a household where using margarine was pretty much as bad as saying a swear word. It was such a great relief when I successfully reintroduced real butter into our diets after years of reacting to all dairy: nothing beats butter in flavour and it's what I use most often for baking. I tend to use salted butter but you can use unsalted if preferred and add a pinch of salt to the recipe.

ghee (clarified butter)

Ghee heats to a high temperature without burning and gives a lovely buttery flavour to foods, without the lactose. I use it to pan-fry, sauté and sometimes even in baking. Because it has no milk solids it keeps well for up to 2 months in a jar at room temperature (although I make fairly small 500g batches that last about 3–4 weeks). Most people tend to use unsalted butter when making ghee, but unsalted is harder to find in NZ and expensive, so I generally use regular salted butter. Most of the salt stays in the sediment at the bottom of the pan and is discarded anyway.

To make ghee, put 500g salted or unsalted butter in a saucepan – when it melts it will foam up, so allow room for this in your pan. Gently melt over low-medium heat, stirring occasionally until starting to boil. Reduce heat to low and simmer gently for around 10 minutes. If you have a splatter screen, now is a good time to use it as the butter will spit a little. After about 10 minutes the splattering will have subsided, the milk solids dropped to the bottom of the pan and turned light golden brown and there will just be a little foam on the surface still. Remove from the heat and set aside for 10 minutes before straining through a fine sieve into a glass jar, leaving behind the sediment in the bottom of the pan. Allow to cool before putting on the lid. Store either at room temperature or in the fridge. Makes approx. 1½ cups (375ml).

virgin coconut oil

Virgin coconut oil is another of my favourite fats to use. It's extremely good for you and is a very stable non-dairy fat to use in high heat cooking. I use it in Asian and Indian cooking and it's invaluable as the setting agent in all raw sweet treats, as it firms up to solid when chilled. In winter it will set solid, so heat gently until liquid once again before adding to a recipe.

olive oil

I use a mild flavoured extra-virgin olive oil for cooking and reserve my more expensive robust flavoured extra-virgin olive oils for finishing off a dish, to drizzle or to use in salad dressings. For years cooking olive oil at high heat was seen as a big no-no, but thankfully new research out in the past few years has now dismissed this claim (and to be honest I've always trusted Italian Nonnas who use it liberally when cooking and have always done so anyway!) Use good-quality extra-virgin olive oils (local, if you can) to reap the benefits.

pure sesame oil

I keep a little bottle of pure sesame oil in my fridge for use in Asian dishes, where a little goes a long way.

mild-flavoured oils

I used to use rice bran and grapeseed oils when I wanted flavourless oil. However, recently it's become much clearer how these oils are extracted using solvents, so I no longer buy or use either of them. If I'm wanting a mild, almost neutral flavoured oil, I'll use macadamia nut oil or a mild extra-virgin olive oil instead.

rice, rice and more rice... and some grains, seeds, nuts + legumes, too

rice

We live off rice and not just because of my husband's Vietnamese background. It's cheap, easy to prepare and can be eaten at any time of the day. Our main types are: white jasmine, medium brown, white basmati and black rice for puddings. I grew up on brown rice and was a teenager before I ate white rice. I adore brown rice for its higher nutrient content, nutty flavour and because it reminds me of home, but when it comes to Asian or Indian food I do prefer the flavour and texture of white jasmine or basmati rice. I believe in the teachings of Chinese and Ayurvedic medicine, which promote eating white rice over brown as it's much gentler on our digestive system. You eat whichever you prefer; I personally like to just mix things up and eat a bit of each.

white rice

Eating an Indian curry would not be the same without a pile of freshly cooked white basmati rice on the side, however, because we eat mostly Asian-style, it's white jasmine rice that we go through the most.

To cook white rice, put 1 cup (215g) white rice (jasmine or basmati) in a saucepan, cover with plenty of water and scrunch and massage the grains with your hands to release the excess starch. Drain the cloudy water off and repeat a couple more times until the water is relatively clear. Drain rice well and put back in the pan. Add 1¼ cups (310ml) cold water to the pan, cover with a tight-fitting lid (it's very helpful if it's glass) and place over high heat. The second the water comes to the boil, reduce heat to the lowest setting without disturbing the rice or lid at all and cook for 12–14 minutes until all the water has been absorbed and there are little tunnels formed in the rice. Remove from the heat, keeping the lid firmly on, and set aside for 10 minutes before fluffing up the rice with a fork to serve. This is the amount that I cook for two adults and two kids (about 3 cups cooked rice), however, if you're feeding a crowd, you can double or triple this amount. If you do so, you can scale back the amount of water per rice – use the same amount as the rice with just an extra few tablespoons of water. So for 2 cups rice I would use 2¼ cups water (not 2½ cups).

brown rice

To cook brown rice, wash and drain 1 cup (200g) brown rice (medium grain, jasmine or basmati) and place in a pan with 1¾ cups (435ml) cold water, cover with a tight-fitting lid and bring to the boil. Reduce heat to the lowest setting and simmer, covered, for about 40–45 minutes until the water is absorbed and rice tender. Remove from heat, keeping the lid on and allow it to stand for 10 minutes before serving. This is the amount that I cook for two adults and two kids (about 3 cups cooked rice).

buckwheat

Although the name suggests it is part of the wheat family, buckwheat is actually a grain from the same family as rhubarb and sorrel. It has a nutty flavour and is extremely good for you, being high in protein, iron, zinc, B vitamins and selenium. It's great in salads or stews. To cook buckwheat, bring 2 cups (500ml) cold water and a pinch of sea salt to the boil in a saucepan. Add 1 cup (180g) raw hulled buckwheat, reduce heat to a simmer, cover and cook for 15–20 minutes or until water is absorbed and buckwheat tender. Remove the lid in the last few minutes of cooking to allow excess liquid to evaporate if needed. Remove from the heat, cover with the lid slightly ajar and allow to cool. Fluff up with a fork. This is about the right amount for 4 people (3 cups of cooked buckwheat).

quinoa

Quinoa (pronounced keen-wa) is labelled as a superfood and for good reason. It's ridiculously high in protein and unlike most other vegetarian protein sources it actually contains all of the nine essential amino acids, meaning it's a complete protein. It's high in iron, calcium, B vitamins and fibre and, while it's not the cheapest thing out, a little does go a long way. You can buy quinoa in shades of black, red and brown; they all work and cook the same, although I find the black and red varieties have a slightly stronger nutty flavour. I often make porridge out of it and love adding it to salads or serve it with stews. I find the easiest way to rinse the teeny little quinoa grains is to place them in a fine sieve and run under cold water while stirring them around a bit. Most quinoa is pre-rinsed these days but if you can track down the Australian grown quinoa from Tasmania by Kindred Organics this will require at least 3–4 good rinses to remove the naturally bitter saponin coating.

To cook quinoa, bring 1½ cups (375ml) water to the boil in a saucepan, add 1 cup (185g) quinoa, cover with a lid and reduce heat to a gentle simmer. Cook for 10–12 minutes until all the water has been absorbed and quinoa is tender. Remove from the heat, leave the lid on and set aside to steam for a further 5 minutes before fluffing up with a fork. This makes about enough for 4 people (3 cups cooked quinoa). If you've soaked the quinoa overnight in cold water (to improve digestibility), reduce the water to 1 cup (250ml).

millet

Millet is one of those underrated grains that I adore (but, to be quite blunt, it's mostly known for its addition to birdseed). The upside to this is that it's one of the cheapest gluten-free grains on the market and I'd be really happy if it stayed that way. Throughout winter I eat warm millet porridge for breakfast and I love adding it to salads or roasted vegetables for a hit of goodness. Like buckwheat and quinoa, millet is high in protein, calcium, iron, B vitamins and zinc, but it has a milder flavour and is a great substitute for rice if you're looking to eat more nutrient-dense foods. You can just simmer the grains in water; however, I really like the flavour and texture if lightly toasted in a little oil or ghee first.

To make about 3 cups cooked millet, heat 1 tablespoon virgin coconut oil, olive oil or ghee in a saucepan, add 1 cup (210g) raw hulled millet and stir constantly for 3–4 minutes until it smells toasty. Carefully add 2 cups (500ml) water (it will splutter a bit) and a pinch of salt, cover the pan and bring to the boil. Reduce heat to the lowest setting and simmer for 20 minutes, by which time all the water will have been absorbed and the millet will be tender. Remove from the heat, keep the lid on and allow to sit for 5 minutes before fluffing up with a fork. If you've soaked the millet overnight in cold water (to improve digestibility), reduce the water to 1½ cups (375ml).

toasting spices, seeds + nuts

Toast whole spices in a dry pan over medium heat, stirring often, for 30–60 seconds or until lightly browned. Remove from the heat and grind to a fine powder using a mortar and pestle or spice grinder.

Toast sesame seeds or pine nuts in a dry frying pan over medium heat for 1–2 minutes, stirring constantly until light golden all over. Watch them like a hawk, as they go from golden to black in a matter of seconds.

To lightly toast cashew nuts or whole almonds, bake at 180ºC (350ºF) for 10–12 minutes, stirring every 5 minutes until golden brown. Toast sliced almonds for just 4–5 minutes; and pecans for 8–10 minutes.

To lightly toast whole peanuts or hazelnuts, bake at 180ºC (350ºF) for 12–15 minutes, stirring every 5 minutes until golden brown and skins start to lift off. You can rub the skins off when cool, if preferred.

legumes

Sitting alongside the jars of grains and seeds in my pantry, you'll find legumes of every colour and shape. I have a tendency to buy every legume I ever come across, but the main ones I use are chickpeas, lentils, black beans and butter beans.

I buy regular brown lentils, which are always cheap, but also have a thing for French Puy-style and Beluga lentils as they keep their shape and texture once cooked. I keep a well-stocked jar of red lentils and use these often for soups and dhals and I buy whole dried chickpeas to use in stews, soups or to make into falafel and hummus.

Make sure you buy un-heat-treated legumes or you'll never get them soft no matter how long you soak and cook them. And, although they are not my first choice, I also keep a few tins of cooked chickpeas, black beans and butter beans for times when I haven't planned ahead. Just go for the no salt varieties (organic if you can) and make sure you rinse and drain them well before use.

dairy alternatives + eggs

We eat very little dairy in our family as lactose is not really our friend. Listed below are the low-lactose dairy products we can tolerate and also the dairy-free alternatives that I like to use at home. I've lumped eggs into this category too, but please don't assume that if you can't tolerate one, you can't tolerate the other. We eat very little dairy in our house but we go through a carton of eggs in the blink of an eye!

yoghurt

I make my own natural yoghurt for a fraction of the cost of store-bought. If you are buying yours, go for a natural plain yoghurt or thick unsweetened Greek yoghurt. Most of the lactose is broken down into lactic acid, so some people, like us, can enjoy it with no problems.

To make yoghurt, bring 1 litre (4 cups) whole full-fat milk to just below boiling point in a large saucepan. As it starts to froth up and reach boiling point, remove from the heat and set aside to cool for approx. 20 minutes. When it has cooled enough for you to hold your finger in for 10–15 seconds without burning, discard the skin from the surface of the milk. Put 2 tablespoons plain live yoghurt (any store-bought natural yoghurt will do) into a 1 litre glass or ceramic jar, pour in a little of the warm milk and whisk to dissolve yoghurt before adding the rest and mixing thoroughly. Cover or put on the lid and keep in a warm place (a hot water cupboard, in the oven with just the light on or wrapped up next to hot water bottles is perfect), undisturbed, for at least 6–8 hours or overnight (in cold weather it can take 12+ hours, if super-hot it can be done in 4–5 hours). Transfer to the fridge and chill overnight. It will keep in the fridge for 1 week, always save 2 tablespoons of yoghurt for your next batch.

labneh

Labneh is strained yoghurt and is a great alternative to cream cheese or cream when lactose is not tolerated. You can find it at selected specialty stores but it's really easy to make yourself and very cost effective to make if using homemade yoghurt.

To make labneh, spoon 1 litre (4 cups) natural plain yoghurt into a square of muslin or cheesecloth. Pull up all four corners and tie. Hang from a wooden spoon that is resting over a bowl or large container (to collect the dripping whey). Leave in the fridge overnight or for up to 48 hours depending on how firm you want your labneh. Check the drip tray occasionally to make sure it's not overflowing (the whey freezes well and can be added to smoothies for an extra vitamin and mineral boost). Makes 1½–2 cups.

feta

Feta is one of the only cheeses we tolerate, with the odd exception of a little bit of mozzarella and haloumi. I buy both firm Greek-style feta and soft Danish feta.

coconut milk + cream

We go through lots of coconut milk and cream in our house. I do sometimes make my own by blending peeled mature coconut flesh with warm water and straining it through my nut-milk bag (cheesecloth or muslin can also be used). Usually, I just buy the tinned stuff. When buying tinned coconut milk and cream it is important that you read the label. It should list only coconut and water (and sometimes ascorbic acid, which is vitamin C used as a natural preservative). Many brands, even some organic ones, contain emulsifiers, thickeners and preservatives. I recommend you always buy full-fat too: the light varieties are simply thinned down with water and then thickeners and emulsifiers are put back in to give the same mouth-feel as full-fat. If you like, you can always use half coconut milk/cream, half water, making the overall fat content less (but also lessening the deliciousness, in my humble opinion).

whipped coconut cream

This is a great alternative to whipped cream for the lactose intolerant. You might have to experiment with different brands of coconut milk to find out which ones set firm in the fridge, as not all do. I find Chef's Choice brand works well, followed by Aroy-D – both made in Thailand and found at your local Asian grocers.

Refrigerate the tin overnight and then give it a gentle shake. If you don't hear any movement in the tin, you should be good to go. If there is movement, reserve that tin for another use and try a different brand. Open the tin, scrape off the solid top layer of 'cream' and place into a clean bowl. Reserve the watery liquid from the bottom for another use (add to your morning porridge in place of milk or use in smoothies). Whisk the cream for 1–2 minutes with electric beaters or a balloon whisk, until thick like regular whipped cream. Sweeten to taste with a touch of honey, maple syrup or pure icing sugar, keeping in mind that you're usually serving with a sweet dessert.

nut + rice milk

The main milks I use are homemade nut and seed milks and store-bought Australian-made rice milk. You can buy almond milk at most supermarkets nowadays, but many contain questionable ingredients such as carrageenan and high-fructose sweeteners such as agave syrup. It's so easy to make it yourself that I can't recommend it enough. Most commercially made nut milks also contain high amounts of phytic acid as the nuts are not always soaked before the milk is made. I have to admit I don't always soak all the nuts that I eat, however if you are consuming large amounts of commercially made nut milk you'd be getting a pretty large daily dose of these enzyme inhibitors. I make almond (or other nut and seed) milk every few days and store it in the fridge in a large glass jar (just shake before using as the solids will settle to the bottom), and I always have cartons of unsweetened Australian-made rice milk (both regular and the high-protein version where chickpeas are added) at hand for use in baking and for times when I haven't made fresh almond milk.

To make nut/seed milk, soak 1 cup of your chosen nuts or seeds (or a combination) overnight in plenty of cold water. Drain well, rinse and transfer to a blender. Add 250ml (1 cup) cold filtered water and a good pinch of fine sea salt and blend on high for 30–45 seconds or until reasonably smooth. Add 500ml (2 cups) cold water and 1–2 tablespoons pure maple syrup, brown rice syrup or 2 soaked dried dates, and blend for a further minute or until smooth. Strain through a nut milk bag or square of muslin or cheesecloth. Store in the fridge for 3 days, making sure you give it a shake before serving as some of the solids will naturally settle down to the bottom.

free-range eggs

We eat eggs so quickly in our house that I just leave them out on the bench, with the exception of high summer when I keep them in the fridge. I recommend you bring your eggs to room temperature for baking; this helps the eggs emulsify with the other ingredients and gives better rise. Either leave out on the bench overnight, or sit them in a bowl of warm water for 5 minutes before using. Because I buy my eggs straight from the farmer, they range in size from 60–64g; this equates to a size 7/large egg in NZ and the UK, but is known as an extra-large egg in Australia.

other bits + bobs...

filtered water

I use filtered water in all my cooking and recommend you do too, to avoid excess chemicals and for better flavour. We have a bench-top water filter that gets a workout on a daily basis, but simple jug filters or larger under-bench water filters are great too.

cocoa powder

I use regular natural unsweetened (non-alkalised) cocoa powder, not Dutch-processed cocoa.

dark chocolate

I use Whittaker's 50% dark chocolate, which is dairy-free.

psyllium husks

More commonly used as a dietary fibre supplement, psyllium husks are amazing in gluten-free baked goods, especially breads. I use them in conjunction with ground linseeds and chia seeds in place of xanthan and guar gums in my gluten-free breads. They suck up moisture and give breads good elasticity to prevent cracking and crumbling. Buy from the health food section of most supermarkets or your local health food store. As you only use in small amounts, one 500g bag will last you a very long time. Store airtight once opened.

tahini

Tahini is a wonderful dairy-free source of calcium. If you can handle the more intense flavour of the unhulled you'll be gaining higher nutritional values. Store tahini in the fridge once opened to prevent the oils turning rancid.

savoury pastry

1 large potato, peeled + roughly chopped
90g (⅔ cup) fine brown rice flour
55g (½ cup) chickpea (chana or besan) flour
35g (⅓ cup) tapioca flour or gluten-free organic cornflour (starch)
½ teaspoon fine sea salt
125g chilled butter, cubed
1 large free-range egg yolk

Place the potato for the pastry in a small saucepan with a little sea salt, cover with water and bring to the boil. Simmer for 10–15 minutes or until soft. Drain, mash and cool. You should have around ¾ cup. This can be done well ahead of time and stored overnight in the fridge in a covered container.

To make pastry, place dry ingredients in the bowl of a food processor and pulse to combine. Add cubed butter and pulse until the mixture resembles fine breadcrumbs. Add cooled potato and egg yolk and pulse a couple more times until combined. Turn mixture out onto a clean, lightly rice-floured bench and bring it together with your hands, kneading a couple of times to form a soft dough. Form into a disc, place in a plastic bag and chill for 30 minutes before using. The pastry can also be frozen for up to 3 months (defrost in the fridge overnight before using).

vegetable stock

2 tablespoons olive oil
2 large onions, unpeeled + cut into quarters
3 large carrots, unpeeled + cut into 4–5 chunks
5–6 celery stalks, cut into 4–5 chunks (leave some of the tender leaves on, too)
15 whole black peppercorns
6 parsley stalks
3 fresh or dried bay leaves
A few thyme sprigs

To make vegetable stock, heat the oil in a large stockpot (8–10 litres would be perfect here) over medium heat. Add onion and cook, stirring often, for 2–3 minutes until starting to soften. Add carrot and celery and cook for a further 6–7 minutes. I like to get a little colour into my vegetables for depth of flavour and sweetness, but for light-coloured stock (perhaps for risotto) just soften the vegetables without browning. Pour in 4 litres (16 cups) cold water and add peppercorns, parsley stalks, bay leaves and fresh thyme, bring to the boil, reduce heat to a gentle simmer and cook for 45 minutes.

Remove from the heat, season to taste with sea salt and set aside until cool enough to handle. Strain stock through a fine sieve set over another large saucepan or bowl. Use immediately or store in the fridge for 2–3 days. Stock can also be frozen for 3–4 months, in which case I tend to divide and freeze in 500ml or 1 litre plastic containers. Makes approx. 3 litres (12 cups).

INGREDIENTS

baking paper = parchment paper
baking soda = bicarbonate of soda; sodium bicarbonate
bird's-eye chilli = small hot red chilli
biscuit = cookie
blackberry = bramble
capsicum = bell pepper
cheesecloth = muslin
chickpea = garbanzo bean
chickpea flour = besan; chana
coriander = cilantro
cornflour = cornstarch
eggplant = aubergine
flat-leaf parsley = Italian parsley
ghee = clarified butter
green chillies = banana or Serrano chillies

ground almonds = almond meal
ground hazelnuts = hazelnut meal
icing sugar = confectioner's sugar
kumara = sweet potato
peanut = groundnut
potato flour = potato starch
pumpkin = winter squash
pumpkin seeds = pepitas
red onion = Spanish onion
rocket = arugula
silverbeet = chard; Swiss chard
snow pea = mangetout; sugar pea
spring onion = scallion
sultana = golden raisin; white raisin
tea towel = dish cloth

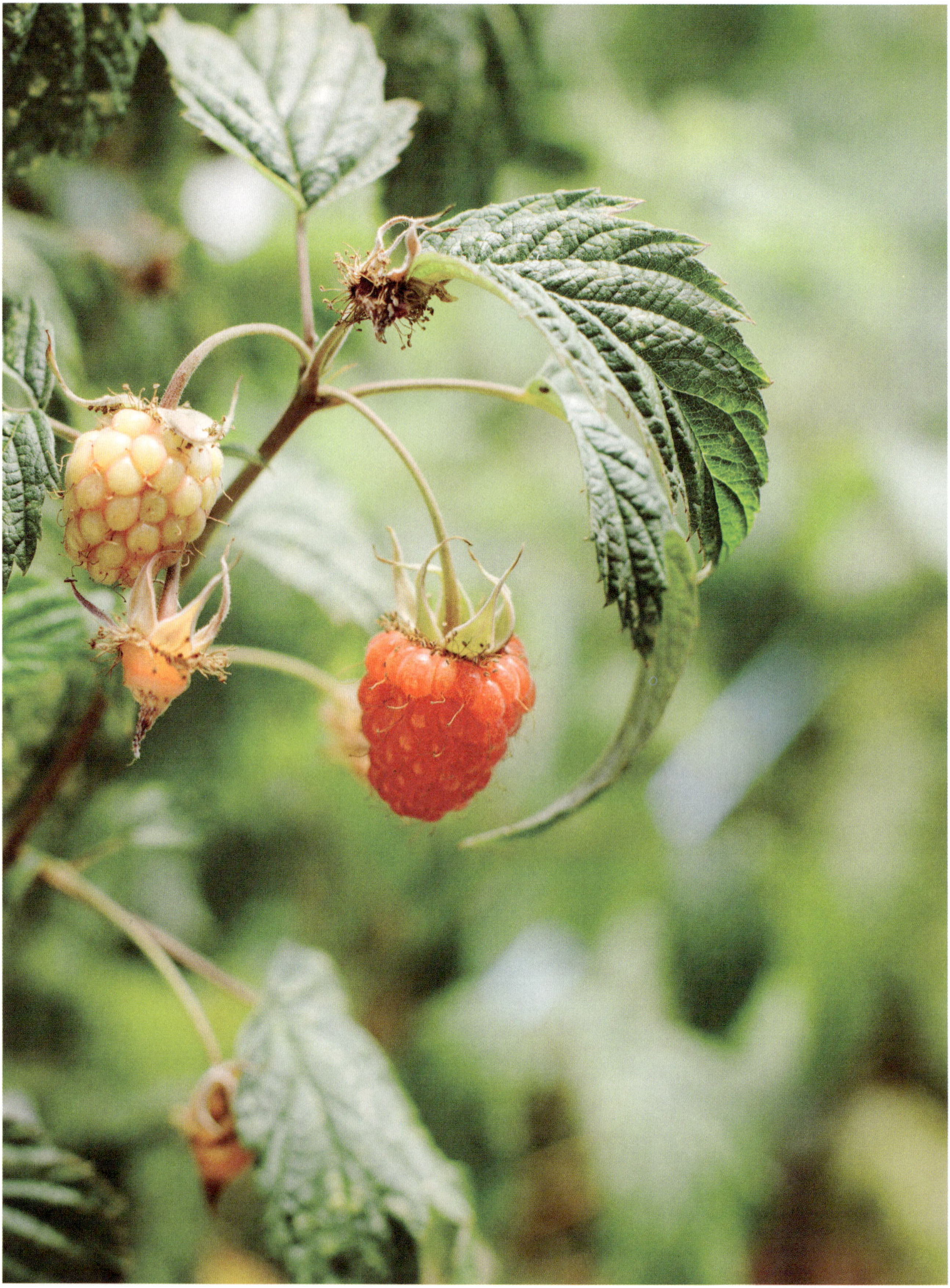

CONVERSIONS

weight

7g = ¼ oz
15g = ½ oz
20g = ¾ oz
30g = 1 oz
60g = 2 oz
90g = 3 oz
125g = 4 oz
155g = 5 oz
185g = 6 oz
220g = 7 oz
250g = 8 oz
280g = 9 oz
315g = 10 oz
345g = 11 oz
375g = 12 oz
410g = 13 oz
440g = 14 oz
470g = 15 oz
500g = 1 lb
750g = 1½ lb
1kg = 2 lb

length

5mm = ¼ in
1cm = ½ in
2cm = ¾ in
2.5cm = 1 in
5cm = 2 in
6cm = 2½ in
8cm = 3 in
10cm = 4 in
13cm = 5 in
15cm = 6 in
18cm = 7 in
20cm = 8 in
23cm = 9 in
25cm = 10 in
28cm = 11 in
30cm = 12 in

liquid measurements

1 teaspoon = 5ml
1 tablespoon (NZ, UK, USA) = 15ml
 (or 3 teaspoons)
1 tablespoon (Australia) = 20ml
 (or 4 teaspoons)
⅛ cup = 30ml = 1 fl oz
¼ cup = 60ml = 2 fl oz
⅓ cup = 80ml = 2½ fl oz
½ cup = 125ml = 4 fl oz
1 cup = 250ml = 8 fl oz

oven temperatures

120° Celsius = 250° Fahrenheit = gas mark ½
135° Celsius = 275° Fahrenheit = gas mark 1
150° Celsius = 300° Fahrenheit = gas mark 2
170° Celsius = 335° Fahrenheit = gas mark 3
180° Celsius = 350° Fahrenheit = gas mark 4
190° Celsius = 375° Fahrenheit = gas mark 5
200° Celsius = 400° Fahrenheit = gas mark 6

WITH THANKS...

Being given the chance to write one cookbook was amazing beyond belief, so to be here again second time around really blows my mind. A thousand thankyous to everyone who made it possible.

To Finlay, Kathy, Sandra, Kimberley + the rest of the HarperCollins team. Thank you for trusting me again and for bringing this baby to life. Thank you to Anna Egan-Reid for her beautiful book design.

Much love and deepest gratitude to my agent Vicki Marsdon. Your belief in me never ceases to amaze.

To Kerry Davies – My Aussie mum. Thank you for being my number one cheerleader. You give so much to those around you and I love you beyond belief.

To Samantha Koch – I don't know what good deed I did to have you come into my life, but I am forever grateful. Your wisdom, big heart + willingness to help never goes unnoticed. I love you to bits.

To Jude Blereau – Thank you for always being the voice of reason + for your reassuring words when I felt lost in the process. Your friendship means the world. Also thanks heaps for allowing us to shoot in your beautiful kitchen!

To Emiko + Lani – thanks so much for taking some of these recipes for a test drive!

To Christine Lim – Thank you for your beautiful shots of me and the kids!

To Patti Mitchley – Thank you for taking a punt on a shy 16 year old ... xx

To my dear friends – Sash, Peggy, Janna, Grace, Anna, Rhyannon, Kara, Aidee, Willa, Lani, Laurinda, Cimmie, Jude, Hayley, Kate, Jacqui, Nat, Trish, Annemarie, Keri + Amy. Your constant love + support means the world.

To Shauna James Ahern, Heidi Swanson, Bryant Terry, Tara O'Brady, Tara Austen Weaver, Aran Goyoaga + Luisa Brimble – You inspire me more than you'll ever know.

To Mum + Dad – Thank you for showing me from a very young age what it means to truly live with the seasons, respect the earth and to nourish our bodies with real food.

To the Galloway + Nguyen tribes – I couldn't ask for two more-food-loving families! Love you all.

To Ada + Kye – I know it's not easy having mum so engrossed in work for months on end. Thank you for your patience, your love, support, cute hands (!) + honest food critiques. Mama loves you both to the moon and back.

And to Si – I owe so much of this to you, thank you for your constant support. I can't wait to restart our life back in NZ and for you to bring magic to our veggie garden in the way only you can. I love you, always.

Finally, to the readers of my website, My Darling Lemon Thyme. It's because of you that I had the opportunity to write my first book. And it is your enthusiastic support of my work that has enabled me to write again. Thank you, a million times over.

INDEX

almonds
  chilli almonds 32
  chocolate, chilli + almond cookies 116
  smoked paprika + almond quinoa 92
amaranth porridge w/ orange + rosemary persimmon 46
apples
  apple, lemon + thyme crumble 102
  apple radish slaw 204
  blackberry, apple + cinnamon slice 228
  cauliflower + apple salad w/ creamy honey mustard dressing 94
  feijoa + apple shortcake 50
apricots
  labneh w/ apricot purée + salted nuts 208
  raspberry, apricot + orange popsicles 212
avocado strawberry shake 170

bananas
  banana cake w/ lemon coconut icing 162
  flourless banana, cherry + chocolate muffins 214
  sunshine smoothie 210
beetroot
  beetroot chocolate cakes 158
  beetroot + fennel soup w/ whipped feta croutons 136
  beetroot gnocchi w/ caper gremolata 122
  celeriac + beet salad w/ lemon, chilli + mint 84
  pickled baby beets 144
  pickled beetroot, lentil + feta salad 146
biscuits, crumbles and slices
  apple, lemon + thyme crumble 102
  chocolate, chilli + almond cookies 116
  chocolate-dipped hazelnut biscuits 114
  fig, millet + dark chocolate bites 56
  grapefruit curd slice w/ rosemary + pine nuts 106
  pumpkin + chocolate brownie 100
  shortbread 106
black pepper tofu w/ cucumber pickle 194
blackberry, apple + cinnamon slice 228
broad beans + garlicky peas w/ egg, feta + dill 138
broccolini + tofu noodles w/ peanut lime sauce 72
broth, carrot + ginger, w/buckwheat noodles 150
brownie, pumpkin + chocolate 100
buckwheat
  buckwheat noodles w/ carrot + ginger broth 150
  buckwheat 'risotto' w/ roasted pumpkin, feta + crispy sage 86
  tomato, eggplant + buckwheat bake 26
burgers, chickpea + carrot, w/ guacamole 124

cakes
  banana cake w/ lemon coconut icing 162
  beetroot chocolate cakes 158
  chocolate zucchini cake 60
  dark chocolate, pear + pistachio cake 118
  feijoa + apple shortcake 50
  flourless chocolate torte 110
  gingerbread loaf w/ coconut icing 108
  little raw carrot cakes w/ whipped orange maple cream 172
  mango, lime + coconut cake 222
  nectarine honey cakes 216
  plum + toasted hazelnut cake 48
  raspberry + peach crumble cake 220
caper gremolata 122
carrots
  buckwheat noodles w/ carrot + ginger broth 150
  chickpea + carrot burgers w/ guacamole 124
  little raw carrot cakes w/ whipped orange maple cream 172
  rainbow carrot salad w/ mint mojo + turmeric pepitas 148
  za'atar roasted carrot + chickpeas w/ pickled chilli, radish + yoghurt 178
cauliflower
  cauliflower + apple salad w/ creamy honey mustard dressing 94
  cauliflower + fennel seed fritters 82
  cauliflower spaghetti w/ lemon, chilli + crispy capers 90
  roasted cauliflower, chickpea + quinoa salad w/ jalapeño lime dressing 76

celeriac + beet salad w/ lemon, chilli + mint 84
chai, rose + cardamom 98
chard pilaf, rainbow 68
cherry, banana + chocolate muffins, flourless 214
chestnut maple purée 52
chickpeas
    chickpea + carrot burgers w/ guacamole 124
    chickpea 'polenta' w/ tomato zucchini stew 202
    chickpea + tomato curry 18
    honeyed eggplant w/ chickpeas + coriander sauce 10
    roasted cauliflower, chickpea + quinoa salad w/ jalapeño lime dressing 76
    tomato + chickpea salad w/ green olive dressing 196
    turmeric mushrooms w/ chickpea crepes 12
    za'atar roasted carrot + chickpeas w/ pickled chilli, radish + yoghurt 178
chilli
    cauliflower spaghetti w/ lemon, chilli + crispy capers 90
    chilli almonds 32
    chocolate, chilli + almond cookies 116
    pickled chillies 180
    sriracha 184
chips, baked kumara w/ oregano, paprika + chilli 16
chocolate
    beetroot chocolate cakes 158
    chocolate, chilli + almond cookies 116
    chocolate-dipped hazelnut biscuits 114
    chocolate éclairs w/ chestnut + maple cream 54
    chocolate icing 54, 60
    chocolate zucchini cake 60
    dark chocolate cinnamon ice cream 226
    dark chocolate, pear + pistachio cake 118
    dark chocolate, pistachio halva ice cream bites 224
    fig, millet + dark chocolate bites 56
    flourless banana, cherry + chocolate muffins 214
    flourless chocolate torte 110

olive oil + chocolate chunk ice cream 174
pumpkin + chocolate brownie 100
chutney, mint 66
coconut
    coconut icing 108
    coconut pikelets w/ lemon curd 156
    curried kumara + coconut soup 70
    lemon coconut icing 162
    lemon, lime + coconut tartlets 104
    mango, lime + coconut cake 222
    spicy coconut noodle soup 134
coriander
    coriander + mint sauce 82
    coriander + pumpkin salsa 40
    coriander sauce 10
corn
    charred corn + red rice salad 192
    sweetcorn soup w/ roasted cherry tomatoes + crispy tortillas 186
chickpea crepes w/ turmeric mushrooms 12
croutons 136
crumble, apple, lemon + thyme 102
curd, grapefruit, slice w/ rosemary + pine nuts 106
curd, lemon 156
curry
    chickpea + tomato curry 18
    curried kumara + coconut soup 70
    curried lentil hand pies 74
    curry paste 140
    pumpkin korma 88
    tempeh curry w/ chilli kang kong 140
custard, vanilla 62

dressings *see* sauces and dressings
dumplings, shiitake, peanut + tofu 28

éclairs, chocolate w/ chestnut + maple cream 54
eggs
    fried tortillas w/ pumpkin + coriander salsa 40
    garlicky peas + broad beans w/ egg, feta + dill 138
    leek + potato frittata 152
eggplant
    honeyed eggplant w/ chickpeas + coriander sauce 10
    tomato, eggplant + buckwheat bake 26

feijoa + apple shortcake 50
fennel + beetroot soup w/ whipped feta croutons 136
fennel, leek + white bean stew 128
feta
    buckwheat 'risotto' w/ roasted pumpkin, feta + crispy sage 86
    garlicky peas + broad beans w/ egg, feta + dill 138
    minty pea + feta purée w/ buttered asparagus on toast 132
    pickled beetroot, lentil + feta salad 146
    pumpkin + feta stuffed jalapeños 6
    silverbeet + feta gözleme 130
    whipped feta croutons 136
    zucchini, feta + mint fritters 182
fig, ginger + orange labneh tart 44
fig, millet + dark chocolate bites 56
five-spice dressing 200
flourless banana, cherry + chocolate muffins 214
flourless chocolate torte 110
frittata, leek + potato 152
fritters, cauliflower + fennel seed 82
fritters, zucchini, feta + mint 182

ginger-roasted pumpkin + quinoa salad w/ mint, chilli + lime 34
gingerbread loaf w/ coconut icing 108
gnocchi, beetroot w/ caper gremolata 122
gözleme, silverbeet + feta 130
grapefruit curd slice w/ rosemary + pine nuts 106
grapefruit, pink + rosemary popsicles 168
gremolata, caper 122

haloumi, grilled w/ roasted grape dressing 198
hazelnuts
    chocolate-dipped hazelnut biscuits 114
    hazelnut romesco 8
    plum + toasted hazelnut cake 48
honey mustard dressing, creamy 94
honeyed eggplant w/ chickpeas + coriander sauce 10
horseradish mash 78

ice cream
    dark chocolate cinnamon ice cream 226

ice cream (cont'd)
   dark chocolate, pistachio halva ice cream bites 224
   olive oil + chocolate chunk ice cream 174
icing
   chocolate 54, 60
   coconut 108
   lemon coconut 162
   whipped orange maple cream 172

jalapeño lime dressing 76
jalapeños, pumpkin + feta stuffed 6

korma, pumpkin 88
kumara
   baked kumara chips w/ oregano, paprika + chilli 16
   curried kumara + coconut soup 70
   roasted kumara, persimmon + rocket salad w/ jalapeño dressing 20
   tandoori-roasted roots w/ fresh mint chutney 66

labneh, fig, ginger + orange tart 44
labneh w/ apricot purée + salted nuts 208
leek, fennel + white bean stew 128
leek + potato frittata 152
lemon
   apple, lemon + thyme crumble 102
   cauliflower spaghetti w/ lemon, chilli + crispy capers 90
   lemon coconut icing 162
   lemon curd 156
   lemon, lime + coconut tartlets 104
   lemony mushroom quinoa w/ chilli almonds 32
lentils
   beetroot, lentil + feta salad 146
   curried lentil hand pies 74
   lentil patties w/ horseradish mash + sauerkraut 78
lime
   jalapeño lime dressing 76
   lemon, lime + coconut tartlets 104
   mango, lime + coconut cake 222
   peanut lime sauce 72

mango, lime + coconut cake 222
millet, fig + dark chocolate bites 56
mint
   mint chutney 66
   mint + coriander sauce 82
   mint mojo 148
   minty pea + feta purée w/ buttered asparagus on toast 132
mojo, mint 148
muffins, flourless banana, cherry + chocolate 214
muffins, rhubarb, strawberry + ginger 166
mushrooms
   lemony mushroom quinoa w/ chilli almonds 32
   mustardy mushroom + toasted quinoa tagliatelle 36
   shiitake, peanut + tofu dumplings 28
   turmeric mushrooms w/ chickpea crepes 12

nectarine honey cakes 216
noodles
   buckwheat noodles w/ carrot + ginger broth 150
   rice noodle salad w/ pickled vegetables + 5-spice dressing 200
   roasted broccolini + tofu noodles w/ peanut lime sauce 72
   spicy coconut noodle soup 134
   spicy tofu noodles 188

olives
   green olive dressing 196
   olive oil + chocolate chunk ice cream 174
   preserved olives 22
orange
   fig, ginger + orange labneh tart 44
   orange + rosemary persimmon 46
   raspberry, apricot + orange popsicles 212
   rhubarb, hibiscus + orange sorbet 164
   roasted strawberry, orange + pink peppercorn popsicles 218
   whipped orange maple cream 172

paprika roasted parsnips w/ hazelnut romesco 8
parsnip soup, creamy w/ smoked paprika + almond quinoa 92
parsnips, paprika roasted, w/ hazelnut romesco 8
pasta
   cauliflower spaghetti w/ lemon, chilli + crispy capers 90
   mustardy mushroom + toasted quinoa tagliatelle 36
pastry 160, 242
patties, lentil w/ horseradish mash + sauerkraut 78
pea, minty + feta purée w/ buttered asparagus on toast 132
peas, garlicky + broad beans w/ egg, feta + dill 138
peach + raspberry crumble cake 220
peanut lime sauce 72
peanut, shiitake + tofu dumplings 28
pear, dark chocolate + pistachio cake 118
persimmon, orange + rosemary, w/ amaranth porridge 46
persimmon, roasted kumara + rocket salad w/ jalapeño dressing 20
pickled baby beets 144
pickled chillies 180
pies, curried lentil 74
pikelets, coconut w/ lemon curd 156
pilaf, rainbow chard 68
pistachio, dark chocolate halva ice cream bites 224
pistachio, dark chocolate + pear cake 118
plums
   plum, cinnamon + quinoa bake 58
   plum + rocket salad w/ almond za'atar 14
   plum + toasted hazelnut cake 48
polenta, chickpea, w/ tomato zucchini stew 202
popsicles
   pink grapefruit + rosemary 168
   raspberry, apricot + orange 212
   roasted strawberry, orange + pink peppercorn popsicles 218
porridge, amaranth w/ orange + rosemary persimmon 46
potato
   beetroot gnocchi w/ caper gremolata 122
   leek + potato frittata 152
   potato salad w/ thyme + mustard red wine vinaigrette 190
pudding, tamarillo sponge w/ vanilla custard 62
pumpkin
   buckwheat 'risotto' w/ roasted pumpkin, feta + crispy sage 86
   ginger-roasted pumpkin + quinoa salad w/ mint, chilli + lime 34
   pumpkin + chocolate brownie 100
   pumpkin + coriander salsa 40

pumpkin + feta stuffed jalapeños 6
pumpkin korma 88
saffron-buttered pumpkin w/ herbed brown rice 24

quinoa
  ginger-roasted pumpkin + quinoa salad w/ mint, chilli + lime 34
  lemony mushroom quinoa w/ chilli almonds 32
  mustardy mushroom + toasted quinoa tagliatelle 36
  plum, cinnamon + quinoa bake 58
  roasted cauliflower, chickpea + quinoa salad w/ jalapeño lime dressing 76
  smoked paprika + almond quinoa 92

radish + apple slaw 204
rainbow carrot salad w/ mint mojo + turmeric pepitas 148
raspberry, apricot + orange popsicles 212
raspberry + peach crumble cake 220
rhubarb
  rhubarb, hibiscus + orange sorbet 164
  rhubarb + rosemary tarts 160
  rhubarb, strawberry + ginger muffins 166
risotto, buckwheat w/ roasted pumpkin, feta + crispy sage 86
rose + cardamom chai 98

saffron-buttered pumpkin w/ herbed brown rice 24
salad
  cauliflower + apple salad w/ creamy honey mustard dressing 94
  celeriac + beet salad w/ lemon, chilli + mint 84
  charred corn + red rice salad 192
  pickled beetroot, lentil + feta salad 146
  plum + rocket salad w/ almond za'atar 14
  potato salad w/ thyme + mustard red wine vinaigrette 190
  pumpkin + coriander salsa 40
  rainbow carrot salad w/ mint mojo + turmeric pepitas 148
  rice noodle salad w/ pickled vegetables + 5-spice dressing 200

roasted cauliflower, chickpea + quinoa salad w/ jalapeño lime dressing 76
roasted kumara, persimmon + rocket salad w/ jalapeño dressing 20
tomato + chickpea salad w/ green olive dressing 196
sauces and dressings
  caper gremolata 122
  coriander sauce 10
  five-spice dressing 200
  green olive dressing 196
  hazelnut romesco 8
  jalapeño lime dressing 76
  mint chutney 66
  mint + coriander sauce 82
  mint mojo 148
  peanut lime sauce 72
  sriracha 184
  thyme + mustard red wine vinaigrette 190
sauerkraut 80
shake, strawberry avocado 170
shiitake, peanut + tofu dumplings 28
shortbread 106
silverbeet + feta gözleme 130
slaw, apple radish 204
sunshine smoothie 210
sorbet, rhubarb, hibiscus + orange 164
soup
  beetroot + fennel w/ whipped feta croutons 136
  buckwheat noodles w/ carrot + ginger broth 150
  creamy parsnip w/ smoked paprika + almond quinoa 92
  curried kumara + coconut 70
  spicy coconut noodle 134
  sweetcorn w/ roasted cherry tomatoes + crispy tortillas 186
spaghetti, cauliflower w/ lemon, chilli + crispy capers 90
stew, chickpea 'polenta' w/ tomato zucchini 202
stew, leek, fennel + white bean 128
stock, vegetable 242
strawberries
  rhubarb, strawberry + ginger muffins 166
  roasted strawberry, orange + pink peppercorn popsicles 218
  strawberry avocado shake 170
sunshine smoothie 210

sweetcorn soup w/ roasted cherry tomatoes + crispy tortillas 186
tacos, smokey tempeh w/ apple radish slaw 204
tamarillo sponge pudding w/ vanilla custard 62
tandoori-roasted roots w/ fresh mint chutney 66
tarts
  fig, ginger + orange labneh tart 44
  lemon, lime + coconut tartlets 104
  rhubarb + rosemary tarts 160
tempeh curry w/ chilli kang kong 140
tempeh tacos w/ apple radish slaw 204
thyme + mustard red wine vinaigrette 190
tofu
  black pepper tofu w/ cucumber pickle 194
  roasted broccolini + tofu noodles w/ peanut lime sauce 72
  shiitake, peanut + tofu dumplings 28
  spicy tofu noodles 188
tomato
  chickpea 'polenta' w/ tomato zucchini stew 202
  chickpea + tomato curry 18
  tomato + chickpea salad w/ green olive dressing 196
  tomato, eggplant + buckwheat bake 26
torte, flourless chocolate 110
tortillas, fried egg w/ pumpkin + coriander salsa 40
turmeric mushrooms w/ chickpea crepes 12
turmeric pepitas 148

vanilla custard 62
vegetable stock 242
vinaigrette, thyme + mustard red wine 190

white bean, leek + fennel stew 128

za'atar roasted carrot + chickpeas w/ pickled chilli, radish + yoghurt 178
zucchini
  chickpea 'polenta' w/ tomato zucchini stew 202
  chocolate zucchini cake 60
  zucchini, feta + mint fritters 182

HarperCollins*Publishers*
First published in 2016
by HarperCollins*Publishers* (New Zealand) Limited
Unit D1, 63 Apollo Drive, Rosedale, Auckland 0632, New Zealand
harpercollins.co.nz

Copyright © Emma Galloway 2016

Emma Galloway asserts the moral right to be identified as the author of this work. This work is copyright. All rights reserved. No part of this publication may be reproduced, copied, scanned, stored in a retrieval system, recorded, or transmitted, in any form or by any means, without the prior written permission of the publisher.

HarperCollins*Publishers*
Unit D1, 63 Apollo Drive, Rosedale, Auckland 0632, New Zealand
Level 13, 201 Elizabeth Street, Sydney NSW 2000
A 53, Sector 57, Noida, UP, India
1 London Bridge Street, London SE1 9GF, United Kingdom
2 Bloor Street East, 20th floor, Toronto, Ontario M4W 1A8, Canada
195 Broadway, New York NY 10007, USA

National Library of New Zealand cataloguing-in-publication data:
Galloway, Emma.
A year in my real food kitchen / Emma Galloway.
978 1 7755 4085 4
Includes index.
1. Cooking. I. Title.
641.563-dc 23

All photographs by Emma Galloway, with the following exceptions:
Author photo on back cover and photo on page 229 by Christine Lim
Internal design by Anna Egan-Reid
Cover design by HarperCollins Design Studio
Typeset in Capita Light
Colour reproduction by Graphic Print Group, Adelaide, South Australia
Printed and bound in China by RR Donnelley